HANDBOOK OF
RESEARCH DESIGN
AND
SOCIAL MEASUREMENT

HANDBOOK OF
RESEARCH DESIGN
AND
SOCIAL MEASUREMENT

Second Edition

DELBERT C. MILLER

PROFESSOR OF SOCIOLOGY AND BUSINESS ADMINISTRATION
INDIANA UNIVERSITY

DAVID McKAY COMPANY, INC.

NEW YORK

HANDBOOK OF RESEARCH DESIGN AND SOCIAL MEASUREMENT

SECOND EDITION, 1970

To

F. STUART CHAPIN and GEORGE A. LUNDBERG

Pioneers in Sociometric Scaling

Preface to the First Edition

THE PURPOSE OF this handbook is to assist the social science researcher in finding information he needs quickly and in brief form when he is designing and conducting research. There are four major areas where aids are commonly required. These are in research functions associated with *research design and sampling, statistical analysis, selection of sociometric scales or indexes,* and, lastly, *research costing and reporting.* Accordingly, the handbook is organized around these functions.

No handbook can replace the training required for qualified research. This handbook is not a text or a substitute for one. It is a compilation of resources organized to provide reference to the essential materials needed in the design of research. Designed research refers to the planned sequence of the entire process involved in conducting a research study. The steps of this sequence are shown in Guide I.1 as:

1. Selection and definition of a sociological problem.
2. Description of the relationship of the problem to a theoretical framework.
3. Formulation of working hypotheses.
4. Design of the experiment or inquiry.
5. Sampling procedures.
6. Establishment of methods of gathering data.
7. Preparation of a working guide.
8. Analysis of results.
9. Interpretation of results.
10. Publication or reporting of results.

The handbook provides guides to accompany most of these steps. No attempt has been made to include guides to methods of gathering data since it is believed that these could not be put into brief form and that it would be better for a researcher to consult books on research methods when he needs guidance. However, he will find a relatively large number of scales in the handbook from which to choose if these prove useful to his problem.

The selection of guides has been made to insure the widest possible use regardless of the problem selected. Aids have been sought that set forth step-by-step procedures. It is hoped that both the professional worker and the graduate student shall find this handbook useful and timesaving.

Another purpose has motivated the development of this guide book. The author seeks to advance a major goal of all research progress, i.e., to improve research and to expedite the design and other operational phases of research. Investigations into leading sociological journals show that replication of research is infrequent. Measures of sociological variables except for such demographic variables as age, sex, religion, race, etc., are not used uniformly. Researchers often tend to ignore the scales available and to construct new ones. Thus, it is impossible to make careful comparisons with previous research and it is also difficult to build an accumulation of empirically verified relationships. Some exceptions show what might be accomplished. Social researchers have made wide use of the *Bogardus Social Distance Scale, Moreno's Sociometry Measures, Chapin's Social Participation Scale,* and other instruments included in this handbook. The psychologists have some relatively standard instruments in the *Minnesota Multiphasic Personality Inventory* and in the *F-Scale* to measure *Authoritarian Personality.* These scales have led to replication, which has produced accumulative research findings.

This handbook seeks to bring together social scales that have, or promise to have, wide utility and validity. It is expected that new scales will continue to be constructed by the hundreds. Certainly, many new and better scales are needed. Meanwhile, we need an inventory and storage house for selected measures that ought to be used unless there are compelling reasons to the contrary. If the scales included herein are not the most useful and valid, then the author invites communication. The handbook should constantly improve as consensus among experts is achieved. Meanwhile, if the selection helps increase replication and speeds research operations, a major goal of this book will have been achieved.

Another possible outcome of this handbook may be its capacity to suggest new research. The graduate student who is looking for a research problem should begin by examining the section containing the sociometric scales and indexes. These are generally measures of the dependent variables of greatest interest to social researchers. Any one of these scales can suggest to a researcher a new hypothesis requiring a test of a relationship not yet carefully demonstrated in a given population. In many ways, the sociometric scales in the storehouse of knowledge constitute the best seedbed for new research ideas and endeavors. The graduate student can play an important role in replicating good research designs of professional researchers. Graduate students now exceed professional researchers in numbers. They represent manpower of such scope that their combined efforts could make a substantial contribution to verified social science knowledge.

Empirical social research is now being actively encouraged not only in all of the traditional social sciences but also in the applied schools of business, education, social work, and law. Newcomers also include recruits from police administration, hospital administration, medical sociology, recreational administration, schools of communication, library administration, and many others.

I am especially indebted to both the College of Arts and Sciences and the Graduate School of Business at Indiana University for opportunities to serve as a research consultant to the faculty and graduate students. I wish to express my appreciation especially to Deans Arthur M. Weimer and W. George Pinnell for an opportunity to serve in the School of Business. Working with candidates for the masters' and doctors' degrees in business administration has more clearly shown me the needs that exist among graduate students in the basic and applied social sciences. I wish to express my appreciation to those devoted graduate students, Charles E. Starnes, Frank Castro, James Barrett, and Charles E. Leinenweber, for their efforts in assembling and classifying much of the material. I am also grateful to Jane Wellman, Jane Sunderland, and Rita Hosler for their enthusiastic help in preparing the manuscript.

DELBERT C. MILLER

Bloomington, Indiana
May 15, 1964

Preface to the Second Edition

THE SECOND EDITION incorporates new features suggested by many of the college teachers, professional researchers, and graduate students who used the first edition. A completely new section introduces the most common methods of social science research and presents a brief set of instructions for the construction of questionnaires, interviews, and scales. The methods are classified under their principal situs of research: library, field, or laboratory.

More attention is given to data collection. Principal social science data archives are listed. Research foundations and institutes are indicated. Materials are incorporated to assist the professional researcher and graduate student in finding sources for research funding.

New scales have been included in the section on sociometric scales. These include scales to measure socioeconomic status, alienation, achievement, and international patterns and norms. There are new comprehensive compilations of sociometric scales of attitudes which have appeared since the handbook was first published. References and lists of the available scales are included to provide wider scope to this section.

Finally, lists of journals and professional meetings are made available to encourage and assist the researcher in the publication and reporting of his research.

The book has been enlarged and revised in every section. All of the inclusions are directed toward the goal of making the handbook a professional tool of increasing utility to research workers. The reception of the work by sociologists, psychologists, political scientists, and researchers in the applied social sciences has shown the importance of professional aids to all steps of the research process from the selection of a problem to the final publication of results. The writer continues to invite correspondence from any researcher who has suggestions for improvements.

I am especially indebted to Charles E. Starnes and Dr. Francisco Suarez who assisted me in the revision.

DELBERT C. MILLER

Bloomington, Indiana
September 1, 1969

Contents

HANDBOOK OF
RESEARCH DESIGN
AND
SOCIAL MEASUREMENT

General Description of the Guides to Research Design and Sampling

PART I CONTAINS guides to accompany the first five steps in the sequence of a planned research proposal. These are (1) selection and definition of a sociological problem, (2) description of the relationship of the problem to a theoretical framework, (3) formulation of working hypotheses, (4) design of the experiment or inquiry, and (5) sampling procedures. The brief treatments of these subjects may be enriched by use of the bibliography placed at the end of Part I.

I.1 AN OUTLINE GUIDE FOR THE DESIGN OF A SOCIAL RESEARCH PROBLEM *

Instructions for Use of Guide I.1.

This outline for the design of social research lists all of the essential considerations in designing a research project. It is recommended that all steps be planned before field or laboratory work is undertaken. Each of the guides in Part I has been selected to aid in planning the first five steps shown in the outline. Other guides in Parts II, III, and IV are available to assist the researcher in most of the steps shown.

I. The Sociological Problem
   1. Present clear, brief statement of the problem with concepts defined where necessary.
   2. Show that the problem is limited to bounds amenable to treatment or test.
   3. Describe the significance of the problem with reference to one or more of the following criteria:
      a. is timely.
      b. relates to a practical problem.
      c. relates to a wide population.
      d. relates to an influential or critical population.
      e. fills a research gap.
      f. permits generalization to broader principles of social interaction or general theory.
      g. sharpens the definition of an important concept or relationship.
      h. has many implications for a wide range of practical problems.
      i. may create or improve an instrument for observing and analyzing data.
      j. provides opportunity for gathering data that is restricted by the limited time available for gathering particular data.

---

* Based on Russell L. Ackoff, *The Design of Social Research* (Chicago: University of Chicago, 1953). Adapted by Delbert C. Miller.

      k. provides possibility for a fruitful exploration with known techniques.

II. The Theoretical Framework

  1. Describe the relationship of the problem to a theoretical framework.

  2. Demonstrate the relationship of the problem to previous research.

  3. Present alternate hypotheses considered feasible within the framework of the theory.

III. The Hypotheses

  1. Clearly state the hypotheses selected for test. (Null and alternate hypothesis should be stated.)

  2. Indicate the significance of test hypotheses to the advancement of research and theory.

  3. Define concepts or variables (preferably in operational terms).

    a. Independent and dependent variables should be distinguished from each other.

    b. The scale upon which variables are to be measured (quantitative, semiquantitative, or qualitative) should be specified.

  4. Describe possible mistakes and their consequences.

  5. Note seriousness of possible mistakes.

IV. Design of the Experiment or Inquiry

  1. Describe ideal design or designs with especial attention to the control of interfering variables.

  2. Describe selected operational design.

    a. Describe stimuli, subjects, environment, and responses with the objects, events, and properties necessary for their specification.

    b. Describe how control of interfering variables is achieved.

  3. Specify statistical tests including dummy tables for each test.

    a. Specify level of confidence desired.

V. Sampling Procedures

  1. Describe experimental and control samples.

    a. Specify the population to which the hypotheses are relevant.

    b. Explain determination of size and type of sample.

    2. Specify method of drawing or selecting sample.

       a. Specify relative importance of Type I Error and Type II Error.

       b. Estimate relative costs of the various sizes and types of samples allowed by the theory.

VI. Methods of Gathering Data

    1. Describe measures of quantitative variables showing reliability and validity when these are known. Describe means of identifying qualitative variables.

    2. Include the following in description of questionnaires or schedules, if these are used.

       a. Approximate number of questions to be asked of each respondent.

       b. Approximate time needed for interview.

       c. The schedule as it has been constructed to this time.

       d. Preliminary testing of interview and results.

    3. Include the following in description of interview procedure, if this is used.

       a. Means of obtaining information, i.e., by direct interview, all or part by mail, telephone, or other means.

       b. Particular characteristics interviewers must have or special training that must be given them.

    4. Describe use to be made of pilot study, pretest, or trial run.

       a. Importance of and means for coping with unavailables, refusals, and response error.

VII. Working Guide

    1. Prepare working guide with time and budget estimates.

       a. Planning.

       b. Pilot Study and Pretests.

       c. Drawing sample.

       d. Preparing observational materials.

       e. Selection and training.

       f. Trial plan.

       g. Revising plans.

       h. Collecting data.

       i. Processing data.

       j. Preparing final report.

    2. Estimate total man hours and cost.

VIII. Analysis of Results

    1. Specify method of analysis.

       a. Use of tables, calculator, sorter, computer, etc.

       b. Use of graphic techniques.

       c. Specify type of tables to be constructed.

  IX. Interpretation of Results

     1. Discuss how conclusions will be fed back into theory.

  X. Publication or Reporting Plans

     1. Write these according to department and graduate school requirements.

     2. Select for journal publication the most significant aspects of the problem in succinct form (probably not in excess of fifteen typewritten pages double spaced). Follow style and format specified by the journal to which the article will be submitted.

I.2. A GENERAL STATEMENT TO GUIDE THE BASIC RESEARCHER IN THE FORMULATION OF RESEARCH PROBLEMS

Instructions for Use of Guide I.2

The first step in the design of research is the selection of a fruitful problem. The range of potential topics for social research is as broad as the range of social behavior itself. The significance of a problem rests on its probable contribution to knowledge. The formulation of the problem becomes of great importance in providing this potential.

Guide I.2 was formulated by a group of researchers to indicate those criteria that should be considered in ensuring that a research proposal will be significant. This guide may be most valuable to the professional researcher, but the graduate student should use it as a standard by which to gauge his work. At the same time, the criteria of significance shown in Guide I.1 should be carefully considered.

Suggested Criteria for Research Problems *

  A. A concern with basic concepts and relationships of concepts, as distinguished from local, particularized, or exclusively applied research, to the end that the knowledge produced may be cumulative with that from other studies.

  B. The development, refinement, and testing of theoretical formulations. At present the theories appropriate as research guides will

---

* From *Report of the Study for the Ford Foundation on Policy and Program* (Detroit, Mich.: Ford Foundation, November, 1949).

be more limited in scope than the comprehensive, speculative systems prominent in the early history of social science.

C. Superior research design, including careful specification of the variables involved and use of the most precise and appropriate methods available.

D. A probable contribution to methodology by the discovery, development, or refinement of practicable tools, techniques, or methods.

E. Full utilization of relevant concepts, theories, evidence, and techniques from related disciplines.

F. The integration of any single study in a planned program of related research to the end that the results become meaningful in a broad context.

G. Adequate provision to train additional research scientists.

H. Provision, wherever feasible, to repeat or check related research of other persons in order to provide a check on the generality of conclusions. A special aspect of this characteristic would be the repetition of studies in more than one culture group.

I.3. THE BEARING OF SOCIOLOGICAL THEORY ON EMPIRICAL RESEARCH

Instructions for Guide I.3.

To advance knowledge, both theory and substantive bodies of fact must be progressively interrelated. Robert K. Merton describes the bearing of theory on empirical research. He says that the "... notion of directed research implies that, in part, empirical inquiry is so organized that if and when empirical discoveries are made, they have direct consequences for a theoretic system." Note the functions of theory that he sets forth. The researcher must often formulate "middle range" or miniature theories that will link his hypotheses to a more inclusive theory. Zetterberg has written that miniature theories delineate convenient research problems. "Granted that our ultimate purpose is a general theory and that this general theory will in part be made up by means of miniature theories, experimental evidence supporting a miniature theory will support also the inclusive theory of which the miniature theory is a special case." [1]

Milton Friedman has listed the following criteria for significant theory: "A theory is 'simpler' the less initial knowledge is needed to make a prediction within a given field of phenomena; it is the more 'fruitful' the more precise the resulting prediction, the wider the area within which the theory yields predictions, and the more additional lines for further research it suggests. ... The only relevant test of the validity of a hypothesis is comparison of prediction with experience." [2]

NOTES

1. Hans L. Zetterberg, *On Theory and Verification in Sociology* (New York: Tressler Press, 1954), p. 15.
2. Milton Friedman, "The Methodology of Positive Economics," *Essays in Positive Economics* (Chicago: University of Chicago Press, 1953), p. 10.

Empirical Generalizations in Sociology *

ROBERT K. MERTON

Not infrequently it is said that the object of sociological theory is to arrive at statements of social uniformities. This is an elliptical assertion and hence requires clarification. For there are two types of statements of sociological uniformities that differ significantly in their bearing on theory. The first of these is the empirical generalization: an isolated proposition summarizing observed uniformities of relationships between two or more variables.[1] The sociological literature abounds with such generalizations that have not been assimilated to sociological theory. Thus, Engel's "laws" of consumption may be cited as examples. So, too, the Halbwachs' finding that laborers spend more per adult unit for food than white-collar employees of the same income class.[2] Such generalizations may be of greater or less precision, but this does not affect their logical place in the structure of inquiry. The Groves-Ogburn finding, for a sample of American cities, that "cities with a larger percentage engaged in manufacturing also have, on the average, slightly larger percentages of young persons married" has been expressed in an equation indicating the degree of this relationship. Although propositions of this order are essential in empirical research, a miscellany of such propositions only provides the raw materials for sociology as a discipline. The theoretic task, and the orientation of empirical research toward

* Reprinted with permission of the publisher from Robert K. Merton, "The Bearing of Sociological Theory on Empirical Research," *Social Theory and Social Structure* (rev. ed.; Glencoe, Ill.: Free Press, 1957), pp. 95-99. Copyright 1949 by The Free Press, copyright 1957 by The Free Press, A Corporation.

theory, first begins when the bearing of such uniformities on a set of interrelated propositions is tentatively established. The notion of directed research implies that, in part,[3] empirical inquiry is so organized that if and when empirical uniformities are discovered, they have direct consequences for a theoretic system. Insofar as the research is directed, the rationale of findings is set forth before the findings are obtained.

Sociological Theory

The second type of sociological generalization, the so-called scientific law, differs from the foregoing inasmuch as it is a statement of invariance derivable from a theory. The paucity of such laws in the sociological field perhaps reflects the prevailing bifurcation of theory and empirical research. Despite the many volumes dealing with the history of sociological theory and despite the plethora of empirical investigations, sociologists (including the writer) may discuss the logical criteria of sociological laws without citing a single instance that fully satisfies these criteria.[4]

Approximations to these criteria are not entirely wanting. To exhibit the relations of empirical generalizations to theory and to set forth the functions of theory, it may be useful to examine a familiar case in which such generalizations were incorporated into a body of substantive theory. Thus, it has long been established as a statistical uniformity that, in a variety of populations, Catholics have a lower suicide rate than Protestants.[5] In this form the uniformity posed a theoretical problem. It merely constituted an empirical regularity that would become significant for theory only if it could be derived from a set of other propositions, a task that Durkheim set himself. If we restate his theoretic assumptions in formal fashion, the paradigm of his theoretic analysis becomes clear:

1. Social cohesion provides psychic support to group members subjected to acute stresses and anxieties.
2. Suicide rates are functions of *unrelieved* anxieties and stresses to which persons are subjected.
3. Catholics have greater social cohesion than Protestants.
4. Therefore, lower suicide rates should be anticipated among Catholics than among Protestants.[6]

This case serves to locate the place of empirical generalizations in relation to theory and to illustrate the several functions of theory.

1. It indicates that theoretic pertinence is not inherently present or absent in empirical generalizations but appears when the generalization is conceptualized in abstractions of higher order (Catholicism–social cohesion–relieved anxieties–suicide rate) that are embodied in more general statements of relationships.[7] What was initially taken as an isolated uniformity is restated as a relation, not between religious affiliation and behavior, but between groups with certain conceptualized attributes (social cohesion) and the behavior. The *scope* of the original empirical finding is considerably extended, and several seemingly disparate uniformities are seen to be interrelated (thus differentials in suicide rates between married and single persons can be derived from the same theory).

2. Once having established the theoretic pertinence of a uniformity by deriving it from a set of interrelated propositions, we provide for the *cumulation* both of theory and of research findings. The differentials-in-suicide-rate uniformities add confirmation to the set of propositions from which they—and other uniformities—have been derived. This is a major function of *systematic theory*.

3. Whereas the empirical uniformity did not lend itself to the drawing of diverse consequences, the reformulation gives rise to various consequences in fields of conduct quite remote from that of suicidal behavior. For example, inquiries into obsessive behavior, morbid preoccupations, and other maladaptive behavior have found these also to be related to inadequacies of group cohesion.[8] The conversion of empirical uniformities into theoretic statements thus increases the *fruitfulness* of research through the successive exploration of implications.

4. By providing a rationale, the theory introduces a *ground for prediction* that is more secure than mere empirical extrapolation from previously observed trends. Thus, should independent measures indicate a decrease of social cohesion among Catholics, the theorist would predict a tendency toward increased rates of suicide in this group. The atheoretic empiricist would have no alternative, however, but to predict on the basis of extrapolation.

5. The foregoing list of functions presupposes one further attribute of theory that is not altogether true of the Durkheim formulation and which gives rise to a general problem that has peculiarly beset sociological theory, at least, up to the present. If theory is to be productive, it must be sufficiently *precise* to be *de-*

terminate. Precision is an integral element of the criterion of *test-ability.* The prevailing pressure toward the utilization of statistical data in sociology, whenever possible, to control and test theoretic inferences has a justifiable basis, when we consider the logical place of precision in disciplined inquiry.

The more precise the inferences (predictions) that can be drawn from a theory, the less the likelihood of *alternative* hypotheses that will be adequate to these predictions. In other words, precise predictions and data serve to reduce the *empirical* bearing upon research of the *logical* fallacy of affirming the consequent.[9] It is well known that verified predictions derived from a theory do not prove or demonstrate that theory; they merely supply a measure of confirmation, for it is always possible that alternative hypotheses drawn from different theoretic systems can also account for the predicted phenomena.[10] But those theories that admit of precise predictions confirmed by observation take on strategic importance since they provide an initial basis for choice between completing hypotheses. In other words, precision enhances the likelihood of approximating a "crucial" observation or experiment.

The internal coherence of a theory has much the same function, for if a variety of empirically confirmed consequences are drawn from one theoretic system, this reduces the likelihood that competing theories can adequately account for the same data. The integrated theory sustains a larger measure of confirmation than is the case with distinct and unrelated hypotheses, thus accumulating a greater weight of evidence.

Both pressures—toward precision and logical coherence—can lead to unproductive activity, particularly in the social sciences. Any procedure can be abused as well as used. A premature insistence on precision at all costs may sterilize imaginative hypotheses. It may lead to a reformulation of the scientific problem in order to permit measurement with, at times, the result that the subsequent materials do not bear on the initial problem in hand.[11] In the search for precision, care must be taken to see that significant problems are not thus inadvertently blotted from view. Similarly, the pressure for logical consistency has at times invited logomachy and sterile theorizing, inasmuch as the assumptions contained in the system of analysis are so far removed from empirical referents or involve such high abstractions as not to permit of empirical inquiry.[12] But the warrant for these criteria of inquiry is not vitiated by such abuses.

NOTES

1. This usage of the term "empirical" is common, as Dewey notes. In this context, *"empirical* means that the subject-matter of a given proposition which has existential inference, represents merely a set of uniform conjunctions of traits repeatedly observed to exist, without any understanding of *why* the conjunction occurs; without a theory which states its rationale." John Dewey, *Logic: The Theory of Inquiry* (New York: Henry Holt, 1938), p. 305.

2. See a considerable collection of such uniformities summarized by C. C. Zimmerman, *Consumption and Standards of Living* (New York: Van Nostrand, 1936), p. 55 ff.

3. "In part," if only because it stultifies the possibilities of obtaining fertile new findings to confine researches *wholly* to the test of predetermined hypotheses. Hunches originating in the course of the inquiry that may not have immediately obvious implications for a broader theoretic system may eventuate in the discovery of empirical uniformities that can later be incorporated into a theory. For example, in the sociology of political behavior, it has been recently established that the larger the number of social cross-pressures to which voters are subjected, the less interest they exhibit in a presidential election [P. F. Lazarsfeld, Bernard Berelson, and Hazel Gaudet, *The People's Choice* (New York: Duell, Sloan & Pearce, 1944), pp. 56-64]. This finding, which was wholly unanticipated when the research was first formulated, may well initiate new lines of systematic inquiry into political behavior, even though it is not yet integrated into a generalized theory. Fruitful empirical research not only tests theoretically derived hypotheses; it also originates new hypotheses. This might be termed the "serendipity" component of research, i.e., the discovery, by chance or sagacity, of valid results that were not sought for.

4. E.g., see the discussion by George A. Lundberg, "The concept of law in the social sciences," *Philosophy of Science*, 5 (1938), 189-203, which affirms the possibility of such laws without including any case in point. The book by K. D. Har, *Social Laws* (Chapel Hill: University of North Carolina, 1930), does not fulfill the promise implicit in the title. A panel of social scientists discussing the possibility of obtaining social laws finds it difficult to instance cases. Herbert Blumer, *An Appraisal of Thomas and Znaiecki's The Polish Peasant in Europe and America* (New York: Social Science Research Council, 1939), pp. 142-50.

5. It need hardly be said that this statement assumes that education, income, nationality, rural-urban residence, and other factors that might render this finding spurious have been held constant.

6. We need not examine further aspects of this illustration, e.g. (1) the extent to which we have adequately stated the premises implicit in Durkheim's interpretation; (2) the supplementary theoretic analysis that would take these premises not as given but as problematic; (3) the grounds on which the potentially infinite regression of theoretic intepretations is halted at one rather than another point; (4) the problems involved in the introduction of such intervening variables as social cohesion that are not directly measured; (5) the extent to which the premises have been empirically confirmed; (6) the comparatively low order of abstraction represented by this illustration; and (7) the fact that Durkheim derived several empirical generalizations from this same set of hypotheses.

7. Thorstein Veblen has put this with typical cogency: "All this may seem like taking pains about trivialities. But the data with which any scientific inquiry has to do are trivialities in some other bearing than that one in which they are of account." *The Place of Science in Modern Civilization* (New York: Russell & Russell, 1961), p. 42.

8. See, e.g., Elton Mayo, *Human Problems of an Industrial Civilization* (New York: Macmillan, 1933), p. 113 *et passim*. The theoretical framework utilized in the studies of industrial morale by Whitehead, Roethlisberger, and Dickson stemmed appreciably from the Durkheim formulations, as the authors testify.

9. The paradigm of "proof through prediction" is, of course, logically fallacious: If A (hypothesis), then B (prediction).
B is observed.
Therefore, A is true.
This is not overdisturbing for scientific research, inasmuch as other than formal criteria are involved.

10. As a case in point, consider that different theorists had predicted war and internecine conflict on a large scale at midcentury. Sorokin and some Marxists, for example, set forth this prediction on the basis of quite distinct theoretic systems. The actual outbreak of large-scale conflicts does not in itself enable us to choose between these schemes of analysis, if only because the observed fact is consistent with both. Only if the predictions had been so *specified*, had been so precise, that the actual occurrences coincided with the one prediction and not with the other, would a determinate test have been instituted.

11. Stuart A. Rice comments on this tendency in public opinion research; see *Eleven Twenty-six: A Decade of Social Science Research,* ed. Louis Wirth (Chicago: University of Chicago, 1940), p. 167.

12. It is this practice to which E. Ronald Walker refers, in the field of economics, as "theoretic blight." *From Economic Theory to Policy* (Chicago: University of Chicago, 1943), chap. IV.

ADDITIONAL READINGS

GREER, SCOTT. *The Logic of Inquiry*. Chicago: Aldine, 1969.

HANSON, N. R. *Patterns of Discovery: An Inquiry into the Conceptual Foundations of Science.* Cambridge, Eng.: Cambridge University, 1958. See chap. IV "Theories."

HEMPEL, CARL G., and OPPENHEIM, P. "Studies in the Logic of Explanation," *Philosophy of Science,* XV (1948), 135-175.

KAPLAN, ABRAHAM. *The Conduct of Inquiry, Methodology for Behavioral Science.* San Francisco: Chandler, 1964. See chap. VIII, "Theories."

STEPHENS, WILLIAM N. *Hypotheses and Evidence.* New York: Crowell, 1968.

WESTIE, FRANK R. "Toward Closer Relations between Theory and Research: A Procedure and an Example," *American Sociological Review,* XXII (April, 1957), 149-154.

ZETTERBERG, HANS L. *On Theory and Verification in Sociology.* 3rd ed. revised. Totowa, N.J.: Bedminster Press, 1965.

I.4. CRITERIA FOR JUDGING USABLE HYPOTHESES *

Instructions for Guide I.4.

The formulation of usable hypotheses is of central importance. The entire study rests upon the potential significance of the hypotheses. In this guide, William J. Goode and Paul K. Hatt prescribe step-by-step methods for evaluating hypotheses against criteria. Note again the emphasis given to the criterion that a hypothesis should be related to a body of theory. It is also important to anticipate the verification problem. Zetterberg has stated three criteria for the acceptance of a working hypothesis: (1) that the empirical data were found to be arranged in the manner predicted by the working hypothesis; (2) that we have disproved the null hypothesis with a certain probability; and (3) that we have disproved alternate hypotheses to the one tested.

WILLIAM J. GOODE and PAUL K. HATT

1. *The hypotheses must be conceptually clear.* The concepts should be clearly defined, operationally if possible. Moreover, they should be definitions that are commonly accepted and communicable rather than the products of a "private world."

What to do: One simple device for clarifying concepts is to write out a list of the concepts used in the research outline. Then try to define them (*a*) in words, (*b*) in terms of particular operations (index calculations, types of observations, etc.), and (*c*) with reference to other concepts to be found in previous research. Talk over each concept with fellow students and other researchers in the field. It will often be found that supposedly simple concepts contain many meanings. Then it is possible to decide which is the desired referent.

2. *Hypotheses should have empirical referents.* It has also been previously pointed out that scientific concepts must have an ultimate empirical referent. No usable hypothesis can embody moral judgments. Such statements as "criminals are no worse than businessmen," "women should pursue a career," or "capitalists exploit their workers," are no more usable hypotheses than is the familiar proposi-

---

* By permission from William J. Goode and Paul K. Hatt, *Methods in Social Research* (New York: McGraw-Hill, 1952), pp. 68-73. Copyright 1952 by McGraw-Hill Book Company, Inc.

tion that "pigs are well named because they are so dirty" or the classical question, "How many yards of buttermilk are required to make a pair of breeches for a black bull?" In other words, while a hypothesis may involve the study of value judgments, such a goal must be separated from a moral preachment or a plea for acceptance of one's values.

What to do: First, analyze the concepts that express attitudes rather than describe or refer to empirical phenomena. Watch for key words such as "ought," "should," "bad," etc. Then transform the notions into more useful concepts. "Bad parents" is a value term but the researcher may have a definite description in mind: parents who follow such practices as whimsical and arbitrary authoritarianism, inducing psychic insecurity in the child, failure to give love, etc. "Should" is also a value term, but the student may simply mean, "If women do not pursue a career, we can predict emotional difficulties when the children leave home, or we can predict that the society will not be able to produce as much goods," etc. When, instead, we find that our referent is simply a vague feeling and we cannot define the operations needed to observe it, we should study the problem further and discover what it is that we really wish to investigate.

3. *The hypotheses must be specific.* That is, all the operations and predictions indicated by it should be spelled out. The possibility of actually testing the hypothesis can thus be appraised. Often hypotheses are expressed in such general terms, and with so grandiose a scope, that they are simply not testable. Because of their magnitude, such grand ideas are tempting because they seem impressive and important. It is better for the student to avoid such problems and instead develop his skills upon more tangible notions.

By making all the concepts and operations explicit is meant not only conceptual clarity but a description of any indexes to be used. Thus, to hypothesize that the degree of vertical social mobility is decreasing in the United States requires the use of indexes. (At present there are many operational definitions of the status levels that define mobility. Therefore, the hypothesis must include a statement of the index that is to be used; see Part III for available indexes.)

Such specific formulations have the advantage of assuring that research is practicable and significant, in advance of the expenditure of effort. It furthermore increases the validity of the results, since the broader the terms the easier it is to fall into the trap of using selective evidence. The fame of most prophets and fortune-tellers lies in their ability to state predictions so that almost any occurrence can be interpreted as a fulfillment. We can express this in almost statistical terms: the more specific the prediction, the smaller the chance that the prediction will actually be borne out as a result of mere accident. Scientific predictions or hypotheses must, then, avoid the trap of selective evidence by being as definite and specific as possible.

What to do: Never be satisfied with a general prediction, if it can be broken into more precise subhypotheses. The general prediction of war is not enough, for example: we must specify time, place, and participants. Predicting the general decline of a civilization is not a hypothesis for testing a theory. Again, we must be able to specify and measure the forces, specify the meaning and time of decline, the population segments involved, etc. Often this can be done by conceptual analysis and the formulation of related hypotheses: e.g., we may predict that urbanization is accompanied by a decline in fertility. However, we gain in precision if we attempt to define our indexes of urbanization; specify which segments will be affected, and how much (since in the United States the various ethnic and religious segments are affected differently); specify the amount of fertility decline, and the type (percentage childless, net reproduction rate, etc.). Forming subhypotheses (1) clarifies the relationship between the data sought and the conclusions; and (2) makes the specific research task more manageable.

4. *Hypotheses should be related to available techniques.* Earlier, the point was repeatedly made that theory and method are not opposites. The theorist who does not know what techniques are available to test his hypotheses is in a poor way to formulate usable questions.

This is not to be taken as an absolute injunction against the formulation of hypotheses that at present are too complex to be handled by contemporary technique. It is merely a sensible requirement to apply to any problem in its early stages in order to judge its researchability.

There are some aspects of the impossible hypothesis that may make its formulation worth while. If the problem is significant enough as a possible frame of reference, it may be useful whether or not it can be tested at the time. The socioeconomic hypotheses of

Marx, for example, were not proved by his data. The necessary techniques were not available either then or now. Nevertheless, Marxian frameworks are an important source of more precise, smaller, verifiable propositions. This is true for much of Emile Durkheim's work on suicide. His related formulations concerning social cohesion have also been useful. The work of both men has been of paramount importance to sociology, even though at the time their larger ideas were not capable of being handled by available techniques.

Furthermore, posing the impossible question may stimulate the growth of technique. Certainly some of the impetus toward modern developments in technique has come from criticisms against significant studies that were considered inadequate because of technical limitations. In any serious sociological discussion, research frontiers are continuously challenged by the assertion that various problems "ought" to be investigated even though the investigations are presently impossible.

What to do: Look for research articles on the subject being investigated. Make a list of the various techniques that have been used to measure the factors of importance in the study. If you are unable to locate any discussions of technique, you may find it wiser to do a research on the necessary research techniques. You may, instead, decide that this lack of techniques means your problem is too large and general for your present resources.

Some items, such as stratification or race attitudes, have been studied by many techniques. Try to discover why one technique is used in one case and not in another. Note how refinements in technique have been made, and see whether one of these may be more useful for your purposes. Look for criticisms of previous research, so as to understand the weaknesses in the procedures followed.

Again, other problems may have been studied with few attempts at precise measurement. Study the literature to see why this is the case. Ascertain whether some subareas (for example, of religious behavior) may be attacked with techniques used in other areas (for example, attitude measurement, stratification measures, research on choice making, etc.).

5. *The hypothesis should be related to a body of theory.* This criterion is one which is often overlooked by the beginning student. He is more likely to select subject matter that is "interesting," without finding out whether the research will really help to refute,

qualify, or support any existing theories of social relations. A science, however, can be cumulative only by building on an existing body of fact and theory. It cannot develop if each study is an isolated survey.

Although it is true that the clearest examples of crescive theoretical development are to be found in the physical and biological sciences, the process can also be seen in the social sciences. One such case is the development of a set of generalizations concerning the social character of intelligence. The anthropological investigations at the end of the nineteenth century uncovered the amazing variety of social customs in various societies, while demonstrating conclusively that there were a number of common elements in social life: family systems, religious patterns, an organization of the socialization process, etc.

The French school of sociology, including Lucien Lévy-Bruhl, Emile Durkheim, Marcel Mauss, Henri Hubert, and others, formulated a series of propositions, at the turn of the century, which suggested that the intellectual structure of the human mind is determined by the structure of the society. That is, perception and thought are determined by society, not alone by the anatomical structure of our eyes, ears, and other senses. Modes of thought vary from society to society. Some of these formulations were phrased in an extreme form that need not concern us now, and they were often vague. Nevertheless, the idea was growing that the intelligence of a Polynesian native could not be judged by European standards; his thinking was qualitatively, not merely quantitatively, different.

At the same time, however, better techniques were being evolved for measuring "intelligence," which came to be standardized in the form of scores on various IQ tests. When these were applied to different groups it became clear that the variation in IQ was great; children of Italian immigrants made lower grades on such tests, as did Negroes. Northern Negroes made higher grades than whites from many Southern states. American children of Chinese and Japanese parents made rather high scores. Since it was generally assumed that these tests measured "innate intelligence," these data were sometimes generalized to suggest that certain "racial" groups were by nature inferior and others superior.

However, such conclusions were opposed on rational grounds, and liberal sentiments suggested that they be put to the test. There were, then, two major sets of conclusions, one suggesting that intelligence is in the main determined by social experience, the other suggesting that the IQ is innately determined. To test such opposing generalizations, a research design was needed for testing logical expectations in more specific situations. If, for example, it is true that the intelligence of individuals who are members of "inferior" groups is really determined biologically, then changes in their environments should not change their IQ. If, on the other hand, the social experience is crucial, we should expect that such changes in social experience would result in definite patterns of IQ change.

Further deductions are possible. If identical twins are separated and are placed in radically different social experiences at an early age, we might expect significant differences in IQ. Or, if a group of rural Negro children moves from the poor school and social experience of the South, to the somewhat more stimulating environment of the North, the group averages would be expected to change somewhat. Otto Klineberg, in a classic study, carried out the latter research. He traced Negro children of various ages after they had moved to the North and found that, in general, the earlier the move to the North occurred, the greater the average rise in the IQ. The later the move, the smaller the increase. Even if one assumes that the "better," more able, and more daring adult Negroes made this move, this does not explain the differences by time of movement. Besides, of course, the subjects were children at the time of the migration.[1]

In this research design a particular result was predicted by a series of deductions from a larger set of generalizations. Further, the prediction was actually validated. In justice to the great number of scholars who have been engaged in refining and developing IQ tests, it should be mentioned that other tests and investigations of a similar order have been carried out by many anthropologists, sociologists, and social psychologists. They do not invalidate the notion that IQ is based in part on "innate" abilities, but they do indicate that to a great extent these abilities must be stimulated by certain types of experience in order to achieve high scores on such tests.

From even so sketchy an outline of a theoretical development as the foregoing is, it can be seen that when research is systematically based upon a body of existing theory, a genuine contribution in knowledge is more likely to result. In other words, to be worth doing, a hypothesis must not only be carefully stated, but it should possess theoretical relevance.

What to do: First, of course, cover the literature relating to your subject. If it is impossible to do so, then your hypothesis probably covers too much ground. Second, try to abstract from the literature the way in which various propositions and sets of propositions relate to one another (for example, the literature relating to Sutherland's theory of differential association in criminology, the conditions for maximum morale in factories, or the studies of prediction of marital adjustment). Third, ascertain whether you can deduce any of the propositions, including your own hypothesis, from one another or from a small set of major statements. Fourth, test it by some theoretical model, such as Merton's "Paradigm for Functional Analysis in Sociology" (*Social Theory and Social Structure,* pp. 50-54), to see whether you have left out major propositions and determinants. Fifth, especially compare your own set of related propositions with those of some classic author, such as Weber on bureaucracy or Durkheim on suicide. If you find this task of abstraction difficult, compare instead with the propositions of these men as explained by a systematic interpreter such as Talcott Parsons in his *Structure of Social Action.* What is important is that, whatever the source of your hypothesis, it must be logically derivable from and based upon a set of related sociological propositions.

NOTE

1. Otto Klineberg, *Negro Intelligence and Selective Migration* (New York: Columbia University, 1935).

I.5. SCIENCE: OBSERVATIONAL, EXPERIMENTAL, HISTORICAL

Instructions for Guides to Study Design. Guides I.5, I.6, I.7, I.8, and I.9

The study design involves such decisions as that of whether a historical analysis, statistical sampling survey, qualitative structured observation, or controlled experimentation is needed. In the following, Raymond Siever, a physical scientist, describes varieties and styles of science and stresses the importance of the problem and its relation to scientific method.

Science: Observational, Experimental, Historical *

RAYMOND SIEVER

A question that has concerned many scientists for about as long as sciences started to differentiate from each other is, "Are there different sciences or is there just one science?" A related question can be put, "Is there *a* scientific method, or are there many scientific methods?" Discussion of these points is usually obfuscated by the speaker's background, in particular, what science he happens to be doing at the moment. It also, of course, is characteristically confused by mixing subject matter with the way in which an investigation is carried out. I will give my idea of how the different conventional groupings of sciences relate to each other and propose some answers to the question of whether there is just one science or many. It is not that these ideas are new. It is more that we need to remind ourselves of our philosophical underpinnings, especially now that branches of science have become more specialized and yet at the same time have joined together in attacks on complex systems.

Observational versus Experimental

The distinction between an observational science and an experimental science is often made. In this context in some people's language, the word "observational" is associated with the thought "solely descriptive" and the word "experimental" is usually associated with an analytical approach. There is an extension of these associations by which some scientists, thereby qualifying themselves as superior, imply that there is "good" or "bad" science by linking observational with bad and experimental with good. This choice of terms is dictated by diplomacy within the scientific community, for it is not good policy to refer to work that one's colleagues in another field are doing as bad; it is much better simply to call it "descriptive." We all know that there are appropriate uses for the words bad and good, but properly only as applied to an individual piece of work.

There are, of course, other terms that we are familiar with. There are the "hard" sciences and, by implication I suppose, the "soft"

* Reprinted from *American Scientist*, 56, No. 1 (1968), 70-77. Copyright by *Sigma Xi*, Princeton, N.J.

sciences. We also know that a good many other words have been juxtaposed to distinguish between "two cultures" within science (Table 1). Without trying to wreck diplomacy, it is worthwhile to point out just how these words, observational, descriptive, experimental, analytical, are being used.

It must be taken as given, I think, that all sciences observe and describe. An example is one product of science that has been with us for a long time, the heat flow equation, an equation that is fundamentally based on simple observation. The laws that Newton first formulated for heat flow are simpler than the more elegant mathematical statements that we now use. But this elegant formulation with which we are able to do so much rests on rather elementary kinds of observations. So it is silly to speak of a non-observational or a non-descriptive science.

There are said to be scientists who describe things and do not wish to make any analysis of them. They say description for its own sake is worthwhile science. It is true, of course, that many sciences in their early stages of development are characterized by an extraordinarily high ratio of data collecting to data analysis. This rarely implies that those who accumulate the data are not thinking about

TABLE 1

WORDS THAT HAVE BEEN USED IN CHARACTERIZING DIFFERENCES
AMONG THE SCIENCES

Analytical	Descriptive
Experimental	Observational
Soft	Hard
Non-mathematical	Mathematical
Good	Bad
Interesting	Dull
"Stamp collecting"	Crucial experimentation
Classical	Modern
The general equation	The encyclopedic monograph
Rigorous	Inexact
Easy	Difficult
Exploding	Mined-out

what they are describing or trying to integrate it into some pattern. It is obvious that those who describe are making a choice of what to describe and that analysis is involved in the selection of the object to be described. We ordinarily do not consider it science for somebody to observe everything that could be catalogued about a particular process, phenomenon, object, or other, though the point may be argued, and probably will be when the first man lands on the moon.

There is no denying that the scientific population includes some who do describe for its own sake, who admit that description is their only goal. As such they bear the same relationship to science as the inventory-taker does to business. But most who solely describe will say that they are only temporarily so engaged, that they are always working toward the goal of analysis (usually put off to some future time).

If it is true that description for its own sake, without any analysis of what to describe or how to integrate it after description, is not what we usually call science, then we really cannot speak of a descriptive or non-descriptive science. When some scientists say of another scientist's work or of another field within science, "It's descriptive," they really mean that it is not science.

The kind of statement made above may also be interpreted to mean, with good grace, that the proportion of description to analysis is high compared to those in some other field. The proportion varies, of course, with the stage of development of the field and it varies, obviously, with the person. Even within a field that is largely beyond the stage where description is in a high ratio to analysis, the invention of a new instrument can lead to new kinds of observations, temporarily producing a great abundance of data relative to analysis.

If one of the major objects of scientific endeavor is to make general laws from specific observations, then it must also be granted that the endeavor is more or less difficult. Physics has come to be, by and large, the domain of those who work where generalizations are relatively easy to make from limited data (though no one would claim physics as an easy field in terms of mental effort). Another way to put it is that the data have small variance and the generalizations are very good. It is also true that in certain fields, of which perhaps the social sciences are the most obvious example, the data have such high variance that the generalizations are either difficult or almost impossible to make. This inevitably leads to differences in the overall logical structure of disciplines. A great many parts of physics are tied together with a strong interconnecting network of fundamental physical theory from which all other parts can be derived, so-called first principles. On the other hand we have fields, such as some areas of engineering, where empiricism is the order of the day simply because there is no generally valid group of first principles from which to operate.

Experiment and Science

Experiments have always been associated with science, and have rightly been considered the most powerful tools of science. Our vision of experiment is largely based on those that have been done in physics and chemistry. But there are a number of ways in which one can look at experiments. They can be divided into controlled and uncontrolled experiments. Alternatively, we can formulate experimentation as either natural or artificial. The artificial experiment we all know about; one chooses the starting materials and conditions of the experiment, then one observes the process in action or the final results.

The natural experiment we are somewhat less familiar with, except for those of us whose primary interest lies in biology, the earth sciences, or astronomy. We may ask what would have happened had Newton one day seen the mythical apple on the ground, somewhat overripe, partly eaten, and decayed. From such an observation, could he have extracted a generalization on gravity? I think it not improbable that he might have, but perhaps at a much greater cost in time and effort and with much less assurance. Many geochemists, for example, have to go about analyzing chemical processes on the earth in a special way. It would be as if someone who wanted to find out what was going on in an elementary chemistry laboratory would go to the laboratory when no one was in it, analyze what he found in the sink, and analyze what he found in the sewer leading from the laboratory. Noting how the laboratory is equipped he could make some deductions as to the experiments that were performed and guess what the starting reagents might have been. So natural experimentation has built into it restricted control and limited information on the nature of the starting materials. Natural experimentation, of course, has the same restrictions as artificial experimentation; one must pick the right observational parameters.

The natural experiment can be refined by looking at separable parts of it or by choosing the chance event that has resulted in a specially controlled or restricted experiment. In a multivariate situation we look for the occasional place or time when the variables are fewer. Those who have spent a good deal of time looking for controlled natural experiments can speak with feeling about the rarity or impossibility of finding the perfectly controlled natural experiment. They all have defects. And so those who work with such data seem always to be trying to draw some generalizations from rather poor experiments.

Restrictions on artificial experimentation possibilities in science are many. The first restriction is the largeness of some systems. Scaling factors are not always available or adequate to reduce the system in size for examination in the laboratory. The two most notable sciences in this regard are astronomy and geology. Here again, restricted bits and pieces of these large systems can be removed and taken to the laboratory, but the interrelatedness of the system itself cannot be reproduced.

The complexity and interrelatedness of some systems restrict the experiment. Warren Weaver (1955) applied the words "strongly coupled" and "weakly coupled" to the sciences. Weaver applied these terms to differentiate the natural from the social sciences, but I think the point can equally be taken to differentiate among the natural sciences. Some aspects of the study of the oceans, for example, the general oceanic circulation, appear to be relatively weakly coupled, in that one considers a few interactions between the motion of the planet, its atmosphere, and the heat budget of the earth and the oceans. Another branch of oceanography, ecology, is a very strongly coupled science. Ecology in the ocean is so strongly coupled that it is difficult even to distinguish the variables from each other. It appears that most natural phenomena of large scale on the earth's surface are rather strongly coupled in the sense that the variables are not separable either for experimental or analytical purposes.

There are, of course, large-scale artificial experiments that have been done and have revealed a great deal of information. I would class the modern air and water pollution disaster as an obvious, though socially evil, experiment. I can offer more examples: Bomb-C^{14} spread through the atmosphere and exchanged with the ocean to give us a much better picture of the circulation of CO_2 and its equilibrium between the ocean and the atmosphere than we had had previously. Attempts to counter the current pollution of the Great Lakes may be an experiment in reversibility; we have the social hope but scientific uncertainty that the Lakes can be cleaned up. Whether reversible or not, the pollution and the counter measures are certainly giving us a good deal of scientific (or engineering?) information.

In the past, social taboos have prevented a whole class of experiments, but it now seems that even these have broken down at some times, most notably with Nazi so-called "experimentation" in some concentration camps. There have been suggestions that warfare in Viet Nam involves certain experimental tests of new equipment and ideas. But it is still largely true that, for scientists, areas considered important in biological experimentation are taboo for what we consider good and sufficient social reasons.

Simulated or "hypothetical" experiments and systems analysis have been used to circumvent social control or for large systems that cannot be taken to the laboratory. But such "experiments" are only as good as the first principles that allow them to be carried on in the mind alone. Theoretical physics is a clear choice for the field in which such experiments have great value. But in most of the world of scientific practice, scientists use hypothetical experiments as a prelude to actual experimentation or further observation. One does not perform hypothetical experiments for their own sake. We grant that as teachers we have frequent recourse to such devices. As research workers in science they are of little value of and for themselves.

It appears then, that experimental science is of many different kinds, that though the nature of experiment is the same no matter where one sees it, the controls may vary and the ability to observe different parts of the experiment may be limited, and finally that there are experiments that simply cannot be done for social reasons.

Historical versus Nonhistorical Science

This topic, a recurring theme in the dialogue on the nature of science (Nagel, 1952), has been explored recently by G. G. Simpson (1963) and R. A. Watson (1966). It appears to me that there is no fundamental difference between historical and nonhistorical science except as it may be economically profitable or culturally desirable to determine as exactly as possible what happened at a certain place and time. Thus we really do not care, as Watson puts it, exactly how the Grand Canyon of the Colorado River was formed. We only care how the generic class of Grand Canyons forms and has formed in the past, assuming that canyon-cutting was not a unique event. This is true in the same way that a chemist does not care what the particular numbers of an individual experiment are. His only concern is in repeating and generalizing that experiment so that the results from his or anybody else's operation of the same kind will fall into the same pattern. In fact, one rarely sees the particular numbers of any experiment. The raw data are of little interest except as an intermediate stage in the calculation of the quantities that are usually of true interest, quantities the significance of which has been established by earlier scientific studies. So, though we measure a particular mass and volume, we quote the important number as the density.

We may differentiate the historical sciences from the so-called nonhistorical sciences by the time scale of the processes involved. Though a chemical reaction has a "history," that history is usually faster than most processes we consider "historical." Even slow chemical reactions are extraordinarily fast compared to geological processes. In astronomy, too, a great many processes are very slow, although there are others that are fast. But even the history of a chemical reaction can be of major importance, for the study of chemical kinetics is just this. Again, though it is a historical event, the chemist studying the course of a reaction is rarely interested in any particular one performed at any particular time in his laboratory, but rather in the general repeatable experiment that anyone can do.

What is different about historical sciences is that many times only one natural experiment is observable, or so few that generalization is difficult if not impossible. We have on this earth, apparently, only one example of organic macroevolution. The general appearance of oxygen in the earth's primitive atmosphere probably happened only once. In modern times, the change in our lives caused by the development of the atomic bomb could happen only once. If the essence of experiment, whether artificial or natural, is that it be repeatable and that one needs at least one degree of freedom in order to make an average or to generalize, then we are destroyed by the uniqueness of some events. This is not to say, of course, that they are unique in the universe; they are only unique as far as our observational capabilities are concerned. It is for this reason that there is interest among biologists about the possibilities of some form of life on the moon or on Mars. They are simply seeking the additional experiment. Almost worse than the unique experiment is the availability of a very few experiments with a high variance. We have on the

Earth only a few continents. In the development of the structure of the North American continent there have been only a few major evolutionary patterns of geosynclines and mountain chain evolution on the borders of the continent. There are only a few terrestrial planets. The social sciences to some extent are plagued by the same. There are as yet only a few nations that have atomic bombs.

Styles in Science

Each scientist selects the discipline he works in for variety of reasons, but many styles can be found in all. I use the word "style" because, as has already become apparent, I reject the notion that there are different kinds of science, or scientific disciplines. There are many different personalities that go into science, and each of these personality types has his own way of doing things, as pointed out by Kubie (1953) and Eiduson (1962). Though there may be some correlation between personality and the discipline selected, I do not wish to discuss that issue.

Style is a word that has many meanings, ranging from a particular historical "school" in any subject (for example, "classical style") to a designation of a particular approach to any intellectual effort that is the product of the interaction of a personality with his time and his subject. It is the latter meaning of the word that I will use exclusively. Styles are probably related to personality, but they are always modified by the field in which that person works. An obvious recent example of different styles is that given by the contrast in the addresses of two recent Nobel laureates in physics, Richard Feynman (1966) and Julian Schwinger (1966). Here two men working in the same field of physics reveal very different styles of tackling the same kind of problem and writing about it.

We can recognize and tag some of the more distinctive styles that are common to all fields. We recognize that some of these are cross-coupled and one may indulge in several styles at different periods or as the mood strikes:

The rigorous formalist.
The brilliant phenomenologist.
The painstaking laboratory methodologist and his equivalent, the
    careful, detailed field observer.
The quick and dirty cream skimmer.
The niche-lover or horizontal monopolist.

The sub-generalist or vertical monopolist.

The dilettante and his brother, the versatile virtuoso, separated by the difference between success and failure.

The older, wiser generalist.

This is a parlor game that anyone can play and apply to his friends and colleagues.

Value judgments are usually made about the relative worth of the various stylists' contribution. But it is probably so that all of these styles are necessary for science to advance, for everyone leans on everyone else. There is some danger at the present time that there will be too much emphasis on certain styles in picking the leaders of science, and that style will be confused with discipline and with fundamental ability of the individual to make advances in science. Pluralism and diversity make for more interest in science as they do elsewhere in life. But let us have differences in style and subject and recognize that invidious distinctions between "kinds" of science serve only to build hierarchies of position and privilege.

REFERENCES

EIDUSON, BERNICE T. *Scientists: Their Psychological World*. New York: Basic Books, 1962.

FEYNMAN, RICHARD P. "The Development of the Space-Time View of Quantum Electrodynamics," *Science*, 153 (1966), 699-708.

KURIE, L. S. "Problems of the Scientific Career," *Scientific Monthly*, 74 (1953). Reprinted in FEIGLE, H., and BRODBECK, M., *Readings in the Philosophy of Science*. New York: Appleton-Century-Crofts, 1953, pp. 688-700.

SCHWINGER, JULIAN. "Relativistic Quantum Field Theory," *Science*, 153 (1966), 949-953.

SIMPSON, G. G. "Historical Science," in ALBRITTON, C. C. JR. (ed.). *The Fabric of Geology*. Reading, Mass.: Addison-Wesley, 1963, pp. 24-27.

WATSON, R. A. "Is Geology Different: A Critical Discussion of 'The Fabric of Geology,' " *Philosophy of Science*, 33 (1966), 172-185.

WEAVER, WARREN. "Science and People," *Science*, 122 (1955), 1255-1259.

At this point one must decide the nature of proof desired, taking into consideration the level of one's hypotheses, the size of one's budget, the amount of personnel and their skills, the time required, etc. It is now generally accepted that the model of the controlled experiment is always a valuable guide even if, in practice, deviation is necessary. *Some Observations on Study Design* (I.6) by Samuel A. Stouffer is regarded as the single most useful statement of design requirements for social investigation.

Hans L. Zetterberg explains the problems facing the researcher who wishes to use controlled observation and explains how alternative hypotheses can be tested with pseudo-experimental designs. See I.7, an excerpt from *On the Evaluation of Designs for the Confirmation of a Working Hypothesis.*

Edward Suchman in I.8 has listed some *General Considerations of Research Design.* These are realistic appraisals often needed when ideal plans must be compromised. The professional researcher keeps these guides before him.

Large-scale group research has grown in volume and in scope. Delbert C. Miller has written *"The Shaping of Research Design in Large-Scale Group Research"* (I.9) to provide a case study for the team research proposal. The breaking down of the problem into manageable parts is illustrated. The importance of individual differences among researchers is highlighted. Note also the progression of research stages. This guide is for the guidance of design in large-scale research only.

I.6 SOME OBSERVATIONS ON STUDY DESIGN *

SAMUEL A. STOUFFER

We must be clear in our own minds what proof consists of, and we must, if possible, provide dramatic examples of the advantages of relying on something more than plausibility. And the heart of our problem lies in study design *in advance,* such that the evidence is not capable of a dozen alternative interpretations.

Basically, I think it is essential that we always keep in mind the model of a controlled experiment, even if in practice we may have

* Reprinted from Samuel A. Stouffer, "Some Observations on Study Design," *The American Journal of Sociology,* 55 (January, 1950), 356-359. Copyright 1950 by the University of Chicago.

to deviate from an ideal model. Take the simple accompanying diagram.

	Before	After	After—Before
Experimental group	x_1	x_2	$d = x_2 - x_1$
Control group	x'_1	x'_2	$d' = x'_2 - x'_1$

The test of whether a difference d is attributable to what we think it is attributable to is whether d is significantly larger than d'.

We used this model over and over again during the war to measure the effectiveness of orientation films in changing soldiers' attitudes. These experiences are described in Volume III of our *Studies in Social Psychology in World War II*.[1]

One of the troubles with using this careful design was that the effectiveness of a single film when thus measured turned out to be so slight. If, instead of using the complete experimental design, we simply took an unselected sample of men and compared the attitudes of those who said they had seen a film with those who said they had not, we got much more impressive differences. This was more rewarding to us, too, for the management wanted to believe the films were powerful medicine. The gimmick was the selective fallibility of memory. Men who correctly remembered seeing the films were likely to be those most sensitized to their message. Men who were bored or indifferent may have actually seen them but slept through them or just forgot.

Most of the time we are not able or not patient enough to design studies containing all four cells as in the diagram above. Sometimes we have only the top two cells, as in the accompanying diagram. In this situation we have two observations of the same individuals or

x_1	x_2

$d = x_1 - x_2$

groups taken at different times. This is often a very useful design. In the army, for example, we would take a group of recruits, ascertain their attitudes, and restudy the same men later. From this we could tell whose attitudes changed and in what direction. (It was almost always for the worse, which did not endear us to the army!) But exactly what factors in the early training period were most responsible for deterioration of attitudes could only be inferred indirectly.

The panel study is usually more informative than a more frequent design, which might be pictured thus:

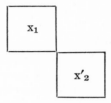

Here at one point in time we have one sample, and at a later point in time we have another sample. We observe that our measure, say, the mean, is greater for the recent sample than for the earlier one. But we are precluded from observing which men or what type of men shifted. Moreover, there is always the disturbing possibility that the populations in our two samples were initially different; hence the differences might not be attributable to conditions taking place in the time interval between the two observations. Thus we would study a group of soldiers in the United States and later ask the same questions of a group of soldiers overseas. Having matched the two groups of men carefully by branch of service, length of time in the army, rank, etc., we hoped that the results of the study would approximate what would be found if the same men could have been studied twice. But this could be no more than a hope. Some important factors could not be adequately controlled, for example, physical conditions. Men who went overseas were initially in better shape on the average than men who had been kept behind; but, if the follow-up study was in the tropics, there was a chance that unfavorable climate already had begun to take its toll. And so it went. How much men overseas changed called for a panel study as a minimum if we were to have much confidence in the findings.

A very common attempt to get the result of a controlled experiment without paying the price is with the design that might be as shown in the accompanying diagram. This is usually what we get

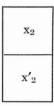

with correlation analysis. We have two or more groups of men whom we study at the same point in time. Thus we have men in the infantry and men in the air corps and compare their attitudes. How much of the difference between x'_2 and x_2 we can attribute to experience in a given branch of service and how much is a function of attributes of the men selected for each branch we cannot know assuredly. True, we can try to rule out various possibilities by matching; we can compare men from the two branches with the same age and education, for example. But there is all too often a wide-open gate through which other uncontrolled variables can march.

Sometimes, believe it nor not, we have only one cell:

When this happens, we do not know much of anything. But we can still fill pages of social science journals with "brilliant analysis" if we use plausible conjecture in supplying missing cells from our imagination. Thus we may find that the adolescent today has wild ideas and conclude that society is going to the dogs. We fill in the dotted cell representing our own yesterdays with hypothetical data, where x_1 represents us and x_2 our offspring. The tragicomic part is that most of the public, including, I fear, many social scientists, are so acculturated that they ask for no better data.

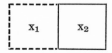

I do not intend to disparage all research not conforming to the canons of the controlled experiment. I think that we will see more of full experimental design in sociology and social psychology in the future than in the past. But I am well aware of the practical difficulties of its execution, and I know that there are numberless important situations in which it is not feasible at all. What I am arguing for is awareness of the limitations of a design in which crucial cells are missing.

Sometimes by forethought and patchwork we can get approximations that are useful if we are careful to avoid overinterpretation. Let me cite an example:

In Europe during the war the army tested the idea of putting an entire platoon of Negro soldiers into a white infantry outfit. This was done in several companies. The Negroes fought beside white soldiers. After several months we were asked to find out what the white troops thought about the innovation. We found that only 7 percent of the white soldiers in companies with Negro platoons said that they disliked the idea very much, whereas 62 percent of the white soldiers in divisions without Negro troops said they would dislike the idea very much if it were tried in their outfits. We have:

	Before	After
Experimental		7%
Control		62%

Now, were these white soldiers who fought beside Negroes men who were naturally more favorable to Negroes than the cross-section of white infantrymen? We did not think so, since, for example, they contained about the same proportion of Southerners. The point was of some importance, however, if we were to make the inference that actual experience with Negroes reduced hostility from 62 to 7 percent. As a second-best substitute, we asked the white soldiers in companies with Negro platoons if they could recall how they felt when the innovation was first proposed. It happens that 67 percent said they were initially opposed to the idea. Thus we could tentatively fill in a missing cell and conclude that, under the conditions obtaining, there probably had been a marked change in attitude.

Even if this had been a perfectly controlled experiment, there was still plenty of chance to draw erroneous inferences. The conclusions apply only to situations closely approximating those of the study. It happens, for example, that the Negroes involved were men who volunteered to leave rear-area jobs for combat duty. If other Negroes had been involved, the situation might have been different. Moreover, they had white officers. One army colonel who saw this study and whom I expected to ridicule it because he usually opposed innovations, surprised me by offering congratulations. "This proves," he said, "what I have been arguing in all my thirty years in the army—that niggers will do all right if you give 'em white officers!" Moreover, the study applied only to combat experience. Other studies would be needed to justify extending the findings to noncombat or garrison duty. In other words, one lone study, however well designed, can be a very dangerous thing if it is exploited beyond its immediate implications.

Now experiments take time and money, and there is no use denying that we in social science cannot be as prodigal with the replications as the biologist who can run a hundred experiments simultaneously by growing plants in all kinds of soils and conditions. The relative ease of experimentation in much—not all—of natural science goes far to account for the difference in quality of proof demanded by physical and biological sciences, on the one hand, and social scientists, on the other.

Though we cannot always design neat experiments when we want to, we can at least keep the experimental model in front of our eyes and behave cautiously when we fill in missing cells with dotted lines. But there is a further and even more important operation we can perform in the interest of economy. That lies in our choice of the initial problem.

NOTE

1. Carl I. Hovland, Arthur A. Lumsdaine, and Fred D. Sheffield, *Experiments on Mass Communication* (Princeton: Princeton University, 1949).

1.7. ON THE DECISIONS IN VERIFICATIONAL STUDIES *

HANS L. ZETTERBERG

The advantages of the experimental design, however, rest with the possibility of a random assignment of cases to the experimental and control groups and on the possibility of producing what the working hypothesis terms the cause. Unfortunately, in sociology we rarely have these possibilities.

Certainly many factors are intentionally introduced into society by politicians, educators, welfare agencies, etc. But these phenomena are seldom or never produced, because they are termed causes in a scientific social theory. Furthermore, when compulsory education, socialized medicine, public housing projects, etc., are introduced into a society, the very complexity of the new phenomena does not make them suitable as indicators of concepts of a theory.

In the second place, we can rarely introduce randomization of the persons supposed to enjoy these intentionally produced phenomena without violating strong moral sentiments. As to the social programs of the welfare state Chapin makes the comment:

> The conventional method of equalizing factors that are known and also unknown (by R. A. Fisher's design of experiment) is to select at random both the experimental group that receives treatment and the control group that serves as a reference group for comparison. In social research the program of social treatment cannot be directed toward a randomly selected group becase the prevailing mores require that this treatment be directed to a group of individuals who are eligible because of greater *need*. Thus precise control of unknown is impossible and the only factors that can be controlled are factors that are known to be in the particular social situation because of previous studies.[1]

It seems that this inability to satisfy the conditions for a profitable use of the experimental design would definitely curtail the sociologist's prospect to verify his theories. However, the situation is by no means disastrous: sciences like meteorology and astronomy have verified theories without the employment of the experimental method.

* From H. L. Zetterberg, *On Theory and Verification in Sociology* (2nd ed. revised; Totowa, N.J.: Bedminster Press, 1963), pp. 61-66.

For control of alternative hypotheses, the sociologist is to a large extent dependent on what might be called *pseudoexperimental* designs. These designs control propositions known as alternative ones, but, unlike the experimental designs, these designs cannot control unknown alternatives.

The most commonly used method in sociology for control of known alternative propositions is multivariate analysis, which has been formalized by Paul Lazarsfeld.[2] Skill in its use has become essential for most sociological research; those who know how to use it deserve to be called "modern sociologists." The technique controls alternative propositions by testing the hypothesis in subsamples that are homogeneous with respect to the determinants specified by the alternative propositions. It can be used to control all known alternative determinants provided the sample used is large enough.

The simplest relation between two variates x and y is a fourfold table:

	X	non-X
Y		
non-Y		

To discover whether a third variable, z, accounts for any of the relations found in such a table, we break it into two parts:

					Z			non-Z
	X	non-X		X	non-X		X	non-X
Y			=			+		
non-Y								

If the relation between x and y still holds in all subclasses of z, we may retain, for the time being, our trust in the proposition that x affects y. To this kind of design many new alternative determinants can be added, and it works equally well for qualitative and quantitative varieties.

However, the advantages do not end here. We can tabulate:

	X	non-X			X	non-X			X	non-X	
Z				Z				Z			
non-Z			=	non-Z			+	non-Z			

and also:

	Y	non-Y			Y	non-Y			Y	non-Y	
Z				Z				Z			
non-Z			=	non-Z			+	non-Z			

The purpose of these tabulations is to discover the actual linkage between the three variables. It would carry us far to review all the rules of interpretation involved here. However, if certain assumptions about the time lag between the variates can be made, it is possible to use such tabulations to disentangle a wide variety of causal chains, as shown in the diagram (opposite) adapted from Dahlström.[3]

Another method of pseudoexperimental control is that of *matching,* advocated by F. S. Chapin.[4] An experimental group and a control group are made equal on some criteria by discarding cases in one group for which no "twin" can be found in the other group. One disadvantage of this procedure is that the matched groups so obtained are not representative of the original groups. When this way of matching is employed, we do not quite know to what population the results can be generalized.

Control in pseudoexperimental design can be obtained through the use of other statistical adjustments. Various applications of the *multiple regression* approach can be made, provided variables fitting the rather rigid assumptions are used. The most common methods are those of partial correlation and analysis of covariance. These

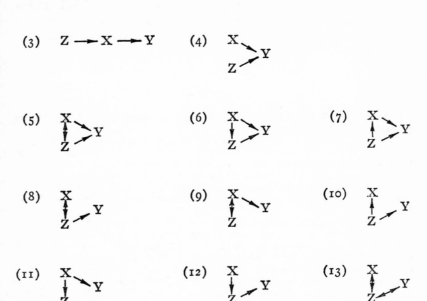

methods become rather laborious if the number of factors to be controlled is more than three or four.

Experimental designs and pseudoexperimental designs may be cross-sectional or longitudinal. We have already pointed out that longitudinal designs are more effective than cross-sectional designs and that experimental designs are more effective than pseudoexperimental designs. We can now reach a typology of designs:

The test of the null-hypothesis

		Cross-sectional	Longitudinal
The control of alterna- tive hypoth- eses	No control		
	Pseudoexperimental		
	Experimental		

The closer a design comes to the longitudinal experimental the better it is. However, we know little or nothing about how to evaluate crosswise combinations of the two criteria. We have no way in which to tell whether a pseudoexperimental longitudinal design (such as a panel with multivariable analysis) is as effective as the cross-sectional experimental design (the conventional laboratory experiment).

NOTES

1. F. Stuart Chapin, "Experimental Designs in Social Research," *American Journal of Sociology*, LV (1950), p. 402.

2. Paul F. Lazarsfeld, "Interpretation of Statistical Relations as a Research Operation" in Paul F. Lazarsfeld and Morris Rosenberg (eds.), *The Language of Social Research* (Glencoe, Ill.: Free Press, 1955), pp. 115-125.

3. Edmund Dahlström, "Analys av surveymaterial" in Georg Karlsson, *et al.* (eds.), *Sociologiska metoder* (Stockholm: Svenska Bokförlaget, 1961), p. 193.

4. F. Stuart Chapin, *Experimental Designs in Sociological Research* (New York: Harper, 1947).

For further reading the advanced student should see F. Stuart Chapin, *Experimental Designs in Sociological Research* (rev. ed.; New York: Harper, 1955); Ernest Greenwood, *Experimental Sociology: A Study in Method* (New York: King's Crown, 1945); Claire Selltiz, Marie Jahoda, Morton Deutsch, and Stuart W. Cook, *Research Methods in Social Relations* (rev., 1 vol.; New York: Henry Holt, 1959) chap. 4; Russell L. Ackoff, *The Design of Social Research* (Chicago: University of Chicago, 1953) chap. 3; Abraham Kaplan, *The Conduct of Inquiry* (San Francisco: Chandler, 1964).

1.8.   GENERAL CONSIDERATIONS OF RESEARCH DESIGN *

EDWARD A. SUCHMAN

1. It seems to us futile to argue whether or not a certain design is "scientific." The design is *the plan of study* and, as such, is present in all studies, uncontrolled as well as controlled and subjective as well as objective. It is not a case of scientific or not scientific, but rather one of good or less good design. The degree of accuracy desired, the level of "proof" aimed at, the state of existing knowledge, etc., all combine to determine the amount of concern one can have with the degree of "science" in one's design.

* From *An Introduction to Social Research,* by John T. Doby (ed.), with the assistance of Edward A. Suchman, John C. McKinney, Roy G. Francis, and John P. Dean, pp. 254-255. By permission of Edward A. Suchman and the Stackpole Company, 1954. The statements above are from chap. 10, "The Principles of Research Design."

2. The proof of hypotheses is never definitive. The best one can hope to do is to make more or less plausible a series of alternative hypotheses. In most cases multiple explanations will be operative. Demonstrating one's own hypotheses does not rule out alternative hypotheses and vice versa.

3. There is no such thing as a single, "correct" design. Different workers will come up with different designs favoring their own methodological and theoretical predispositions. Hypotheses can be studied by different methods using different designs.

4. All research design represents a compromise dictated by the many practical considerations that go into social research. None of us operates except on limited time, money, and personnel budgets. Further limitations concern the availability of data and the extent to which one can impose upon one's subjects. A research design must be *practical*.

5. A research design is not a highly specific plan to be followed without deviation, but rather a series of guideposts to keep one headed in the right direction. One must be prepared to discard (although not too quickly) hypotheses that do not work out and to develop new hypotheses on the basis of increased knowledge. Furthermore, any research design developed in the office will inevitably have to be changed in the face of field considerations.

I.9. THE SHAPING OF RESEARCH DESIGN IN LARGE-SCALE GROUP RESEARCH *

DELBERT C. MILLER

This paper examines some of the problems and opportunities in the shaping of research design posed by a large-scale group research project undertaken by the University of Washington for the United States Air Force.

The project began in June 1951 under a contract with the Human Resources Research Institute calling for an exploration of human relations problems of Air Force personnel manning isolated Air Defense radar stations "with reference to job requirements, morale factors, and leadership under stressful noncombat conditions and to develop methods for improving effectiveness." The contract was

* Reprinted from *Social Forces*, XXXIII (May, 1955), 383-390.

concluded in December, 1953. During the 32 months of active research, the project moved from exploration to descriptive and diagnostic study. Some cross-sectional experimental studies were undertaken in the final phase. The full research program included a national survey of the United States Air Defense Command Aircraft Control and Warning Stations, a study of the Japan Air Defense Command (A. C. and W.), and numerous investigations in the 25th Division of the Pacific Northwest. All of these undertakings centered about personnel problems and squadron efficiency.

It is the theme of this paper that research design in a group project is a product of a social process. That process is influenced by a number of organizational demands as well as by the dynamic interplay of personalities and experiences that are encountered by the group as research penetration continues. It is believed that it is entirely fallacious to consider group research as individual research simply grown big.

Research design for group research must be sensitive to needs of individual researchers, to organizational demands, and to research growth through contact with the problem. Indeed, it should be clearly recognized that individual researchers do not become group researchers merely by joining group research. The problem of research design becomes one of wedding the logic of scientific method to the social pressures of many internal and external considerations. Four major factors affected research design on the Air Site Project. These were: (I) the characteristic imperatives of group research; (II) the personal wants of researchers; (III) the demands of education; and (IV) the accumulation of empirical and theoretical knowledge.

I. The Characteristic Imperatives of Group Research

A. *The Restrictions of Interdependent Research Relationships.* The individual researcher confronting group research is asked to change many research habits that he may value highly. The change in habits may be experienced as a set of onerous restrictions. He may find that he cannot choose his problem, and the problem assigned to him may require collaboration with others that reduces still further his area of free movement. He discovers that he has come to live in a web of interrelationships in which his work is intertwined. His own methods of work undergo close scrutiny of the group. He is subordinate to the final approval of a research director.

Status and craft comparisons may clearly become causes of inter-personal conflict.[1] If the researcher does not or cannot adjust to this new social environment, conflict processes are intensified and spread to the group. In this atmosphere, even interpretation of words can become a serious source of wrangling.[2] Learning to live together in close interdependence does not come easy. And in group research for a client, many additional pressures are added.

B. *The Demands of a Time Schedule.* Group research for a client usually has a number of deadlines. Our military client required quarterly, interim, and final reports on given dates. No longer could researchers regard as indefinite the date for concluding a study. The demand for a report often meant intensified work, and this brought to some workers a sense of frustration that quality had been sacrificed for lack of time to do one's best.

C. *Conciliation of Other Pressures.* The client—or, as in our project, the monitoring agent—may offer suggestions and instructions as the research proceeds. These are usually accepted as persuasions to modify or intensify work in a given direction. These come to the project director and are transmitted through his actions or instructions to the group researchers. Sometimes the reason is not understood, or it may be understood but resented as an outside idea, foreign to the group process, and emotionally rejected.

Scientific canons of rigor may be opposed by demands for exploratory or applied research on problems for which hypotheses and measurement tools cannot be readied. A researcher whose pride system has incorporated strict and rigid standards of craftsmanship may quail before problems whose solution requires simple exploration or vulgar practicality (especially if he does not see how he can get a published paper from it).

The requirements of expense accounts, security clearances, permission for entry to the research field, "logistic support," and numerous matters of red tape are often further irritations—a headache to researchers and director alike.

The airmen and officers in the research field also exert subtle pressure on the researchers. The questions, "What's this all about? What are you trying to find out?" are continuous and require some kind of answer. The challenge, "You won't be able to do any good" is even more difficult to meet. It can undermine the feeling of acceptance and make fieldwork a resented rather than a welcome experience.

All of these new elements call for personal adjustments. It is apparent that a number of strains must be borne by group researchers who have not confronted these factors before. Who are these researchers that come into the group and what do they want?

II. The Personal Wants of Researchers

A. *Motivations of Researchers.* Young researchers are attracted to group research. If they are graduate students, the prospect of funds and a thesis presents an opportunity both to do research and to eat. Young Ph.D.'s see opportunity for publication, promotion, and freedom from teaching. Both of these groups are seeking to build research reputations through publication. This motive serves to make the burdens of fieldwork sufficiently acceptable to get the necessary data collecting done, but marriage, parenthood, and sedentary proclivities all contrive to make absence from the home an increasing burden. The influence of wives on the shaping of research design is an unknown but promising area of investigation.

B. *Security Needs of Researchers.* Research staffs are often recruited from among those persons who are seeking permanent employment. When contracts are on a year-to-year basis with no fixed guarantee as to their duration, a job insecurity is added to the social influences that bear upon the researchers' morale and productivity. As individual contracts begin to approach termination, personal insecurities mount and are intensified by group interaction. The feelings of insecurity are expressed in many different ways, which may include demands for more say in both policy and administrative decisions, safeguards for individual publication rights, and almost single-minded preoccupation with the acquisition of the *next* research contract.

A research design is under the stress of individual wants, for group thinking is colored every step of the way by these personal concerns. Each person wants to know what part of the design he can claim for his research publications. Each person wants to have an opportunity to guide his fieldwork in such a way as to minimize its burdens. Each wants the maximum opportunity to determine his working conditions.

C. *Role of the Research Director.* The research director takes his place in the center of all the forces that have been described. His role is to direct group processes, ascertain group sentiment, and make decisions so that research can be designed and executed with harmony and efficiency. He must see that role definitions for each member are clearly outlined. He must interpret the external demands on the project and relate them to his research personnel so that appropriate action is taken. He must come to recognize that he will get little opportunity to do field research himself. And he must accept the fact that some interpersonal friction will accompany his most valiant efforts to make group research palatable, especially during the early period when a number of individual researchers are learning to live together as group researchers. He will come to understand that each member of the group is concerned with his reputation as the result of his membership. He wants to have his say as to what others do when he feels his own standards are being violated. This is at once a source of group power and of group conflict. The director will often be challenged as to how these group motivations can be channeled.

A research director who wishes to manage by the use of democratic methods must know the dilemmas of leadership in the democratic process and find his own way to cope with them.[3] Softhearted, inexperienced democratic leadership rivals autocratic blindness in creating poor conditions for efficiency and morale.

III. The Demands of Education

The major problem facing organization of group research within a university is to secure opportunity for each researcher to have maximum freedom to apply his talents to a project whose major problems have been outlined in a contract for him. This is no little task. A professional researcher, we have said, wants to choose his problem, be given the proprietary right of publication for his work, and have control over his working conditions. The university is concerned that graduate students receive broad research training and not be employed at mere clerical tasks. The research design must be constructed in recognition of these concerns and the staff organized in optimum-size working groups so that the best combination of professional staff and graduate students may be obtained.

The basic research unit of the Air Site Project was made up of a professional sociologist and two graduate students; in 1952-53, there were four such units in the Project. Graduate students alternated fieldwork and classwork so that both types of training were secured. In the close association of professional sociologist and graduate student, both educational and research functions were served.

IV. The Accumulation of Empirical and Theoretical Knowledge

Research progress on a central problem usually proceeds through stages—first, exploration of the social setting of the problem, the factors involved, and the criteria that may be used to measure or appraise the problem; then descriptive and diagnostic study may be possible. Hypotheses are set up, factors are isolated, measured, and relationships ascertained. Still later, experimental studies may be undertaken. Research design keeps changing as hypotheses are modified, eliminated, and substituted. Each stage of research requires the use of new skills, the recasting of theory, the introduction of new revised factors, and perhaps reinterpretation of results.[4]

A. *Exploratory Study.* The Air Site Project began as a military requirement to investigate the morale and personnel problems of Air Force personnel in radar squadrons. We agreed to go to the research field and discover the personnel problems and personnel needs. At the same time we were to find the most significant problems for basic research into morale and motivation. Three professional sociologists developed a plan of sampling and interviewing and devoted three months between July and October 1951 to field visits and analysis of seven squadrons in one Air Defense Division.[5] Detailed interviews were held with a representative sample of Air Force personnel in each squadron. We lived with and observed the operations and leisure activities of each squadron for a number of days. From our interviews and notes a common record was prepared by the research team for each squadron. This record ranked the major personnel problems as reported to us in each squadron, the needs as expressed by Air Force personnel, and research clues that we determined through our experiences in the field. Table 1 gives a record of major personnel needs and research clues for one Air Force squadron.

Interviews were coded and an analysis of major personnel problems was made to determine possible associations with age, marital status, education, length of service, and isolation of site. Various tables were constructed to show analyses of interview data—Analysis of Management Problems, Impact of Isolation on Operating Problems, and Personnel Needs as Defined by Site Personnel. All of these tables were prepared especially for top military leaders and were presented in briefing sessions to them for their guidance. On

TABLE 1

MAJOR PERSONNEL NEEDS AND RESEARCH CLUES
FOR ONE AIR FORCE SQUADRON

Problems Encountered

1. Recreational outlets on the base.
2. Access to city or large town.
3. Degree of supervision.
4. Housing for the married man and his family.
5. Living on Indian Reservation and adjustment to Indian people.
6. Restrictions imposed on minors.
7. Career misassignment.
8. Pressures from division and group commands.
9. Irritations from G.I. regulations.
10. Inequities in promotions and advancements.
11. Supply problems.
12. Access to weapon and monotony of tracking.
13. Organizational change to larger unit.
14. Relative deprivation.
15. Organizational cleavages.

Basic Research Clues for Possible Future Study

1. Study relationship between humor and tension. Compare a tense and relaxed site, watching for differences.
2. Study of emotional outbursts as manifested in attitude and in behavior such as A.W.O.L., chewing out, or fighting.
3. Time sampling study of a group of highly motivated and poorly motivated personnel.
4. A study of newcomers over an extended time period to watch acculturation.
5. A study of the effect of increasing size on organizational and morale changes.
6. Relations of age, marital status, military experience, and residence and education to adjustment of highly and poorly adjusted persons.
7. A validation of relative deprivation.
8. A study of language functions, especially jargon and argot.
9. Socialization of the civilian to military culture.
10. Description of military culture.
11. The relation of job satisfaction to civilian training, experience, and goals.
12. Extent to which realization alone of choice of job is related to job satisfaction.

Continued on page 48.

Observation Clues for Possible Future Measurement

1. Evaluate condition of uniform and military bearing at spot point.
2. Number of persons found in various places—barracks, dayroom, mess hall (goldbricking).
3. Count number who leave camp every day—check those who leave on 2-day-off periods.
4. Turnover as a generalized aspect of military organizations.
   —among officers (upward mobility involves spatial mobility).
   —among airmen (stay only 18 months in a site).
5. What is relation of high turnover to problem of morale, organization, and leadership, to identification with the site, fellows, C.O.?

the basis of these facts and others, new facilities were subsequently made available to the squadrons.

Meanwhile, research clues were combed to find the most significant research problems. General clusters of factors that we called research sectors were set forth as the ones we believed to be most directly related to the adjustment of Air Force personnel.[6] We selected (1) The Job and the Career, (2) Organization and Communication, (3) Leadership, and (4) Morale and Motivation. We pressed forward without an overall theory; [7] rather, research teams were formed and these teams selected a research sector, set up hypotheses, and began field research in the fall of 1951.

B. *Descriptive and Diagnostic Study.* In January, 1952, six months after the initiation of the project, the research design was composed of the parts shown on page 49. The central problem had become the adjustment of the person to a military organization. Morale, motivation, and management or personnel problems had been chosen as the principal objects of study. Guttman scaling techniques were being applied to the study of various attitude areas. Nonverbal indices, such as rate of promotion, were being developed. Later, as a squadron efficiency rating system was developed by the officers of one Air Division (assisted by the Air Site Project), this criterion was introduced. Against these criteria we sought to determine the relationship of many social and social-psychological variables.

The illustration on page 49, Basic Generalities of Social Organization, became our overall design. It was based essentially on the importance of studying certain difficult sociological problems *in-*

ASIC GENERALITIES of SOCIAL ORGANIZATION

Relationships Validated in the Air Defense Command

anagement
formation
anuals

Basic
Science
Contributions

↑

EXTENSIVE INTERSITE RESEARCH DESIGNS

Relationships Validated in the 25th Air Division A.D.C.

Site 1	Site 2	Site 3	Site 4	Site 5	Site 6	Site 7	Site 8	Site 9	Site 10
A.C.&W.	E.W.	A.C.&W	A.C.&W	A.C.&W.	E.W.	E.W.	A.C.&W.	A.C.&W.	E.W.

VARIABLES AND RELATIONSHIPS READY FOR INTER-SITE TESTS

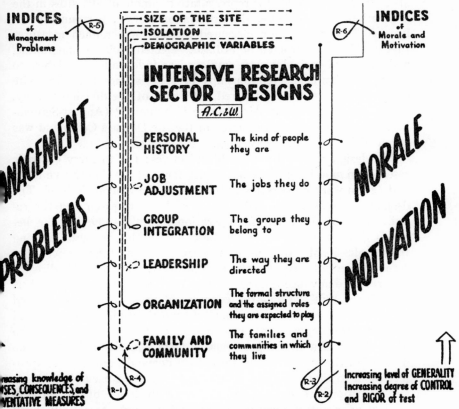

INDICES
of
Management
Problems

(R-5)

SIZE OF THE SITE
ISOLATION
DEMOGRAPHIC VARIABLES

(R-6)

INDICES
of
Morale and
Motivation

INTENSIVE RESEARCH SECTOR DESIGNS

A.C.&W.

PERSONAL HISTORY — The kind of people they are

JOB ADJUSTMENT — The jobs they do

GROUP INTEGRATION — The groups they belong to

LEADERSHIP — The way they are directed

ORGANIZATION — The formal structure and the assigned roles they are expected to play

FAMILY AND COMMUNITY — The families and communities in which they live

MANAGEMENT PROBLEMS

MORALE MOTIVATION

(R-5) (R-4) (R-1) (R-3) (R-2)

easing knowledge of
SES, CONSEQUENCES, and
VENTATIVE MEASURES

Increasing level of GENERALITY
Increasing degree of CONTROL
and RIGOR of test

The general research design of large-scale investigation into the human factors affecting morale, motivation, and efficiency of radar sites.

49

tensively while ascertaining the full scope of other problems *extensively*. The six research sectors that received intensive study were those of Personal History, Job Adjustment, Group Integration, Leadership, Organization, and Family and Community. In these sectors researchers attempted to find relationships in areas where it was difficult to secure the relevant data and in which understanding could come only through patient, skillful, and persistent study. Such study was usually confined to one or two sites.[8] As crucial variables were identified and quantitative measures were developed, these variables were considered ready for extensive intersite test. The intersite design called for a testing of variables on a selected sample of Air Force men in all (or representative sample of all) sites in the population studied. Here, the criteria of morale, personnel problems, and efficiency were measured by the most refined measures that could be constructed or utilized. Selected social, demographic, and ecological variables were employed as independent variables to determine significant relationships to criteria measures. Intersite questionnaires were administered in 12 sites of one division [9] (May, 1952), and in the Japan Air Defense Command [10] (August-September, 1952); and a national survey of the Air Defense Command was executed in April and May 1953.

The design reflects the twofold objectives: (1) to carry on basic research in morale (or personal adjustment) at the descriptive level, and (2) to work on personnel problems at the diagnostic level. The design thus reflects both the canons of basic research and the requirements of the client for operational results. The balance between these two foci was often beset by subtle pressures deriving from professional standards, on the one hand, and the practical concerns of the military officials, on the other. The research director who seeks to advance knowledge must see that the research work is so designed that the long-run concerns of basic science are carried along while, at the same time, good diagnostic studies of operational problems are produced that convince his client that research can be of service to him on the problems he faces *now*. He must persuade his staff of the importance of these twin demands, and he must protect them so that there is ample opportunity to achieve both basic and operational research. The basic research design of the Air Site Project grew out of these pressures, and it sought to satisfy them.

But more than this, the design must be understood as an expression of the researcher's desire for freedom to attack his problem in his own way. Some researchers took to the field at once to explore their problem. Others began to devise measuring instruments and to work out sampling plans. Some planned much observational work in the field; others planned fieldwork only to make pretests of questionnaires and scales. These differences seemed to be explained sometimes by differences in research approach (interactionists versus statistical testers) and sometimes by different adjustments to fieldwork. The deprivations of fieldwork and the new role relationships of a fieldworker (in contrast to those of the classroom teacher and library researcher) presented adjustment problems to all staff members. Some found field contact exciting and satisfying; others found absence from home and from customary routines of office a deprivation and sought to center their research in the university. It has already been suggested that the home plays an influential role in shaping the attitudes of the field researcher and thus indirectly the research work itself.

C. *Experimental Study.* Samuel Stouffer has written that "the necessary condition for dealing with a collection of variables is to isolate and identify them and, in addition, it is useful if they can also be measured. Until the relevant variables can be identified, empirical tests of a conceptual scheme involving these variables hardly can be expected." [11]

In the Air Site Project we identified the objects of study and were able to measure some of them. We ascertained many relationships between our criteria and social, demographic, and ecological factors. Many hypotheses were tested by field teams. Experimental work of a cross-sectional type was carried out.[12] Perhaps one of the most important relationships tested was that between morale in a squadron and the efficiency of the squadron. It is widely believed that good human relations are related positively to high efficiency. However, only a few tests have been made under experimental conditions involving a control group.[13]

The assignment of Air Force men is made according to the training specialty of available personnel and according to organizational needs. The assignment of men who are drawn out to fill quotas results in near stratified-random selection. As a result it is possible to find squadrons that have almost identical characteristics as to mean age, length of service, marital status, education, rank structure, degree of isolation, work conditions, and living conditions. In one division we studied 12 squadrons. Efficiency ratings of these squadrons were made each quarter by the responsible division officials. We constructed Guttman type scales or items measuring such areas of morale as satisfaction with air site, satisfaction with Air Force, job satisfaction, and acceptance of mission goals. The relationship of morale to efficiency under controlled conditions was ascertained in our population. Because of the randomization in the squadron populations, control by frequency distribution could be employed. Squadrons were selected from the total universe (one division) and matched on variables believed to affect efficiency. The significance of differences between means was determined. Replication of this design was made on our larger universe of squadrons from all divisions.[14]

D. *Projected Experimentation.* Plans had been made for moving to the stage of true experimental study by taking before and after measures of experimental and control groups under controlled conditions. This would have consummated the direction of research movement. Unfortunately, the sharp curtailment of funds for human relations research in 1953 made it impossible to proceed into this type of experimentation. Projected experiments were not undertaken earlier because needed measures of morale, leadership, and efficiency had to be constructed first. Moreover, a high degree of confidence and cooperation from line military officers had to be earned before such work would have been possible. This is a hard social fact that cannot be ignored.

Conclusion

Four major factors influenced the shaping of research design on one large-scale group research project. These were: the characteristic imperative of group research; the personal wants of researchers; the demands of education; and the accumulation of empirical and theoretical knowledge.

These factors created both problems and opportunities. Problems have been considered in much of this paper, but opportunities were also abundant. Adequate financing of research brings professional, clerical, and technical assistance, permitting a rapid increase in the quantity and quality of research. Access to the research field and cooperation within it opens a new wealth of social data. A long-standing weakness of social science research has been the inability to get enough individual cases or organizational units so that relationships could be validated through replication. This is possible in large-scale group research. These opportunities can be capitalized, but only as the social processes of group research are marshaled. Social processes ever blend with scientific thinking to mold research design. As an end product of group research, it is a precipitate of personal feelings, thoughts, habits, and hopes.

NOTES

* This paper is based on the conclusions of the writer as director of the Air Site Project. Other members of the project have contributed in many different ways to the experiences described. Appreciation is acknowledged to: Orvis F. Collins (Southern Illinois University), Edward Gross (University of Washington), F. James Davis (California State College at Fullerton), Glenn C. McCann (North Carolina State College), Nahum Z. Medalia (Chatham College), Charles D. McGlamery (University of Alabama), professional sociologists; David S. Bushnell, Donald L. Garrity, Robert Hagedorn, John Hudson, Harold Kant, Alvin S. Lackey, Robert Larson, Herman Loether, Duane Strinden, Wes Wager, Shirley Willis, and David Yaukey, research fellows; all are now professional sociologists in the United States.

The research was supported in part by the United States Air Force under contract number AF-33-038-26823, monitored by the Human Resources Research Institute, Air Research and Development Command, Maxwell Air Force Base, Alabama. Permission is granted for reproduction, translation, publication, and disposal in whole and in part by or for the U.S. Government.

I am especially indebted to the continuous encouragement of Dr. Raymond V. Bowers, Director of the Institute from 1949-52, and to Dr. Abbott L. Ferriss, Chief of the Human Relations Division, whose administrative efforts made possible our access to many research fields.

1. Joseph W. Eaton, "Social Process of Professional Teamwork," *American Sociological Review*, 16 (October, 1951), 707-713; Alfred M. Lee, "Individual and Organizational Research in Sociology," *American Sociological Review,* 16 (October, 1951), 701-707.

2. Urie Bronfenbrenner and Edward C. Devereux, "Interdisciplinary Planning for Team Research on Constructive Community Behavior," *Human Relations,* V (1952), 187-203; William Caudill and Bertram H. Roberts, "Pitfalls in the Organization of Interdisciplinary Research," *Human Organization,* 10 (Winter, 1951), 12-15.

3. Chester I. Barnard, "Dilemmas of Leadership in the Democratic Process," *Organization and Management* (Cambridge: Harvard University, 1949), pp. 24-50.

4. Robert K. Merton, "The Bearing of Empirical Research Upon the Development of Social Theory," *American Sociological Review,* 13 (October, 1948), 505-515.

5. Squadrons varied in size from approximately 100 to 300 men, depending on type and function of the station.

6. For a full report of this exploratory survey see F. James Davis, Edward Gross, and Delbert C. Miller, *Survey Report on Military Management Problems in Aircraft Control and Warning Stations in the Air Defense Command* (Human Resources Research Institute, Air University, Maxwell Air Force Base, Ala., 1951).

7. This was a source of much concern to some of our researchers, and we held many staff meetings groping for such a theory. Some members of the staff believed we should not set out at all until a fully-developed theory was in hand. Others believed theory should wait until the research and field experience were more advanced.

8. For published reports of this work see: F. James Davis, "Conceptions of Official Leader Roles in the Air Force," *Social Forces*, 32 (March, 1954), 253-258; F. James Davis and Robert Hagedorn, "Testing the Reliability of Systematic Field Observations," *American Sociological Review*, 19 (June, 1954), 345-348; F. James Davis, Robert Hagedorn, and J. Robert Larson, "Scaling Problems in the Study of Conceptions of Air Force Leader Roles," *Public Opinion Quarterly*, 18 (Fall, 1954), 279-286; Edward Gross, "Some Functional Consequences of Primary Controls in Formal Work Organizations," *American Sociological Review*, 18 (August, 1953), 368-373; Edward Gross, "Primary Functions of the Small Group," *American Journal of Sociology*, 60 (July, 1954), 24-29; Herman J. Loether, "Propinquity and Homogeneity as Factors in the Choice of Best Buddies in the Air Force," *Pacific Sociological Review*, 3 (Spring, 1960), 18-22; C. D. McGlamery, "Developing an Index of Work Group Communications," *Research Studies, State College of Washington*, 21 (1953), 225-230; Nahum Z. Medalia, "Unit Size and Leadership Perception," *Sociometry*, 17 (February, 1945), 64-67; Nahum Z. Medalia, "Authoritarianism, Leader Acceptance, and Group Cohesion," *Journal of Abnormal and Social Psychology*, 51 (September, 1955), 207-213.

9. The Human Resources Research Institute published interim reports in 1952.

10. A final report has been prepared for Human Resources Research Institute by Edward Gross and Orvis Collins, *American Air Sites in Japan: An Analysis of Human Relations in A. C. & W. Detachment Within the Japan Air Defense Force* (January 12, 1953).

11. Samuel A. Stouffer, *et al.*, *The American Soldier* (Princeton: Princeton University, 1949), I, 34.

12. Stouffer writes, "I would trade a half dozen army-wide surveys on attitudes toward officers for one good controlled experiment. Keeping the model of the controlled experiment as an ideal, it is sometimes possible for one to approximate it. . . . Ingenuity in locating ready-made situations is much needed. In any program of future research, I would put far more emphasis on this than ever has been done in the past." Robert K. Merton and Paul F. Lazarsfeld (eds.), *Studies in the Scope and Method of "The American Soldier"* (Glencoe, Ill.: Free Press, 1950), p. 211.

13. See Daniel Katz, Nathan Maccoby, and Nancy C. Morse, *Productivity, Supervision and Morale in an Office Situation*, Part I (Ann Arbor: Institute for Social Research, University of Michigan, 1950); Daniel Katz, Nathan Maccoby, Gerald Gurin, and Lucretia G. Floor, *Productivity, Supervision, and Morale Among Railroad Workers* (Ann Arbor: Survey Research Center, University of Michigan, 1951); Irving R. Weschler, Murray Kahane, and Robert Tannenbaum, "Job Satisfaction, Productivity and Morale: A Case Study," *Occupational Psychology*, I (January, 1952), 1-14; Gunner Westerlund, *Group Leadership, A Field Experiment* (Stockholm: Nordisk Rotogravyr, 1952).

14. This research is described by Nahum Z. Medalia and Delbert C. Miller in "Human Relations Leadership and the Association of Morale and Efficiency in Workgroups: A Controlled Study with Small Military Units," *Social Forces*, 33 (May, 1955), 348-352. See also D. C. Miller and N. Z. Medalia, "Efficiency, Leadership, and Morale in Small Military Organizations," *The Sociological Review*, 3 (July, 1955), 93-107; Edward Gross and D. C. Miller, "The Impact of Isolation on Worker Adjustment in Military Installations of the United States and Japan,"

Estudios de Sociologia, Buenos Aires, I (Fall, 1961), 70-86; Glenn C. McCann, Nahum Z. Medalia, and Delbert C. Miller, "Morale and Human Relations Leadership as Factors in Organizational Effectiveness," *Studies of Organizational Effectiveness,* ed. R. V. Bowers (Washington, D.C.: Air Force Office of Scientific Research, 1962), pp. 85-114.

I.10. THE SAMPLING CHART

Instructions for Use of Guide I.10.

A sample is a smaller representation of a larger whole. The use of sampling allows for more adequate scientific work by making the time of the scientific worker count. Instead of spending much of his time analyzing a large mass of material from one point of view, he can use that time to make a more intensive analysis from many points of view. The researcher can also save much time and money by sampling, thus making possible investigations that could not otherwise be carried out.

The sampling problems may be divided into those that affect (1) the definition of the population, (2) the size of the sample, and (3) the representativeness of the sample. In regard to the definition of the population, the important problem is to decide the group about which the researcher wishes to generalize his findings. In regard to size of sample, consideration must be given to the persistent disappearance of cases in a breakdown analysis. This disappearance should be foreseen as clearly as possible. Dummy tables help provide for such planning. The third and perhaps most intricate sampling problem arises in connection with the method of securing a representative sample. The essential requirement of any sample is that it is as representative as possible of the population or universe from which it is taken.

Three methods of sampling are commonly used. These are *random sampling, stratified sampling,* and *judgmental* or *"purposive" sampling.*

1. *Random sampling.* A random sample is one that is drawn in such a way that every member of the population has an equal chance of being included. The most rigorous method of random sampling employs a table of random numbers. In this method, a number is assigned to each member of the population. Those members are in-

cluded in the sample whose numbers are taken from the table of random numbers in succession until a sample of predetermined size is drawn. A more common method is to write the names or numbers of the members of a population on cards or discs, shuffling these, and then drawing. A convenient method, known as systematic sampling, which is not exactly equivalent to random sampling, but is often close enough for practical purposes, is to take every n^{th} item in the population, beginning at some random member in the population.

2. *Stratified sampling.* The aforementioned methods assume that the composition of the total group is not known, and that a representative sample will be best approximated by a strictly random selection or a selection by regular intervals. In some cases the more or less exact composition of the total group with respect to some significant characteristics is known before we select our sample. For example, we may know the exact ratio of men to women in the population and that sex differences are related to the variables we wish to test. In such cases we can increase the chances of selecting a representative sample by selecting subsamples proportionate in size to the significant characteristics of the total population. Thus, we can select a sample that is mathematically absolutely representative with regard to some significant characteristics. There are numerous forms of stratified random sampling techniques as shown in the Ackoff Sampling Chart, which follows on pages 57-58.

3. *Judgment or "purposive" sampling.* When practical considerations preclude the use of probability sampling, the researcher may seek a representative sample by other means. He looks for a subgroup that is typical of the population as a whole. Observations are then restricted to this subgroup, and conclusions from the data obtained are generalized to the total population. An example would be the choice of a particular state or county as a barometer of an election outcome, relying upon the results of past elections as evidence of the representativeness of the sample for the nation or state. Sampling errors and biases cannot be computed for such samples. For this reason judgmental sampling should be restricted to the following situations: (1) when the possible errors are not serious and (2) when probability sampling is practically impossible. Data from judgmental samples at best suggest or indicate conclusions, but in general they cannot be used as the basis of statistical testing procedures.

Sampling Chart *

Type of Sampling	Brief Description	Advantages	Disadvantages
A. Simple random	Assign to each population member a unique number; select sample items by use of random numbers	1. Requires minimum knowledge of population in advance 2. Free of possible classification errors 3. Easy to analyze data and compute errors	1. Does not make use of knowledge of population which researcher may have 2. Larger errors for same sample size than in stratified sampling
B. Systematic	Use natural ordering or order population; select random starting point between 1 and the nearest integer to the sampling ratio (N/n); select items at interval of nearest integer to sampling ratio	1. If population is ordered with respect to pertinent property, gives stratification effect, and hence reduces variability compared to A 2. Simplicity of drawing sample; easy to check	1. If sampling interval is related to a periodic ordering of the population, increased variability may be introduced 2. Estimates of error likely to be high where there is stratification effect
C. Multistage random	Use a form of random sampling in each of the sampling stages where there are at least two stages	1. Sampling lists, identification, and numbering required only for members of sampling units selected in sample 2. If sampling units are geographically defined, cuts down field costs (i.e., travel)	1. Errors likely to be larger than in A or B for same sample size 2. Errors increase as number of sampling units selected decreases
1. With probability proportionate to size	Select sampling units with probability proportionate to their size	1. Reduces variability	1. Lack of knowledge of size of each sampling unit before selection increases variability
D. Stratified 1. Proportionate	Select from every sampling unit at other than last stage a random sample proportionate to size of sampling unit	1. Assures representativeness with respect to property which forms basis of classifying units; therefore yields less variability than A or C 2. Decreases chance of failing to include members of population because of classification process 3. Characteristics of each stratum can be estimated, and hence comparisons can be made	1. Requires accurate information on proportion of population in each stratum, otherwise increases error 2. If stratified lists are not available, may be costly to prepare them; possibility of faulty classification and hence increase in variability
2. Optimum allocation	Same as 1 except sample is proportionate to variability within strata as well as their size	1. Less variability for same sample size than 1	1. Requires knowledge of variability of pertinent characteristic within strata
3. Disproportionate	Same as 1 except that size of sample is not proportionate to size of sampling unit but is dedicated by analytical considerations or convenience	1. More efficient than 1 for comparison of strata or where different errors are optimum for different strata	1. Less efficient than 1 for determining population characteristics; i.e., more variability for same sample size

* Reprinted from Russell L. Ackoff, *The Design of Social Research* (Chicago: University of Chicago, 1953), p. 124. By permission of The University of Chicago Press. Copyright 1953 by The University of Chicago.

Type of Sampling	Brief Description	Advantages	Disadvantages
E. Cluster	Select sampling units by some form of random sampling; ultimate units are groups; select these at random and take a complete count of each	1. If clusters are geographically defined, yields lowest field costs 2. Requires listing only individuals in selected clusters 3. Characteristics of clusters as well as those of population can be estimated 4. Can be used for subsequent samples, since clusters, not individuals, are selected, and substitution of individuals may be permissible	1. Larger errors for comparable size than other probability samples 2. Requires ability to assign each member of population uniquely to a cluster; inability to do so may result in duplication or omission of individuals
F. Stratified cluster	Select clusters at random from every sampling unit	1. Reduces variability of plain cluster sampling	1. Disadvantages of stratified sampling added to those of cluster sampling 2. Since cluster properties may change, advantage of stratification may be reduced and make sample unusable for later research
G. Repetitive: multiple or sequential	Two or more samples of any of the above types are taken, using results from earlier samples to design later ones, or determine if they are necessary	1. Provides estimates of population characteristics which facilitate efficient planning of succeeding sample, therefore reduces error of final estimate 2. In the long run reduces number of observations required	1. Complicates administration of fieldwork 2. More computation and analysis required than in nonrepetitive sampling 3. Sequential sampling can only be used where a very small sample can approximate representativeness and where the number of observations can be increased conveniently at any stage of the research
H. Judgment	Select a subgroup of the population which, on the basis of available information, can be judged to be representative of the total population; take a complete count or subsample of this group	1. Reduces cost of preparing sample and field work, since ultimate units can be selected so that they are close together	1. Variability and bias of estimates cannot be measured or controlled 2. Requires strong assumptions or considerable knowledge of population and subgroup selected
1. Quota	Classify population by pertinent properties; determine desired proportion of sample from each class; fix quotas for each observer	1. Same as above 2. Introduces some stratification effect	1. Introduces bias of observers' classification of subjects and nonrandom selection within classes

These three forms of sampling do not exhaust the range of sampling procedures. The Ackoff Sampling Chart lists such types as multistage random sampling, cluster, stratified cluster, and repetitive sampling. A description of these forms may be found in Russell Ackoff, *The Design of Social Research* (copyright 1953 by the University of Chicago Press), pp. 123-126. He writes:

From practical as well as purely scientific purposes it is necessary to use selection procedures whose errors are measurable. A procedure should be capable of characterization relative to bias and variability. The fundamental procedure satisfying these conditions is simple random sampling, a method in which each individual has an equal chance of being selected. Simple random sampling is performed with the aid of random numbers, while systematic sampling is a variation which proceeds from a random start to select elements at a preset interval.

By breaking the population into subgroups, we may select a sample in stages. If a random sample is selected at each stage, we have a multistage random sample. If a complete count of sampling units is taken at one stage other than the last, we have a stratified sample. If a complete count is made at the last stage, we have a cluster sample. The probability of selecting any subgroup may be made proportionate to some function of the size of the subgroup, and the number of units selected from any subgroup may also be made proportionate to some such function. Proportionate sampling tends to reduce sampling errors. Stratification and clustering can be combined to yield efficient samples, particularly where stratification and/or clustering is based on geographic properties (i.e., in area sampling). Area sampling reduces the complexity of preparing sampling lists and permits the clustering of subjects so that they come in bunches.

In double sampling a first sample can be used to provide information which can in turn be used to design an efficient second sample. Such sampling can also be used to reduce the number of observations required, on the average, for coming to a conclusion. When double sampling is generalized, it yields sequential sampling, a method of drawing one item or set of items at a time and using the data obtained to decide whether to continue sampling or not.

—The ultimate basis for selecting a sampling procedure should be minimization of the cost of getting the sample and the expected cost of errors which may result from using the method. Expert assistance should be employed in making such evaluations.

The sampling chart summarizes in a very brief way the description, advantages, and disadvantages of the various sampling procedures discussed.

I.11.   A SELECTED BIBLIOGRAPHY ON RESEARCH DESIGN

ACKOFF, RUSSELL L. *The Design of Social Research.* Chicago: University of Chicago Press, 1953.

BORGATTA, EDGAR F. (ed.) *Sociological Methodology.* San Francisco: Jossey-Bass, 1969.

BROSS, IRWIN D. J. *Design for Decision.* New York: The Macmillan Company, 1953.

CAMPBELL, DONALD T., and STANLEY, JULIAN C. *Experimental and Quasi Experimental Design.* Chicago: Rand McNally & Company, 1966.

CANNON, WALTER BRADFORD. *The Way of an Investigator.* New York: Hafner Publishing Company, Inc., 1961.

CHAPIN, F. S., *Experimental Designs in Sociological Research.* Rev. ed. New York: Harper & Row, Publishers, Inc., 1955.

CHURCHMAN, C. W. *Theory of Experimental Inference.* New York: The Macmillan Company, 1948.

COCHRAN, W. G., and COX, G. N. *Experimental Designs.* 2nd ed. New York: John Wiley & Sons, Inc., 1957.

COHEN, MORRIS, and NAGEL, E. *An Introduction to Logic and Scientific Methods.* Rev. ed. New York: Harcourt, Brace & World, Inc., 1960.

DiRENZO, GORDON J. (ed.). *Concepts, Theory, and Explanation in the Behavioral Sciences,* see especially Paul F. Lazarsfeld, Chapter VII, "Concept Formation and Measurement." New York: Random House, 1967, pp. 144-202.

EDWARDS, ALLEN L. *Experimental Design in Psychological Research.* New York: Holt, Rinehart and Winston, Inc., 1960.

FESTINGER, L., and KATZ, DANIEL (eds.). *Research Methods in the Behavioral Sciences.* New York: The Dryden Press, Inc., 1953.

FISHER, R. A. *The Design of Experiments.* 7th rev. ed. New York: Hafner Publishing Company, Inc., 1960.

GLOCK, CHARLES Y. *Survey Research in the Social Sciences,* New York: Russell Sage Foundation, 1967.

GOODE, WILLIAM J., and HATT, PAUL K. *Methods in Social Research.* New York: McGraw-Hill Book Company, 1952.

GREER, SCOTT. *The Logic of Social Inquiry.* Chicago: Aldine Publishing Co., 1969.

HAMMOND, P. E. (ed.). *Sociologists at Work: Essays on the Craft of Social Research.* New York: Basic Books, Inc., 1964.

HYMAN, HERBERT. *Survey Design and Analysis: Principles, Cases, and Procedures.* Glencoe, Ill.: The Free Press, 1955.

KAPLAN, ABRAHAM. *The Conduct of Inquiry.* San Francisco: Chandler Press, 1964.

NORTHROP, F. S. C. *The Logic of the Sciences and the Humanities.* New York: The Macmillan Company, 1947.

PHILLIPS, BERNARD S. *Social Research: Strategy and Tactics.* New York: The Macmillan Company, 1966.

POPPER, KARL R. *The Logic of Scientific Discovery.* New York: Basic Books, 1959.

RILEY, MATILDA WHITE. *Sociological Research: A Case Approach.* New York: Harcourt, Brace & World, Inc., 1963.

SELLTIZ, C., DEUTSCH, M., and COOK, S. W. *Research Methods in Social Relations.* Rev. ed. New York: Holt, Rinehart & Winston, Inc., 1959.

STOUFFER, SAMUEL. *Social Research to Test Ideas.* New York: The Free Press, 1962.

SUCHMAN, EDWARD A. *Evaluative Research, Principles and Practice in Public Service and Social Action Programs.* New York: Russell Sage Foundation, 1968.

WHITEHEAD, ALFRED N. *A Philosopher Looks at Science.* New York: Philosophical Library, 1965.

ZETTERBERG, HANS L. *On Theory and Verification in Sociology.* 3rd rev. ed. Totowa, N.J.: The Bedminster Press, 1965.

Guides to Methods and Techniques of Collecting Data in Library, Field, and Laboratory; Social Science Data Libraries and Research Centers

THE COLLECTION OF DATA is the crucial operation in the execution of a good research design. The quality of the research rests upon the quality of the data. In this section the methods and techniques of social research are presented according to their common situs of research: library, field, and laboratory. Advantages and disadvantages of principal methods are pointed out. Guides to the construction of questionnaires, interviews, and scales are described.

A listing of social science data libraries is given. These social science archives are available to research scholars and offer many excellent opportunities for research. The collection of data is expensive and the ability to use data previously collected offers the possibility of superior research at a greatly lowered cost.

Finally, directories and lists of research centers in the United States, Europe, Latin America, and the world generally are given to aid the researcher. These are especially valuable contact points to determine the status of current research and to determine comparative research advances in various fields.

II.1. OUTLINE GUIDE TO SITUSES, PRINCIPAL METHODS, AND TECHNIQUES OF THE SOCIAL SCIENCE RESEARCHER

The collection of data occurs in a designed inquiry only after a long series of steps including:

1. The definition of the problem.
2. The construction of the theoretical framework.
3. The stating of hypotheses.
4. The establishment of the design of inquiry.
5. The determination of sampling procedures.

This section introduces the most common methods of social science research and presents a brief set of instructions for the construction of questionnaires, interviews, and scales. These instructions will assist the researcher in evaluating the appropriate method for his problem. He should consult methods books for a thorough explanation of each method or technique.

Methods are handmaidens of designed inquiry. It is important to distinguish carefully between four terms: *methodology, situs, methods,* and *techniques.*

Methodology is a body of knowledge that describes and analyzes methods, indicating their limitations and resources, clarifying their presuppositions and consequences, and relating their potentialites to research advances. In this part the methods of social science are first examined in order to set forth the advantages and disadvantages of each method. The aim is to help the researcher to understand the process of gathering data and what his choice of method entails.

Situs refers to the place in which the data is gathered. For most sciences, the most used situses are the library, the field, and the laboratory.

Method refers to the means of gathering data that are common to all sciences or to a significant part of them. Thus methods include such procedures as the making of observations and measurements, performing experiments, building models and theories, or providing explanations and making predictions. The social sciences use docu-

SITUS	METHODS	TECHNIQUES
Library	(1) Analysis of historical records: primary records—letters, diaries, etc.; secondary interpretations of events (2) Analysis of documents: statistical and non-statistical records of formal agencies (3) Literature search for theory and previous research in books, journals, and monographs	Recording of notes Content analysis Tape and film listening and analysis Statistical compilations and manipulations Reference and abstract guides Content analysis
Field	(1) Mail questionnaire	Identification of social and economic background of respondents Use of sociometric scales to ascertain such variables as social status, group structure, community and social participation, leadership activity, and family adjustment Use of attitude scales to measure morale, job satisfaction, marital adjustment, etc.
	(2) Personal interview Structured interview schedule	Interviewer uses a detailed schedule with open and closed questions Sociometric scales may be used
	(3) Focused interview	Interviewer focuses attention upon a given experience and its effects; he knows in advance what topics or questions he wishes to cover
	(4) Free story interview	Respondent is urged to talk freely about the subjects treated in the study

Situs	Methods	Techniques
Field, *continued*	(5) Group interview	Small groups of respondents are interviewed simultaneously; any of the above techniques may be used
	(6) Telephone survey	Used as a survey technique for information and for discerning opinion May be used for follow-up of a questionnaire mailing to increase return
	(7) Case study and life history	For case study, cross-sectional collection of data for intensive analysis of a person emphasizing personal and social factors in socialization For life history, longitudinal collection of data of intensive character also emphasizing socialization over an extended period of time
	(8) Non-participant direct observation	Use of standard score cards and observational behavior scales
	(9) Participant observation	Interactional recording; possible use of tape recorders and photographic techniques
	(10) Mass observation	Recording mass or collective behavior by observation and interview using independent observers in public places
Laboratory	Small group study of random behavior, play, problem solving, or stress behavior of individuals and/or groups	Use of contrived and non-constructed situations; use of confederates; use of audio-visual recording devices; use of observers behind one-way mirror.

mentary analysis, the mailed questionnaire and the personal interview, most frequently.

Techniques refer to specific procedures which are used in a given method. For example, the field method worker may employ such techniques as use of sociometric scales to measure social variables and personality inventories to identify personal traits. The research worker such as a demographer may draw heavily on statistical documents and use various statistical techniques to describe relationships or gain statistical control over his data.

The following aids first present an outline of methods and techniques as employed in the three situses: library, field, and laboratory. Then aids are presented for the most common methods and techniques. A list of reference books is given which describes various methods and techniques in detail.

II.2. DESCRIPTION OF IMPORTANT DOCUMENTARY RESOURCES AVAILABLE IN THE LIBRARY *

Statistical Sourcebooks

The social science researcher commonly uses reference books to assist him. Among the most useful are:

1. U.S. BUREAU OF THE CENSUS. *Historical Statistics of the United States: Colonial Times to 1957.* A Statistical Abstracts Supplement. Washington, D.C.: U.S. Government Printing Office, 1960. Pp. xii + 789.

    Arranged in twenty-six chapters: population; vital statistics and health and medical care; migration; labor; prices and price indexes; national income and wealth; consumer income and expenditures; social statistics; land, water, and climate; agriculture; forestry and fisheries; minerals; construction and housing; manufactures; transportation; communication; power; distribution and services; foreign trade and other international transactions; business enterprise; productivity and technological development; banking and finance; government; colonial statistics. Index of names and subjects. Clothbound.

2. U.S. BUREAU OF THE CENSUS. *Historical Statistics of the United States: Colonial Times to 1957—Continuation to 1962 and Revisions.* A Statistical Abstract Supplement. Washington, D.C.: U.S. Government Printing Office, 1965. Pp. iv. + 154.

* This guide was assembled by John Pease, University of Maryland.

Arranged in two parts: continuation of series in "historical statistics"; revisions of series in "historical statistics." Source notes. Paperbound.

3. U.S. BUREAU OF THE CENSUS. *Statistical Abstract of the United States, 1966.* 87th ed. Washington, D.C.: U.S. Government Printing Office, 1966. Pp. xii + 1039.

Arranged in thirty-three sections: population; vital statistics, health, and nutrition; immigration and naturalization; education; law enforcement, federal courts, and prisons; area, geography, and climate; public lands, parks, recreation, and travel; labor force, employment, and earnings; national defense and veterans affairs; social insurance and welfare services; income, expenditures, and wealth; prices; elections; federal government finances and employment; state and local government finances and employment; banking, finance, and insurance; business enterprise; communications; power; science; transportation—land; transportation—air and water; agriculture—farms, land, and finances; agriculture—production, marketing, and trade; forests and forest products; fisheries, mining and mineral products; construction and housing; manufactures; distribution and services; foreign commerce and aid; outlying areas under the jurisdiction of the United States; comparative international statistics. Three appendixes. Index of names and subjects. Clothbound.

4. *United States Census of Population by States.* Washington, D.C.: U.S. Government Printing Office, 1963.

Contains the following information for most urban places of 2500 or more: size of population by sex; major occupational groups by sex; income for stated year of total families and unrelated individuals; major industry groups by sex; color of population by sex; age of population by sex; years of school completed; marital status of males and females, fourteen years and above; country of birth of foreign born white (a decennial publication).

5. *World Handbook of Political and Social Indicators* by RUSSETT, BRUCE M., ALKER, HAYWARD R., JR., DEUTSCH, KARL W. and LASSWELL, HAROLD D. New Haven: Yale University Press, 1964.

An extensive compilation of seventy-five variables for one hundred thirty-three states and colonies based on indices covering human resources, government and politics, communication, wealth, health, education, family and social relations, distribution of wealth and income, and religion. A matrix of intercorrelation is presented for the seventy-five variables and an analysis of trends and patterns is presented showing how the data can be used to investigate a wide variety of political and social questions.

6. City Directories

Often useful in giving a wide range of information about industries and social organizations of the community. Contains alphabetical lists of persons and typically lists occupation and address of each adult.

7. *The County and City Data Book.* Washington, D.C.: U.S. Government Printing Office.

Lists numerous tables for each county and cities of 25,000 or more. Contains such tables as labor force, income, elections, banking and finance, business enterprises, and education.

8. *The Municipal Year Book.* Chicago: The International City Managers' Association. (Issued yearly)

Authoritative reference book on municipal governments. Facts available about the role of city governments including education, housing, welfare, and health make it possible to compare any city with other cities on hundreds of items.

For specialized purposes consult:

U.S. Census of Manufacturers, Area Statistics

U.S. Census of Population, Census Tract Bulletin

Poor's Register of Directors and Executives

Rand McNally's International Bankers' Directory

Moody's Industrial Manual

Editor and Publisher Market Guide

Sales Management, Survey of Buying Power

Fortune Magazine Directory of 500 Largest Corporations

The Economic Almanac

Labor Fact Book

Directory of National and International Labor Unions in the United States

Who's Who in America, Who's Who in the East, Who's Who in the Midwest, Who's Who in the South and Southwest, Who's Who on the Pacific Coast

Directory of Scholars, Social and Behavioral Sciences

Who's Who in Commerce and Industry

Who's Who in Labor

DEWHURST, FREDERICK, et. al., *America's Needs and Resources,* Twentieth Century Fund, 1961.

WOYTINSKI, W. S., and WOYTINSKI, E. S. *World Population and Production,* Twentieth Century Fund, 1955.

Abstracts

Abstracts of the Papers of the Annual Meetings of the American Sociological Association. Sociological Abstracts, Inc., 2315 Broadway, New York, New York 10024.

1961. Annually. Table of contents. Abstracts. Author index. Published as a supplement to *Sociological Abstracts*.

Catholic University of America Studies in Sociology Abstract Series. Catholic University of America Press, 620 Michigan Avenue, N. W., Washington, D.C. 20017.

1950. Irregularly. Abstracts of dissertations in sociology from the Catholic University of America.

Sociological Abstracts. Sociological Abstracts, Inc., 2315 Broadway, New York, New York 10024.

1952. Octannually. Classified table of contents. List of abbreviations. Abstracts arranged in twenty-four major information areas: methodology and research technology; sociology—history and theory; social psychology; group interactions; culture and social structure; complex organizations (management); social change and economic development; mass phenomena; political interactions; social differentiation; rural sociology and agricultural economics; urban structures and ecology; sociology of the arts; sociology of education; sociology of religion; social control; sociology of science; demography and human biology; the family and socialization; sociology of health and medicine; social problems and social welfare; sociology of knowledge; community development; planning, forecasting, and speculation. Author index. Cumulative index for each volume is published as the last (eighth) issue and includes: table of contents; subject index; periodical index; monograph index; author index; list of abbreviations. *Abstracts of the Papers of the Annual Meetings of the American Sociological Association* is published annually as a supplement and includes: table of contents; abstracts; author index.

Sociology of Education Abstracts. School of Education, University of Liverpool, 19 Abercromby Square, Liverpool 7, England.

1965. Quarterly. Education study areas index. Sociological study areas index. List of abstractors.

Almanacs

GENDELL, MURRAY, and ZETTERBERG, HANS L. (eds.). *A Sociological Almanac for the United States.* 2nd ed. New York: Charles Scribner's Sons, 1964. Pp. xv + 94.

Three essays—"The United States Summed Up by Browsing in a Sociological Almanac," "The Organization of a Sociological Almanac," and "How to Read a Table"—and ninety-six tables about American society organized in terms of nine major topics: human resources; non-human resources; polity and order; economy and prosperity; science and knowledge; religion and sacredness; art and beauty; ethics and virtue; community—local and national. Paperbound.

Bibliographies

International Bibliography of the Social Sciences—Sociology. Aldine Publishing Co., 320 West Adams Street, Chicago, Ill. 60606.

1952-1954, volumes I-IV published in *Current Sociology;* 1955-1959, volumes V-IX published as *International Bibliography of Sociology,* 1960. Annually. List of periodicals consulted. Classification scheme. Bibliography. Author index. Subject index.

Dictionaries and Glossaries

BORGARDUS, EMORY S. "Selected Sociological Concepts for Beginning Students in Sociology," *Sociology and Social Research,* XLIV (January-February, 1960), 200-208.

A brief definition of and discussion about fifty-two sociological concepts which are recommended to beginning sociology students.

FAIRCHILD, HENRY PRATT (ed.). *Dictionary of Sociology.* New Students Outline Series. Paterson, N.J.: Littlefield, Adams and Co., 1961. Pp. viii + 342.

This is a reprint, unchanged, of the original edition which first appeared in 1944. Paperbound.

GOULD, JULIUS, and KOLB, WILLIAM L. (eds.). *A Dictionary of Social Science.* New York: The Free Press, 1964. Pp. xvi + 761.

Each entry outlines a brief history of usage and discusses the variations in current usage. Foreword by the Secretariat of UNESCO. Clothbound.

MIHANOVICH, CLEMENT S., McNAMARA, ROBERT J., and TOME, WILLIAM N. (eds.). *Glossary of Sociological Terms.* Milwaukee, Wis.: The Bruce Publishing Co., 1957. Pp. iv + 36.

MITCHELL, G. DUNCAN (ed.). *A Dictionary of Sociology.* Chicago: Aldine Publishing Co., 1968. Pp. 232.

Especially prepared to introduce students to the language of the discipline.

THEODORSON, GEORGE A. (ed.). *Modern Dictionary of Sociology.* New York: Thomas Y. Crowell Co., 1969.

Encyclopedias

SELIGMAN, EDWIN R. A., and JOHNSON, ALVIN (eds.). *Encyclopaedia of the Social Sciences.* New York: Macmillan Co., 1930-1935. 15 vols. (Now issued in an eight volume set.)

Volume I, in addition to regular articles, includes twenty-three essays in two introductory sections: "The Development of Social Thought and Institutions," and "The Social Sciences as Disciplines." Volume XV, in addition to regular articles, includes a complete index.

SILLS, DAVID L. (ed.). *International Encyclopedia of the Social Sciences.* New York: Macmillan Co. and The Free Press, 1968. 17 vols. Foreword by Alvin Johnson. Volume XVII is a complete index.

Guides to the Literature

BLAU, PETER M., and MOORE, JOAN W. "Sociology," in *A Reader's Guide to the Social Sciences.* Edited by BERT F. HOSELITZ. Glencoe, Ill.: The Free Press, 1959. Chap. vi, pp. 158-187.

Arranged in two major sections. The first section, "The Development of Sociology," includes: early social philosophy; the separation of state and society; inevitable evolutionary forces; concern with social reform; history and sociology; the scientific study of social facts; implications and reactions. The second section, "Contemporary Sociological Literature in Selected Areas," includes: social theory; interviewing surveys; social psychology; demography and human ecology; social differentiation in community and nation; formal and informal organization.

LEWIS, PETER R. "Sociology," *The Literature of the Social Sciences: An Introductory Survey and Guide.* London: The Library Association, 1960, chap. x, pp. 183-203.

Arranged in five parts: bibliographies, guides, and reference books; sociological theory; sources on social conditions; social services; libraries and library problems.

MUKHERJEE, A. K. "Sociology, Social Psychology, and Allied Topics," *Annotated Guide to Reference Materials in the Human Sciences.* London: Asia Publishing House, 1962, pt. II, chaps. iv, v, and vi, pp. 177-256.

Chapter Four is arranged in eight parts: dictionary; encyclopedia; year book; directory; handbook; bibliography; abstract and index; historical material. Chapter Five covers "Specialized Journals." Chapter Six is arranged in sixteen parts: basic source material and standard treatise—sociology; rural and urban sociology; social change; social problems; family and kinship; social survey and methodology; social case work; race problems; social psychology; culture and personality; personality study; ethno-psychology; somato-psychology; author index; subject index.

ZETTERBERG, HANS L. "Sociology," in *Sources of Information in the Social Sciences: A Guide to the Literature.* Edited by Carl M. White. With an annotated bibliography by THOMPSON M. LITTLE and CARL M. WHITE. Totowa, N.J.: The Bedminster Press, 1964, chap. iv, pp. 183-228.

Zetterberg's essay is arranged in twenty parts, organized under four major headings: general orientation; sociological theory; topics of sociology; methods of sociology. Little and White's bibliography is organized under the following fourteen headings; guides to the literature; reviews of the literature; abstracts and digests; bibliographies—current; bibliographies—retrospective; dictionaries; encyclopedias and encyclopedic sets; directories and biographical information; atlases and pictorial works; handbooks, manuals, compendia; yearbooks; statistical sources; sources of scholarly contributions; sources of unpublished information.

Handbooks, Sourcebooks, and Reviews

BLUMER, HERBERT (ed.). "Special Semicentennial Issue," *The American Journal of Sociology,* L (May, 1945), 421-548.

An editorial foreword and fourteen articles especially prepared for this issue and arranged in four parts: developments in the last fifty years; fifty years of sociology in the United States; the proximate future of American sociology; trends in sociology.

FARIS, ROBERT E. L. (ed.). *Handbook of Modern Sociology.* Chicago: Rand McNally and Co., 1964. Pp. viii + 1088.

A collection of twenty-seven articles written especially for this volume and aimed at summarizing "all major growing research areas of modern sociology." Each article includes an extensive bibliography. Index of names. Index of subjects. Clothbound.

GITTLER, JOSEPH B. (ed.). *Review of Sociology: Analysis of a Decade.* New York: John Wiley and Sons, Inc., 1957. Pp. ix + 588.

A collection of fourteen articles and five bibliographical appendixes especially prepared for this volume and aimed at "presenting and evaluating the significant literature in American sociology" during the decade 1945-1955. Clothbound.

HANDY, ROLLO, and KURTZ, PAUL. "Sociology," *A Current Appraisal of the Behavioral Sciences.* Great Barrington, Mass.: Behavioral Research Council, 1964, chap. ii, pp. 25-34.

Arranged under the following nine headings: working specification of the field, other specifications of the field; schools, methods, techniques; results achieved; contemporary controversy; problems of terminology; comment and evaluation; selected bibliographies; germane journals.

LAZARSFELD, PAUL F., SEWELL, WILLIAM H., and WILENSKY, HAROLD L. (eds.). *The Uses of Sociology.* New York: Basic Books, Inc., 1967. Pp. xi + 902.

Introduction and thirty-one other articles written especially for this volume and arranged in six parts: sociological perspectives; the uses of sociology in the professions; the uses of sociology in establishments; social problems and formal planning; rapid social change; institutional problems in applied sociology. Index of names. Index of subjects. Clothbound.

LIPSET, SEYMOUR MARTIN, and SMELSER, NEIL J. (eds.). *Sociology, the Progress of a Decade: A Collection of Articles.* Englewood Cliffs, N.J.: Prentice-Hall, Inc., 1961. Pp. xi + 635.

Introduction and sixty-four other articles arranged in four parts: the discipline of sociology; the major boundaries of social systems; the production and allocation of wealth, power, and prestige; the balance between stability and change in society. Clothbound.

MERTON, ROBERT K., BROOM, LEONARD, COTTRELL, LEONARD S., JR. (eds.). *Sociology Today: Problems and Prospects.* New York: Basic Books, Inc., 1959. Pp. xxxiv + 623.

Introduction and twenty-five other articles written especially for this volume and arranged in five parts: problems in sociological theory and methodology; problems in the sociology of institutions; the group and the person; problems in demographic and social structure; selected applications of sociology. Index of names and subjects. Clothbound. (This is also available in a two-volume paperbound set from Harper and Brothers of New York.)

PARSONS, TALCOTT (ed.). *American Sociology: Perspectives, Problems, Methods.* New York: Basic Books, Inc., 1968. Pp. xxii + 346.

Introduction and twenty-four other essays especially prepared for this volume and arranged in six parts and a conclusion: components of social systems; methods of investigation; functional subsystems; sociology of culture; strain, deviance, and social control; total societies and their change; conclusion. Index of names and subjects. Clothbound.

ROUCEK, JOSEPH S. (ed.). *Readings in Contemporary American Sociology.* New Student Outline Series. Paterson, N.J.: Littlefield, Adams and Company, 1961. Pp. xi + 261.

Thirty-five essays arranged in three sections: framework; trends in the United States; some applications of sociology. Index of names. Paperbound. This is a reprint, unchanged, of the first three sections of: ROUCEK, JOSEPH S. (ed.), *Contemporary Sociology* (New York: The Philosophical Library, 1958). The original edition is no longer in print.

II.3. GUIDES FOR SELECTION AND CONSTRUCTION OF QUESTIONNAIRES AS UTILIZED IN FIELD RESEARCH

The mail questionnaire is a list of questions for information or opinion which is mailed to potential respondents who have been chosen in some designated manner. The respondents are asked to complete the questionnaire and return it by mail.

This means of gathering information is very popular because it promises to secure data at a minimum of time and expense. The popularity of the method is often defeating because many respondents are overburdened by the number which reach them. In the competition for his time, the respondent increasingly examines the purpose of the study, the sponsorship, the utility of findings to him, the time required to fill it out, the clarity and readability of the type, and perhaps, the quality of the paper.

Decision making criteria: Every researcher who chooses the mail questionnaire should consider himself as a seller in a highly competitive environment in which the majority of respondents will probably not complete and return his questionnaire. He should examine carefully the advantages and disadvantages described below. The disadvantages are shown first to emphasize their importance. If the advantages override these disadvantages, and if the method fits his study, then the questionnaire is appropriate. A guide to questionnaire construction follows which should prove useful. Also note the guide to techniques for increasing percentage of returns.

Disadvantages of the Mail Questionnaire *

    1. MAJOR WEAKNESS: Problem of non-returns.
        a. Most ordinary studies as conducted by private and relatively unskilled persons yield only from 10 to 25 percent of returns.
        b. The questionnaire must be short to have a greater probability of return.

* Cf. David Wallace, "A Case For—and Against—Mail Questionnaires," *Public Opinion Quarterly,* 18 (1954), pp. 40-52.

      i. Norton found 78.5 percent returned with less than five questions.

     ii. Stanton reported 28.3 percent returned a three-page questionnaire while 50.2 percent answered a double postcard containing a single question which could be answered by making a single check.

   c. Sletto found an altruistic appeal increased returns to 67 percent in a college trained population.

   d. Shuttleworth found a questionnaire containing a 25-cent coin prompted a return of 52 percent; questionnaires without the coin produced 19 percent returns.

   e. The percentage of returns is about double for a regular stamped envelope over the business reply envelope.

2. Those who answer the questionnaires may differ from the non-respondents thereby biasing the sample.

3. Validity depends on the ability and willingness of the respondent to provide information.

4. Possibility of misinterpretation of the question.

5. No follow-through on misunderstood questions or evasive answers; no observation of apparent reluctance or evasiveness.

Advantages of Mail Questionnaire

1. Permits wide coverage for minimum expense both in money and effort.

2. Affords wider geographic contact.

3. Reaches people who are difficult to locate and interview.

4. Greater coverage may yield greater validity through larger and more representative samples.

5. Permits more considered answers.

6. More adequate in situations in which the respondent has to check his information.

7. More adequate in situations in which group consultations would give more valid information.

8. Greater uniformity in the manner in which questions are posed.

9. Gives respondent a sense of privacy.

10. Affords a simple means of continual reporting over time.

11. Lessens interviewer effect.

Guide to Questionnaire Construction

A. Re-clarify the relation of the method to problem and hypotheses. Obtain a thorough grasp of the area to be studied and a clear understanding of the objectives of the study and the nature of the data needed.

In a *descriptive* inquiry the investigator is seeking to estimate as precisely and comprehensively as possible a problem area; in an *explanatory* inquiry of a theoretical type he is seeking to test some particular hypothesis about the determinants of a dependent variable or factor. In either type, economy and efficiency are important criteria. The rule is: gather the data you need but not more than is needed. Know how you will use and analyze your data. Make your dummy tables now if possible and challenge their adequacy for describing the possible distributions or relationships that are related to your problem or hypotheses.

B. Formulate questions.

1. Keep the language pitched to the level of the respondent.

    Interviews given only to specialized respondents can use the terminology with which they are familiar. But interviews given to the general public must use language with more common usage.

2. Try to pick words that have the same meaning for everyone.

    A questionnaire involving American and British respondents might ask, "How often do you have tea?" To the American, tea would refer to a drink. To the British, tea would refer to a light meal.

3. Avoid long questions.

    When questions become long they often become ambiguous and confusing.

4. Do not *a priori* assume that your respondent possesses *factual* information, or first hand opinions.

    A mother may be able to report what books her child reads, but a child himself must be questioned to know how he feels about reading those books.

5. Establish the frame of reference you have in mind.

    Don't ask: How many magazines do you read?

    Ask: Which magazines do you read?

6. In forming a question, either suggest all possible alternatives to the respondent or don't suggest any.

    Don't ask: Do you think the husband should help with dressing and feeding the small children when he's home?

    Ask: Do you think the husband should help with dressing and feeding the small children when he's home, or do you think it's the wife's job in any case?

        Or: Who should dress and feed the children when the husband is home?

7. Protect your respondent's ego.

    Don't ask: Do you know the name of the Chief Justice of the Supreme Court?

          Ask: Do you happen to know the name of the Chief Justice of the Supreme Court?

8. If you're after unpleasant orientations, give your respondent a chance to express his positive feelings first so that he's not put in an unfavorable light.

    Ask: What do you like about X?

    Then: What don't you like about X?

9. Decide whether you need a direct question, an indirect question, or an indirect followed by a direct question.

      Direct: Do you ever steal on the job?

    Indirect: Do you know of anyone ever stealing on the job?

    Combina- Do you know of anyone ever stealing on the job?

      tion: Have you ever taken anything from the job?

10. Decide whether the question should be open or closed.

    Open: It is believed that some people in this community have too much power. Do you think this is true? Who are they?

    Closed: It is believed that some people in this community have too much power. Is this statement ☐ True, ☐ False, ☐ Don't know. If true, who are they? ☐ Negroes, ☐ Jews, ☐ Poles, ☐ Italians, ☐ ───────.

11. Decide whether general or specific questions are needed.

    It may be enough to ask: How well did you like the book?

    It may be preferable to also ask: Have you recommended the book to anyone else?

12. Avoid ambiguous wording.

    Don't ask: Do you usually work alone?

          Ask: ☐ No, I never work alone, ☐ Yes, I work alone less than half the time, ☐ Yes, I work alone most of the time

13. Avoid biased or leading questions.

    Don't ask: Did you exercise your right as an American citizen to vote in the last election?

          Ask: Did you vote in the last election?

14. Phrase questions so that they are not unnecessarily objectionable.

Instead of: Did you graduate from high school?
  Ask: What is the highest grade in school you completed?

15. Decide whether a personal or impersonal question will obtain the better response.

Impersonal: Are working conditions satisfactory or not satisfactory where you work?
  Personal: Are you satisfied or dissatisfied with working conditions in the plant where you work?

16. Questions should be limited to a single idea or a single reference.

Don't ask: Do you favor or oppose increased job security and the guaranteed annual wage?
  Ask: Do you favor or oppose increased job security?
  And: Do you favor or oppose the guaranteed annual wage?

C. Organize the questionnaire.
  1. Start with easy questions that the respondent will enjoy answering.
    Don't start with age, occupation, or marital status.
    Ask questions to arouse interest.
  2. Don't condition answers to subsequent questions by preceding ones.
    a. Go from the general to the specific
      How do you think this country is getting along in its relations with other countries?
      How do you think we are doing in our relations with Russia?
    b. Go from the easy to the difficult.
  3. Use the sequence of questions to protect the respondent's ego. Save the personal questions such as income for later.
  4. Decide whether one or several questions will best obtain the information for a given objective.
  5. With free-answer questions, it is sometimes helpful to have the questions in pairs, asking for the pros and cons of a particular issue.
  6. Open-ended questions which require most thought and writing should be kept to a minimum. Generally, these should be placed at the end to assure that the closed questions will be answered.
  7. The topics and questions should be arranged so that they make the most sense to the respondent. The aim is to secure a sequence that is natural and easy for the respondent.

D. Pre-test the questionnaire.
   1. Select a number of respondents representative of those you expect to survey and interview them. Encourage them to ask any questions that they have as they respond to your items. Watch for misunderstanding, ambiguity, and defensiveness. Ask them how they would restate a question that is difficult to understand or to answer.
   2. Never omit pre-testing!
E. Select paper and type carefully. The use of type-print can produce a mimeographed questionnaire on good paper that looks like a printed copy.
F. Consider how you can present the strongest possible sponsorship. The person, persons, or group that will support your efforts through a covering letter is important. Note the increase of 17 percent return reported in the technique guide for increasing percentage of returns.
G. Examine each of the techniques for increasing return of the questionnaire and decide which will maximize returns for you.

TECHNIQUES FOR INCREASING PERCENTAGE OF RETURNS

Method	Possible Increase of Total % of Returns	Optimal Conditions
Follow-up *	40%	More than one follow-up may be needed. If possible, returns may be increased by using double postcards with the most important questions on follow-ups. The telephone can often be used effectively for follow-up. Researcher should find out if respondent needs another copy of the questionnaire (which he may have destroyed or misplaced). Sewell and Shaw report a 87.2% return on 9007 from parents of Wisconsin high school students using 3 waves of mailed questionnaires and final telephone interview. *American Sociological Review*, 33 (April, 1968), p. 193.

* The Bureau of Social Science Research, Inc., 1200 Seventeenth St. N.W., Washington, D.C. 20036, has compiled completion rates in mail surveys undertaken by B.S.S.R. Data compiled by Lenore Reid. They report as many as four follow-ups. Covering letter from institutional sponsor is believed very important.

Methods	Possible Increase of Total % of Returns	Optimal Conditions
Sponsor	17%	John K. Norton found that people the respondent knew produced the best results. A state headquarters received the second best rate. Others following in order were: a lower status person in a similar field, a publishing firm, a college professor or student, and a private association or foundation.
Length	22%	If a questionnaire is short, then the shorter the better. A double postcard should produce the best results. However, if the questionnaire is over 10 pages at the minimum, length may cease to be a factor. Sewell and Shaw used a double postcard in the study reported.
Introductory Letter	7%	An altruistic appeal seems to have better results than the idea that the respondent may receive something good from it.
Type of Questions	13%	Questionnaires asking for objective information receive the best rate and questionnaires asking for subjective information receive the worst.
Inducements	33%	Shuttleworth found that a questionnaire containing a quarter produced better results than one without. However, the population and the type of questionnaire could make such inducements unnecessary. Consider promise of report to respondent.
Method of Return	not known	A regular stamped envelope produces better results than the business-reply envelope.
Time of Arrival	not known	The questionnaire, if sent to the home, should arrive near the end of the week.

Methods	Possible Increase of Total % of Returns	Optimal Conditions
Format	not known	Sletto found a need for an esthetically pleasing cover, a title which would arouse interest, an attractive page format, a size and style of type easily readable under poor illumination and by people with poor vision, and photographs to illustrate the questionnaire.
Selection of Respondents	Respondent selection can rarely increase returns to above a total of 80%	1. Non-readers and non-writers are excluded from participation. 2. Interest in, or familiarity with, the topic under investigation is a major factor in determining the rate of return. 3. The better educated are more likely to return questionnaires. 4. Professionals are more likely to return questionnaires. One of the highest returns reported in the research literature is that by Rensis Likert. In a study of the League of Women Voters (commissioned by the League) a cross sectional sample of 2,905 League members and officers showed the following percent of return: 79% of members 95% of board members 100% of chapter presidents (Rensis Likert, *New Patterns of Management,* p. 145)

H. Examine the sample page from a questionnaire designed by Raymond F. Sletto. Note how attention has been given to appearance, spacing, ease of response. Note how the open and closed questions are presented, how the data are recorded.

YOUR EXPERIENCES

Please give your answers to the following questions by writing in the appropriate spaces or by marking an X in the blanks as indicated.

1. What is your present job, or last job if unemployed? (Please be specific so that responses can be accurately classified. For example, wholesale hardware salesman, retail sales clerk in department store, high school teacher of English, owner of drug store, housewife, etc.)

   Clinic nurse + technician

   Housewife

2. What was your first full-time job after leaving the University?

   medical technician

3. How did you obtain this first full-time job? (You may check more than one.)

   - [x] By direct application
   - [ ] Through friends
   - [ ] Through relatives
   - [ ] Approached by employer
   - [ ] By financial investment
   - [ ] Through an advertisement

   - [ ] Through University Employment Office
   - [ ] Through other University assistance
   - [ ] Through other employment office
   - Other, please specify:
   _____
   _____

4. How did you obtain your present job? (You may check more than one.)

   - [x] By direct application
   - [ ] Through friends
   - [ ] Through relatives
   - [ ] By financial investment
   - [ ] Through an advertisement

   - [ ] Through an employment office
   - [ ] Through previous employer
   - Other, please specify:
   _____
   _____

5. How many hours per week on the average do you spend on your job? *38*

6. How closely related is your present job to your chosen field of specialization at the University?

   - [ ] Same field   [x] Related field   [ ] Different field

II.4. GUIDES FOR SELECTION AND USE OF PERSONAL INTERVIEWS AS UTILIZED IN FIELD RESEARCH

The interview represents a personal contact between an interviewer and a respondent usually in the home or office of the respondent. The interview can range from a highly structured situation with a planned series of questions to a very informal talk with no structure except for some areas of discussion desired by the interviewer. The degrees of freedom represent opportunity and danger: opportunity to explore many subjects with intensity but with the danger that the interview may not yield the appropriate data. It is often not susceptible to codification and comparability.

The researcher may not appreciate that every open-ended question will take considerable interview time. The analysis of open-ended questions requires a code guide and careful independent observers to establish the validity and reliability of the coding for each question. In general the rule is: Present closed rather than open-ended questions. If you must employ open-ended questions, choose a few with care and with the precise aims of the study in mind. If hypotheses are to be tested, make sure that the questions bear directly upon them. Open-ended questions are appropriate and powerful under conditions that require probing of attitude and reaction formations and ascertaining information that is interlocked in a social system or personality structure.

In general, keep the interview within a 45-minute time span. Public opinion interviewers have reported that most respondents begin to weary and show less interest in the interview at this point. It is true that some respondents will "warm up" as the interview proceeds and there are examples of six- and eight-hour interviews in the literature. (Robert Dahl with community leaders in New Haven, Connecticut, and Neal Gross in planned interviews with Massachusetts School Superintendents in Cambridge, Massachusetts).* These long interviews are exceptional and can only occur under specially prepared conditions.

The interview may be identified in three forms: (1) The Structured Interview Schedule, (2) The Focused Interview and (3) The Free Story. These forms and their characteristics are shown in the outline Guide to Situses, Principal Methods, and Techniques of the Social Science Researcher. Common techniques that may be employed include inclusion of scales to measure social factors, attitudes, and personality traits. Secret ballots and panel techniques are often employed.

The guide that follows lists advantages and disadvantages of the

---

* Robert A. Dahl, *Who Governs* (New Haven: Yale University, 1961), p. 334. Neal Gross, Ward S. Mason, and Alexander W. McEachern, *Explorations of Role Analysis: The Superintendency Role* (New York: Wiley, 1958), p. 85.

interview. Use it as a check list noting with a plus mark those advantages that are important or essential; mark a minus for the disadvantages that will affect your use of the interview. You now have an adequate base for your choice or rejection of the personal interview.

Other field methods are available including the group interview, telephone interview, case study and life history, direct observation, participant observation, and mass observation. Guides have not been prepared for these methods, but a list of reference books is appended to this part describing in detail all of the methods and techniques.

Guide for Appraisal of Personal Interview for Data Collection

The researcher should check the advantages important for his study. Then check the disadvantages that cannot be overcome. Appraise the choice. Reconsider documentary analysis, mail questionnaire, observation, or other methods suggested in the Outline Guide to Situses, Principal Methods, and Techniques of the Social Science Researcher.

Advantages of Personal Interview

1. The personal interview usually yields a high percentage of returns, for most people are willing to cooperate.
2. It can be made to yield an almost perfect sample of the general population because practically everyone can be reached by and can respond to this approach.
3. The information secured is likely to be more correct than that secured by other techniques since the interviewer can clear up seemingly inaccurate answers by explaining the questions to the informant. If the latter deliberately falsifies replies, the interviewer may be trained to spot such cases and use special devices to get the truth.
4. The interviewer can collect supplementary information about the informant's personal characteristics and environment which is valuable in interpreting results and evaluating the representatives of the persons surveyed.
5. Scoring and test devices can be used, the interviewer acting as experimenter to establish accurate records of the subject.
6. Visual material to which the informant is to react can be presented.

7. Return visits to complete items on the schedule or to correct mistakes can usually be made without annoying the informant. Thus greater numbers of usable returns are assumed than when other methods are employed.
8. The interviewer may catch the informant off guard and thus secure more spontaneous reactions than would be the case if a written form were mailed out for the informant to mull over.
9. The interviewer can usually control which person or persons answer the questions, whereas in mail surveys several members of the household may confer before the questions are answered. Group discussions can be held with the personal interview method if desired.
10. The personal interview may take long enough to allow the informant to become oriented to the topic under investigation. Thus recall of relevant material is facilitated.
11. Questions about which the informant is likely to be sensitive can be carefully sandwiched in by the interviewer. By observing the informant's reactions, the investigator can change the subject if necessary or explain the survey problem further if it appears that the interviewee is about to rebel. In other words, a delicate situation can usually be handled more effectively by a personal interview than by other survey techniques.
12. More of the informant's time can be taken for the survey than would be the case if the interviewer were not present to elicit and record the information.
13. In cases where a printed schedule is not used (cf. #2, below) the language of the survey can be adapted to the ability or educational level of the person interviewed. Therefore, it is comparatively easy to avoid misinterpretations or misleading questions.

Disadvantages of Personal Interview

1. The transportation costs and the time required to cover addresses in a large area may make the personal interview method unfeasible.
2. The human equation may distort the returns. If an interviewer has a certain economic bias, for example, he may unconsciously ask questions so as to secure confirmation of his views. In opinion studies especially, such biases may operate. To prevent such coloring of questions, most opinion surveyors instruct their interviewers to ask the question *exactly* as printed on the schedule.
3. Unless the interviewers are properly trained and supervised, the

data recorded may be inaccurate and incomplete. A few poor enumerators may make a much higher percentage of returns unusable than if the informants filled out and mailed the interview form to survey headquarters.

4. The organization required for selecting, training, and supervising a field staff is more complex than that needed for surveys conducted by other methods.

5. It is usually claimed that costs per interview are higher when field investigators are employed than when telephone or mail surveys are used. This may not be true if the area to be covered is not too great. If the general public in a community is to be surveyed, the costs of securing a *representative* sample by telephone or mail inquiries will probably equal or exceed the cost by the personal interview method, since in the end personal follow-up will be necessary to round out the sample.

6. The personal interview usually takes more time than the telephone interview providing the persons who can be reached by telephone are a representative sample of the type of population to be covered by the survey. However, for a sample of the general public, a telephone inquiry is not a substitute for a personal interview. The lowest income groups often do not have telephones.

7. If the interview is conducted in the home during the day, the majority of the informants will be housewives. If a response is to be obtained from a male member of the household, most of the field work will have to be done in the evening or on week ends. Since only an hour or two can be used for evening interviewing, the personal interview method requires a large staff for studies requiring contacts with the working population.

II.5. GUIDES FOR THE SELECTION AND CONSTRUCTION OF SOCIAL SCALES AND INDICES

Scaling techniques play a major role in the construction of instruments for collecting standardized, measurable data. Scales and indices are significant because they provide quantitative measures that are amenable to greater precision, statistical manipulation, and explicit interpretation. However, before constructing a new scale, it is exceedingly important that a very careful survey of the literature be made to ascertain if an appropriate scale is already available to measure the dependent or independent variables in a given study.

The general rule is: use the available scale if it has qualities of validity, reliability, and utility (and in that order of priority). With such a scale comparative and accumulative research is possible. The need to develop a new scale can almost be considered a disciplinary failure unless the variable represents a factor never before considered as open to measurement. We shall begin, therefore, at the point at which the literature has not revealed an appropriate scale and the researcher decides he must construct an index or scale.

How does one "think up" a number of indicators to be used in empirical research?

This question is answered by Paul F. Lazarsfeld and Morris Rosenberg as follows:

"The first step seems to be the creation of a rather vague image or construct that results from the author's immersion in all the detail of a theoretical problem. The creative act may begin with the perception of many disparate phenomena as having some underlying characteristic in common. Or the author may have observed certain regularities and is trying to account for them. In any case, the concept, when first created, is some vaguely conceived entity that makes the observed relations meaningful. Next comes a stage in which the concept is specified by elaborate discussion of the phenomena out of which it emerged. We develop "aspects," "components," "dimensions," or similar specifications. They are sometimes derived logically from the overall concept, or one aspect is deduced from another, or empirically observed correlations between them are reported. The concept is shown to consist of a complex combination of phenomena, rather than a simple and directly observable item. In order to incorporate the concept into a research design, observable indicators of it must be selected." *

Indices and scales are often used interchangeably to refer to all sorts of measures, absolute or relative, single or composite, the product of simple or elaborate techniques of measurement.

Indices may be very simple. For example, one way to measure morale is to ask the direct question, "How would you rate your morale? Very good, good, fair, poor, very poor." This might be refined slightly so that the responses are placed on a numerical scale. Note that there are nine points on the following scale.

* Paul F. Lazarsfeld and Morris Rosenberg (eds.), *The Language of Social Research: A Reader in the Methodology of Social Research* (Glencoe, Ill.: Free Press 1962), p. 15.

How Would You Rate Your Morale?								
Very good		Good		Fair		Poor		Very poor
I	2	3	4	5	6	7	8	9

The basis for construction is logical inference and the use of a numerical scale requires the assumption of a psychological continuity which the respondent can realistically act upon in his self rating. Face validity is usually asserted for such a scale although it would be possible to make tests of relations with criteria such as work performance, absenteeism, lateness, amount of drinking, hours of sleep, etc.

A composite index is one or a set of measures, each of which is formed by combining simple indexes. For example, morale may be considered as a composite of many dimensions.

Four measures can be combined by such questions as

How satisfied are you with your job?
How satisfied are you with your company or organization?
How satisfied are you in your personal life?
How satisfied are you with your community?

Response choices of very good, good, fair, poor, and very poor may be offered for each question with weights of 5, 4, 3, 2, and 1. A range from 4 to 20 points is possible. Such a composite index may improve precision, reliability, and validity.

Rigor is introduced as greater attention is paid to tests of validity and reliability. At a certain point a given means of measurement reaches its limit of improvement and a more refined technique becomes necessary for greater precision. Many scaling techniques concern themselves with linearity and equal intervals or equal-appearing intervals. This means that the scale follows a straight line model and that a scoring system is devised, preferably based on interchangeable units and subject to statistical manipulation. This is a major attribute of the Thurstone attitude scaling technique.

Unidimensionality or homogeneity is another desired attribute assuring that only one dimension is measured and not some mixture of factors. This is a prime concern of the Guttman scaling technique.

Reproducibility is a characteristic that enables the researcher to predict the patern of a respondent's answers by knowing only the total scale score. This attribute is built into Guttman scaling techniques.

The intensity of feeling is introduced in the Likert technique. The respondent is usually asked to indicate his feelings on a five-point scale ranging from strongly agree to strongly disagree. Tests of item discrimination are applied.

There is no single method that combines the advantages of all of them.* It is, therefore, important that we understand their respective purposes and the differences between them.

II.5.a. Thurstone Equal-Appearing Interval Scale

NATURE: This scale consists of a number of items whose position on the scale has been determined previously by a ranking operation performed by judges. The subject selects the responses which best describe how he feels.

UTILITY: This scale approximates an interval level of measurement. This means that the distance between any two numbers on the scale is of known size. Parametric and non-parametric statistics may be applied. See Part III, Guide 5 of this handbook.

CONSTRUCTION:

1. The investigator gathers several hundred statements conceived to be related to the attitude being investigated.
2. A large number of judges (50-300) independently classify the statements in eleven groups ranging from most favorable to neutral to least favorable.
3. The scale value of a statement is computed as the median position to which it is assigned by the group of judges.
4. Statements which have too broad a spread are discarded as ambiguous or irrelevant.
5. The scale is formed by selecting items which are evenly spread along the scale from one extreme to the other.

Example: Brayfield and Roethe's Index of Job Satisfaction. This index is reproduced in the handbook (Part IV, Section C). The Thurstone technique is used in the initial development of the scale

---

* The Scale Discrimination Technique developed by Allen Edwards makes an excellent attempt to secure a combination of the Thurstone, Likert, and Guttman features. See the following pages.

to provide equal-appearing intervals. The full scale contains eighteen items with Thurstone scale values ranging from 1.2 to 10.0 with approximately .5 step intervals. Some items from the scale representing the job satisfaction continuum are:

My job is like a hobby to me.
I am satisfied with my job for the time being.
I am often bored with my job.
Most of the time I have to force myself to go to work.

RESEARCH APPLICATIONS: Scales have been constructed to measure attitudes toward war, the church, capital punishment, the Chinese, the Negroes, whites, and institutions.

II.5.b. Likert-Type Scale

NATURE: This is a summated scale consisting of a series of items to which the subject responds. The respondent indicates his agreement or disagreement with each item on an intensity scale. The Likert technique produces an ordinal scale which generally requires non-parametric statistics. See Part III, Guide 5 of this handbook.

UTILITY: This scale is highly reliable when it comes to a rough ordering of people with regard to a particular attitude or attitude complex. The score includes a measure of intensity as expressed on each statement.

CONSTRUCTION:

1. The investigator assembles a large number of items considered relevant to the attitude being investigated and either clearly favorable or unfavorable.
2. These items are administered to a group of subjects representative of those with whom the questionnaire is to be used.
3. The responses to the various items are scored in such a way that a response indicative of the most favorable attitude is given the highest score.
4. Each individual's total score is computed by adding his item scores.
5. The responses are analyzed to determine which items differentiate most clearly between the highest and lowest quartiles of total scores.
6. The items which differentiate best (at least six) are used to form a scale.

Example: Rundquist and Sletto Scales of Morale and General Adjustment. See the Minnesota Survey of Opinions (long and short form) as reproduced in the handbook (Part IV, Section C). The scales to measure morale and general adjustment, and also inferiority, family, law, and economic conservatism, are examples of the Likert attitude scale technique. A significant characteristic is that each selected statement has been carefully researched to determine its discrimination through a criterion of interval consistency. A second feature is the addition of the intensity dimension to each statement as follows:

The Future Looks Very Black
Strongly agree[5] Agree[4] Undecided[3] Disagree[2] Strongly disagree[1]
Most People Can Be Trusted
Strongly agree[1] Agree[2] Undecided[3] Disagree[4] Strongly disagree[5]

II.5.c. Guttman Scale-Analysis

NATURE: The Guttman technique attempts to determine the unidimensionality of a scale. Only items meeting the criterion of reproducibility are acceptable as scalable. If a scale is unidimensional, then a person who has a more favorable attitude than another should respond to each statement with equal or greater favorableness than the other.

UTILITY: Each score corresponds to a highly similar response pattern or scale type. It is one of the few scales where the score can be used to predict the response pattern to all statements. Only a few statements (five to ten) are needed to provide a range of scalable responses. Note the analysis below showing how fourteen subjects responded

RESPONDENT	Item 7	Item 5	Item 1	Item 8	Item 2	Item 4	Item 6	Item 3	Score
7	yes	yes	yes	yes	yes	yes	yes	—	7
9	yes	yes	yes	yes	yes	yes	yes	—	7
10	yes	yes	yes	yes	yes	yes	—	—	6
1	yes	yes	yes	—	yes	yes	—	yes	6
13	yes	yes	yes	yes	yes	yes	—	—	6
3	yes	yes	yes	yes	yes	—	—	—	5
2	yes	yes	yes	yes	—	—	—	—	4
6	yes	yes	yes	yes	—	—	—	—	4
8	yes	yes	yes	—	—	yes	—	—	4
14	yes	yes	yes	yes	—	—	—	—	4
5	yes	yes	yes	—	—	—	—	—	3
4	yes	yes	—	—	—	—	—	—	2
11	—	—	—	—	yes	—	—	—	1
12	yes	—	—	—	—	—	—	—	1

(yes) to several different statements and how scores reflect a given pattern of response.

CONSTRUCTION:

1. Select statements that are felt to apply to the measurable objective.
2. Test statements on a sample population (about 100).
3. Discard statements with more than 80 percent agreement or disagreement.
4. Order respondents from most favorable responses to fewest favorable responses. Order from top to bottom.
5. Order statements from most favorable responses to fewest favorable responses. Order from left to right.
6. Discard statements that fail to discriminate between favorable respondents and unfavorable respondents.
7. Calculate coefficient of reproducibility.
   a. Calculate the number of errors (favorable responses that do not fit pattern)

   b. Reproducibility $= 1 - \dfrac{\text{Number of errors}}{\text{Number of responses}}$

   c. If reproducibility equals .90, a unidimensional scale is said to exist.
8. Score each respondent by the number of favorable responses.

Example: This handbook reproduces two scales constructed by the Guttman attitude scaling technique. These are the Guttman Scales of Military Base Morale (Part IV, Section C) and a Guttman Scale for Measuring Women's Neighborliness (Part IV, Section E). The statements must permit a range of opinions and evoke a definite feeling. Note the statements which scaled on Air Force personnel reflecting their satisfaction with the Air Force.

> I have a poor opinion of the Air Force most of the time.
> Most of the time the Air Force is not run very well.
> I am usually dissatisfied with the Air Force.
> The Air Force is better than any of the other services.
> If I remain in military service I would prefer to remain in the Air Force.

II.5.d. Scale-Discrimination Technique

NATURE: This technique seeks to develop a set of items that meet the requirements of a unidimensional scale, possess equal-appearing intervals, and measure intensity. Aspects of the construction of Thurstone's equal-appearing intervals, Likert's summated scales, and Guttman's scale analysis are combined in this technique of Edwards and Kilpatrick.

UTILITY: Three distinct advantages of separate scaling techniques are combined. The interval scale quality of the Thurstone technique can be achieved. The discriminability between respondents and the addition of an intensity measure are derived from the Likert technique, and unidimensionality from the Guttman technique. Caution: Item analysis will eliminate items in the middle of the scale.

CONSTRUCTION:
1. Select a large number of statements that are thought to apply to the attitude being measured.
2. Discard items that are ambiguous or too extreme.
3. Give the statements to judges and have them judge the favorableness of each statement and place it in one of eleven categories.
4. Discard half the items with the greatest scatter or variance.
5. Assign scores to the remaining items as the median of the judges scores.
6. Formulate the statements in the form of a summated scale and give to a new set of judges.
7. Perform an item analysis to determine which questions discriminate best between the lowest and highest quartiles.
8. Select twice the number of items that are wanted in the final scale. Select from each scale interval the statements that discriminate best.
9. Divide these statements in half.
10. Submit halves to separate test groups.
11. Determine coefficients of reproducibility for each test group and use if .90 or above.

II.5.e. Rating Scales

NATURE: This technique seeks to obtain an evaluation or a quantitative judgment of personality, group, or institutional characteristics based upon personal judgments. The rater places the person or object being rated at some point along a continuum or in one of an ordered series of categories; a numerical value is attached to the point or the category.

UTILITY: Rating scales can be used to assess attitudes, values, norms, social activities, and social structural features.

CONSTRUCTION:

1. Divide the continuum to be measured into an optimal number of scale divisions (approximately 5-7).
2. The continuum should have no breaks or divisions.
3. The positive and negative poles should be alternated.
4. Introduce each trait with a question to which the rater can give an answer.
5. Use descriptive adjectives or phrases to define different points on the continuum.
6. Decide beforehand upon the probable extremes of the trait to be found in the group in which the scale is to be used.
7. Only universally understood descriptive terms should be used.
8. The end phrases should not be so extreme in meaning as to be avoided by the raters.
9. Descriptive phrases need not be evenly spaced.
10. Pre-test. Ask respondents to raise any questions about the rating and the different points on the continuum if they are unclear.
11. To score, use numerical values as assigned.

Example: Miller's Scale Battery of International Patterns and Norms reproduced in this handbook (Part IV, Section H) contains fifteen rating scales to ascertain important norms and patterns within national cultures. The significant feature is the meaningful continuum that can be developed with approximately worded statements or adjectives for each point on the continuum. The scale can be designed so that the researcher or the respondent may make the rating. An example of a rating scale is item 7, Moral Code and Role Definitions of Men and Women, taken from the Miller Scale Battery of International Patterns and Norms.

7. MORAL CODE AND ROLE DEFINITIONS OF MEN AND WOMEN

1	2	3	4	5	6
Single code of morality prevails for men and women. Separate occupational and social roles are not defined for men and women. Similar amounts and standards of education prevail.		Variations between moral definitions for men and women exist for certain specified behaviors. Occupational and social role definitions vary in degree. Varying educational provisions for the sexes.		Double code of morality prevails. Separate occupational and social roles for men and women exist and are sharply defined. Amount and standards of education vary widely between the sexes.	

II.5.f. Latent Distance Scales

NATURE: A technique for scalogram analysis based on a probability model, that attempts to apply to qualitative data the principles of factor analysis providing ordinal information. The basic postulate is that there exists a set of latent classes such that the manifest relationship between any two or more items on a questionnaire can be accounted for by the existence of these latent classes and by these alone.

UTILITY: Unlike scalogram analysis, this technique includes imperfect scale types in the analysis without considering them as mistakes.

CONSTRUCTION:
1. List questions believed to be related to the latent attitude.
2. Dichotomize answers to questions in terms of positive-negative, favorable-unfavorable, etc.
3. Calculate proportion of respondents who demonstrate latent attitude in each response.
4. Arrange items in terms of their manifest marginals.
5. Compute the latent class frequencies through inverse-probability procedures.
6. Rank response patterns in terms of average latent position or use an index to characterize each response pattern.

Example: Latent Distance Scale on Neurotic Inventory
1. Have you ever been bothered by pressure or pains in the head?
   Positive answer: Yes, Often or Yes, Sometimes or No
               Answer   13.8%
2. Have you ever been bothered by shortness of breath when you were not exercising or working hard?
   Positive answer: Yes, Often or Yes, Sometimes or No
               Answer   30.7%
3. Do your hands ever tremble ever enough to bother you?
   Positive answer: Yes, Often or Yes, Sometimes or No
               Answer   43.1%
4. Do you often have trouble in getting to sleep or staying asleep?
   Positive answer: Very Often or No Answer   57.1%

COMPLETE ANALYSIS OF LATENT DISTANCE SCALE ON
NEUROTIC INVENTORY

Response Pattern				Percent of each pattern in latent class:						Fitted Total	Actual Total
I	2	3	4	n_I	n_{II}	n_{III}	n_{IV}	n_V			
+	+	+	+	94.9%	4.2%	0.8%	0.1%	0.0%	100%	76.8	75
+	+	−	+	90.0	3.9	0.7	4.6	0.8	100%	14.6	10
+	+	+	−	90.4	4.0	0.7	0.1	4.8	100%	5.8	8
+	−	+	+	66.8	2.9	24.5	5.0	0.8	100%	16.3	14
−	+	+	+	2.5	79.3	14.7	3.0	0.5	100%	108.3	110
−	−	+	+	0.3	8.8	73.5	14.9	2.5	100%	145.4	141
−	+	−	+	1.3	38.9	7.2	45.1	7.5	100%	39.7	49
+	−	−	+	24.5	1.1	9.0	56.1	9.3	100%	8.0	11
−	−	−	+	0.0	1.4	11.9	74.3	12.4	100%	161.9	161
+	+	−	−	36.7	1.6	0.3	1.9	59.5	100%	2.6	3
−	+	+	−	1.3	40.7	7.6	1.5	48.9	100%	15.2	11
+	−	+	−	25.9	1.2	9.5	1.9	61.5	100%	3.0	8
−	−	+	−	0.1	1.5	12.8	2.6	83.0	100%	60.2	64
−	+	−	−	0.1	2.5	0.5	2.9	94.0	100%	44.0	41
+	−	−	−	1.3	0.0	0.5	3.0	95.2	100%	10.9	9
−	−	−	−	0.0	0.1	0.5	3.0	96.4	100%	287.3	285
Total in each class				109.9	129.5	161.3	181.4	417.9		1,000.0	1,000

The above items were taken from a neurotic inventory presented by Samuel A. Stouffer, *The American Soldier: Measurement and Prediction*, Vol. 4 (Princeton, Princeton University, 1949), p. 445. Consult the book for instruction in this technique or see Section II.9 of this handbook. The bibliography on Index and Scale Construction will prove useful. Paul F. Lazarsfeld developed latent structure analysis. See Lazarsfeld, "Recent Developments in Latent Structure Analysis," *Sociometry*, 18 (December, 1955), 647-659.

II.5.g. Paired Comparisons

NATURE: This technique seeks to determine psychological values of qualitative stimuli without knowledge of any corresponding respondent values. By asking respondents to select the more favorable of a pair of statements or objects over a set of several pairs, an attempt is made to order the statements or objects along a continuum. It is sometimes called the forced choices technique. Note how it is applied in the Neal and Seeman Powerless Scale reproduced in Part IV, Section G.

UTILITY: The ordering by paired comparisons is a relatively rapid process for securing a precise and relative positioning along a continuum. Comparative ordering generally increases reliability and validity over arbitrary rating methods.

CONSTRUCTION:

1. Select statements that relate to the attribute being measured.
2. Combine statements in all possible combination of pairs. $\dfrac{N(N-1)}{2}$
3. Ask judges to select which statement of each pair is the more favorable.
4. Calculate the proportion of judgments each statement received over every other statement.
5. Total the proportions for each statement.
6. Translate the proportions into standardized scale values.
7. Apply an internal consistency check by computing the absolute average discrepancy.
8. Present statements to respondents and ask them to indicate favorableness or unfavorableness to each statement.
9. Respondent's score is the median of his favorable responses.

Example: Hill's Scale of Attitudes Toward Involvement in the Korean War *

Item set favorable to U.S. Involvement in Korea	Paired Comparison Scale Score
1. I suppose the United States has no choice but to continue the Korean War.	0.00
2. We should be willing to give our allies in Korea more money if they need it.	0.74
3. Withdrawing our troops from Korea at this time would only make matters worse.	0.98
4. The Korean War might not be the best way to stop Communism, but it was the only thing we could do.	1.07
5. Winning the Korean War is absolutely necessary whatever the cost.	1.25
6. We are protecting the United States by fighting in Korea.	1.46
7. The reason we are in Korea is to defend freedom.	1.71

* From Richard J. Hill, "A Note on Inconsistency in Paired Comparison Judgments," *American Sociological Review*, 18 (October, 1953), 564-566. Richard Ofshe and Ronald E. Anderson have translated Hill's Korea items to Viet Nam and the Viet Nam scale is described in "Testing a Measurement Model," in Edgar F. Borgatta (ed.), *Sociological Methodology* (San Francisco: Jossey-Bass, 1969).

II.6. Social Science Data Libraries in the United States *

MEMBERS OF THE COUNCIL OF SOCIAL SCIENCE DATA ARCHIVES [a]

Name of Data Library	Address	Type of Data	Subject Matter
Archive on Political Elites in Eastern Europe	Dept. of Political Science 1028H Cathedral of Learning University of Pittsburgh Pittsburgh, Pa. 15213	Biographical Information	Political elites in Eastern Europe
Archive on Comparative Political Elites	Dept. of Political Science University of Oregon Eugene, Oregon 97403		
Bureau of Applied Social Research	Columbia University 605 West 115th Street New York, New York 10025	Sample Surveys	Health & Welfare occupations & professions, mass communications, politics, education, organizations
**Bureau of Labor Statistics	United States Department of Lab.		
Carleton University, Social Science Data Archive	Dept. of Political Science Carleton University Colonel By Drive Ottawa 1, Canada	Sample Surveys Biographies, Election Statistics, Census Data	Politics and public opinion
Center for International Studies Data Bank	Mass. Inst. of Technology E53-365, Hermann Building Cambridge, Mass. 02139	Sample Surveys	Politics, social behavior, public opinion
Columbia University School of Public Health and Administrative Medicine Research Archives	630 West 168th Street New York, New York 10032	Sample Surveys Operational data	Administrative medicine, public health
Council for Inter-Societal Studies	Northwestern University 1818 Sheridan Road Evanston, Illinois 60201		

Graduate School of Industrial Administration	Carnegie Inst. of Technology Pittsburgh, Pennsylvania 15213		French cantons: election & demographic statistics
Human Relations Area Files	Yale University P.O. Box 2054 Yale Station New Haven, Connecticut 06520	Some machine-readable data; reports; bibliographies; texts	Social structure, organization: diet practices; kinship
**International Data Library and Reference Service	Survey Research Center 2220 Piedmont Ave. University of California Berkeley, California 94720	Sample Surveys	Politics, communication, social behavior. Emphasis on Asia, Latin America
International Development Data Bank	Michigan State University 322 Union Building East Lansing, Michigan 48823		List of Archive holdings is available
**Inter-University Consortium for Political Research	University of Michigan P.O. Box 1248 Ann Arbor, Michigan 48106	Sample Surveys	Political behavior Public opinion
Laboratory for Political Research	Dept. of Political Science University of Iowa Iowa City, Iowa 52240	Sample Surveys Voting studies	Politics; biography data on American and Argentine legislators
**Louis Harris Political Data Center	Dept. of Political Science University of North Carolina Cardwell Hall Chapel Hill, North Carolina 27514	Public Opinion Surveys	Politics in individual states in U.S.

* Assembled and described by David Nasatir, Asst. Research Sociologist, Survey Research Center, University of California, Berkeley, Calif. *The American Sociologist*, 2 (November, 1967), 207-212.
** General purpose, service oriented libraries. Materials in these libraries are routinely available to the entire community of social scientists.
[a] This is not an exhaustive list of data libraries as it contains only those currently affiliated with the Council of Social Science Data Archives. Individuals desiring further information about these data libraries or wishing to inform the council of their own activities in this area are advised to contact Professor William Glaser, Executive Director, GSSDA, 605 West 115th Street, New York, New York 10025.

Name of Data Library	Address	Type of Data	Subject Matter
National Opinion Research Center	University of Chicago 6030 South Ellis Avenue Chicago, Illinois 60637	Sample Surveys	Health and welfare, mass communication, community problems
Political Science Research Library and Political Data Program	Yale University 89 Trumbell Street New Haven, Connecticut 06520	Sample Surveys	Studies from Roper ICPR in political science
Public Opinion Survey Unit	Research Center, School of Business & Public Administ. University of Missouri Columbia, Missouri 65201	Sample Surveys	Politics & public opinion in Missouri, U.S.
Project Talent Data Bank	132 N. Bellefield Avenue Pittsburgh, Pennsylvania 15213	Sample Surveys	High school student attitudes surveys, career plans, aptitude tests
**Roper Public Opinion Research Center	Williams College Williamstown, Massachusetts 01267	Sample Surveys	Politics, economics, business, education, public opinion
**Social Science Data and Program Library Service	Social Systems Research Inst. Rm. 4451, Social Science Bldg. University of Wisconsin Madison, Wisconsin 53703	Sample Surveys	Economics, demography
Survey Research Laboratory	437 David Kinley Hall University of Illinois Urbana, Illinois 61801	Sample Surveys Statistics	Politics, economics, public opinion
U.C.L.A. Political Behavior Archive	Dept. of Political Science University of California Los Angeles, California 90024		
Yale Growth Center	Yale University 52 Hillhouse Avenue New Haven, Connecticut 06520	National accounts	Country analysis of under-developed nations

II.7. DIRECTORIES OF SOCIAL RESEARCH CENTERS IN THE UNITED STATES, ENGLAND, AND THE WORLD GENERALLY

Research Centers in the United States

Research Centers Directory, Gale Research Co., Detroit, Michigan, 1965, 2nd edition.

Lists 3200 research centers in the following:

1. Agriculture, Home Economics, and Nutrition
2. Astronomy
3. Business, Economics, and Transportation
4. Conservation
5. Education
6. Engineering and Technology
7. Government and Public Affairs
8. Labor and Industrial Relations
9. Law
10. Life Sciences
11. Mathematics
12. Physical and Earth Sciences
13. Regional and Area Studies
14. Social Sciences, Humanities, and Religion
    A total of 376 centers are listed including Anthropology, Communications, Human Development, Population, Religion, Sociology, History, Ethnic Folklore, Linguistics, Journalism, Creativity, Family Study, Behavior, Race Relations.
15. Multidisciplinary Programs
16. Research Coordinating Offices

A typical entry shows the information given:

2750 Columbia University
BUREAU OF APPLIED SOCIAL RESEARCH
605 West 115th Street
New York, New York   10025
Dr. Allen H. Barton, Director   Phone UN-5-4000
                                       Founded 1937

Integral unit of graduate faculties of Columbia University. Supported by parent institution, U.S. Government, state and local agencies, foundations, non-profit social organizations, and industry. Staff: 24 research professionals, 16-20 graduate research assistants, 10 others, plus research fellows, interns, and part-time student interviewers, coders, and statistical clerks.

Principal fields of research: Communication and opinion formation; political behavior; consumer and family behavior; manpower and populations; professions of education, law and medicine; religious, industrial, and social organizations; mental health. Also collects cases of application of social research to practical problems, codifies social research methods, develops new methods for study of aggregate aspects of mass social behavior, and provides empirical social science research training for graduate students and visiting foreign scholars. Maintains its own IBM data processing equipment.

Research results published in books, monographs, professional journals, project reports, and graduate student doctoral dissertations. Publication: *Bureau Reporter* (monthly). Holds periodic seminars on sociological problems and application of social science research methodology.

World Directory of Research Institutes

The World of Learning 1967-1968, 18th ed. Europe Publications, Ltd., 18 Bedford Square, W.C. 3, London, England.

A compilation, for all countries of the world, of academies, learned societies, research institutes, libraries, museums, art galleries, and universities (including lists of faculty) in all fields of knowledge. This coverage is excellent for most purposes but often fails to include research organizations within academic departments and the university generally.

In the United States the Gale *Research Centers Directory* is superior. For additional information consult the Social Science Research Council, 230 Park Avenue, New York, New York 10017.

International Organizations in the Social Sciences

Consult UNESCO reports and papers in the Social Sciences No. 5: *International Organizations in the Social Sciences,* 1956.

II.8.a. LIST OF IMPORTANT SOCIAL RESEARCH CENTERS IN EUROPE

These European centers are engaged in collaborative research (with the Survey Research Center of the University of Michigan as an American member) on Time-Budget Activity Analysis.*

---

* The list of research participants was accurate in April, 1966, and was described in *The American Behavioral Scientist,* II, No. 4 (December, 1966), 4-5.

RESEARCH PARTICIPANTS

Institut de Sociologie de l'Université Libre de Bruxelles (Belgium)	*Prof. Pierre Feldheim* *Mr. Claude Javeau*
Scientific Research Group of the Trade Union Council, Sofia (Bulgaria)	*Mr. Zachari Staikov*
Institut National de la Statistique et des Etudes Economiques, Paris (France)	*Mr. Claude Goguel*
Sociological Research Group of the Hungarian Academy of Sciences, Budapest (Hungary)	*Mr. Làsló Cseh-Szombathy*
Central Statistical Office, Budapest (Hungary)	*Mrs. Suzanne Ferge*
Institut des Sciences Politiques et Sociales, Université Catholique de Louvain (Belgium) Director of the Research Group at Lima (Peru)	*Prof. Rodolphe Rezsohazy*
Institute of Philosophy and Sociology of the Polish Academy of Sciences, Warsaw (Poland)	*Mr. Zygmunt Skorzynski*
Labor Institute, Warsaw (Poland)	*Mrs. Helen Strzeminska*
Research Group on Living Standards, Institute for Economics, Berlin-Karlshorst (German Democratic Republic)	*Dr. Günther Manz* *Mr. Gerhardt Lippold*
Institute for International Comparative Research in Social Sciences, University of Cologne (Federal Republic of Germany)	*Prof. Erwin K. Scheuch* *Miss Annerose Schneider*
Institute for Social Research of the University of Münster, Dortmund (Federal Republic of Germany)	*Prof. Dieter Claessens* *Mr. Bernard von Rosenbladt*
Sociological Laboratory of the Prague Polytechnical Institute, Prague (Czechoslovakia)	*Prof. Bedrich Weiner*
Institute for Economy and Organization of Industrial Production of the USSR Academy of Sciences, Novosibirsk (U.S.S.R.)	*Prof. German A. Proudenski* *Mr. Vassili D. Patrouchev*
Survey Research Center of the University of Michigan, Ann Arbor, Mich. (United States)	*Prof. Philip Converse* *Dr. John Robinson*
Institute for Sociology, Belgrade (Yugoslavia)	*Prof. Vladimir Raskovic* *Mr. Predrag Aleksic*
Institute for Philosophy and Sociology of the University of Ljubljana (Yugoslavia)	*Mrs. Katja Boh*

SECRETARIAT OF THE PROJECT

European Co-ordination Center for Research and Documentation
in Social Sciences
1010 Vienna, Franz-Josefs Kai 3 (Austria)

DIRECTOR OF THE PROJECT	SECRETARY OF THE PROJECT
Professor Alexander Szalai, Hungarian Academy of Sciences (Budapest)	M. Henri Raymond, Scientific Secretary of the European Co-ordination Center for Research and Documentation in Social Sciences (Vienna)

II.8.b. LIST OF IMPORTANT SOCIAL RESEARCH CENTERS IN LATIN AMERICA

Argentina

1. Centro de Investigaciones Económicas. Instituto Torcuato Di Tella. Virrey del Pino 3210. Buenos Aires (26). Cables: INSTELLA. Tel.: 76-7484, 76-9311, 76-3370.
   Director: Dr. Mario S. Brodersohn.
   (1) Informe Reunión.
2. Centro de Sociología Comparada. Instituto Torcuato Di Tella. Verrey del Pino 3230, Buenos Aires. Cables: INSTELLA. Tel.: 73-7771, 73-2825.
   Director: Dr. Jorge García Bouza.
   (1) Revista Latinoamericana de Sociología.
   (2) Informe Reunión.
3. Instituto de Desarrollo Económico y Social (IDES). Cangallo 1615, piso 7º, of. 72. Buenos Aires. Tel.: 35-0361.
   Presidente: Dr. Oscar Cornblit.
   (1) Folleto del IDES.
   (2) Programa de Consolidación y Expansión 1967-1969.
4. Centro de Estudios de Coyuntura. Instituto de Desarrollo Económico y Social (IDES). Cangallo 1615, piso 7º, Buenos Aires. Tel: 49-3941.
   Coordinator: Dr. Aldo Ferrer
5. Facultad de Ciencias Económicas. Instituto de Investigaciones Económicas. Universidad de Buenos Aires. Córdoba 2122. Buenos Aires.
   Director: Doctor Julio H. G. Olivera.
6. Centro de Estudios Regionales y Urbanos. Canning 2257 Buenos Aires. Tel.: 72-4087.
   Director: Arq. Jorge Enrique Hardoy.
   (1) Centro de Estudios Urbanos y Regionales, Informe Reunión.
7. Instituto Torcuato Di Tella. Florida 936. Buenos Aires. Cables: INSTELLA. Tel.: 31-4721 al 26.
   Director: Enrique Oteiza.
   (1) Folleto del Instituto.
8. Fundación de Investigaciones Económicas Latinoamericanas. Esmeralda 320, 4º piso. Buenos Aires. Cable: FIEL.
   Director: Doctor José María Dagnino Pastore.
9. Instituto de Economía y Finanzas. Facultad de Ciencias Económicas. Universidad de Córdoba. Ciudad Universitaria, Urquiza 161, Córdoba. Casilla 622. Tel.: 6634, 99.808, 24.200.
   Director: Doctor Aldo A. Arnaudo.

10. Instituto de Investigaciones Económicas. Facultad de Ciencias Económicas. Universidad Nacional de Tucumán. 25 de Mayo 456. Tucumán. Casilla de Correo 209. Tel.: 20.934.
Director: Dr. Victor Jorge Elías.
(1) Proyecto de Reestructuración del Plan de Estudios para la Licenciatura y Doctorado en Economía.
(2) Informe Reunión.
11. Centro de Historia Económica y Social. Instituto de Desarrollo Económico y Social. Cangallo 1615. Buenos Aires.
Director: Dr. Tulio Halperín Donghi.
12. Instituto para la Integración de América Latina (INTAL). Cerrito 264—2ọ piso. Casilla de Correo 39—Sucursal 1—Buenos Aires. Argentina. Cables: INTAMBANC. Tel.: 35-5513, 35-7842.
Director: Dr. Gustavo Lagos Matus.
(1) Informe Reunión.

Brazil

1. Instituto Brasileiro de Economía. Fundacão Getúlio Vargas. Praía Botafogo 186. Río de Janeiro.
Director: Doctor Julián M. Chacel.
(1) Personal de Formação Universitaria.
(2) Escola de Pos-graduação em Economía.
(3) Régimen Interno.
(4) O Instituto Brasileiro de Economía.
2. Instituto de Pesquisas Económicas. Facultad de Ciencias Económicas. Universidad de Sao Paulo. Caixa Postal 8030. Sao Paulo.
Director: Dr. Antonio Delfim Netto.
3. Instituto de Ciencias Sociais. Universidad Federal de Río Janeiro. Rua Marquês de Olinda, 64, Botafogo. Río de Janeiro. Tel.: 46-7362.
Director: Doctor Evaristo de Moraes.
(1) Informe Reunión.
4. Departamento de Ciência Política. Universidade Federal de Minas Gerais. Edif. Da Reitoria, 7ọ Andar. Caixa Postal 1621. Belo Horizonte—Minas Gerais. Tel.: 23.144.
Director: Dr. Tocari Assis Bastos.
5. Centro de Sociología Indusrial. Universidad de Sao Paulo. Sao Paulo.
Director: Profesor Florestan Fernández.
6. Instituto de Investigaciones Económicas. Facultad de Ciencias Económicas. Universidad Federal do Rio Grande do Sul. Avenida João Pesoa, Nọ 31. Caixa Postal 2394. Porto Alegre—Rio Grande do Sul. Tel.: 8417.
Director: Dr. Jorge Bermejo.
(1) Informe Reunión.

7. Centro de Pesquisas. Facultad de Aministração. Universidad de Bahia. Salvador (Bahia).
   Director: Dr. Perceu Amaral.
8. Centro Latinoamericano de Pesquisas en Ciencias Sociais. Rua Dona Mariana 73—Botafogo. Caixa Postal 12—ZC 02. Río de Janeiro. Brasil Cables: CENTRO. Tel.: 46-5253.
   Director: Dr. Manoel Diégues Júnior.
   (1) Centro Latinoamericano de Investigaciones en Ciencias Sociales —Informe.
   (2) Plano de Actividades para 1967-68.

Central America

1. Instituto Universitario Centroamericano de Investigaciones Sociales (ICAI). Universidad de Costa Rica. Ciudad Universitaria. San José —Costa Rica. A. C. Cables: ICAI. Tel.: 6750.
   Director: Dr. Oscar Chaves Esquivel.
   (1) Informe Reunión.

Chile

1. Instituto de Economía. Universidad de Chile. Casilla 3861 Santiago de Chile. Casilla 3861 Santiago—Condell 343. Cables: INVEC. Tel.: 25-2253.
   Director: Ing. Roberto Maldonado V.
   (1) Informe Reunión.
2. Centro de Investigaciones Económicas. Universidad Católica de Chile (C.I.E.U.C.). Avda. Bernardo O'Higgins 340 Casilla 114-D. Santiago. Tel.: 30.095, anexo 325.
   Director: Dr. Rolf Lüders.
   (1) Informe Reunión.
3. Centro de Investigaciones So-Santiago. Tel.: 30.091.
   Director: Prof. Hernán Godoy Urzua.
   (1) Informe Reunión.
4. Escuela de Economía y Administración. Universidad de Concepción. Barros Arana 1765. Casilla 1987. Concepción. Tel.: 23.933, 23.756.
   Decano Director: Ing. Ignacio Pérez Salgado.
   (1) Informe Reunión.
5. Comité Interdisciplinario de Desarrollo Urbano (C.I.D.U.). Universidad Católica de Chile. Mardoqueo Fernández Nº 15. Depto. 74. Santiago. Tel.: 46-1930.
   Director: Arq. Ricardo Jordán
   (1) Informe Reunión.
   (2) Programa Docencia: Cursos sobre Programación del Desarrollo Comunal. Prog. Materias. CIDU/PD.3/DD.2.

(3) Programa Docencia: Cursos Interdisciplinarias de Desarrollo Urbano. 2º Sem. 1966. CIDU/PD. 1/DF. 2.

(4) Programa de Investigaciones: Modelo general de las relaciones existentes entre el desarrollo económico y social y el proceso de urbanización: Un enfoque para la investigación. CIDU/PI. o/DD. 3.

(5) Programa de Docencia: Programa de entrenamiento en Desarrollo Comunal del Ministerio de la Vivienda y Urbanismo. CIDU/PD. 3/DD. 1.

6. Centro Latinoamericano de Demografía (CELADE). Casilla 3721. Santiago. Chile.
   Director: Dra. Carmen Miró.
   (1) Lista de Publicaciones.
   (2) Origen, Objectivos y Organización.

7. Facultad Latinoamericana de Ciencias Sociales (FLACSO). Av. J. P. Alessandri 832. Casilla 3213. Santiago. Chile. Cables: FLACSO. Tel.: 46-0096.
   Director: Dr. Glaucio Dillon Soares.

8. Instituto Latinoamericano de Planificación Económica y Social. Casilla 1567—José M. Infante 9. Santiago. Chile. Cables: INSTI-TUTO.
   Director General Adjunto: Lic. Cristóbal Lara.
   (1) Instituto Latinoamericano de Planificación Económica y Social.
   (2) Lista de Publicaciones y Documentos.
   (3) Informe Reunión.

9. Comisión Económica para América Latina. Casilla 179 D. Santiago. Chile. Cables: UNATIONS.
   Secretario Ejecutivo: Dr. José Antonio Mayobre.
   (1) Guía Básica de la Comisión y de su Secretaría.

10. Centro de Investigaciones de Historia Americana. Facultad de Filosofía y Educación. Universidad de Chile. Calle Castro 158 B. Casilla 1483. Santiago.
    Director: Prof. Alvaro Jara.

11. Centro para el Desarrollo Económico y Social de América Latina (DESAL). Casilla 9990. Santiago. Cables: DESAL.
    Director: P. Roger Vekemans.

Colombia

1. Centro de Estudios sobre Desarrollo Económicó (CEDE). Facultad de Economía. Universidad de Los Andes. Apartado Aéreo 4976. Bogotá. Cable: UNIANDES.
   Director Asistente: Francisco J. Ortega.

(1) Detalle de Algunas Investigaciones.

(2) Folleto del CEDE.

2. Programa Latinoamericano de Estudios del Desarrollo. Facultad de Ciencias Sociales. Universidad Nacional de Colombia. Bogotá. Director: Luis Ratinoff.

Ecuador

1. Centro de Estudios del Desarrollo. Caracas 172 y Salinas. Casilla Postal No 2321. Quito. Cables: CENDES. Tel.: 31.069, 32.621, 35.670. Director Ejecutivo: Ec. Germánico Espinosa Z.

Mexico

1. Centro de Estudios Económicos y Demográficos. El Colegio de México. Guanajuato 125. México 7—D.F. Cables: COLMEX. Tel.: 28-6861. Director: Víctor L. Urquidi.

   (1) Informe Reunión.

2. Instituto de Investigaciones Sociales. Universidad Nacional Autónoma de México. Ciudad Universitaria. México 20—D. F. Director: Dr. Pablo González Casanova.

3. Instituto de Investigaciones Económicas. Escuela Nacional de Economía. Universidad Nacional Autónoma de México. Ciudad Universitaria. México 20—D. F. Director: Lic. Diego López Rosado.

   (1) Informe Reunión.

4. Centro de Investigaciones Económicas. Facultad de Economía. Universidad de Nuevo León. Abasolo 907. Oriente. Monterrey—N. L. Director Interino: Lic. Ernesto Bolaños.

5. Centro de Economía Agrícola Escuela de Posgraduados. Escuela Nacional de Agricultura. Chapingo. Presidente: Ing. Ramón Fernández y Fernández.

Peru

1. Instituto de Estudios Peruanos. Horacio Urteaga 694 (Campo de Marte). Lima. Cables: IEPERU. Tel.: 35.228. Director: Dr. José Matos Mar.

   (1) Informe Reunión.

2. Instituto de Investigaciones Económicas. Facultad de Ciencias Económicas y Comerciales. Universidad Nacional Mayor de San Marcos. Avda. Nicolás de Piérola, No 1254. Parque Universitario. Lima. Tel.: 70.779, 80.685. Director: Dr. Carlos Capuñay Mimbela.

   (1) Informe Reunión.

3. Instituto de Investigaciones Sociologicas, Universidad Nacional, Mayor de Marcos.
Director: Dr. José Mejia Valera.

Uruguay

1. Instituto de Economía. 25 de Mayo 395. Facultad de Ciencias Económicas y de Administración. Universidad de la República del Uruguay. Montevideo. Cables: Instituto Económico. 25 de Mayo 395. Tel.: 985.421.
Director: Contador Enrique V. Iglesias.
   (1) Reseña de Actividades y Programas.
2. Instituto de Ciencias Sociales. Facultad de Derecho y Ciencias Sociales. Universidad de la República del Uruguay. Mercedes 1703. Montevideo. Tel.: 48.311.
Director: Dr. Aldo E. Solari.
   (1) Informe Reunión.

Venezuela

1. Centro de Estudios del Desarrollo. Universidad Central de Venezuela. Apartado 6622. Caracas. Cables: CENDESUC.
Director: Dr. Luis Lander.
   (1) Informe Reunión.
2. Instituto de Investigaciones Económicas (U.C.A.B.). Universidad Católica Andrés Bello. A. P. 422. Caracas. Cables: UNICABE. Tel.: 81-5191.
Director: Reverendo Padre Manuel Pernaut.
   (1) Instituto de Investigaciones Económicas.
3. Instituto de Investigaciones Económicas. Facultad de Economía. Universidad Central de Venezuela. Ciudad Universitaria—Edif. de la Biblioteca, Piso 11. Caracas. Tel.: 61-9811 al 14. Ext. 2424 y 2425.
Director: Dr. D. F. Maza Zavala.
   (1) Informe Reunión.
4. Universidad de Oriente. Cerro Colorado. Cumaná—Edo. Sucre. Cables: UNIVORIENT.
Vicerrector: Marco Tulio Bruni Celli.
   (1) Universidad de Oriente.
   (2) El Instituto Oceonográfico.
   (3) Esquema de trabajo de la Escuela de Ciencias Sociales.
   (4) Dirección de Planificación.
   (5) Oficina Coordinadora de Investigación y Extensión.
   (6) Prospecto General 1966.

5. Centro de Investigaciones Administrativas y Sociales (C.I.A.S.). Escuela de Administración Pública. Comisión de Administración Pública. Avda. Universidad, Esquina de Traposos. Edif. Banco Industrial, 5ọ piso. A. P. 6494. Caracas. Tel.: 41-8742 al 45. Director: Doctora Ligia Valladares.
   (1) Informe Reunión.

6. Departamento de Investigaciones. Económicas y Administrativas. Facultad de Ciencias Económicas y Sociales. Universidad del Zulia. La Ciega—Apartado 1354. Maracaibo. Tel.: 4587, 4588. Director: Doctor Rubén S. Margheritti.
   (1) Informe Reunión.

7. Instituto de Investigaciones Económicas. Facultad de Economía. Universidad de Los Andes. Mérida. Tel.: 2877. Director: Doctor Leocadio Hontoria.
   (1) Informe Reunión.

8. Instituto Venezolano de Investigaciones Científicas (IVIC). Altos de Pipe, Km. 14. Carretera Panamericana. Edo. Miranda. Director: Dr. Marcel Roche.

9. Instituto para el Desarrollo Económico y Social (IDES). Edif. Gran Avenida—6ọ piso. Caracas. Director Encargado: Dr. Luis E. Alcalá.

10. Escuela de Sociología y Antropología de la U. C. V. Caracas. Director: Dr. Alfredo Chacón.

II.9. A BIBLIOGRAPHY OF METHODS GUIDES

Documents

ALLPORT, GORDON. *The Use of Personal Documents in Psychological Science.* New York: Social Science Research Council, 1942.

GOTTSCHALK, L., KLUCKHOHN, K., and ANGEL, R. *The Use of Personal Documents in History, Anthropology, and Sociology.* New York: Social Science Research Council, 1945.

THOMAS, W. I., and ZNANECKI, F. *The Polish Peasant in Europe and America.* New York: Dover Publications, Inc., 1958.

Direct Observation

BALES, ROBERT. *Interaction Process Analysis.* Reading, Mass.: Addison-Wesley Publishing Company, Inc., 1949.

WEBB, EUGENE J., CAMPBELL, DONALD T., SCHWARTZ, RICHARD D., and SECHREST, LEE. *Unobtrusive Measures: Nonreactive Research in the Social Sciences,* Chicago: Rand McNally & Company, 1966.

Participant Observation

BRUYN, SEVERYN T. *The Human Perspective in Sociology: The Methodology of Participant Observation.* Englewood Cliffs, N.J.: Prentice-Hall, Inc., 1966.

POWDERMAKER, HORTENSE. *Stranger and Friend, The Way of an Anthropologist.* New York: W. W. Norton & Company, 1966.

Questionnaire Construction

LAZARSFELD, PAUL F., and BARTON, ALLEN, "Some General Principles of Questionnaire Classification," *The Language of Social Research.* Edited by PAUL F. LAZARSFELD and MORRIS ROSENBERG. Glencoe, Ill.: The Free Press, 1962, pp. 83-92.

OPPENHEIM, A. N. *Questionnaire Design and Attitude Measurement.* New York: Basic Books, Inc., 1966.

Interview

HYMAN, HERBERT H., *et al. Interviewing in Social Research.* Chicago: The University of Chicago Press, 1954.

KAHN, ROBERT L., and CANNELL, CHARLES F. *The Dynamics of Interviewing.* New York: John Wiley & Sons, Inc., 1957.

MERTON, ROBERT K. *et al. The Focused Interview: A Manual of Problems and Procedures.* Glencoe, Ill.: The Free Press, 1956.

Index and Scale Construction

BAUER, RAYMOND A. (ed.). *Social Indicators.* Cambridge, Mass.: The M.I.T. Press, 1966.

EDWARDS, ALLEN. *Technique of Attitude Scale Construction.* New York: Appleton-Century-Crofts, Inc., 1957.

OPPENHEIM, A. N. *Questionnaire Design and Attitude Measurement.* New York: Basic Books, Inc., 1966.

RILEY, MATILDA W., RILEY, JOHN W., and TOBY, JACKSON, *Sociological Studies in Scale Analysis.* New Brunswick, N.J.: Rutgers University Press, 1954.

SHAW, MARVIN E., and WRIGHT, JACK M. *Scales for the Measurement of Attitudes.* New York: McGraw-Hill Book Company, 1967.

SHELDON, ELEANOR B., and MOORE, WILBERT E. *Indicators of Social Change: A Symposium on Concepts and Measures.* New York: Russell Sage Foundation, 1968.

STOUFFER, SAMUEL, *et al. The American Soldier: Measurement and Prediction.* Vol. 4. Princeton: Princeton University Press, 1949. See chapters by Louis Guttman on scaling and by Paul F. Lazarsfeld on latent structure analysis.

TORGERSON, W., *Theory and Methods of Scaling*, New York: John Wiley & Sons, Inc., 1958.

YOUNG, PAULINE, and SCHMID, CALVIN P. *Scientific Social Surveys and Research*. 4th ed. Englewood Cliffs, N.J.: Prentice-Hall, Inc., 1968. Includes chapters on scaling techniques and graphic presentation.

PART III

Guides to Statistical Analysis

THIS PART INCLUDES guides that should prove useful to the researcher as he seeks statistical tools to test hypotheses. He may find it necessary to reformulate his initial hypotheses in order to use the most precise statistical test. Qualitative and quantitative variables require appropriate statistics to provide tests of association or of significant differences between groups. In Part III the researcher will find statistical tests organized to deal with these two kinds of variables. Also the question of the probability of normal distribution of the data forces the researcher to make a distinction between parametric and nonparametric statistics in drawing inferences from samples. These distinctions will be set forth in the description of the statistics presented.

No limited set of guides can replace a good text in statistics. However, it is believed that the researcher can find an array of concepts so organized here that he may be able to survey the dimensions of his problem. The most space has been given to the importance of qualitative variables and their statistical treatment. Computation guides have been included for the use of the most commonly used statistical measures.

The bibliography placed at the end of this part has been selected to provide additional information on statistics, tables, and graphic presentation. Each reference enables the reader to follow step-by-step explanations.

III.1. THE IMPERTINENT QUESTIONER: THE SCIENTIST'S GUIDE TO THE STATISTICIAN'S MIND *

WILLIAM LURIE

Instructions for Guide III.1.

This article should sharpen the researcher's awareness of the dimensions of his hypotheses as he prepares to test them. As Lurie puts it: "It is the scientist's responsibility to decide exactly what his hypotheses are, what these hypotheses are about, and how sure he wants to be of their correctness. . . . And the more the scientist becomes aware of his responsibilities, and takes them into account in his work, so much more accurate and valid will his conclusions be, and so much more properly related to the reality with which he deals."

Prologue

It has become fashionable to ornament science with statistical embellishments. No equation is complete without at least a double summation sign somewhere in it, sub-ij's attach themselves to familiar X's, Y's and Z's; and phrases like "polymodal distribution," "inverse reciprocal correlation," and "multivariate deviations" now can be seen on practically every other page of "The Journal of the Society for Thus-and-So," "The Transactions of the Association for Such-and-Such," and "The Proceedings of the Symposium on Etc., Etc."

But in addition to providing mathematical and linguistic ornamentation for these publications, the statistician, if he is really to assist the scientist, must perform a necessary, but irritatingly annoying task: he must ask the scientist impertinent questions. Indeed, the questions, if bluntly asked, may appear to be not only impertinent but almost indecently prying—because they deal with the foundations of the scientist's thinking. By these questions, unsuspected weaknesses in the foundations may be brought to light, and the exposure of weaknesses in one's thinking is a rather unpleasant occurrence.

* *American Scientist,* 46 (March, 1958), 57-61.

The statistician will, then, if he is wise in the ways of human beings as well as learned in statistics, ask these questions diplomatically, or even not ask them as questions at all. He may well guide the discussion with the scientist in such a way that the answers to the questions will be forthcoming without the questions having been even explicitly asked.

And if happily the scientific and statistical disciplines reside within one mind, and it is the scientist's statistical conscience that asks him these questions, instead of impertinent questioning there is valid scientific soul-searching.

Regardless, then, of whether these questions arise inside or outside the scientist's own mind, what are they? These:

1. With respect to the experiment you are performing, just what are your ideas?
2. With respect to the scientific area to which these ideas refer, just what are they about?
3. How sure do you want to be of the correctness of these ideas?

In order to understand the statistician's reasons for asking these questions, let us first see how the scientist's activities look to the statistician.

From the statistician's point of view, what the scientist does, is: performs experiments and/or makes observations to obtain data relating to *an idea he has* about the organization of *that portion of the world he is interested in,* so that he can decide *whether his idea was correct or not.*

For each of these italicized aspects of the scientist's activity, there is a corresponding question.

Let us, then, examine each of these aspects of the scientist's activities, and the purpose for and consequences of the question concerning it.

An Idea He Has

The impertinent questioner must take the risk of appearing to imply that the scientist is not thinking clearly. And, of course, even an implication to this effect is not calculated to endear the implier to the heart of the implyee. But it is exactly this implication that, perhaps innocently, is associated with the question, "Just what are your ideas?"

Why does the statistician ask this impertinent question? Because it is a precondition for the statistician's being able to help the scientist accomplish his objective. A hazily formulated idea not only can be discussed, at best, with difficulty, but further, it is practically impossible to test its correctness. Therefore, the statistician has a rule, his name for which is: EXPLICIT HYPOTHESIZATION. This rule expresses the requirement that the idea, whose correctness is to be determined by the experiment, should be stated in as clear, detailed, and explicit form as possible, preferably before the experiment is conducted. This idea can relate either to the influence of one factor or to the influence of several factors, or to the numerical characterization of a property (or properties) of whatever is being experimented on. In the early stages of an investigation, where what are being sought are the influential factors (i.e., those which, when they are at varying levels, give rise to sufficiently varied results), the idea (or hypothesis) need not be specific, but it must be explicit. The hypothesis can be broad, but it must be explicitly broad:—that is, even though it is not a hypothesis about details, its boundary must be sharply delineated.

For example, "Factors A, B, C, and D individually influence the results, "Factors A and B, acting in conjunction, influence the results differently than would be expected from the effects of A alone and B alone," "Factors A, B, and C, acting in conjunction, etc., etc." Or later in the investigation, and more specifically, "The measurement of the effect of factor A at level a_1, will result in the numerical value $N \pm n$."

To emphasize unmistakably the requirement for explicit hypothesization, let us use an obviously exaggerated example dealing with a particular subject: the task of an industrial psychologist who has been given the job of finding out why the accounting clerks are making too many errors in addition. (The problem of deciding how many errors are "too many" is another statistical problem, which will not be considered here.)

The psychologist, for the purposes of this example, may say to himself: "My training as a psychologist tells me that the situation in which a person operates affects his behavior. So let me find out what the situation is that is causing the clerks to make these errors." If the formulation of the psychologist's idea goes no further than this, he can obviously continue to attempt to find out what the situation is, from now on forever, since "The Situation" has no boundaries.

It might, for example, not only include the working circumstances of the clerks, but their home circumstances, their childhood histories, their dream life; and it is seen that the possibilities are unlimited. As then is obvious, the hypothesis has not been sufficiently explicitly formulated, nor the situation covered by it clearly enough delineated, for a decision to be able to be arrived at as to the correctness of the hypothesis.

But now, let the psychologist's statistical conscience awaken, and his ideas begin to crystallize out of their original diffuseness. "The Situation?—Well, to be more specific, let's just consider the office situation. And within the office situation, I'll pick three factors that I believe affect the performance of the clerks. The factors I'm selecting to study for their effects are: Temperature, Humidity, and Noise. And now, my explicit hypothesis: It makes a difference what the levels of temperature, humidity, and noise are with respect to the number of errors in addition made by the accounting clerks." The hypothesis could (and probably should) have been even more explicitly formulated (e.g., including as factors Illumination Level, Desk Space per employee, etc.) but the direction of the path to statistical virtue has been pointed out, and further travel along that path is left to the reader.

Now, assuming that the hypothesis has been sufficiently explicitly formulated, the scientist and statistician can together review the plan (or design) of the experiment, and assure themselves that such data will be obtained as will be sufficient to determine the correctness (or noncorrectness) of the scientist's idea.

That Portion of the World He Is Interested In

Again, the impertinent questioner must be careful in asking: "Just what are your ideas about?" Even though one may admit that his ideas are not as clearly and explicitly formulated as he would like, the question "Just what are your ideas about?" carries with it, to the person being asked, the implication that he isn't clear about the subject-matter of his ideas, surely not a flattering implication. The statistician has a reason for his implied aspersion on the basis of the scientist's self-esteem. The statistician's reason can be stated to the scientist thus: "It's for your own good. If I am to help you decide, on the basis of the experimental facts, whether your ideas are correct or not, I have to know, as explicitly as possible, not only what your ideas are, but *what they are about*. My name for this requirement is: MODEL FORMULATION." Technically, model formulation establishes the requirement that a clear differentiation be made as to whether the scientist's ideas are intended to be applicable only to the conditions of the experiment (the narrower range of application) or to conditions (i.e., levels of the factors) other than those specific ones under which the experiment is being conducted (the broader range of application). Why the necessity for this differentiation? Because, when the experimental data have been obtained, the analysis of the data is carried on in different ways, depending on whether the hypotheses are intended to have the broader or narrower range of application.

Let us again, for exemplification, return to our industrial psychologist. And, let us say, his experimental conditions are, for temperature, 40°, 55°, and 70°F.; for humidity, 40, 55, and 70 percent; and for noise level, 40, 55, and 70 decibels.

It may well make a difference in the way the experimental data are analyzed to arrive at conclusions (i.e., decisions as to correctness of ideas), and whether any conclusions can be arrived at, and, if so, what they are, depending on whether the scientist wants his conclusions to apply only to the three levels of temperature, humidity, and noise level that have been used in the experiment, or also to other (unspecified) temperature, humidity, and noise levels. Data that support narrow conclusions may not be sufficient to support broader conclusions. Therefore, the scientist must have clearly in mind what his hypotheses are about, and whether, consequently, his conclusions will be broad or narrow; and the statistician's effort to assure that the scientist does have this clearly in mind, may well, to the scientist, appear to be impertinent.

Whether His Idea Was Correct or Not

The statistician's third question—"How sure do you want to be of the correctness of your ideas?" is the least impertinent of the three. This question, unlike the other two, does not probe the foundations of the scientist's thinking, but rather requests him to quantify a previously unquantified aspect of it. (In fact, the request is in accordance with the scientist's own predilection for quantitative data.) This aspect is that dealing with levels of assurance, for which ordinary language supplies us with qualitatively descriptive terms (somewhat sure, rather sure, quite sure, extremely sure). But these terms are not sufficiently explicit for scientific use. Therefore, the statistician asks the scientist to decide upon and express his desired level of assurance in quantitative terms, so that it can be determined, by analysis of the quantitative data, whether the desired level of assurance of the conclusions has been achieved. The statistician's name for the choice and quantitative expression of the desired level of assurance is: SIGNIFICANCE LEVEL SELECTION. And how does the statistician help the scientist choose the desired level of assurance? By bringing to the forefront of the scientist's consciousness his already unconscious awareness of the inherent variability of events (i.e., that, because of chance alone, no repetition of an experiment will give exactly the same results); by helping the scientist decide what assurance is desired that the hypothesis has not been "confirmed" just by the operation of chance alone; and by furnishing the mathematical tools to decide, on the basis of the experimental data, whether the desired level of assurance has been attained. Say, for example, in the temperature-humidity-noise level experiment, when all the data have been accumulated, and the scientist is preparing them for analysis so that he may decide whether his hypotheses were correct or not, the statistician will then say to him: "You know, of course, that if you did the experiment over, under as near the same conditions as possible, you'd get slightly, or even somewhat different results. The results might even, just by chance, be different enough to lead you to believe that temperature does affect accuracy, even though it really doesn't. Or even if you didn't do the experiment over again, the particular experiment you've just done might be the one in which the data are such that you'd believe temperature has an effect though it really doesn't. *But I can test these data of yours.* I can assure you that when you state the conclusion, say, that temperature does affect accuracy, you'll have only a 5 percent, or 1 percent, or 1/10th of 1 percent chance of being wrong, as a result of that off chance I told you about. Now—what chance do you want to take? If you select a very small chance of being wrong in saying there is a temperature effect when there really isn't you're taking a bigger chance of saying there isn't a temperature effect when there really might be. I can figure this out for you also. So again, what chance do you want to take?"

When the scientist has selected the chance he is willing to take of being wrong (or what is equivalent, how sure he wants to be that he is correct) in his conclusions, the statistician can analyze the data and tell the scientist what conclusions he can validly draw (i.e., what decisions he can make about the correctness of his ideas).

Epilogue

One final word. *It is the statistician's responsibility to ask these questions, not to answer them.* It is the scientist's responsibility to decide exactly what his hypotheses are, what these hypotheses are about, and how sure he wants to be of their correctness.

The statistician, in asking his impertinent questions, is just explicitly bringing to the scientist's attention responsibilities that the scientist may not have been aware that he had. And the more the scientist becomes aware of his responsibilities, and takes them into account in his work, so much more accurate and valid will his conclusions be, and so much more properly related to the reality with which he deals.

III.2. A NOTE ON STATISTICAL ANALYSIS IN THE AMERICAN SOCIOLOGICAL REVIEW *

DAVID GOLD

University of California at Santa Barbara

Instructions for Guide III.2.

This analysis of statistics used by social scientists provides a basis for evaluating the kinds of statistics most commonly used in research. Note the large importance given to qualitative analysis. It is also significant to learn that "rarely does the sociologist have occasion to deal simultaneously with more than two quantitative variables." This limitation may change with new knowledge about matrices and the use of the computer.

In order to get some notions about the nature of the data and the kinds of statistical analysis that do and do not occur in sociological research, an examination has been made of all articles published in the *American Sociological Review* from 1944 through

* *American Sociological Review*, 22 (June, 1957), 332-333.

1953. (Prof. Gold wrote in January, 1969: "To the best of my knowledge such an examination has not been replicated since the above analysis was completed.")

Roughly 48 percent of these articles reported data that conceivably could be subjected to some sort of statistical analysis. This classification uses the broadest possible definition of statistical analysis, assuming that any ordering of statistical data, qualitative or quantitative, represents statistical analysis. Included in the 48 percent are some reports that present incomplete data for purposes of possible statistical analysis but from which it can be inferred that the investigator has more complete data, which he did not present.[1]

The other 52 percent of the articles were discussions or studies whose data could not be subjected to any sort of statistical analysis. Included in the 52 percent are some articles that refer to statistical data and/or the results of statistical analysis in other reports but indicate no statistical manipulation by the writer. The proportion of such "nonstatistical" articles has steadily decreased in the ten-year period examined, from almost two-thirds in 1944 to less than one-third in 1953.

Eleven percent of the "statistical" articles were strictly in the area of demography, population, and census analysis. The remaining "statistical" articles (37 percent), a total of 272 reports, run the gamut of sociological research. For the purposes of this investigation, these latter reports were subjected to intensive examination.

In 38 percent (102 of the 272)[2] of these research reports, no statistical analysis other than presentation of the data in tables was performed. It is significant to note that in all but four of these 102 reports, the investigator was dealing exclusively with qualitative variables.[3] Apparently when dealing with qualitative data the investigator often feels he can do nothing but present the data and reach inferences about the degree and significance of relationships by inspection. However, if he is dealing with quantitative data, the investigator invariably performs some sort of statistical analysis beyond tabular presentation.

With respect to tests of significance, it is perhaps just as well that they are not used. There is widespread confusion between substantive significance and statistical significance as well as questionable legitimacy of application and interpretation in many instances.[4] Sophisticated and rigorous statistical tests are certainly not desirable per se. The research design and the quality of the data must merit such treatment. However, most data, if worth reporting at all, merit some statistical analysis at the descriptive level. The omission of an index of degree of relationship can be serious. In a simple fourfold table, it may seem unnecessary. But often the investigator must compare the relationship displayed in one fourfold table with that in another; and this is not always easy by inspection.

TABLE 1

ARTICLES IN THE *American Sociological Review*, 1944 THROUGH 1953

Nonstatistical			386
Statistical			357
Demographic		85	
Other		272	
Quantitative Data	19		
Qualitative Data	149		
Both	104		
Total *			743

* Articles in the "Notes on Research and Teaching" section were counted if "statistical" but were ignored if "nonstatistical."

In only 7 percent of the articles does the author use a computed measure of degree of relationship among qualitative variables. In another 29 percent of the articles, there is a statement that clearly implies an inference about the degree of relationship among qualitative variables but which is based on no computed index of degree. Included here are those cases in which the analyst mistakenly based statements of degree of relationship on tests of significance. It is evident that, on the most elementary descriptive level, there is markedly inadequate statistical analysis of qualitative data.

And qualitative data are by far the most common data with which the sociologist concerns himself. In 55 percent of the research reports nothing but qualitative data occur. In another 38 percent there are both qualitative and quantitative data; and in only 7 percent are quantitative data the only kind that occur. It can additionally be noted that in 23 percent of the articles not only are qualitative data the only kind that occur, but none of the variables makes up an ordered set of categories.

The proportion of reports in which legitimately quantitative variables actually occur is considerably less than the aforementioned figures would indicate. For included in the "quantitative" classification are scores on tests and some indexes which, in fact, are order statistics only. The possible effects upon substantive conclusions of treating such data as if they represent equal-interval measurement has yet to be systematically examined.

Rarely does the sociologist [in the material here examined] have occasion to deal simultaneously with more than two quantitative variables. During the ten-year period there appeared only eight reports in which multiple and/or partial correlation was used; in addition, there were four reports involving the use of factor analysis.[5] There were no instances in which the investigator confined himself to tabular presentation only when dealing with three or more quantitative variables. On the other hand, in 27 percent (73) of the articles there appeared some statement or direct question concerning the nature of the relationship among three or more qualitative variables but no accompanying statistical analysis involving more than two variables. That is, not even the joint frequencies for more than two variables simultaneously were presented.

It seems clear that in sociological research most variables are of the nature of manifold classification or order statistics rather than quantitative or continuous. We count the number of cases that fall into each of a set of categories that, not too infrequently, are not even mutually exclusive. More often than not there is no particularly meaningful way in which such categories can be rank ordered.

The emphasis in the development of applied statistics has been on techniques for the analysis of data that represent strict quantitative measurement, i.e., with fixed units of magnitude. These research reports seem to indicate that what the sociologist most needs are appropriate measures of association, measures of differences between contingency tables, descriptive measures that will perform a task somewhat analogous to multiple and partial correlation. In other words, he needs statistical techniques for describing the nature of the relationship among qualitative variables.

NOTES

1. A question can, of course, be raised concerning the reliability of this content analysis. All the coding and classification were done by the writer only.
2. All the following percents refer to this base of 272.

3. Any variable that was operationally treated in terms of nominal classification (a set of two or more categories) or ordinal measurement only (ranks) was classified as qualitative.

4. Hanan C. Selvin, "A Critique of Statistical Tests in Survey Research," paper presented at the annual meeting of the American Sociological Society, September, 1956.

5. A change has occurred here. Greater use of multiple and partial correlation, analysis of variance, and factor analysis is being made. An analysis of the recent articles in the *American Sociological Review* for 1963 shows trends as reported by David Gold except for an increase in statistical analysis. Sixty percent show use of statistical analysis, still highly qualitative in character.   D. C. M.

III.3. THE IDEA OF PROPERTY-SPACE IN SOCIAL RESEARCH *

ALLEN H. BARTON

Instructions for Use of Guide III.3.

This guide presents a technique of classifying qualitative data so that associations may be discovered. Arranging data in "property-space" is particularly useful in permitting the effects of various background variables to be compared, while other variables are held constant in each case. The concept of property space is valuable because it becomes a way of thinking about qualitative data and the way in which relations may be ascertained. Hans Zeisel, *Say It With Figures* (5th ed. revised; New York: Harper, 1968), presents a more elaborate description of causal analysis and the role of cross tabulation for the reader who wishes additional knowledge. The more advanced student should consult Herbert Hyman, *Survey Design and Analysis: Principles, Cases, and Procedures* (Glencoe, Ill.: Free Press, 1955). See also the selected readings on causal models and multivariate analysis in the bibliography at the end of Part III.

Everyone is familiar with the idea of indicating location in space by means of coordinates. Every point on this page can be described by two numbers: its distance from the left-hand side and its distance from the bottom (or from any other pair of axes we choose). The location of any point on the earth's surface can be indicated by giving its latitude and longitude, using as base lines the equator and the Greenwich meridian.

* Reprinted by permission from Paul F. Lazarsfeld and Morris Rosenberg (eds.), *The Language of Social Research* (Glencoe, Ill.: Free Press, 1955), pp 40-44. Copyright 1955 by The Free Press, A Corporation.

Other properties besides location in physical space can likewise be indicated by coordinates. A man can be characterized by his scores on tests of mathematical and linguistic ability, just as by his latitude and longitude. These two scores locate him in a "property-space" with the two dimensions of mathematical ability and linguistic ability. We can chart this property-space on paper by using mathematics score as one axis and linguistic score for the other, just as we can chart the earth's surface. Of course in the latter case we are making a spatial representation of actual spatial dimensions, only on a smaller scale. In the former our distances on paper represent the numbers of correct answers to questions given by people taking tests, or in a larger sense, the ability of their minds to perform certain tasks.

The dimensions on which we "locate" people in property-space can be of different kinds. Most psychological test scores are for all practical purposes *continuous variables,* but they usually do not have equal intervals or a meaningful zero point. They provide only a relative ordering of people. Once we have located a representative sample of the United States population in our mathematical-linguistic property-space, we can say that a man is in the fifth percentile of the population in mathematical ability and in the fortieth in linguistic ability. Sometimes social scientists do work with continuous variables that do have a zero-point and equal intervals, at least formally; age, income, size of community, number of hours spent watching television.

More often, probably, the dimensions will be qualitative properties, which locate cases in one of a number of classes, like "state of birth," "military rank," or "occupation." State of birth locates everyone born in the continental U.S. in one of 51 *unordered classes* (counting District of Columbia). Military rank locates members of the armed forces in what is by definition a set of *rank-ordered classes,* ranging from buck private up to five-star general. Occupations in themselves do not necessarily form a set of ranked classes, although some of them are specifically defined in terms of degree of "skill." We might simply list them arbitrarily, as in alphabetical order. Or we might draw upon outside information about them— for example average income, as known from census data, or prestige status, as discovered through surveys—to arrange them in one or another rank-order.

The simplest type of property by which an object can be characterized is a *dichotomous attribute,* such as voter/nonvoter, white/ nonwhite, male/female, or Democrat/Republican. It is always possible to simplify a more complex property by reducing the number of classes that are distinguished. A continuous variable can be cut up to form a set of ranked classes, like income brackets or age levels. A set of ranked classes, in turn, can be simplified by combining all those above a certain point into one class and all those below into a second class, forming a dichotomy. This is done when we reduce the military hierarchy to the distinction between officers and enlisted men, or the income brackets to above or below a certain amount. By picking out one aspect of a set of unordered classes we can sometimes order them into a dichotomy, as when we classify states as east or west of the Mississippi, or occupations as manual or nonmanual.

When we chart the property-space formed by two qualitative characteristics the result is not, of course, a continuous plane, but an array of cells each representing one combination of values on two properties. For example, a study of the 1952 election described people's "political position" in October 1952 in terms of the two dimensions of "usual party affiliations" and "degree of political interest." If one asks Americans what their usual party affiliation is almost everyone falls into three categories: Republicans, Democrats, and independents. These are natural divisions. Degree of interest on the other hand can be divided into any number of ranked categories we please, depending on the alternatives we offer the respondent. In the present case they could rate themselves as having high, medium, or low interest. These two trichotomous dimensions then define a ninefold property-space as shown in Table 1.

TABLE 1

A QUALITATIVE PROPERTY-SPACE OF POLITICAL POSITION

USUAL PARTY AFFILIATION

		Republican	Democratic	Independent
DEGREE OF POLITICAL INTEREST	High			
	Medium			
	Low			

We can locate a person within this property-space by giving as coordinates his usual party affiliation and his degree of political interest.

TABLE 2

A THREE-DIMENSIONAL ATTRIBUTE-SPACE LAID OUT
IN TWO DIMENSIONS

FATHER MANUAL
OCCUPATION

Son's Occupation

SON'S PARTY		Manual	Nonmanual
	Democrat		
	Republican		

FATHER NONMANUAL
OCCUPATION

Son's Occupation

SON'S PARTY		Manual	Nonmanual
	Democrat		
	Republican		

There is no reason why we cannot characterize objects by as many properties as we want. We can add a test in historical knowledge to tests in mathematics and language, and characterize our subjects by three coordinates. These can still be presented in the form of a physical model, by using a box in which everyone is located by distance from the left-hand side, from the front, and from the bottom. If we add a fourth test, for instance, of reading speed, we can give our subjects four coordinates and locate them in a four-dimensional property-space. Thus we can say that someone is in the fifth percentile of the U.S. population in mathematics, the fortieth in language skill, the sixtieth in historical knowledge, and the twenty-ninth in reading speed. We can no longer represent this by a physical model, but we can perform mathematical operations on the four coordinates just as well as on two or three.

In dealing with qualitative property-spaces which have limited numbers of categories on each dimension, we can still chart the property-space on paper even though it is three-dimensional or even higher-dimensional. Let us take the two dimensions of occupation, dichotomized as manual/nonmanual, and political preference, dichotomized as Democratic/Republican. These give us a fourfold table. If we add the dimension of father's occupation, again dichotomized as manual/nonmanual, we now have a "two-story" fourfold table: occupation and party of sons of manual workers and occupation and party of sons of nonmanually employed people. This can be physically represented by a cube with eight cells, with the original fourfold table repeated on both the "first floor" and the "second floor." If we want to represent this cube on a flat piece of paper, all we have to do is to lay the two "stories" side by side, as an architect would two floor plans. (See Table 2 on page 130.)

Now suppose that we ask a fourth question, for example, the father's usual party, again dichotomized as Democratic/Republican. Our property-space then becomes a four-dimensional "cube." But we can still lay out each level on this fourth dimension on paper just as we did those on the third. (See Table 3 on page 132.)

The combination of dichotomous attributes produces a type of property-space that may be labeled "dichotomous attribute-space." [1] Position in a dichotomous attribute-space can be indicated as a response-pattern of plus and minus signs, where we have assigned these values (arbitrarily or otherwise) to the two sides of each dichotomy and arranged the dimensions in some order. Thus a Democratic manual worker, whose father was a Democratic manual worker, might be indicated by the coordinates $(+ + + +)$. A Republican nonmanually employed person, whose father was a Democratic manual worker, would have the coordinates $(- - + +)$, and so on. (This system of notation is often used in "political score-sheets" that show how congressmen voted on a series of bills, a plus sign showing a "correct" vote and a minus sign a "wrong" vote, in terms of a given political viewpoint or economic interest.)

TABLE 3

A FOUR-DIMENSIONAL ATTRIBUTE-SPACE LAID OUT IN TWO DIMENSIONS

	FATHER MANUAL OCCUPATION	FATHER NONMANUAL OCCUPATION
	Son's Occupation	Son's Occupation
	Manual Nonmanual	Manual Nonmanual
FATHER DEMOCRAT	Son Democrat · Republican	Son Democrat · Republican
FATHER REPUBLICAN	Son Democrat · Republican	Son Democrat · Republican

If we are particularly interested in one of the dimensions as a criterion or dependent variable, we may present a dichotomous attribute-space in abbreviated form by showing only the "background" factors as dimensions in the chart, and filling in each cell with a figure showing the percent who are "positive" on the criterion behavior. No information is lost since the attribute is a dichotomy, and all those not positive are classified as "negative" on the attribute. It is as if we had raised three-dimensional bars from the two-dimensional chart of background characteristics with a height proportional to the positive answers on the criterion behavior, and then replaced them with figures indicating their height just as altitudes are shown on a flat map. Thus Table 3 could be presented as an eightfold table showing the dimensions of father's occupation, father's party, and son's occupation; the cells would be filled in with figures showing "percent Democrat" (or vice versa). (See Table 4.)

TABLE 4

ABBREVIATED PRESENTATION OF A FOUR-DIMENSIONAL
ATTRIBUTE-SPACE

FATHER'S OCCUPATION

	Manual		Nonmanual	
	SON'S OCCUPATION		SON'S OCCUPATION	
	Manual	Nonmanual	Manual	Nonmanual
Democratic	——% Dem.	——% Dem.	——% Dem.	——% Dem.
FATHER'S PARTY				
Republican	——% Dem.	——% Dem.	——% Dem.	——% Dem.

Such tables are particularly useful in permitting the effects of the various background variables to be compared, holding the others constant in each case.[2]

To suggest how far the use of very high-dimension property-spaces has actually developed in social research, we need only note that the results of each interview in a survey are normally punched on an IBM card containing 80 columns, each with twelve rows. Such a card provides for an 80-dimensional property-space, with each property having twelve classes. In practice one never uses all eighty dimensions simultaneously to characterize a respondent; however, they are all available to use in whatever smaller combinations we select. If we consider each position in the 80 by 12 matrix as representing a dichotomous attribute (each can either be punched or not punched), we have the possibility of locating each respondent in a dichotomous attribute-space of 960 dimensions.

NOTES

1. This has special characteristics that are used in latent-structure analysis, but this will not be discussed here. A dichotomous system is also equivalent to a binary number system, or an "off/on" system of information, as used in computing machines and in communication theory.

2. Many concrete examples can be found in Chap. X in Hans Zeisel, *Say It With Figures* (New York: Harper, 1968).

III.4. SUMMARY OF COMMON MEASURES OF ASSOCIATION *

Instructions for Use of Guide III.4.

Statistical methods enable us to study and to describe precisely averages, differences, and relationships. The number of statistical tests has risen considerably in the last thirty years and has become so large that not even a professional statistician can keep all of them at his fingertips. As these tests have become more numerous so have the kinds of hypotheses that can be tested by statistical procedures. Common questions that the researcher often asks are:

Is there a significant difference between these two (or more) groups on this variable? What confidence can I have that observed differences did not occur by chance?

Is there an association between these two (or more) variables? If so, how close is the association?

* From Allen L. Edwards, *Statistical Analysis* (2nd ed.; New York: Holt, 1946), pp. 127-28 and A. L. Edwards, *Statistical Methods for the Behavioral Sciences* (New York: Holt, 1967).

To ascertain significance of differences and the existence of possible associations between variables, the most common statistics used include: t, z, χ^2, r, r_s, and F. Consult the bibliography, Guide III.8 for a statistical text describing these measures. Note that computation guides have been included in this handbook for the very useful statistics, t, r, χ^2, and r_s.

Guide III.4, which follows, summarizes common measures of association. Since a major object of scientific inquiry is to discover relationships, these measures become standard equipment in the training of the scientist who uses statistical tests to ascertain relationships.

    a. Pearson product-moment r: For measuring relationships between two variables when both are continuous and the relationship is rectilinear. The coefficient of correlation is most reliable when based upon a large number of pairs of observations. An *r* based upon 15 pairs of observations would have to be at least .64 to indicate that the correlation in the population from which the sample was drawn was not zero, for example, whereas the same inference might be made for an *r* of .18 if the sample consisted of 200 cases.

    b. The correlation ratio: For measuring relationships between two variables that are related in a curvilinear fashion. The correlation ratio, unlike the correlation coefficient, is overestimated when the number of class intervals of X is large so that but a few cases are found in each class. Obviously, if only a single case were present in each column, then the variance of the means of the columns would be as great as the total variance of Y, and the correlation ratio would be 1.00. However, if N is sufficiently large and the grouping of X is in terms of 8 to 10 intervals, each interval is apt to have a sufficient number of cases in it to make the obtained correlation ratio approximately accurate.

    c. Biserial r: For measuring relationships when one variable is recorded in terms of a dichotomy and the other is continuous. Biserial *r* assumes that the individuals in each of the two categories represent a complete distribution (i.e., not just the two extremes), that the dichotomized variable is really continuous and normally distributed, and that the relationship between the two variables is rectilinear.

    d. Point biserial r: For measuring the relationship between a truly dichotomous variable and a continuous variable.

e. Phi coefficient: For measuring the relationship between two variables that are truly dichotomous. Cf. with Yule's Q for appropriate use.

f. Pearson r estimated by ϕ and tetrachoric r: For measuring the relationship between two variables, when each one is recorded in terms of a dichotomy. It is assumed that both variables are essentially continuous and normally distributed and that the measures in each of the categories represent a complete distribution, and that the relationship is rectilinear.

g. Contingency coefficient: For measuring the relationship between two variables that can be classified in two or more categories, but when the categories themselves are not quantitative.

h. Rank difference coefficient: For measuring the relationship between two variables, each of which is arranged in terms of rank order.

i. Multiple correlation coefficient: For measuring the maximum relationship that may be obtained between a combination of several variables and some other one variable.

j. Partial correlation coefficient: For measuring the relationship between two variables with the effects of a third (or several others) held constant.

k. Coefficient of concordance: For measuring the degree of agreement among m sets of n ranks. If we have a group of n objects ranked by each of m judges, the coefficient of concordance tells us the degree of agreement among the m sets of ranks.

III.5. FOUR LEVELS OF MEASUREMENT AND THE STATISTICS APPROPRIATE TO EACH LEVEL

Instructions for Use of Guide III.5.

In Part IV many sociometric scales have been included to measure social variables. These scales may be *nominal, ordinal, interval,* and *ratio* types.

A Nominal or Classificatory Scale refers to a level of measurement when number or other symbols are used simply to classify an object, person, or characteristic. Example: Folkways, Mores, Laws.

The Ordinal or Ranking Scale refers to a level of measurement when objects in various categories of a scale stand in some kind of *relation* to the categories. Given a group of equivalence classes, if the relation greater than holds between some but not all pairs of classes we have a partially ordered scale. If the relation greater than holds for all pairs of classes so that a complete rank ordering of classes arises, we have an ordinal scale. Example: Socioeconomic status as conceived by Warner in his ranking from Lower Lower to Upper Upper.

The Interval Scale refers to a level of measurement when a scale has all the characteristics of an ordinal scale, and when in addition the distances between any two numbers on the scale are of known size. Then, measurement considerably stronger than ordinality has been achieved. Example: Thurstone's Equal-Appearing Interval Scale.

The Ratio Scale refers to a level of measurement when a scale has all the characteristics of an interval scale and in addition has a true zero point as its origin. The ratio of any two scale points is independent of the unit of measurement. Example: Centigrade temperature scale.

FOUR LEVELS OF MEASUREMENT AND THE STATISTICS APPROPRIATE
TO EACH LEVEL *

Scale	Defining Relations	Examples of Appropriate Statistics	Appropriate Statistical Tests
Nominal	(1) Equivalence	Mode Frequency Contingency coefficient	Nonparametric test
Ordinal	(1) Equivalence (2) Greater than	Median Percentile Spearman r_s Kendall T Kendall W	Nonparametric test
Interval	(1) Equivalence (3) Greater than (3) Known ratio of any two intervals	Mean Standard deviation Pearson product-moment correlation Multiple product-moment correlation	Nonparametric and parametric tests
Ratio	(1) Equivalence (2) Greater than (3) Known ratio of any two intervals (4) Known ratio of any two scale values	Geometric mean Coefficient of variation	Nonparametric and parametric tests

Each of these scales has defining relations that make particular statistical tests appropriate. Nominal and ordinal scales require nonparametric tests; only interval and ratio scales may permit use of parametric tests. Since most indexes and scales are ordinal, the nonparametric test is of especial importance. It is necessary to match the appropriate statistic with the defining characteristics of the scale. The guide summarizes these relations between type of scale and appropriate statistic.

III.6. NONPARAMETRIC STATISTICAL TESTS APPROPRIATE TO VARIOUS TYPES OF SCALES

Instructions for Use of Guide III.6.

In the development of modern statistical methods, the first techniques of inference that appeared were those that made many assumptions about the nature of the population from which the scores were drawn. Since population values are "parameters" these statistical techniques are called *parametric*. For example, a technique of inference may be based on the assumption that the scores were drawn from a normally distributed population. Or the technique of inference may be based on the assumption that both sets of scores were drawn from populations having the same variance (σ^2) or spread of scores. Such techniques produce conclusions that contain qualifications, i.e., "If the assumptions regarding the shape of the population(s) are valid, then we may conclude that...."

More recently a large number of techniques of inference have been developed that do not make stringent assumptions about parameters. These newer nonparametric techniques are "distribution free," so that "Regardless of the shape of the population(s), we may conclude that...."

In the computation of parametric tests, we add, divide, and multiply the scores from samples. When these arithmetic processes are used on scores that are not truly numerical, they naturally introduce distortions in those data and thus throw doubt on conclusions from the test. Thus it is permissible to use the parametric techniques only with scores that are truly numerical. The mean and standard deviation are the central concepts of position and dispersion. Many nonparametric tests, on the other hand, focus on the order or ranking of the scores, not on their "numerical" values. The advantages of

LEVEL OF MEASURE-MENT	One-Sample Case	Two-Sample Case		k-Sample Case		NONPARAMETRIC MEASURE OF CORRELATION
	Col. 1	Col. 2 Related Samples (Chap. 5)	Col. 3 Independent Samples (Chap. 6)	Col. 4 Related Samples (Chap. 7)	Col. 5 Independent Samples (Chap. 8)	Col. 6
	(Chap. 4)					(Chap. 9)
Nominal	Binomial test, pp. 36-42 χ^2 one-sample test pp. 42-47	McNemar test for the significance of changes, pp. 63-67	Fisher exact probability test, pp. 96-104 χ^2 test for two independent samples, pp. 104-11	Cochran Q test, pp. 161-66	χ^2 test for k independent samples, pp. 175-79	Contingency coefficient: C, pp. 196-202
Ordinal	Kolmogorov-Smirnov one-sample test, pp. 47-52 One-sample runs test, pp. 52-58	Sign test, pp. 68-75 Wilcoxon matched-pairs signed-ranks test, pp. 75-83 ‡	Median test, pp. 111-16 Mann-Whitney U test, pp. 116-27 Kolmogorov-Smirnov two-sample test, pp. 127-36 Wald-Wolfowitz runs test, pp. 136-45 Moses test of extreme reactions, pp. 145-52	Friedman two-way analysis of variance by ranks, pp. 166-72	Extension of the median test, pp. 179-84 Kruskal-Wallis one-way analysis of variance by ranks, pp. 184-93	Spearman rank correlation coefficient: r_s, pp. 202-13 Kendall rank correlation coefficient: r, pp. 213-23 Kendall partial rank correlation coefficient: $r_{xy.z}$, pp. 223-29 Kendall coefficient of concordance: W, pp. 229-38
Interval		Walsh test, pp. 83-87 Randomization test for matched pairs, pp. 88-92	Randomization test for two independent samples, pp. 152-56			

* Each column lists, cumulatively downward, the tests applicable to the given level of measurement. For example, in the case of k related samples, when ordinal measurement has been achieved both the Friedman two-way analysis of variance and the Cochran Q test are applicable.
† For use of this table, consult Sidney Siegel, *Nonparametric Statistics for the Behavioral Sciences* (New York: McGraw-Hill, 1956).
‡ The Wilcoxon test requires ordinal measurement not only within pairs, as is required for the sign test, but also of the differences between pairs. See the discussion on pp. 75-76 of Siegel.

order statistics for data in the behavioral sciences are especially pronounced since so many "numerical" scores are numerical in appearance only.

Guide III.6 presents a wide range of various nonparametric statistical tests. Note that each row divides the tests into those appropriate for nominal, ordinal, and interval scales. The first column contains those tests that may be used when one wishes to determine whether a single sample is from a specified sort of population. Columns 2 and 3 contain tests that may be used when one wishes to compare the scores obtained from two samples—one set considers tests for two related samples, while the other considers tests for two independent samples. Columns 4 and 5 are devoted to significance tests for k (3 or more) samples; one of these presents tests for k related samples and the other presents tests for k independent samples. Column 6 gives nonparametric measures of association and the tests of significance that are useful with some of these.

The field of statistics has developed to the extent that we now have, for almost all research designs, alternative statistical tests that might be used in order to come to a decision about a hypothesis. Having alternative tests, the researcher has two choices—read carefully about criteria to follow in choosing among various tests applicable to a given research design or get advice from a professional statistician. Preferably, he should do both. In order to use Guide III.6 intelligently, the researcher should note where his problem falls within the table and then consult Sidney Siegel, *Nonparametric Statistics for the Behavioral Sciences* (New York: McGraw-Hill, 1956).

III.7. COMPUTATION GUIDES

Instructions for Use of Computation Guide III.7.

The computation guides that follow describe procedures for computing four statistics commonly needed by research workers in the behavioral sciences. Statistics t and r are parametric statistics, assuming randomness and normality of the populations; χ^2 *and* r_s are nonparametric or "distribution free," only randomness is generally assumed.

The computation design for the t test of the significance of the difference between two means is for the case of two independent samples. This is the test commonly used to test the difference between two means because we are often dealing with small samples, and we cannot assume that our data and values of t derived from them are normally distributed as are the parameters of large samples of 500 or more observations. However, it is assumed that the observations are drawn from normally distributed populations. The computation design for r, Pearson's product-moment coefficient of correlation, is useful when the number of cases is relatively large and the correlation chart is desired as a substitute for machine calculation. Pearson's r is for measuring relationships between two variables when both are continuous and the relationship is rectilinear. Both t and r may be used when the scores under analysis result from measurement in the strength of at least an *interval scale*.

The computation design for χ^2 is for testing significance of association between two attributes; for the general $r \times s$ case and for the special 2×2 table. This is the most widely used statistic for use with qualitative variables. The Spearman rank order coefficient r_s is the nonparametric statistic corresponding to the parametric Pearsonian r. This statistic is based on two sets of rankings of the same set of items. The Spearman rank order coefficient is not limited by the restrictions of normality and linearity imposed upon the Pearsonian product-moment r. While χ^2 is a test of the *existence* of a possible association, r_s provides a measure of the *degree of relationship* between two sets of rankings. Both χ^2 and r_s may be used when the scores under analysis result from measurements of *ordinal* or *nominal scales*.

III.7.a.   t Test of Significance Between Two Means of Independent Samples

Computation Design for t Test of the Difference Between Two Means, for Two Independent Samples *

$$from \; S_1: \overline{X}_1 = \Sigma X_{1i}/N_1$$
$$\Sigma x_1{}^2 = \Sigma X_{1i}{}^2 - (\Sigma X_{1i})^2/N_1$$

$$from \; S_2: \overline{X}_2 = \Sigma X_{2i}/N_2$$
$$\Sigma x_2{}^2 = \Sigma X_{2i}{}^2 - (\Sigma X_{2i})^2/N_2$$

Continued on page 142.

* From Morris Zelditch, Jr., *A Basic Course in Sociological Statistics* (New York: Holt, 1959), p. 245. See Theodore R. Anderson and Morris Zelditch, Jr., *A Basic Course in Statistics: With Sociological Applications* (2nd ed.: New York: Holt, 1968), pp. 272-277 for further discussion.

1. H_0: (See below for instructions.)

2. $s_{\bar{x}1 - \bar{x}2} = \sqrt{\left(\dfrac{\Sigma x_1{}^2 + \Sigma x_2{}^2}{N_1 + N_2 - 2} \right) \left(\dfrac{1}{N_1} + \dfrac{1}{N_2} \right)}$

$=$

3. $t = \dfrac{\overline{X}_1 - \overline{X}_2}{s_{\bar{x}1 - \bar{x}2}} =$

4. d.f. $= N_1 + N_2 - 2 =$

5. $P =$

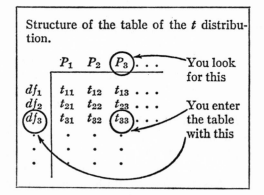

Structure of the table of the t distribution.

1. Formulate the null hypothesis you wish to test. This will determine whether you are to make a two-sided or one-sided test. The chief null hypotheses are $\mu_1 = \mu_2$ (two-sided), $\mu_1 \leqq \mu_2$, or $\mu_1 \geqq \mu_2$ (both one-sided). Write the hypothesis on line 1.

2. Compute the standard error of the difference by pooling estimates of the sums of squares. Enter on line 2.

3. Assume that both samples are normally and independently distributed; assume also that they have equal variances; then the distribution of t, which is the difference between the means divided by the estimated standard error of the difference, follows the t distribution with $N_1 + N_2 - 2$ degrees of freedom. Enter t on line 3 and d.f. on line 4.

4. With the value of t and d.f. you enter the table of t. You are looking for P, the probability that a value of t this large or larger would have been obtained by chance if the null hypothesis were

true. P will be shown along the head of the table, d.f. down the side, and the values of t will be shown in the body of the table. The probability shown will be two-tailed (i.e. the *sum* of the probability to the right of t and to the left of $-t$) ; if the hypothesis is one-sided, use one-half the tabled probability.

5. If P is equal to, or less than, 0.05, reject the null hypothesis. (Set the level of significance at 0.01 if you prefer greater certainty.) If P is greater than 0.05, accept the null hypothesis.

IIII.7.b.   Pearsonian r to Measure Linear Correlation Between Two Variables

Instructions for Calculation of r from Coded Group Data by Means of a Correlation Chart *

After the scatter diagram has been completed, and the distribution has been judged to be rectilinear, the data are then transferred to some standard product-moment correlation chart. It is much cheaper, quicker, and more reliable to use a printed correlation chart than it is to lay one out by hand. The correlation chart that will be used in the present discussion was devised by Professor F. Stuart Chapin, formerly of the University of Minnesota.[1]

The following instructions summarize the various steps to be observed in computing a coefficient of correlation with this type of chart, which is shown on pages 144-145.

The class-intervals for both the X- and Y-variables should be written in the spaces at the top and left-hand side of the correlation chart and the number of cases recorded in the proper cells. The frequencies for the two variables should also be entered on the chart. This operation involves merely a transferral of the essential data from the scatter diagram to the correlation chart. In selecting the zero-intervals for the two variables, an attempt should be made to choose intervals in which the means of the respective distributions are most likely to occur. In this problem, 69 was chosen to represent the zero-interval for the X-variable and 140 to 149 for the Y-variable.

2. For the X-variable determine the products of (f) (d_x) and record them in the fd_x row. Multiply (f) (d_y) for the Y-variable and

---

* Calvin F. Schmid in Pauline V. Young, *Scientific Social Surveys and Research* (4th ed.; Englewood Cliffs, N.J.: Prentice-Hall, 1966), pp. 311–314. © 1966. By permission of Prentice-Hall, Inc.

Correlation chart table. Column header row shows X values from -10 to $+9$ (deviation units), with class marks 61–77. Row header shows Y values from $+10$ to -10 with associated class intervals. Printed cell values form the $d_x \cdot d_y$ product grid; handwritten tallies indicate observed frequencies.

Y \ X	−10	−9	−8 61	−7 62	−6 63	−5 64	−4 65	−3 66	−2 67	−1 68	0 69	+1 70	+2 71	+3 72	+4 73	+5 74	+6 75	+7 76	+8 77	+9
+10	100	90	80	70	60	50	40	30	20	10	0	10	20	30	40	50	60	70	80	90
+9	90	81	72	63	54	45	36	27	18	9	0	9	18	27	36	45	54	63	72	81
+8	80	72	64	56	48	40	32	24	16	8	0	8	16	24	32	40	48	56	64	72
+7	70	63	56	49	42	35	28	21	14	7	0	7	14	21	28	35	42	49	56	63
+6 (200–209)	60	54	48	42	36	30	24	18	12	6	0 *(1)*	6	12 *(1)*	18	24	30 *(1)*	36	42	48	54
+5 (190–199)	50	45	40	35	30	25	20	15	10	5	0 *(1)*	5	10 *(1)*	15	20	25	30	35	40	45
+4 (180–189)	40	36	32	28	24	20	16	12	8	4	0 *(1)*	4 *(2)*	8	12	16 *(4)*	20 *(3)*	24	28	32	36
+3 (170–179)	30	27	24	21	18	15	12	9	6 *(1)*	3	0 *(3)*	3 *(3)*	6 *(2)*	9 *(2)*	12 *(1)*	15 *(2)*	18 *(1)*	21	24	27
+2 (160–169)	20	18	16	14	12	10	8	6	4	2 *(4)*	0 *(5)*	2 *(7)*	4 *(8)*	6 *(9)*	8 *(3)*	10 *(2)*	12	14	16 *(1)*	18
+1 (150–159)	10	9	8	7	6	5 *(1)*	4 *(2)*	3 *(4)*	2 *(6)*	1 *(4)*	0 *(11)*	1 *(9)*	2 *(3)*	3 *(4)*	4 *(3)*	5	6	7	8	9
0 (140–149)	0	0	0	0	0	0	0 *(1)*	0 *(5)*	0 *(2)*	0 *(20)*	0 *(−8 +)*	0 *(12)*	0 *(9)*	0 *(4)*	0 *(4)*	0	0 *(1)*	0	0	0
−1 (130–139)	10	9	8	7	6	5	4 *(2)*	3 *(5)*	2 *(12)*	1 *(7)*	0 *(7)*	1 *(5)*	2 *(3)*	3 *(1)*	4	5	6	7	8	9
−2 (120–129)	20	18	16 *(1)*	14	12 *(3)*	10 *(4)*	8 *(4)*	6 *(5)*	4 *(4)*	2 *(4)*	0 *(4)*	2 *(2)*	4 *(4)*	6 *(1)*	8	10	12	14	16	18
−3 (110–119)	30	27	24	21	18 *(1)*	15 *(1)*	12 *(1)*	9	6 *(2)*	3 *(3)*	0 *(1)*	3	6	9	12	15	18	21	24	27
−4 (100–109)	40	36	32	28	24	20	16 *(1)*	12	8	4	0	4	8	12	16	20	24	28	32	36
−5 (90–99)	50	45	40	35	30	25	20 *(1)*	15	10	5	0	5	10	15	20	25	30	35	40	45
−6	60	54	48	42	36	30	24	18	12	6	0	6	12	18	24	30	36	42	48	54
−7	70	63	56	49	42	35	28	21	14	7	0	7	14	21	28	35	42	49	56	63
−8	80	72	64	56	48	40	32	24	16	8	0	8	16	24	32	40	48	56	64	72
−9	90	81	72	63	54	45	36	27	18	9	0	9	18	27	36	45	54	63	72	81
−10	100	90	80	70	60	50	40	30	20	10	0	10	20	30	40	50	60	70	80	90
f			2	0	4	6	11	19	27	42	41	38	27	22	15	8	2	0	1	
d_x	−10	−9	−8	−7	−6	−5	−4	−3	−2	−1	0	+1	+2	+3	+4	+5	+6	+7	+8	+9
fd_x			−16	0	−24	−30	−44	−57	−54	−42	Σ 267	38	54	66	60	40	12	0	8	Σ +27
fd_x^2	100	81	64 /128	49 /0	36 /144	25 /150	16 /176	171	108	42	0	38	108 /198	240	200	72	0	64	81 /64	

Correlation Chart by F. Stuart Chapin

d_y	fd_y	fd_y^2	Σfd_{xy}^+	Σfd_{xy}^-
+10		100		
+9		81		
+8				
+7				
+6	18	=108	42	
+5	5	=25	10	
+4	44	=176	144	
+3	45	.135	99	6
+2	78	.156	160	8
+1	47	.47	39	41
0	237	0		
−1	−42	.42	54	14
−2	−60	.120	178	6
−3	−27	.81	66	
−4	−4	=16	16	
−5	−5	=25	40	
−6	Σ −138	=		
−7				
−8				
−9		81		
−10		100		

$\Sigma fd_y = +99$

$= +11$

$^2 = 1839$

$\Sigma fd_y^2 = 931$

$\Sigma fd_{xy}^+ = 848$

$\Sigma fd_{xy}^- = 75$

$\Sigma fd_{xy} = +.773$

$$r = \frac{N\Sigma fd_{xy} - [\Sigma fd_x][\Sigma fd_y]}{\sqrt{N\Sigma fd_x^2 - [\Sigma fd_x]^2} \cdot \sqrt{N\Sigma fd_y^2 - [\Sigma fd_y]^2}}$$

$$= \frac{265[773] - [11][99]}{\sqrt{265[839] - [11]^2} \cdot \sqrt{265[931] - [99]^2}}$$

$$= \frac{204,845 - 1,089}{\sqrt{487,335 - 121} \sqrt{246,715 - 9801}}$$

$$= \frac{203,756}{\sqrt{487,214} \sqrt{236,914}}$$

$$= \frac{203,756}{339,746.53} = +.59973 \text{ or } .60$$

X Height

Y Weight

r = +.59973

S.E.$_r$ = .039

COMPUTED BY _____ DATE _____

enter in the fd_y column. Care should be taken to observe signs. Determine the algebraic sums of the fd_x row and the fd_y column. In the chart on pages 144-145 it will be observed that $\Sigma fd_x = +11$ and $\Sigma fd_y = +99$.

3. The respective values of fd_x^2 are next obtained, as are also the values of fd_y^2, and recorded on the chart. Add the fd_x^2 row and the fd_y^2 column. In the problem, $\Sigma fd_x^2 = 1,839$ and $\Sigma fd_y^2 = 931$. It will be recalled that the second and third steps are identical with those used in computing the standard deviation.

4. The fourth operation is different from anything that has thus far been discussed. First, note the small figures printed in the upper left-hand corner of each cell. Second, observe the signs for each of the quadrants indicated in the center of the field of the chart. The lower left-hand quadrant and the upper right-hand quadrant are plus $(+)$ and the other two are minus $(-)$. Multiply the number of cases in each cell by the corresponding printed figure in the cell, observing signs. The products are entered in either the $\Sigma fd_{xy} +$ or the $\Sigma fd_{xy} -$ column, depending on the sign. Let us illustrate this step by performing the computations in the row 130 to 139 in the chart on pages 144–145. Multiply each of the frequencies in the row designated by the class-interval 130 to 139 by the small printed figures in each of the corresponding cells. The products for the numbers located in the plus quadrant are as follows: $(4)(2) = 8$; $(3)(5) = 15$; $(2)(12) = 24$; and $(1)(7) = 7$. The sum of these products, which is 54, is entered in the $\Sigma fd_{xy} +$ column. The products of the numbers for this row that are located in the minus quadrant are: $(3)(1) = -3$; $(2)(3) = -6$; and $(1)(5) = -5$. By adding these products together we have -14, which is recorded in the $\Sigma fd_{xy} -$ column. The figures in each of the columns are added and entered on the chart. The next step is to determine the algebraic sum of $\Sigma fd_{xy} +$ and $\Sigma fd_{xy} -$. In the problem the figures are: $848 - 75 = 773$.

5. This completes all the preliminary computations on the chart. The final step is to substitute in the formula on the right side of the chart and proceed with the calculations. It will be observed from the chart that the proper substitutions have been made in the formula and the coefficient of correlation has been computed for the illustrative problem. The coefficient of correlation between height and weight for this sample of 265 men students is $r = +.60$. The standard error is $\pm.039$. S.E.$_r = (1 - r^2)/\sqrt{N}$.

NOTE

1. All of the printed forms for computing the coefficient of correlation are very similar. A few of the better known charts are: (1) Thurstone (published by C. H. Stoelting Company, Chicago); (2) Otis (World Book Company, New York); (3) Cureton and Dunlop (Psychological Corporation, New York); (4) Tryon (University of California); (5) Ruch-Stoddard (University of Iowa); (6) Holzinger (University of Chicago); (7) Kelley (World Book Company, New York); and (8) Durost-Walker (World Book Company).

III.7.c. χ^2 Test of Association

Computation Design for χ^2 for Testing Significance of Association Between Two Attributes; for the General $r \times s$ Case and for the Special 2×2 *

n_{11}	n_{12}	n_{13}	$\ldots$	n_{1s}	$n_{1.}$
n_{21}	n_{22}	n_{23}	$\ldots$	n_{2s}	$n_{2.}$
n_{31}	n_{32}	n_{33}	$\ldots$	n_{3s}	$n_{3.}$
$\cdot$	$\cdot$	$\cdot$		$\cdot$	$\cdot$
$\cdot$	$\cdot$	$\cdot$		$\cdot$	$\cdot$
$\cdot$	$\cdot$	$\cdot$		$\cdot$	$\cdot$
n_{r1}	n_{r2}	n_{r3}	$\ldots$	n_{rs}	$n_{r.}$
$n_{.1}$	$n_{.2}$	$n_{.3}$	$\ldots$	$n_{.s}$	N

	1	2	3	4	5
	O	E	$O - E$	$(O - E)^2$	$(O - E)^2/E$
	n_{11}	$n_{1.}n_{.1}/N$			
	n_{12}	$n_{1.}n_{.2}/N$			
	n_{13}	$n_{1.}n_{.3}/N$			
	$\cdot$	$\cdot$			
	$\cdot$	$\cdot$			
	$\cdot$	$\cdot$			
	n_{rs}	$n_{r.}n_{.s}/N$			

$$\chi^2 = \Sigma[(O - E)^2/E]$$
$$\text{d.f.} = (r - 1)(s - 1)$$

* From Morris Zelditch, Jr., *op. cit.*, p. 290. See also Theodore R. Anderson and Morris Zelditch, Jr., *A Basic Course in Statistics: With Sociological Applications* (2nd edition; New York: Holt, Rinehart & Winston, Inc., 1968), pp. 256-264.

1. Enter the observed frequencies in column 1.
2. Calculate the expected values, E, as follows: find the marginal in the row containing the cell ij and the marginal in the column containing the cell, and multiply them together, giving $n_i.n._j$; then divide by N, the total number of observations in the table, giving $n_i.n._j/N$, and enter in column 2.
3. Subtract the expected values from the observed, column 2 from 1, and enter the result in column 3.
4. Square the differences obtained and enter in column 4.
5. Divide each entry in column 4 by the expected values in column 2 and enter in column 5.
6. Add up column 5. This gives you χ^2.
7. To find the number of degrees of freedom with which you enter the table, take one less than the number of rows times one less than the number of columns $(r - 1)$ $(s - 1)$.

Interpretation of χ^2 as a Test of Relationship Between Variables

As reported by David Gold in "A Note on Statistical Analysis in the American Sociological Review," "qualitative data are by far the most common data with which the sociologist concerns himself. —It is evident that, on the most elementary descriptive level, there is markedly inadequate statistical analysis of qualitative data."

These statements should alert the social science researcher to the importance of the correct use and interpretation of χ^2. It is this coefficient which appears most frequently in social science research as a test of association and significance. The following article by Thomas J. Duggan and Charles W. Dean should be "must" reading for all social scientists.

III.7.d. Common Misinterpretations of Significance Levels in Sociological Journals *

Thomas J. Duggan and Charles W. Dean

Periodically, the uses and misuses of probability statistics in social and behavioral science research have been reviewed. For instance, in 1949 Lewis and Burke pointed to several misuses of the chi-square test [1] and in 1959 an article by Selvin stimulated discussion on the general question of using statistics in social surveys.[2] Most recently,

* Reprinted from *The American Sociologist*, 3 (February, 1968), 45-46.

Skipper, Guenther, and Nass reviewed the discussion of substantive interpretation associated with significant levels.[3] While such discussions have served to clarify some of the technical requirements and have corrected some of the misunderstandings often associated with the use of statistical tests, one crucial matter has received relatively little attention. This concerns the substantive interpretation of significance tests and the consequences of such interpretations.

The frequently used chi-square test, and the interpretations given to data analyzed by this statistic, will serve to illustrate the problem. This statistic can be used to test goodness of fit or independence although it is the latter which is more frequenly used in reporting research. Since this is a test of the independence of variables, significant values of chi-square are often taken to indicate a dependence on relationship between variables. In interpreting such relationships, there are two serious problems which are often overlooked.

TABLE 1

Variable Y	Variable X			
	Very High	High	Low	Very Low
High	5	24	17	9
Moderate	12	18	9	3
Low	19	22	16	2

$\chi^2 = 14.0, P < .05, G = -.30.$

TABLE 2

Variable Y	Variable X		
	High	Moderate	Low
High	24	18	10
Moderate	19	12	7
Low	19	18	21

$\chi^2 = 6.2, P < .20, G = .22.$

The first concerns the strength of relationship and the second the form of relationship.

Strength of Relationship

As to the first problem, if the chi-square is significant at the chosen level, then the investigator routinely rejects the null hypothesis of independence and tentatively accepts the alternate hypothesis that the variables are dependent or are related. Regardless of how low the probability associated with the obtained value of chi-square, nothing can be inferred about the strength or degree of that relationship. However, in practice, this point is often overlooked.

Consider Table 1 which was reported in a major sociological journal within the last year.[4] According to the author's interpretation, the significance level of the chi-square test was so high that if variables X and Y were not clearly separate measures, "We would suspect the relationship to be tautological." Since the authors failed to report the degree of association, Goodman and Kruskels' gamma was computed. In this instance, gamma equalled −.30 which suggests a relationship which is far from tautological. The difference in the interpretation based on chi-square and gamma should be noted and emphasized. In contrast to the above data, consider Table 2 which was presented in the same article.

In this case, the probability is such that the sociologist normally would accept the null hypothesis of independence. However, gamma was computed for these data and G equalled .22. Here, data non-

TABLE 3

A COMPARISON OF LEVEL OF SIGNIFICANCE AND STRENGTH
OF RELATIONSHIP (n = 45 articles)

Level of Signifi- cance	Strength of Relationship								
	.00 to .09	.10 to .19	.20 to .29	.30 to .39	.40 to .49	.50 to .59	.60 to .69	.70 to .79	.80 to .89
.001	3	2	2	8	..	1	..	2	3
.01	1	..	6	..	2	..	..	..	..
.05	4	3	..	..	..	..	..	..	..
.10	1	..	1	..	..	..	..	..	..
.20	1	1	1	..	..	..	..	..	..
.30+	..	3	..	..	..	..	..	..	..

significant according to chi-square has a relationship only slightly lower than that of the preceding example, where it was concluded that the variables were highly related. To further demonstrate the need for sensitivity to the difference between significance level and strength of association, Table 3 was constructed.[5]

Table 3 clearly demonstrates that while chi-square, properly used, may be sensitive to the dependence of variables, after dependence is shown the usefulness of this statistic is exhausted. As the data of Table 3 show, significance at the .001 level could mean that the relationship between the variables could be less than .09 or more than .80. At the .001 level, the distribution of the strength of association appears to approach randomness. While these data do show that non-significance, or significance at or about the arbitrary .05 level, will usually result in a relationship which is consistently weaker, the relationship is as likely to be above .10 at the .30 level as at the .05 level. Still, all three tables reporting significance above the .30 level had gammas ranging between .10 and .19. In contrast, of the seven tables reporting significance a .05, only three had gammas in the .10 to .19 range, while four tables had gammas below .10. If more non-significant tables were reported in the journals, the distribution of measures of association would probably be even broader. Generally, the lower the significance level, the greater the probability of a low relationship, but this cannot be assumed. These data emphatically demonstrate that a measure of strength of association is necessary before statements about strength of relationship can be made.

These data illustrate the serious problem in interpreting significance levels of the chi-square test of independence and indicate the need for a reminder that statistical significance is not equatable with

TABLE 4

Variable Y	Variable X		
	Frequent	Occasional	Infrequent
High	3	9	6
Moderate	14	30	12
Low	17	12	6

χ^2 (4df) $= 8.51$; $P < .05$.

practical significance. A significant chi-square value at best, permits one to say that *probably* there is some dependence between variables in the population, but the extent of dependence may be virtually zero *regardless of the significance level.* The consequences for understanding the phenomena under investigation and for the construction of theories require constant awareness of the limited interpretations which can be given to statistical significance.

Form of Relationship

The second problem refers to the form of relationship between variables. In using tables three by three or larger, users of the chi-square are often prone to think and interpret results in terms of linear relationships, but the contingency table and the chi-square statistic are not sensitive to and provide no basis for assuming the existence of this form of relationship.

The data of Table 4, also presented in a major sociological journal within the last year illustrate the error in interpreting the direction of the relationship in linear terms. The author stated that the data of this table confirmed the hypothesis that the greater the degree of variable X, the greater the degree of variable Y. An inspection of the table reveals that this is not the case. As Table 4 indicates, the largest number of subjects ranking in the "frequent" category of variable X rank in the low category of variable Y. However, the largest number of subjects in the "occasional" and "infrequent" categories of variable X rank in the "moderate" category of variable Y. Only those ranking "low" on variable Y are distributed in the expected pattern.

Another team of authors in a recent edition of another sociological journal presented data similar to that of Table 4 to test the hypothesis that the greater the degree of variable A, the higher the degree of variable B. They computed chi-square values for their data table and stated, "The relationship shown is significant beyond the .001 level; therefore, the hypothesis is accepted." Throughout the article, the authors made similar statements from similar data about linear relationships.

While the above authors did not attempt to disguise their acceptance of linearity, frequently, other researchers state a linear hypothesis, present the data, table, accept the hypothesis on the basis of the chi-square probability and then discuss only those proportions of the table which fit the linear model. This more subtle but equally erroneous procedure appears frequently in the sociological literature.

A linear relationship exists only if the pattern of concentration of subjects lies along a diagonal of the table. If this is not the case, the relationship cannot be interpreted as a linear one. If the phenomenon of possible nonlinearity is not taken into account or if the implication of linearity is made in interpreting chi-square, serious consequences again arise in interpreting data and in developing explanatory theories. This problem can be averted by inspecting the data table, outlining the pattern of concentration and describing the pattern.

Conclusion

To avoid these errors of confusing significance with strength of association and of misinterpreting form of relationship, two elementary safeguards can be exercised in reporting results. One is routinely to compute and report a measure of degree of association in addition to the statistical test whenever this is possible. The second safeguard is the introduction of care and caution in the verbal interpretation of data tables and the inferred association of variables.

In this day when computer technology is so drastically improving the analytical tools of the sociologist, it seems paradoxical that there is a need to remind researchers of such basic rules of interpretation.

NOTES

1. Don Lewis and C. J. Burke, "The Use and Misuse of The Chi-square Test," *Psychological Bulletin,* 46 (1949), 433-489.

2. Hanan Selvin, "A Critique of Tests of Significance in Survey Research," *American Sociological Review,* 22 (October, 1957), 519-527.

3. James K. Skipper, Anthony L. Guenther, and Gilbert Nass, "The Sacredness of .05: A Note Concerning the Uses of Statistical Levels of Significance in Social Science," *The American Sociologist,* 2 (February, 1967), 16-18.

4. Since the purpose of these tables is to illustrate peculiarities in the use of chi-square rather than to criticize individual research, no tables will identify either author, journal or original variables actually treated. However, all tables were reported in refereed sociological journals within a year prior to the writing of this piece.

5. These data were derived from major sociological journals published between 1955 and 1965 in a systematic search for three by three tables. both variables ordinal.

III.7.e. Spearman's Rank Order Correlation

Computation Design for Spearman Rank Order Correlation Coefficient, r_s *

K_i designates an ordered position. K_{xi} designates the position of the ith observation in an array of the X variable; K_{yi} designates the position of the *same* observation in the Y array. If, for example, the first observation, O_1, is first in the X array and fourth in the Y array, the first row of the layout form below should read

$$K_{x1} = 1, K_{y1} = 4, K_{x1} - K_{y1} = -3, (K_{x1} - K_{y1})^2 = 9$$

(1) O_i	(2) K_{xi}	(3) K_{yi}	(4) d	(5) d^2
O_1	K_{x1}	K_{y1}	$K_{x1} - K_{y1}$	$(K_{x1} - K_{y1})^2$
O_2	K_{x2}	K_{y2}	$K_{x2} - K_{y2}$	$(K_{x2} - K_{y2})^2$
.	.	.	.	.
.	.	.	.	.
.	.	.	.	.
O_N	K_{xN}	K_{yN}	$K_{xN} - K_{yN}$	$(K_{xN} - K_{yN})$

$$\Sigma(K_{xi} - K_{yi})^2 = \Sigma d^2 =$$

$$r_s = 1 - \frac{6\Sigma d^2}{N(N^2 - 1)} =$$

$$t = r_s \sqrt{\frac{N-2}{1 - r_s^2}} = \qquad , \text{d.f.} = N - 2.$$

1. Form an array of the observations on the X variable. (Start with the "best," "smallest," "highest." You may choose the starting point at will, but you must be consistent on both X and Y, or the sign of r_s will be meaningless.) Order the observations on the variable Y in the same manner.

2. Replace the X value of each observation by its rank in the X array and the Y value of each observation by its rank in the Y array. In column 2 at the right enter ranks of the observations on the X variable and in column 3 enter ranks of the observations on the Y variable. Ranks in the same row must be for the *same* observation.

---

* From Morris Zelditch, Jr., *op. cit.*, p. 326. See also, Theodore R. Anderson and Morris Zelditch, Jr., *A Basic Course in Statistics: With Sociological Applications* (2nd edition; New York: Holt, Rinehart & Winston, Inc., 1968), pp. 126-132.

3. Take the difference between ranks and enter in column 4.

4. Square these differences, enter in column 5, and sum column 5.

5. Compute r_s from the formula shown above.

6. For $N > 10$, to test H_0: $\rho_s = 0$, use t, computed form the formula shown above with $(N - 2)$ d.f. (ρ_s [read "rho sub-s"] is the population parameter corresponding to r_s.)

III.8. A BIBLIOGRAPHY OF STATISTICAL GUIDES

The following books are especially valuable as reference books when the researcher is seeking a readable step-by-step explanation or procedure. The selections are based on the simplicity of the description and the inclusion of illustrative examples.

1. ANDERSON, THEODORE R., and ZELDITCH, MORRIS, JR. *A Basic Course in Statistics: With Sociological Applications.* 2nd ed. New York: Holt, Rinehart and Winston, Inc., 1968. (Has step-by-step computation guides for all basic statistics; well illustrated.)

2. ARKIN, HERBERT, and COLTON, RAYMOND R. *An Outline of Statistical Methods.* 5 ed. New York: Barnes & Noble, Inc., 1968. (A guide to elementary statistics.)

3. BERNSTEIN, ALLEN L., *A Handbook of Statistical Solutions for the Behavioral Sciences.* New York: Holt, Rinehart and Winston, 1964. (Presents solutions to typical problems.)

4. CONWAY, FREDA. *Sampling: An Introduction for Social Scientists.* New York: Humanities Press, Inc., 1967. (Lucid, neatly organized book on statistics using large sample theory.)

5. CROWLEY, FRANCIS J., and COHEN, MARTIN. *Basic Facts of Statistics.* New York: Collier Books, 1963. (Digests elementary statistics in a very brief and comprehensive manner within 62 pages.)

6. EDWARDS, ALLEN. *Statistical Methods.* 2nd ed. New York: Holt, Rinehart and Winston, Inc., 1967. (Statistical techniques and methods presented for the student with a minimum amount of mathematical knowledge. Parametric and nonparametric methods are integrated into the text.)

7. FREUND, JOHN E., LIVERMORE, PAUL E., and MILLER, IRVIN. *Manual of Experimental Statistics.* Englewood Cliffs, N.J.: Prentice-Hall, Inc., 1960. (Presents in outline form the most frequently used statistical techniques, including appropriate computing formulas and completely worked-out examples of each method.)

8. MARK, MARY LOUISE. *Statistics in the Making: A Primer in Statistical Survey Method.* Columbus, Ohio: Ohio State University

Bureau of Business Research, 1958. (Shows how to produce statistical tables of "journal" quality.)

9. MAXWELL, ALBERT E. *Analyzing Qualitative Data.* New York: John Wiley & Sons, Inc., 1961. (The book, which might have been given the title χ^2 tests, aims at providing the research worker with a simple but up-to-date account of statistical techniques available for the analysis of qualitative data.)

10. MORONEY, M. J. *Facts from Figures.* Baltimore: Penguin Books, Inc., 1956. (Lucid explanation of the background of statistics, well illustrated.)

11. MUELLER, JOHN H., and SCHUESSLER, KARL F. *Statistical Reasoning in Sociology.* Boston: Houghton Mifflin Company, 1961. (Emphasis is placed on reasons supporting statistical analysis.) The second edition, 1970, by Karl Schuessler and Herbert Costner has many new features.

12. SCHMID, CALVIN F. *Handbook of Graphic Presentation.* New York: The Ronald Press Company, 1954. (Methods for presenting social statistics in a visual manner.)

13. SMITH, G. MILTON. *A Simplified Guide to Statistics for Psychology and Education.* 3rd ed. New York: Holt, Rinehart and Winston, Inc., 1962. (Integrates most commonly used tools.)

14. WALKER, HELEN M. *Mathematics Essential for Elementary Statistics: A Self-Teaching Manual.* Rev. ed. New York: Henry Holt and Company, 1951. (Material permits student to proceed with mathematical training by self-instruction.)

15. WEISS, ROBERT S. *Statistics in Social Research.* New York: John Wiley & Sons, Inc., 1968. (The traditional topics are treated from the point of view of someone guiding a student through the research process.)

16. ZEISEL, HANS. *Say It with Figures.* 5th edition, revised. New York: Harper & Row, Publishers, Inc., 1968. (A guide to the assembly and interpretation of social statistics.)

III.9. A SPECIALIZED BIBLIOGRAPHIC SECTION FOR THE ADVANCED STUDENT

SELECTED READINGS ON CAUSAL MODELS AND MULTIVARIATE ANALYSIS

BLALOCK, HUBERT M., JR. "Correlational Analysis and Causal Inferences," *American Anthropologist,* 62 (August, 1960), 624-631.

————. "Correlation and Causality: the Multivariate Case," *Social Forces*, 39 (March, 1961), 246-251.

————. "Evaluating the Relative Importance of Variables," *American Sociological Review*, 26 (December, 1961), 866-874.

————. "Spuriousness versus Intervening Variables: The Problem of Temporal Sequences," *Social Forces*, 40 (May, 1962), 330-334.

————. "Further Observations on Asymmetric Causal Models," *American Sociological Review*, 27 (August, 1962), 542-545.

————. "Four-Variable Causal Models and Partial Correlation," *American Journal of Sociology*, 48 (September, 1962), 182-194.

————. *Causal Inferences in Non-Experimental Research*. Chapel Hill: University of North Carolina Press, 1964.

————. and BLALOCK, ANN B. (eds.). *Methodology in Social Research*. New York: McGraw-Hill Book Company, 1968.

BLAU, PETER M. "Determining the Dependent Variable in Certain Correlations," *Public Opinion Quarterly*, 19 (Spring, 1955), 100-105.

GLASER, BARNEY G., and STRAUSS, ANSELM L. *The Discovery of Grounded Theory: Strategies for Qualitative Research*. Chicago: Aldine Publishing Company, 1967.

GRAWOIG, DENNIS E. *Decision Mathematics*. New York: McGraw-Hill Book Company, 1967.

HYMAN, HERBERT. *Survey Design and Analysis: Principles, Cases, and Procedures*. Glencoe, Ill.: The Free Press, 1955, pp. 242-329 (chaps. 6 and 7).

KENDALL, PATRICIA, and LAZARSFELD, PAUL. "Problems of Survey Analysis," in *Continuities in Social Research*. Edited by R. K. Merton and P. Lazarsfeld. Glencoe, Ill.: The Free Press, 1950, pp. 133-196.

LAZARSFELD, PAUL F. "Interpretation of Statistical Relations as a Research Operation," in *The Language of Social Research*. Edited by P. Lazarsfeld and M. Rosenberg. Glencoe, Ill.: The Free Press, 1955, pp. 115-125.

NOWAK, S. "Some Problems of Causal Intepretation of Statistical Relationships," *Philosophy of Science*, 27 (January, 1960), 23-38.

ORCUTT, GUY H. "Actions, Consequences and Causal Relations," *The Review of Economics and Statistics*, 34 (1952), 305-314.

POLK, KENNETH. "A Note on Asymmetric Causal Models," *American Sociological Review*, 27 (August, 1962), 539-542.

ROBINSON, W. S. "Asymmetric Causal Models: Comments on Polk and Blalock," *American Sociological Review*, 27 (August, 1962), 545-548.

ROSE, ARNOLD M. "A Weakness of Partial Correlation in Sociological Studies," *American Sociological Review*, 14 (August, 1949), 536-539.

SIMON, HERBERT A. "Causal Ordering and Identifiability," in *Studies in Econometric Methods*. Edited by W. C. Hood and T. C. Koopmans. New York: John Wiley & Sons, Inc., 1953, pp. 49-74.

————. "Spurious Correlation: A Causal Interpretation," *Journal of the American Statistical Association,* 49 (September, 1954), 467-479.
————. *Models of Man: Social and Rational.* New York: John Wiley & Sons, Inc., 1957, pp. 37-49.
WOLD, HERMAN. "Causal Inference from Observational Data," *Journal of the Royal Statistical Society,* Vol. 119, Ser. A, Pt. I (1956), 28-60.
————, and JUREEN, L. *Demand Analysis: A Study in Econometrics.* New York: John Wiley & Sons, Inc., 1953.

SELECTED BIBLIOGRAPHY FOR THE APPLICATION OF MATHEMATICS TO SOCIAL ANALYSIS

COLEMAN, JAMES S. *Introduction to Mathematical Sociology.* Glencoe, Ill.: The Free Press, 1964. The emphasis in this book is on mathematics as a tool for the elaboration of sociological theory.
DODD, STUART C., and CHRISTOPHER, STEFAN C. "The Reactants Models," in *Essays in Honor of George Lundberg.* Great Barrington, Mass.: Behavioral Research Council, 1968, pp. 143-179. A search for laws of communicative behavior by fitting curves to diffusion data as item moves through a population.
GOLDBERG, SAMUEL. *Introduction to Difference Equations.* New York: John Wiley & Sons, Inc., 1958. Revised edition of monograph on difference equations written in 1954 at the invitation of SSRC Committee on the Mathematical Training of Social Scientists.
HARMAN, HARRY H. *Modern Factor Analysis.* Chicago: University of Chicago Press, 1960.
KEMENY, JOHN G., and SNELL, LAURIES J. *Mathematical Models in the Social Sciences.* Boston: Blaisdell, 1962. This book is for a mathematics course, not a social science course; the problems in the social sciences are introduced only as an incentive to learn mathematics.
LAZARSFELD, PAUL F. "Notes on the History of Quantification in Sociology—Trends, Sources, and Problems," in *Quantification.* Edited by Harry Woolf. Indianapolis: The Bobbs-Merrill Company, Inc., 1961.
LAZARSFELD, PAUL F. (ed.). *Mathematical Thinking in the Social Sciences.* Glencoe, Ill.: The Free Press, 1954.
LUNDBERG, GEORGE A. "Statistics in Modern Social Thought," *Contemporary Social Theory.* Edited by Harry Elmer Barnes, Howard Becker, and Francis Bennett Becker. New York: Appleton Century, 1940, pp. 110-140. Historical account of the rise of social statistics.
MARTINDALE, DON. "Limits to the Uses of Mathematics in the Study

of Sociology," *Mathematics and the Social Sciences*. Edited by James C. Charlesworth. Philadelphia: American Academy of Political and Social Science, June 1963, pp. 95-121.

McGINNIS, ROBERT. *Mathematical Foundations for Social Analysis*. Indianapolis: The Bobbs-Merrill Company, Inc., 1965. Provides an introduction to mathematical procedures which are being increasingly employed in sociology: sets, relations, real numbers, matrices, and limits.

RASHEVSKY, NICHOLAS. *Mathematical Biology of Social Behavior*. Chicago: University of Chicago Press, 1950. Application of mathematical methods to study of social stratification.

SOLOMON, HERBERT (ed.). *Mathematical Thinking in the Measurement of Behavior*. Glencoe, Ill. The Free Press, 1960. Includes contributions by James S. Coleman on mathematics and small group research; Ernest W. Adams on utility theory; and Herbert Solomon on factor analysis.

STONE, RICHARD. "Mathematics in the Social Sciences," *Scientific American*, 211, No. 3 (September, 1964), 168-186.

WHITE, HARRISON. "Uses of Mathematics in Sociology," in *Mathematics and the Social Sciences*. Edited by James C. Charlesworth. Philadelphia: American Academy of Political and Social Science, June, 1963, 77-94.

————. *An Anatomy of Kinship*. Englewood Cliffs, N.J. Prentice-Hall, Inc., 1963. Attempt to analyze logic underlying kinship systems by mathematical methods.

ZIPF, GEORGE KINGSLEY. *Human Behavior and the Principle of Least Effort*. Cambridge: Addison-Wesley Publishing Company, Inc., 1949.

PART IV

Selected Sociometric Scales and Indexes

Introduction

There are literally thousands of scales and indexes to measure social variables. Social scientists have often elected to construct new measures even when scales of high reliability and validity have been available. This practice is wasteful of time, energy, and money. In addition, it makes replication and accumulation of research findings difficult if not impossible. The selection of scales to be found in this handbook was based on such criteria as validity, reliability, and utility. The variables most commonly used in social measurement were studied and measures for them were sought. Those with the highest reliability and validity were selected. It is hoped that this handbook will encourage greater use of these scales or stimulate the search for better ones.

In general, three groups of variable factors need to be observed and measured in any research design that seeks to test a basic hypothesis or social relationship.

First, there is the dependent variable, the effect we wish to observe and describe.

Second, there is the independent variable that has been designated as the causal factor. Sometimes this factor must be broken down into the component parts that operate more or less as a unit pattern.

Third, there are intervening or other independent variables that must be controlled lest they obscure the relationship we wish to measure by use of experimental design.

Sociometric scales have been constructed in substantial numbers to permit quantitative description of these factors in human relations.

Three areas of social measurement can be identified. These are:

1. Psychometric and social psychological scales: psychological measurements including intelligence scales, personality tests and scales, attitude tests and scales.

   Examples of these scales that are included in this part are the Minnesota Multiphasic Personality Inventory, the Authoritarian Personality (F) Scale, Morale and Job Satisfaction Scales, as well as attitude scales to measure leisure satisfactions; community attitudes, achievement orientation, and alienation.

2. Demographic Scales: measurements of the forms or results of social behavior in large units such as the community, state, or nation.

Examples in this part include community rating scales, community services activity, citizen political activity, and a community solidarity index.

3. Sociometric Scales: measurements of the social structure and process.*

Examples in this part include sociometric tests to measure informal friendship constellations, measurements of social participation, of social distance, and of group cohesiveness. Other scales are provided to assess marital adjustment and group dimensions. The measurement of social status is of such crucial importance that a number of scales are included, such as *Alba Edwards' Socioeconomic Scale, Warner's Revised Occupational Scale for Social Class, Hatt-North Occupational Prestige Scores,* and the 1960 U.S. Census Socioeconomic Status Scores.

In 1967 three very useful bibliographic compilations of social and attitude scales have appeared. The most comprehensive is the work of Charles M. Bonjean, Richard J. Hill, and S. Dale McLemore, *Sociological Measurement* (San Francisco: Chandler, 1967). They examined every article and research note in each issue of the *American Sociological Review, The American Journal of Sociology, Social Forces,* and *Sociometry* from 1954 through 1965. The table below shows the fifty most frequently used and cited measures.

Most Frequently Used and Cited Measures, 1954-1965 †

Measure	Frequency of Use and Citations
1. Occupational Status (Census, Edwards)	91
2. California F Scale and Modifications	53
3. Occupational Prestige (North, Hatt)	53
4. Leadership (Reputational Approach)	35

† Charles M. Bonjean, Richard J. Hill, and S. Dale McLemore, *Sociological Measurement* (San Francisco: Chandler, 1967), pp. 13-14. Copyright © 1967 by Chandler Publishing Co. The complete scale is available for most of these measures. In all cases, research which employed the scale is cited.

* Cf. F. Stuart Chapin, *Experimental Designs in Sociological Research* (New York: Harper, 1947), chap. VI, "Sociometric Scales," pp. 140-164. This chapter summarizes rationale for scales and contains a compilation of selected scales.

Measure	Frequency of Use and Citations
5. Stereotype Check List (Katz, Braly)	33
6. Indexes of Social Position (Hollingshead)	30
7. Anomia (Srole)	28
8. Social Rank (Shevky, Williams, Bell)	28
9. Index of Status Characteristics (Warner)	27
10. Urbanization (Shevky, Williams, Bell)	26
11. Segregation (Shevky, Williams, Bell)	25
12. Sociometric Status and Structure (Various Measures)	19
13. Marital Adjustment (Burgess, Cottrell, Locke)	18
14. Social Distance (Bogardus)	18
15. Social Participation (Chapin)	17
16. Achievement Motivation (Murray, McClelland, Atkinson)	16
17. Occupational Status (Census, Edwards Related)	16
18. Occupational Status (Warner)	16
19. Ethnocentrism (California E Scale)	15
20. Segregation (Duncan, Duncan)	15
21. Occupational Mobility, Intergenerational (Census, Edwards Related)	12
22. Occupational Mobility, Intergenerational (North, Hatt Related)	10
23. Social Class: Judges or Informants	10
24. Occupational Status (Duncan)	9
25. Socioeconomic Status (Sewell)	8
26. American Council on Education Psychological Examination	8
27. Centralization	8
28. Consideration (Ohio State Leader Behavior Description Questionnaire and Related Measures)	8
29. Delinquency Proneness, Social Responsibility (Gough))	8
30. Initiating Structure (Ohio State Leader Behavior Description Questionnaire and Related Measures)	8
31. Occupational Status (Hollingshead)	8
32. Status Crystallization (Lenski)	8
33. Dogmatism (Rokeach)	7
34. Segregation (Cowgill, Cowgill)	7
35. Segregation (Jahn, Schmid, Schrag)	7
36. Social Distance, Summated Differences Technique (Westie)	7
37. Achievement Training (Winterbottom)	6
38. Administrative Rationality (Udy)	6
39. Alienation (Nettler)	6
40. Alienation, Powerlessness (Neal)	6
41. California Test of Personality (Tiegs, Clark, Thrope)	6
42. Conservatism (McClosky)	6
43. Delinquent Behavior Checklist (Nye, Short)	6
44. Edwards Personal Preference Schedule	6
45. Marital Satisfaction (Burgess, Wallin)	6
46. Religious Orthodoxy (Putney, Middleton)	6
47. Social-Emotional Reactions (Bales)	6
48. Status Concern (Kaufman)	6
49. Urbanization (Davis)	6
50. Values (Allport, Vernon, Lindzey)	6

If you do not find a scale that fits your particular research interest, consult the inventory of measures used by researchers represented in the *American Sociological Review* during 1965-1968. This inventory has been placed at the end of Part IV.

Also presented at the end of Part IV is the list of attitude scales from Marvin E. Shaw and Jack M. Wright, *Scales for the Measurement of Attitudes* (New York: McGraw-Hill, 1967). The complete scale can be found in their book.

The third compilation lists more than 100 scales of political attitudes. See John P. Robinson, Jerrold G. Rusk, and Kendra B. Head, *Measures of Political Attitudes* (Ann Arbor, Mich.: Institute for Social Research, University of Michigan, 1968).

Scale construction yields four types of scales: the *nominal* scale, consisting simply of distinguishable categories with no implication of "more" or "less"; the *ordinal* scale, on which positions can be identified in a rank order with no implication as to the distance between positions; the *interval* scale, which has equal distance between any two adjacent positions on the continuum; and the *ratio* scale, which has not only equal intervals but an absolute zero.

The ideal scale is a ratio scale, but with the possible exception of the procedures for measuring certain psychophysical phenomena, none of the measurement techniques currently used fits the requirements for a ratio scale. The nominal scale permits neither rank ordering nor a metric scale. It is so elemental as a classification scheme that such scales are generally regarded as first approximations toward the quantification of a social variable. The result is that ordinal and interval scales are the most frequent types in use. There is considerable disagreement over whether an ordinal or interval scale provides the most appropriate model for social data. Some writers have taken the view (see David Gold in this handbook, pp. 123-127) that few, if any, of the techniques now in use provide data that can be considered appropriate to more than ordinal scales. Others believe that various types of scales may properly be treated as conforming to interval scales. Still others have taken the position that, although most of the measurements used do not go beyond ordinal scales, little harm is done in applying statistics to them that are appropriate to interval scales.

The result is that statistics appropriate to interval scales continue to be widely used in the analysis of social data whether the assumptions are met or not. However, there is also an increasing use of statistics that are specifically appropriate to ordinal scales. The statistical tools included in Part III of the handbook are for the use of the ordinal and interval scales included in this section.

The selection of a good scale involves weighing a number of criteria. Frequency of use is one useful criterion for choice of a scale, because of the possibility of maximizing accumulated research in the test of hypotheses. In the selection of scales for the revised edition this frequency criterion has been utilized. However, it is not the only determinant. Frequency can be misleading, especially when recorded as far back as 1954. New and better scales are constantly appearing. Moreover, use of a scale by others does not guarantee that they have chosen the "best" scale as described by rigorous criteria. For this reason the scales selected for this section may not be high on frequency count, but it is believed that they are the scales the researcher should use *now*. The most important single consideration is validity. Does the scale measure what it purports to measure? How much and what kind of evidence is available? Does the scale fit the problem selected for study?

Other considerations include its reliability, its precision, its simplicity and ease of administration. In recent years there has been considerable emphasis on unidimensionality. The Guttman technique enables the researcher to identify and construct scales of a single dimension. This may be very important in increasing the precision and predictability of a given variable. However, two qualifications must be kept in mind. Such a scale may not be the most effective either for measuring attitudes toward complex objects or for making predictions about behavior in relation to such objects. It must also be remembered that a given scale may be unidimensional for one group of individuals but not for another.

The scales assembled in this part include those constructed by arbitrary or judgmental ranking, by item analysis techniques, by Thurstone's equal-appearing interval method, by Guttman's technique of scale analysis, and by factor analysis. Regardless of the method used in construction, what the researcher seeks is the scale that best fits his problem, has the highest reliability and validity, is precise, and is relatively easy to apply.[1] When he has made his selection he must be aware of the statistical techniques he may subsequently apply. Generally, he will be using nonparametric statistics for ordinal scales and parametric statistics for interval scales and for those ordinal scales that do not deviate too far from the assumptions of randomness and normal distribution.

NOTE

1. For an excellent discussion of these criteria, see Paul F. Lazarsfeld and Morris Rosenberg, *The Language of Social Research* (Glencoe, Ill.: Free Press, 1955); Hans Zeisel, *Say It with Figures*, 5th ed., rev. (New York: Harper, 1968), pp. 76-102.

Social Status

Social class or status is one of the most important variables in social research. The socioeconomic position of the person affects his chances for education, income, occupation, marriage, health, friends, and even life expectancy. The variable has proved difficult to measure in a pluralistic, equalitarian, and fluid society such as exists in the United States. However, many researchers have tried to identify the social strata and to measure them. There are four scales presented here for the researcher's choice. These are:

1. Alba M. Edwards' Social-Economic Grouping of Occupations
2. Hatt-North Occupational Prestige Ratings (with O. D. Duncan's Extensions)
3. 1960 United States Census Socioeconomic Status Scores
4. The Revised Occupational Rating Scale from Warner, Meeker, and Eells' Index of Status Characteristics

Choose Edwards' socioeconomic grouping if a relatively broad classification is satisfactory for your problem. This grouping makes it possible to use the United States Census for many kinds of comparative purposes. This nominal scale has been widely used in research on occupational mobility and occupational trends generally. The most often cited criticisms of the Edwards' classifications concern the lack of homogeneity of the categories and the weak scale properties of hierarchical grouping.

Choose the Hatt-North Occupational Prestige Ratings if the problem requires a greater range of ratings. Although the rankings rest on subjective assessments, many researchers believe they are highly valid because they represent a composite of factors and higher predictive power can be attained. O. D. Duncan has developed prestige indices for all 446 occupations listed in Detailed Classification of the Bureau of the Census.

Choose the United States 1960 Census Socioeconomic Status Scores if a wide range of occupations is to be included. Two hundred ninety-seven occupational categories are scored using a multiple item index by combining data on occupation, educational attainment, and family income. The socioeconomic status scores were designed for comparative analysis and have limited absolute meaning. They may be most useful where the analyst wants to compare different areas or population subgroups or where socioeconomic status is needed as a control in studying other relationships.

Choose the Warner, Meeker, Eell's Occupational Rating Scale if a broad classification is desired and where house type and dwelling area is important (in addition to occupation and source of income). The scale provides scores ranging from 12 to 84 but occupations are grouped into 7 classifications. The scale is comparable to Edwards' socio-economic groupings but the Warner scale obtains greater rigor by increased homogeneity of its classifications.

IV.A.1. INDEX: ALBA M. EDWARDS' SOCIAL-ECONOMIC GROUPING OF OCCUPATIONS

VARIABLE MEASURED: Socioeconomic position.

DESCRIPTION: Occupations are classified into six major groups with each group purported to have a somewhat distinct economic standard of life and to exhibit intellectual and social similarities. The two major dimensions for the ranking order are income and education.

WHERE PUBLISHED: Alba M. Edwards, *Comparative Occupation Statistics for the United States.* (Washington, D.C.: U.S. Government Printing Office, 1934), pp. 164-169; U.S. Bureau of the Census, 1960 Census of Population, *Classified Index of Occupations and Industries* (Washington, D.C.: U.S. Government Printing Office, 1960).

RELIABILITY: Occupational grouping shows high comparability with similar occupational ranking systems such as Barr-Taussig, Beckman Goodenough and Anderson, Centers, etc.

VALIDITY: Major occupational groups can be ranked on the two dimensions of income and education with relatively high correspondence as shown for the following ocupational groups.

Occupational Group	Adults with Some College Education (1957) (a)	Median (1959) Income (b)
	Percentage	Male Workers
Professional, technical, and kindred workers	78.7	$6,725
Business managers, officials, and proprietors	40.6	6,315
Clerical and kindred workers	30.2	4,904
Craftsman, foreman, and kindred workers	14.7	5,355
Operatives and kindred workers	9.0	4,281
Laborers, except farm and mine	8.3	3,150

(a) Bureau of the Census, *Current Population Reports,* Ser. P-20, No. 83 (August, 1958), 18.
(b) Bureau of the Census, *Current Population Reports,* Ser. P-60, No. 35 (January, 1961), 41-42.
For full report see the 1960 U.S. Census of Population, *Occupation by Earnings and Occupation,* Final Rept. PC(2)-7B (Washington, D.C.: U.S. Government Printing Office, 1963). More recent data will not be available until 1970 census is analyzed.

UTILITY: This is the most widely used scale of social-economic groupings of gainful workers in the United States. It is the basis on which the United States Census has grouped workers since 1930 in the decennial census.

The universe of gainful workers is fully enumerated every ten years. Any research worker can check his sample against enumeration parameters and can draw generalizations with high confidence.

RESEARCH APPLICATIONS: ANDERSON, H. DEWEY, and DAVIDSON, PERCY E. *Occupational Trends in the United States.* Stanford: Stanford University Press, 1940.
―――. *Occupational Mobility in an American Community.* Stanford: Stanford University Press, 1937.
BLAU, PETER M., and DUNCAN, OTIS D. *The American Occupational Structure in the United States.* New York: John Wiley & Sons, Inc., 1967.
DAVIDSON, PERCY E., and ANDERSON, DEWEY. *Ballots and the Democratic Class Struggle.* Stanford: Stanford University Press, 1943.
GLENN, NORVAL D., and ALSTON, JOHN P. "Cultural Distances Among Occupational Categories," *American Sociological Review,* 33 (June, 1968), 365-382.

JAFFE, A. J., and CARLETON, R. O. *Occupational Mobility in the United States, 1930-1960.* New York: Columbia University Press, 1954.

LIPSET, SEYMOUR MARTIN, and BENDIX, REINHARD. *Social Mobility and Industrial Society.* Berkeley: University of California Press, 1959.

TAUSSIG, F. W., and JOSLYN, C. S. *American Business Leaders.* New York: The Macmillan Company, 1932.

WARNER, W. LLOYD, and ABEGGLEN, JAMES C. *Occupational Mobility in American Business and Industry, 1928-1952.* Minneapolis: University of Minnesota Press, 1955.

SOCIAL-ECONOMIC GROUPING OF OCCUPATIONS

After *Alba M. Edwards*

(Present United States Census Classification
of Occupational Groups)

1. Professional, technical, and kindred workers
2. Business managers, officials, and proprietors
    a. Nonfarm managers, officials, and proprietors
    b. Farm owners and managers
3. Clerical and sales workers
    a. Clerical and kindred workers
    b. Sales workers
4. Craftsmen, foremen, and kindred workers
5. Operatives and kindred workers
6. Unskilled, service, and domestic workers
    a. Private household workers
    b. Service workers, except private household
    c. Farm laborers, unpaid family workers
    d. Laborers, except farm and mine

IV.A.2. INDEX: HATT-NORTH OCCUPATIONAL PRESTIGE RATINGS

VARIABLE MEASURED: Stratification is measured through occupational prestige and esteem.

DESCRIPTION: A nationwide cross-section of Americans (National Opinion Research Center Sample of 2,930) were asked to rate the standing of ninety occupations. These occupations were chosen from a wide range of white collar and manual occupations.

Respondents were asked—"For each job mentioned, please pick out the statement that best gives your own personal opinion of the general standing that such a job has: 1. *Excellent* standing, 2. *Good* standing, 3. *Average* standing, 4. *Somewhat below average* standing, 5. *Poor* standing. I don't know where to place that one." Ranking the ninety occupations was made possible by a procedure devised to translate the percentage ratings on each of the jobs into a single general score. When the "Don't Know" answers were excluded, the scoring theoretically allowed a maximum of 100 points for any job receiving only "excellent" ratings and a minimum of 20 points for work that was unanimously rated as poor. The actual range became 33-96.

WHERE PUBLISHED: Paul K. Hatt and C. C. North, "Jobs and Occupations: A Popular Evaluation," *Opinion News* (September, 1947), 3-13.

RELIABILITY: Reliability of raters is known to be highest in the higher and lower extremes of the prestige continuum and least reliable in the midrange. Social stratification of subjects has an effect on judgments in this field. Reliability is also lowered whenever the respondent is asked to rate unfamiliar occupations. In 1963, the National Opinion Research Center conducted a replication of the 1947 study with a r = .99 between the scores. See Robert W. Hodge, Paul M. Siegel, and Peter Rossi, "Occupational Prestige in the United States, 1925-63," *American Journal of Sociology*, 70 (November, 1964), 286-302.

VALIDITY: Numerous prestige studies exist, and correspondence between independent samples of respondents is quite high.

For an excellent comparative analysis see Lawrence Thomas, *The Occupational Structure and Education* (Englewood Cliffs, N.J.: Prentice-Hall, 1956), pp. 181-182.

Hatt later reexamined his own data to discover whether occupational prestige could be considered as a single dimension. The Guttman scaling technique was employed and responses were examined. They were not scalable, but occupational subgroups or families all proved to be scalable or to have reproducibilities high enough to consider them so. These occupational families and situs are shown:

1. Political	2. Professional
National	Free Professions
Local	Pure Sciences
	Applied Sciences
	Community Professionals

3. Business
   Big Business
   Small Business
   Labor Organization
   White Collar Employees

4. Recreation and Aesthetics
   High Arts
   Journalism and Radio
   Recreation

5. Agriculture
   Farming
   Employed on Farms

6. Manual Work
   Skilled Mechanics
   Construction Trades
   Outdoor Work
   Factory Work
   Unskilled Labor

7. Military
   Army
   Navy
   Marine Corps
   Coast Guard
   Air Force

8. Service
   "Official Community"
   "Unofficial Community
   Personnel"

The researcher who is working with subgroups should be aware of these occupational situses. For further information see Paul K. Hatt, "Occupation and Social Stratification," *American Journal of Sociology,* 55 (May, 1950), 538-543.

Theodore Caplow also insists that occupational prestige ranking is not unidimensional. See his *Sociology of Work* (Minneapolis: University of Minnesota, 1954), pp. 33-57.

RESEARCH APPLICATIONS:

BLAU, PETER M. "Occupational Bias and Mobility," *American Sociological Review,* 22 (August, 1957), 392-399.

BLOOM, RICHARD, WHITEMAN, MARTIN, and DEUTSCH, MARTIN. "Race and Social Class as Separate Factors Related to Social Environment," *American Journal of Sociology,* 70 (January, 1965), 471-476.

CLARKE, ALFRED C. "The Use of Leisure and Its Relation to Levels of Occupational Prestige," *American Sociological Review,* 21 (June 1956), 301-307.

CROCKETT, HARRY J., JR. "The Achievement Motive and Differential Occupational Mobility in the United States," *American Sociological Review,* 27 (April, 1962), 191-204.

ELLIS, EVELYN. "Social Psychological Correlates of Upward Social Mobility among Unmarried Career Women," *American Sociological Review,* 17 (October, 1952), 558-563.

EMPEY, LA MAR T. "Social Class and Occupational Aspirations: A Comparison of Absolute and Relative Measurement," *American Sociological Review,* 21 (December, 1956), 703-709.

INKELES, A., and ROSSI, P. "National Comparisons of Occupational Prestige," *American Journal of Sociology*, 61 (1956), 329-339.

JACKSON, ELTON F. "Status Consistency and Symptoms of Stress," *American Sociological Review*, 27 (August, 1962), 469-480.

LANDIS, JUDSON R., and SCARPITTI, FRANK R. "Perceptions Regarding Value Orientations and Legitimate Opportunity: Delinquents and Non-Delinquents," *Social Forces*, 44 (September, 1965), 83-91.

SEWELL, W. H., HALLER, A. O., and STRAUS, M. "Social Status and Educational and Occupational Aspiration," *American Sociological Review*, 22 (February, 1957), 67-73.

SIMPSON, RICHARD L., and SIMPSON, IDA H. "Correlates and Estimation of Occupational Prestige," *American Journal of Sociology*, 66 September, 1960), 135-140.

STRAUS, MURRAY A. "Deferred Gratification, Social Class, and the Achievement Syndrome," *American Sociological Review*, 27 (June, 1962), 326-335.

OCCUPATIONAL RATINGS

Paul K. Hatt and C. C. North

Occupation	Score
U.S. Supreme Court Justice	96
Physician	93
State Governor	93
Cabinet member in the federal government	92
Diplomat in the U.S. Foreign Service	92
Mayor of a large city	90
College professor	89
Scientist	89
United States Representative in Congress	89
Banker	88
Government scientist	88
County judge	87
Head of a department in a state government	87
Minister	87
Architect	86
Chemist	86
Dentist	86
Lawyer	86
Member of the board of directors of a large corporation	86
Nuclear physicist	86
Priest	86

OCCUPATIONAL RATINGS—(Continued)

Paul K. Hatt and C. C. North

Occupation	Score
Psychologist	85
Civil engineer	84
Airline pilot	83
Artist who paints pictures that are exhibited in galleries	83
Owner of factory that employs about 100 people	82
Sociologist	82
Accountant for a large business	81
Biologist	81
Musician in a symphony orchestra	81
Author of novels	80
Captain in the regular army	80
Building contractor	79
Economist	79
Instructor in the public schools	79
Public school teacher	78
County agricultural agent	77
Railroad engineer	77
Farm owner and operator	76
Official of an international labor union	75
Radio announcer	75
Newspaper columnist	74
Owner-operator of a printing shop	74
Electrician	73
Trained machinist	73
Welfare worker for a city government	73
Undertaker	72
Reporter on a daily newspaper	71
Manager of a small store in a city	69
Bookkeeper	68
Insurance agent	68
Tenant farmer—one who owns livestock and machinery and manages the farm	68
Traveling salesman for a wholesale concern	68
Playground director	67
Policeman	67
Railroad conductor	67
Mail carrier	66
Carpenter	65
Automobile repairman	63

OCCUPATIONAL RATINGS—(Continued)

Paul K. Hatt and C. C. North

Occupation	*Score*
Plumber	63
Garage mechanic	62
Local official of a labor union	62
Owner-operator of a lunch stand	62
Corporal in the regular army	60
Machine operator in a factory	60
Barber	59
Clerk in a store	58
Fisherman who owns his own boat	58
Streetcar motorman	58
Milk routeman	54
Restaurant cook	54
Truck driver	54
Lumberjack	53
Filling station attendant	52
Singer in a nightclub	52
Farmhand	50
Coal miner	49
Taxi driver	49
Railroad section hand	48
Restaurant waiter	48
Dock worker	47
Night watchman	47
Clothes presser in a laundry	46
Soda fountain clerk	45
Bartender	44
Janitor	44
Share cropper—one who owns no livestock or equipment and does not manage farm	40
Garbage collector	35
Street sweeper	34
Shoe shiner	33
AVERAGE	69.8

A major limitation of Hatt-North scores is that such scores are available only for occupations encompassing, in the aggregate, less than half of the labor force. Otis D. Duncan has extended index scores for the 446 occupations listed in the detailed classification of the Bureau of the Census. He constructed the occupational socioeconomic index in terms of the relationship between the NORC prestige ratings X_1 and socioeconomic characteristics of the occupations, such as education X_2 and income X_3 with a multiple correlation of $R_{123} = 0.91$. A researcher needing a longer list of occupational prestige ratings is referred to Albert J. Reiss, with Otis D. Duncan, Paul K. Hatt, and C. C. North, *Occupations and Social Status* (Glencoe, Ill.: The Free Press, 1961), pp. 109-161 and Appendix B.

IV.A.3. INDEX: UNITED STATES 1960 CENSUS SOCIOECONOMIC STATUS SCORES

DESCRIPTION: The socioeconomic status score is a multiple-item measure derived by averaging scores for the component items of occupation, education, and family income. A second socioeconomic measure was developed in connection with the 1960 Census program. This is a status consistency measure which indicates whether the components of the multiple-item score are at about the same or different levels and, if at different levels, the pattern of their inconsistency. These indexes were derived from chief income recipients in families, and assigned to other family members, and for non-family members.

WHERE PUBLISHED: U.S. Bureau of the Census, *Methodology and Scores of Socioeconomic Status,* Working Paper No. 15 (Washington, D.C.: U.S. Government Printing Office, 1963).

RELIABILITY: The socioeconomic scores for detailed occupations were based upon the data most recently available at the time of analysis, i.e. for those males 14 years old and over in the experienced civilian labor force as of 1950. The Pearsonian coefficient of correlation between the 1950 scores and scores based upon 1960 data is .96. However for a few specific occupations there was a substantial discrepancy. Charles B. Nam and Mary G. Powers, "Variations in Socioeconomic Structure by Race, Residence, and the Life Cycle," *American Sociological Review,* 30 (February, 1965), 97-103.

VALIDITY: Negative relationship exists between socioeconomic scores and non-white persons in 1960.

Highest scores correlated with urban fringe areas of large cities; lowest in rural areas.

Rates of unemployment for males were inversely related to level of socioeconomic status.

Relatively more persons age 45 and over than under 45 years of age had low status scores. Scores for non-white remained generally lower than those for the total population at each age. U.S. Bureau of the Census, Current Population Reports, *Socioeconomic Characteristics of the Population, 1960,* Technical Studies, Series P. 23, No. 12 (Washington, D.C.: U.S. Government Printing Office, July 31, 1964).

UTILITY: A socioeconomic score for 297 occupational categories can be quickly assigned. Comparisons with United States Census research can be made. This means any sample can be compared with a United States national population. Range of scores: 1–99.

RESEARCH APPLICATIONS:

NAM, CHARLES B., and POWERS, MARY G. "Variations in Socioeconomic Structure by Race, Residence, and Life Cycle," *American Sociological Review,* 30 (February, 1965), 97-103.

————. "Changes in the Relative Status Level of Workers in the United States, 1950-1960," paper read at annual meeting of the American Sociological Association, San Francisco, Calif., August 30, 1967.

U.S. BUREAU OF THE CENSUS, U.S. Census of Population, 1960. *Socioeconomic Status,* Final Rept. PC(2)-5C (Washington, D.C.: U.S. Government Printing Office, 1967).

SOCIOECONOMIC STATUS SCORES FOR CATEGORIES OF
OCCUPATION COMPONENT *
(Based on Average Levels of Education and Income for Males)

Score	Category
	Professional, technical and kindred workers
92	Accountants and auditors
84	Actors
96	Airplane pilots and navigators
98	Architects
88	Artists and art teachers
60	Athletes
93	Authors
89	Chiropractors
67	Clergymen
96	College presidents, professors, and instructors (n.e.c.)
61	Dancers and dancing teachers
99	Dentists
91	Designers

* Charles B. Nam, Chief, Education and Social Stratification Branch, Population Division, U. S. Bureau of the Census, Washington, D.C., had the major responsibility for the preparation of the scores.

Score   Category

Professional, technical and kindred workers—*Cont'd.*

Score	Category
65	Dietitians and nutritionists
87	Draftsmen
95	Editors and reporters

Engineers, technical

Score	Category
97	Aeronautical
98	Chemical
96	Civil
97	Electrical
95	Industrial
96	Mechanical
97	Metallurgical, and metallurgists
97	Mining
96	Not elsewhere classified

Score	Category
48	Entertainers (n.e.c.)
94	Farm and home management advisors
78	Foresters and conservationists
83	Funeral directors and embalmers
98	Lawyers and judges
64	Librarians
72	Musicians and music teachers
	Natural scientists
94	Chemists
95	Other natural scientists

Score	Category
71	Nurses, professional
50	Nurses, student professional
96	Optometrists
99	Osteopaths
96	Personnel and labor relations workers
95	Pharmacists
73	Photographers
99	Physicians and surgeons
95	Public relations men and publicity writers
90	Radio operators

Score	Category
84	Recreation and group workers
63	Religious workers
85	Social and welfare workers, except group
96	Social scientists
87	Sports instructors and officials

Score   Category

Engineers, technical—*Cont'd.*

71 Surveyors
89 Teachers (n.e.c.)

73 Technicians, medical and dental
80 Technicians, electrical and electronic
80 Technicians, other engineering and physical sciences
85 Technicians (n.e.c.)
81 Therapists and healers (n.e.c.)
95 Veterinarians
86 Professional, technical, and kindred workers (n.e.c.)

Managers, officials, and proprietors, except farm
92 Buyers and department heads, store
51 Buyers and shippers, farm products
73 Conductors, railroad
92 Credit men
79 Floormen and floor managers, store
Inspectors, public administration
89   Federal public administration and postal service
81   State public administration
82   Local public administration

41 Managers and superintendents, building
79 Officers, pilots, pursers, and engineers, ship
Officials & administrators (n.e.c.), public administration
94   Federal public administration
90   State public administration
79   Local public administration
82 Officials, lodge, society, union, etc.
82 Postmasters
92 Purchasing agents and buyers (n.e.c.)

Managers, officials, and proprietors (n.e.c.)—Salaried
84   Construction
95   Manufacturing
87   Transportation
93   Communications, and utilities and sanitary services
90   Wholesale trade
    Retail trade
78   Food and dairy products stores
70   Eating and drinking places

Score	Category

Managers, officials, and proprietors, except farm—*Cont'd.*
Retail trade—*Cont'd.*

Score	Category
90	General merchandise and limited price variety stores
89	Apparel and accessories stores
89	Furniture, housefurnishings, and equipment stores
88	Motor vehicles and accessories retailing
63	Gasoline service stations
87	Hardware, farm implement, & building material retailing
84	Other retail trade
96	Banking and other finance
96	Insurance and real estate
96	Business services
76	Automobile repair services and garages
81	Miscellaneous repair services
78	Personal services
89	All other industries (incl. not reported)

Managers, officials, & proprietors (n.e.c.)—Self-employed

Score	Category
79	Construction
88	Manufacturing
73	Transportation
72	Communications, and utilities and sanitary services
85	Wholesale trade
	Retail trade
54	Food and dairy products stores
71	Eating and drinking places
72	General merchandise and limited price variety stores
88	Apparel and accessories stores
86	Furniture, housefurnishings, and equipment stores
89	Motor vehicles and accessories retailing
63	Gasoline service stations
90	Hardware, farm implement, & building material retailing
75	Other retail trade
97	Banking and other finance
95	Insurance and real estate
91	Business services
68	Automobile repair services and garages
60	Miscellaneous repair services
68	Personal services
76	All other industries (incl. not reported)

Score   Category

Clerical and kindred workers

Score	Category
90	Agents (n.e.c.)
50	Attendants and assistants, library
56	Attendants, physician's and dentist's office
54	Baggagemen, transportation
75	Bank tellers
73	Bookkeepers
69	Cashiers
66	Collectors, bill and account
73	Dispatchers and starters, vehicle
85	Express messengers and railway mail clerks
73	File clerks
89	Insurance adjusters, examiners, and investigators
80	Mail carriers
43	Messengers and office boys
69	Office machine operators
73	Payroll and timekeeping clerks
73	Postal clerks
73	Receptionists
82	Secretaries
58	Shipping and receiving clerks
82	Stenographers
73	Stock clerks and storekeepers
33	Telegraph messengers
75	Telegraph operators
72	Telephone operators
82	Ticket, station, and express agents
82	Typists
73	Clerical and kindred workers (n.e.c.)

Sales workers

Score	Category
90	Advertising agents and salesmen
67	Auctioneers
62	Demonstrators
08	Hucksters and peddlers
89	Insurance agents, brokers, and underwriters
20	Newsboys
86	Real estate agents and brokers
94	Stock and bond salesmen

Score   Category

Sales workers—*Cont'd.*
Salesmen and sales clerks (n.e.c.)

88   Manufacturing
85   Wholesale trade
61   Retail trade
77   Other industries (incl. not reported)

Craftsmen, foremen, and kindred workers

50   Bakers
31   Blacksmiths
59   Boilermakers
69   Bookbinders
50   Brickmasons, stonemasons, and tile setters
48   Cabinetmakers
35   Carpenters
34   Cement and concrete finishers
79   Compositors and typesetters
52   Cranemen, derrickmen, and hoistmen
67   Decorators and window dressers
74   Electricians
81   Electrotypers and stereotypers
75   Engravers, except photoengravers
57   Excavating, grading, and road machinery operators

Foremen (n.e.c.)
65   Construction
        Manufacturing
76   Metal industries
82   Machinery, except electrical
82   Electrical machinery, equipment, and supplies
84   Transportation equipment
71   Other durable goods
66   Textiles, textile products, and apparel
79   Other nondurable goods (incl. not specified mfg.)
61   Railroads and railway express service
74   Transportation, except railroad
79   Communications, and utilities and sanitary services
73   Other industries (incl. not reported)
51   Forgemen and hammermen
66   Furriers
57   Glaziers
58   Heat treaters, annealers, and temperers

Score   Category

Craftsmen, foremen, and kindred workers—*Cont'd.*
48 Inspectors, scalers, and graders, log and lumber
Inspectors (n.e.c.)
76   Construction
65   Railroads and railway express service
74   Transportation, etc. RR., commun. & other public util.
71   Other industries (incl. not reported)

63 Jewelers, watchmakers, goldsmiths, and silversmiths
64 Job setters, metal
76 Linemen and servicemen, telegraph, telephone, and power
68 Locomotive engineers
76 Locomotive firemen
32 Loom fixers
68 Machinists
Mechanics and repairmen
61   Air conditioning, heating, and refrigeration
79   Airplane
52   Automobile
66   Office machine
62   Radio and television
52   Railroad and car shop
61   Not elsewhere classified

39 Millers, grain, flour, feed, etc.
62 Millwrights
41 Molders, metal
73 Motion picture projectionists
72 Opticians, and lens grinders and polishers
37 Painters, construction and maintenance
22 Paperhangers
74 Pattern and model makers, except paper
84 Photoengravers and lithographers
54 Piano and organ tuners and repairmen
46 Plasterers
64 Plumbers and pipe fitters
77 Pressmen and plate printers, printing
54 Rollers and roll hands, metal
34 Roofers and slaters
22 Shoemakers and repairers, except factory
72 Stationary engineers
44 Stone cutters and stone carvers
66 Structural metal workers

Score   Category

Craftsmen, foremen, and kindred workers—*Cont'd.*

Score	Category
40	Tailors
68	Tinsmiths, coppersmiths, and sheet metal workers
77	Toolmakers, and die makers and setters
53	Upholsterers
62	Craftsmen and kindred workers (n.e.c.)
36	Former members of the Armed Forces

Operatives and kindred workers
Apprentices

Score	Category
46	Auto mechanics
57	Bricklayers and masons
50	Carpenters
61	Electricians
59	Machinists and toolmakers
60	Mechanics, except auto
60	Plumbers and pipe fitters
49	Building trades (n.e.c.)
55	Metalworking trades (n.e.c.)
57	Printing trades
51	Other specified trades
55	Trade not specified

Score	Category
63	Asbestos and insulation workers
61	Assemblers
44	Attendants, auto service and parking
33	Blasters and powdermen
50	Boatmen, canalmen, and lock keepers
71	Brakemen, railroad
65	Bus drivers
47	Chainmen, rodmen, and axmen, surveying
61	Checkers, examiners, and inspectors, mfg.
61	Conductors, bus and street railway
59	Deliverymen and routemen
35	Dressmakers and seamstresses, except factory
36	Dyers
57	Filers, grinders, and polishers, metal
19	Fruit, nut, and vegetable graders and packers, exc. factory
45	Furnacemen, smeltermen, and pourers
14	Graders and sorters, mfg.
56	Heaters, metal
47	Knitters, loopers, and toppers, textile

Score   Category

Operatives and kindred workers—*Cont'd.*

Score	Category
37	Laundry and dry cleaning operatives
60	Meat cutters, except slaughter and packing house
73	Milliners
	Mine operatives and laborers (n.e.c.)
18	Coal mining
70	Crude petroleum and natural gas extraction
36	Mining and quarrying, except fuel
28	Motormen, mine, factory, logging camp, etc.
64	Motormen, street, subway, and elevated railway
44	Oilers and greasers, except auto
38	Packers and wrappers (n.e.c.)
47	Painters, except construction and maintenance
65	Photographic process workers
78	Power station operators
40	Sailors and deck hands
10	Sawyers
39	Sewers and stitchers, mfg.
20	Spinners, textile
40	Stationary firemen
72	Switchmen, railroad
37	Taxicab drivers and chauffeurs
40	Truck and tractor drivers
27	Weavers, textile
62	Welders and flame—cutters

Operatives and kindred workers (n.e.c.)
    Manufacturing
        Durable goods
            Sawmills, planing mills, and misc. wood products

Score	Category
12	Sawmills, planing mills, and mill work
25	Miscellaneous wood products
27	Furniture and fixtures
	Stone, clay, and glass products
50	Glass and glass products
29	Cement, and concrete, gypsum, and plaster products
31	Structural clay products
49	Pottery and related products
41	Misc. nonmetallic mineral and stone products

Score	Category
	Operatives and kindred workers—*Cont'd.*
	Operatives and kindred workers (n.e.c.)—*Cont'd.*
	Manufacturing—*Cont'd.*
	Durable goods—*Cont'd.*
	Sawmills, planing mills, and mill work—*Cont'd.*
	Metal industries
	Primary metal industries
49	Blast furnaces, steel works, and rolling and finishing mills
39	Other primary iron and steel industries
47	Primary nonferrous industries
	Fabricated metal industries (incl. not spec. metal)
48	Cutlery, handtools, and other hardware
48	Fabricated structural metal products
48	Miscellaneous fabricated metal products
47	Not specified metal industries
	Machinery, except electrical
59	Farm machinery and equipment
67	Office, computing, and accounting machines
57	Miscellaneous machinery
62	Electrical machinery, equipment, and supplies
	Transportation equipment
61	Motor vehicles and motor vehicle equipment
71	Aircraft and parts
41	Ship and boat building and repairing
56	Railroad and misc. transportation equipment
	Professional and photographic equipment, and watches
57	Professional equipment and supplies
73	Photographic equipment and supplies
62	Watches, clocks, and clockwork-operated devices
42	Miscellaneous manufacturing industries
	Nondurable goods
	Food and kindred products
43	Meat products
53	Dairy products
26	Canning and preserving fruits, vegetables, and sea foods
36	Grain-mill products
38	Bakery products
34	Confectionery and related products
48	Beverage industries
32	Misc. food preparations and kindred products
46	Not specified food industries

Score   Category

Operatives and kindred workers (n.e.c.)—*Cont'd.*
   Manufacturing—*Cont'd.*
      Nondurable goods—*Cont'd.*
         Food and kindred products—*Cont'd.*

Score	Category
13	Tobacco manufactures
	Textile mill products
47	Knitting mills
38	Dyeing & finishing textiles, exc. wool & knit goods
44	Floor coverings, except hard surface
14	Yarn, thread, and fabric mills
33	Miscellaneous textile mill products
	Apparel and other fabricated textile products
39	Apparel and accessories
36	Miscellaneous fabricated textile products
	Paper and allied products
51	Pulp, paper, and paperboard mills
37	Paperboard containers and boxes
52	Miscellaneous paper and pulp products
60	Printing, publishing, and allied industries
	Chemicals and allied products
51	Synthetic fibers
57	Drugs and medicines
51	Paints, varnishes, and related products
55	Miscellaneous chemicals and allied products
	Petroleum and coal products
79	Petroleum refining
44	Miscellaneous petroleum and coal products
	Rubber and misc. plastic products
59	Rubber products
42	Miscellaneous plastic products
	Leather and leather products
37	Leather: tanned, curried, and finished
31	Footwear, except rubber
36	Leather products, except footwear
44	Not specified manufacturing industries
	Nonmanufacturing industries (incl. not reported)
38	Construction
42	Railroads and railway express service
53	Transportation, except railroad
52	Communications, and utilities and sanitary services
38	Wholesale and retail trade

Score	Category
	Operatives and kindred workers (n.e.c.)—*Cont'd.*
	Nonmanufacturing industries (incl. not reported)—*Cont'd.*
45	Business and repair services
29	Personal services
50	Public administration
36	All other industries (incl. not reported)

	Private household workers
07	Baby sitters, private household
	Housekeepers, private household
25	Living in
32	Living out
	Laundresses, private household
09	Living in
09	Living out
	Private household workers (n.e.c.)
26	Living in
07	Living out

	Service workers, except private household
38	Attendants, hospital and other institution
46	Attendants, professional and personal service (n.e.c.)
26	Attendants, recreation and amusement
37	Barbers
46	Bartenders
35	Boarding and lodging house keepers
02	Bootblacks
18	Chambermaids and maids, except private household
15	Charwomen and cleaners
31	Cooks, except private household
41	Counter and fountain workers
28	Elevator operators
37	Hairdressers and cosmetologists
61	Housekeepers and stewards, except private household
18	Janitors and sextons
18	Kitchen workers (n.e.c.), except private household
51	Midwives
16	Porters
32	Practical nurses

Score   Category

Service workers, except private household—*Cont'd.*
Protective service workers
73   Firemen, fire protection
38   Guards, watchmen, and doorkeepers
44   Marshals and constables
Policemen and detectives
74   Public
67   Private
66   Sheriffs and bailiffs
39   Watchmen (crossing) and bridge tenders
34   Ushers, recreation and amusement
39   Waiters
18   Service workers, except private household (n.e.c.)

Laborers, except farm and mine
16   Carpenters' helpers, except logging and mining
11   Fishermen and oystermen
24   Garage laborers, and car washers and greasers
19   Gardeners, except farm, and groundskeepers
25   Longshoremen and stevedores
04   Lumbermen, raftsmen, and wood choppers
13   Teamsters
28   Truck drivers' helpers
28   Warehousemen (n.e.c.)

Laborers (n.e.c.)
    Manufacturing
        Durable goods
            Sawmills, planing mills, and misc. wood products
04   Sawmills, planing mills, and mill work
09   Miscellaneous wood products
19   Furniture and fixtures
            Stone, clay, and glass products
31   Glass and glass products
22   Cement, and concrete, gypsum, and plaster products
19   Structural clay products
30   Pottery and related products
23   Misc. nonmetallic mineral and stone products
            Metal industries
                Primary metal industries
35   Blast furnaces, steel works, and rolling and finishing mills

Score   Category

                    Laborers, except farm and mine—*Cont'd.*
              Laborers (n.e.c.)—*Cont'd.*
                Manufacturing—*Cont'd.*
                   Durable goods—*Cont'd.*
                      Metal industries—*Cont'd.*
                         Primary metal industries—*Cont'd.*

Score	Category
18	Other primary iron and steel industries
34	Primary nonferrous industries
	Fabricated metal industries (incl. not spec. metal)
27	Cutlery, hand tools, and other hardware
27	Fabricated structural metal products
27	Misc. fabricated metal products
28	Not specified metal industries
	Machinery, except electrical
38	Farm machinery and equipment
45	Office, computing, and accounting machines
32	Miscellaneous machinery
45	Electrical machinery, equipment and supplies
	Transportation equipment
42	Motor vehicles and motor vehicle equipment
51	Aircraft and parts
19	Ship and boat building and repairing
31	Railroad and misc. transportation equipment
	Professional and photographic equipment, and watches
37	Professional equipment and supplies
41	Photographic equipment and supplies
29	Watches, clocks, and clockwork-operated devices
28	Miscellaneous manufacturing industries
	Nondurable goods
	Food and kindred products
32	Meat products
34	Dairy products
15	Canning and preserving fruits, vegetables, and sea foods
23	Grain-mill products
30	Bakery products
33	Confectionery and related products
34	Beverage industries
17	Misc. food preparations and kindred products
40	Not specified food industries
10	Tobacco manufactures

Score	Category
	Laborers, except farm and mine—*Cont'd.*
	Laborers (n.e.c.)—*Cont'd.*
	Manufacturing—*Cont'd.*
	Durable goods—*Cont'd.*
	Nondurable goods—*Cont'd.*
	Textile mill products
12	Yarn, thread, and fabric mills
14	Other textile mill products
21	Apparel and other fabricated textile products
	Paper and allied products
27	Pulp, paper, and paperboard mills
31	Paperboard containers and boxes
30	Miscellaneous paper and pulp products
50	Printing, publishing, and allied industries
	Chemical and allied products
30	Synthetic fibers
48	Drugs and medicines
42	Paints, varnishes, and related products
18	Miscellaneous chemicals and allied products
	Petroleum and coal products
59	Petroleum refining
26	Miscellaneous petroleum and coal products
41	Rubber and miscellaneous plastic products
27	Leather and leather products
26	Not specified manufacturing industries
	Nonmanufacturing industries (incl. not reported)
16	Construction
20	Railroads and railway express service
28	Transportation, except railroad
18	Communications, and utilities and sanitary services
28	Wholesale and retail trade
26	Business and repair services
01	Personal services
29	Public administration
07	All other industries (incl. not reported)
33	Occupation not reported
63	Present members of the Armed Forces

IV.A.4. INDEX: REVISED OCCUPATIONAL RATING SCALE FROM W. L. WARNER, M. MEEKER, AND K. EELL'S INDEX OF STATUS CHARACTERISTICS

VARIABLE MEASURED: Social class position according to a seven point rating.

DESCRIPTION: The rating of occupations is one measure included in the Index of Status Characteristics. The Index is composed of four status characteristics: Occupation, Source of Income, House Type, and Dwelling Area. Each of these is rated on a seven point scale, and this rating is then weighted according to its separate contributions to the total Index. The weighted ratings are totaled to yield the scores that are appropriate to the various classes. The scores on the Index of Status Characteristics range from 12 to 84. The ranges are calculated by validating preliminary scores using the Evaluated Participation method of determining social class position. Occupation is the single measure most highly correlated with class position.

WHERE PUBLISHED: W. Lloyd Warner, Marchia Meeker, and Kenneth Eells, *Social Class in America* (Chicago: Science Research Associates, 1949), pp. 121-159. The occupational rating scale is shown on pp. 140-41.

VALIDITY OF INDEX OF STATUS CHARACTERISTICS:
1. Accuracy in prediction: 85 percent of the Old Americans in *Yankee City* were placed correctly or within one point. Not as valid for ethnics.
2. Correlation with the Evaluative Participation Method as reported by Warner, *et. al.*, on p. 168.

Occupation	$r = .91$
Source of Income	$r = .85$
House Type	$r = .85$
Dwelling Area	$r = .82$
I.S.C. (all four measures)	$r = .97$

3. Comparative Study by John L. Haer.
   Five indexes of social stratification were compared and evaluated by examining their capacities for predicting variables that have been shown in previous studies to be related to measures of stratification. These five indexes include Centers' class identification question, an open end question, occupation, education, and Warner's Index of Status Characteristics. An overall comparison

reveals that coefficients are higher for the Index of Status Characteristics than for other indexes in 18 out of 22 comparisons. Its greater efficiency may be due to the fact that it is a composite index that provides a continuous series of ranks. These features make it possible to discern minute variations in relation to other variables. John L. Haer, "Predictive Utility of Five Indices of Social Stratification," *American Sociological Review*, 22 (October, 1957), 541-546.

VALIDITY OF THE OCCUPATION SCALE: Joseph A. Kahl and James A. Davis selected 19 single measures of socioeconomic status and measured their intercorrelations. They report a product moment correlation of .74 between occupation (Warner) and status of friends, and a multiple correlation of .80 between occupation plus education and status of friends—". . . our data agree with Warner's that occupation (as he measures it) is the best predictor of either social participation or the whole socioeconomic cluster represented by the general factor identified by factor analysis." "A Comparison of Indexes of Socio-Economic Status," *American Sociological Review*, 20 (June, 1955), 317-325.

Stanley A. Hetzler reports the following coefficients between seven rating scales and ratings of social class and social position.

Rating Scales	*Social Class*	*Social Position*
Occupational Prestige	.69	.57
Residential Area	.54	.46
Family Background	.53	.48
Personal Influence	.49	.52
Dwelling Unit	.47	.39
Family Wealth	.45	.45
Personal Income	.34	.44

The four rating scales showing the highest coefficients were occupational prestige, family background, residential area, and personal influence. The multiple correlation of these four scales with social class is .75; with social position it is .68. "An Investigation of the Distinctiveness of Social Classes," *American Sociological Review*, 18 (October, 1953), 493-497. *See also* J. L. Haer, "A Test of the Unidimensionality of the Index of Status Characteristics," *Social Forces*, 34 (1955), 56-58.

UTILITY: The Index of Status Characteristics presents a comparatively objective means of determining social class postion. The limits defined for the various seven-point ratings are sufficiently precise to eliminate to a great degree any subjective judgment. All one needs to know is a person's name, occupation, and address; the source of income can generally be derived from the occupation, and the house type and dwelling area can be evaluated through the address. This eliminates extensive, time-consuming interviewing.

The Occupation Scale is the best single predictor of social class position within a seven-point range. The high correlation it exhibits with the evaluative participative method of social class position ($r = .91$) commends occupation as a single dimension. Researchers will achieve a high degree of predictive efficiency by use of the one scale. Cf. Hollingshead's use of a two-factor index of social position in August B. Hollingshead and Frederick C. Redlich, *Social Class and Mental Illness: A Community Study* (New York: Wiley, 1958), pp. 390-391.

RESEARCH APPLICATIONS:

FREEMAN, HOWARD E., and SIMMONS, OZIE G. "Social Class and Post-Hospital Performance Levels," *American Sociological Review,* 24 (1959), 345-351.

LAWSON, EDWIN D. and BOCK, WALTER E. "Correlations of Indexes of Families' Socioeconomic Status," *Social Forces,* 39 (December, 1960), 149-152.

STONE, GREGORY P., and FORM, WILLIAM H. "Instabilities in Status: The Problem of Hierarchy in the Community Study of Status Arrangements," *American Sociological Review,* 18 (April, 1953), 149-162.

————. "The Local Community Clothing Market: A Study of the Social and Social Psychological Contexts of Shipping," Technical Bulletin 247. East Lansing, Mich.: Michigan State University, June, 1955.

SWINEHART, JAMES W. "Socioeconomic Level, Status Aspiration, and Maternal Role," *American Sociological Review,* 28 (June, 1963), 391-399.

WARNER, W. LLOYD, *et al. Democracy in Jonesville.* New York: Harper & Brothers, 1949.

WHITE, MARTHA STURM. "Social Class, Child Rearing Practices and Child Behavior," *American Sociological Review,* 22 (December, 1957), 704-712.

WARNER, MEEKER, EELLS'S REVISED SCALE FOR RATING OCCUPATION

Rating Assigned to Occupation	Professionals	Proprietors and Managers	Business Men	Clerks and Kindred Workers, Etc.	Manual Workers	Protective and Service Workers	Farmers
1	Lawyers, doctors, dentists, engineers, judges, high-school superintendents, veterinarians, ministers (graduated from divinity school), chemists, etc., with postgraduate training, architects	Businesses valued at $75,000 and over	Regional and divisional managers of large financial and industrial enterprises	Certified Public Accountants			Gentlemen farmers
2	High-school teachers, trained nurses, chiropractors, undertakers, ministers (some training), newspaper editors, librarians (graduate)	Businesses valued at $20,000 to $75,000	Assistant managers and office and department managers of large businesses, assistants to executives, etc.	Accountants, salesmen of real estate and insurance, postmasters			Large farm owners, farm owners

Rating Assigned to Occupation	Professionals	Proprietors and Managers	Business Men	Clerks and Kindred Workers, Etc.	Manual Workers	Protective and Service Workers	Farmers
3	Social workers, grade-school teachers, optometrists, librarians (not graduate), undertaker's assistants, ministers (no training)	Businesses valued at $5,000 to $20,000	All minor officials of businesses	Auto salesmen, bank clerks and cashiers, postal clerks, secretaries to executives, supervisors of railroad, telephone, etc., justices of the peace	Contractors		
4		Businesses valued at $2,000 to $5,000		Stenographers, bookkeepers, rural mail clerks, railroad ticket agents, sales people in dry goods stores, etc.	Factory foreman, electricians, plumbers, carpenters, watchmakers (own business)	Dry cleaners, butchers, sheriffs, railroad engineers and conductors	
5		Businesses valued at $500 to $2,000		Dime store clerks, hardware salesmen, beauty operators, telephone operators	Carpenters, plumbers, electricians (apprentice), timekeepers, linemen, telephone or telegraph, radio repairmen, medium skilled workers	Barbers, firemen, butcher's apprentices, practical nurses, policemen, seamstresses, cooks in restaurant, bartenders	Tenant farmers

6	Businesses valued at less than $500	Moulders, semi-skilled workers, assistants to carpenter, etc.	Baggage men, night police-men and watchmen, taxi and truck drivers, gas station attendants, waitresses in restaurants	Small tenant farmers, laborers
7		Heavy labor, migrant work, odd-job men, miners	Janitors, scrubwomen, newsboys	Migrant farm laborers

Group Structure and Dynamics

This section contains five scales, each of which measures a different variable relating to group structure and dynamics. Hemphill's Index of Group Dimensions, which ascertains thirteen dimensions of a group, is the most ambitious attempt to measure the structural properties of groups. Bales's Interactional Process Analysis is a nominal scale, widely used to assess the characteristics of personal interaction in problem-solving groups. Seashore's Group Cohesiveness Index provides a measure of the strength of a group to maintain its identity and to persist. The Sociometry Scales of Sociometric Choice and Sociometric Preference reveal the interpersonal attractions of members in groups. These scales may be widely adapted to suit many different kinds of situations. They are useful not only to a researcher seeking basic relationships, but also to the action researcher or social worker. New groupings of individuals can be quickly arranged and new measurements of morale or productivity can be made. The Bogardus Social Distance Scale may also be adapted to many different purposes. The social distance between two persons, person and group, or between groups can be measured in such diverse situations as that involving an outgroup member and a country, a community, or an organization.

IV.B.1. INDEX: HEMPHILL'S INDEX OF GROUP DIMENSIONS

VARIABLE MEASURED: The index is designed to measure group dimensions or characteristics.

DESCRIPTION: The index is built upon thirteen comparatively independent group dimensions: autonomy, control, flexibility, hedonic tone, homogeneity, intimacy, participation, permeability, polarization, potency, stability, stratification, and viscidity. The 150 items are answered on a five-point scale. The dimensions were selected from a list of group adjectives used by authorities. Items were suggested from a free-response type questionnaire administered to 500 individuals, and 5 judges then put the items into the dimensional categories.

WHERE PUBLISHED: John K. Hemphill, *Group Dimensions: A Manual for Their Measurement,* Research Monograph Number 87 (Columbus, Ohio: Bureau of Business Research, Ohio State University, 1956).

RELIABILITY: Split-half reliabilities range from .59 to .87. The relationship between an item and high-low categories ranges from .03 to .78 with a median of .36 on the keyed items and from .01 to .36 with a median of .12 on the randomly selected items. Intercorrelation of dimension scores ranges from $-.54$ to .81, with most within $+.29$ (which has a .01 significance level). Agreement between different reporters of the same group ranges from .53 to .74.

VALIDITY: The dimension scores describing the characteristics of two quite different groups vary accordingly, while those describing the characteristics of two similar groups are quite similar.

UTILITY: The index can be useful in studying the relationships between the behavior of leaders and characteristics of groups in which they function. Although fairly long, it is comparatively easy to administer and score.

RESEARCH APPLICATIONS: Validation and reliability studies on 200 descriptions of 35 groups.
BENTZ, V. J. "Leadership: A Study of Social Interaction," unpublished report, Bureau of Business Research, Ohio State University.
HEMPHILL, JOHN K., and WESTIE, CHARLES M. "The Measurement of Group Dimensions," *The Journal of Psychology,* 29 (April, 1950), 325-342.
SEEMAN, M. "A Sociological Approach to Leadership: The Case of the School Executive," unpublished report, Bureau of Business Research, Ohio State University.

GROUP DIMENSIONS DESCRIPTIONS QUESTIONNAIRE

Directions:

Record your answer to each of the items on the answer sheet for the group you are describing. Make no marks on the question booklet itself.

In considering each item go through the following steps:

1. Read the item carefully.
2. Think about how well the item tells something about the group you are describing.
3. Find the number on the answer sheet that corresponds with the number of the item you are considering.
4. After each number on the answer sheet you will find five pairs of dotted lines lettered A, B, C, D, or E.

If the item you are considering tells something about the group that is definitely true blacken the space between the pair of dotted lines headed by A.

If the item you are considering tells something that is mostly true, blacken the space between the pair of lines headed by B.

If the item tells something that is to an equal degree both true and false, or you are undecided about whether it is true or false, blacken the space between the pair of lines headed by C.

If the item you are considering tells something that is mostly false, blacken the space between the pair of lines headed by D.

If the item you are considering tells something about the group that is definitely false, blacken the space between the pair of dotted lines headed by E.

5. When blackening the space between a pair of lines, fill in all the space with a heavy black line. If you should make an error in marking your answer, erase thoroughly the mark you made and then indicate the correct answer.
6. In rare cases where you believe that an item does not apply at all to the group or you feel that you do not have sufficient information to make any judgment concerning what the item tells about the group, leave that item blank.
7. After you have completed one item, proceed to the next one in order. You may have as long as you need to complete your

description. Be sure the number on the answer sheet corresponds with the number of the item being answered in the booklet.

Questions:

The questions that follow make it possible to describe objectively certain characteristics of social groups. The items simply describe characteristics of groups; they do not judge whether the characteristic is desirable or undesirable. Therefore, in no way are the questions to be considered a "test" either of the groups or of the person answering the questions. We simply want an objective description of what the group is like.

1. The group has well understood but unwritten rules concerning member conduct.
2. Members fear to express their real opinions.
3. The only way a member may leave the group is to be expelled.
4. No explanation need be given by a member wishing to be absent from the group.
5. An individual's membership can be dropped should he fail to live up to the standards of the group.
6. Members of the group work under close supervision.
7. Only certain kinds of ideas may be expressed freely within the group.
8. A member may leave the group by resigning at any time he wishes.
9. A request made by a member to leave the group can be refused.
10. A member has to think twice before speaking in the group's meetings.
11. Members are occasionally forced to resign.
12. The members of the group are subject to strict discipline.
13. The group is rapidly increasing in size.
14. Members are constantly leaving the group.
15. There is a large turnover of members within the group.
16. Members are constantly dropping out of the group but new members replace them.
17. During the entire time of the group's existence no member has left.
18. Each member's personal life is known to other members of the group.
19. Members of the group lend each other money.

20. A member has the chance to get to know all other members of the group.
21. Members are not in close enough contact to develop likes or dislikes for one another.
22. Members of the group do small favors for one another.
23. All members know each other very well.
24. Each member of the group knows all other members by their first names.
25. Members are in daily contact either outside or within the group.
26. Members of the group are personal friends.
27. Certain members discuss personal affairs among themselves.
28. Members of the group know the family backgrounds of other members of the group.
29. Members address each other by their first names.
30. The group is made up of individuals who do not know each other well.
31. The opinions of all members are considered as equal.
32. The group's officers hold a higher status in the group than other members.
33. The older members of the group are granted special privileges.
34. The group is controlled by the actions of a few members.
35. Every member of the group enjoys the same group privileges.
36. Experienced members are in charge of the group.
37. Certain problems are discussed only among the group's officers.
38. Certain members have more influence on the group than others.
39. Each member of the group has as much power as any other member.
40. An individual's standing in the group is determined only by how much he gets done.
41. Certain members of the group hold definite office in the group.
42. The original members of the group are given special privileges.
43. Personal dissatisfaction with the group is too small to be brought up.
44. Members continually grumble about the work they do for the group.
45. The group does its work with no great vim, vigor, or pleasure.
46. A feeling of failure prevails in the group.
47. There are frequent intervals of laughter during group meetings.
48. The group works independently of other groups.
49. The group has support from outside.
50. The group is an active representative of a larger group.
51. The group's activities are influenced by a larger group of which it is a part.

52. People outside the group decide on what work the group is to do.
53. The group follows the examples set by other groups.
54. The group is one of many similar groups that form one large organization.
55. The things the group does are approved by a group higher up.
56. The group joins with other groups in carrying out its activities.
57. The group is a small part of a larger group.
58. The group is under outside pressure.
59. Members are disciplined by an outside group.
60. Plans of the group are made by other groups above it.
61. The members allow nothing to interfere with the progress of the group.
62. Members gain a feeling of being honored by being recognized as one of the group.
63. Membership in the group is a way of acquiring general social status.
64. Failure of the group would mean little to individual members.
65. The activities of the group take up less than ten percent of each member's waking time.
66. Members gain in prestige among outsiders by joining the group.
67. A mistake by one member of the group might result in hardship for all.
68. The activities of the group take up over ninety percent of each member's waking time.
69. Membership in the group serves as an aid to vocational advancement.
70. Failure of the group would mean nothing to most members.
71. Each member would lose his self-respect if the group should fail.
72. Membership in the group gives members a feeling of superiority.
73. The activities of the group take up over half the time each member is awake.
74. Failure of the group would lead to embarrassment for members.
75. Members are not rewarded for effort put out for the group.
76. There are two or three members of the group who generally take the same side on any group issue.
77. Certain members are hostile to other members.
78. There is constant bickering among members of the group.
79. Members know that each one looks out for the other one as well as for himself.
80. Certain members of the group have no respect for other members.
81. Certain members of the group are considered uncooperative.
82. There is a constant tendency toward conniving against one another among parts of the group.

83. Members of the group work together as a team.
84. Certain members of the group are responsible for petty quarrels and some animosity among other members.
85. There are tensions among subgroups that tend to interfere with the group's activities.
86. Certain members appear to be incapable of working as part of the group.
87. There is an undercurrent of feeling among members that tends to pull the group apart.
88. Anyone who has sufficient interest in the group to attend its meetings is considered a member.
89. The group engages in membership drives.
90. New members are welcomed to the group on the basis "the more the merrier."
91. A new member may join only after an old member resigns.
92. A college degree is required for membership in the group.
93. A person may enter the group by expressing a desire to join.
94. Anyone desiring to enter the group is welcome.
95. Membership is open to anyone willing to further the purpose of the group.
96. Prospective members are carefully examined before they enter the group.
97. No applicants for membership in the group are turned down.
98. No special training is required for membership in the group.
99. Membership depends upon the amount of education an individual has.
100. People interested in joining the group are asked to submit references which are checked.
101. There is a high degree of participation on the part of members.
102. If a member of the group is not productive he is not encouraged to remain.
103. Work of the group is left to those who are considered most capable for the job.
104. Members are interested in the group but not all of them want to work.
105. The group has a reputation for not getting much done.
106. Each member of the group is on one or more active committees.
107. The work of the group is well divided among members.
108. Every member of the group does not have a job to do.
109. The work of the group is frequently interrupted by having nothing to do.
110. There are long periods during which the group does nothing.

111. The group is directed toward one particular goal.
112. The group divides its efforts among several purposes.
113. The group operates with sets of conflicting plans.
114. The group has only one main purpose.
115. The group knows exactly what it has to get done.
116. The group is working toward many different goals.
117. The group does many things that are not directly related to its main purpose.
118. Each member of the group has a clear idea of the group's goals.
119. The objective of the group is specific.
120. Certain members meet for one thing and others for a different thing.
121. The group has major purposes which to some degree are in conflict.
122. The objectives of the group have never been clearly recognized.
123. The group is very informal.
124. A list of rules and regulations is given to each member.
125. The group has meetings at regularly scheduled times.
126. The group is organized along semimilitary lines.
127. The group's meetings are not planned or organized.
128. The group has an organization chart.
129. The group has rules to guide its activities.
130. The group is staffed according to a table of organization.
131. The group keeps a list of names of members.
132. Group meetings are conducted according to "Robert's Rules of Order."
133. There is a recognized right and wrong way of going about group activities.
134. Most matters that come up before the group are voted upon.
135. The group meets at any place that happens to be handy.
136. The members of the group vary in amount of ambition.
137. Members of the group are from the same social class.
138. Some members are interested in altogether different things than other members.
139. The group contains members with widely varying backgrounds.
140. The group contains whites and Negroes.
141. Members of the group are all about the same ages.
142. A few members of the group have greater ability than others.
143. A number of religious beliefs are represented by members of the group.
144. Members of the group vary greatly in social background.
145. All members of the group are of the same sex.
146. The ages of members range over a period of at least 20 years.

147. Members come into the group with quite different family backgrounds.
148. Members of the group vary widely in amount of experience.
149. Members vary in the number of years they have been in the group.
150. The group includes members of different races.

SCORING KEY AND DIRECTIONS FOR SCORING

A subject's score for a particular dimension is the sum of the item scores for that dimension. For example, the raw score for the dimension "Control" is the sum of the scores for items 1 to 12 inclusive. The total (raw) score for this dimension can range from 12 to 60.

Occasionally a respondent may fail to indicate his answer. Such omissions are scored as C responses (neither true nor false). However, if the number of omitted items exceeds half the total number of items assigned to a given dimension, no score for that dimension is assigned. In general, experience has shown that few respondents deliberately omit items.

The answers are marked on a separate answer sheet (IBM Answer Sheet No. 1100 A 3870). A separate blank answer sheet may be used for preparing a scoring key for each dimension.

Control	A	B	C	D	E
1	5	4	3	2	1
2	5	4	3	2	1
3	5	4	3	2	1
4	1	2	3	4	5
5	5	4	3	2	1
6	5	4	3	2	1
7	5	4	3	2	1
8	1	2	3	4	5
9	5	4	3	2	1
10	5	4	3	2	1
11	5	4	3	2	1
12	5	4	3	2	1

Stability	A	B	C	D	E
13	1	2	3	4	5
14	1	2	3	4	5
15	1	2	3	4	5
16	1	2	3	4	5
17	5	4	3	2	1

Intimacy	A	B	C	D	E
18	5	4	3	2	1
19	5	4	3	2	1
20	5	4	3	2	1
21	1	2	3	4	5
22	5	4	3	2	1
23	5	4	3	2	1
24	5	4	3	2	1
25	5	4	3	2	1
26	5	4	3	2	1
27	5	4	3	2	1
28	5	4	3	2	1
29	5	4	3	2	1
30	1	2	3	4	5

Stratification	A	B	C	D	E
31	1	2	3	4	5
32	5	4	3	2	1
33	5	4	3	2	1
34	5	4	3	2	1
35	1	2	3	4	5
36	5	4	3	2	1
37	5	4	3	2	1
38	5	4	3	2	1

Stratification	A	B	C	D	E
39	1	2	3	4	5
40	5	4	3	2	1
41	5	4	3	2	1
42	5	4	3	2	1

Hedonic Tone	A	B	C	D	E
43	5	4	3	2	1
44	1	2	3	4	5
45	1	2	3	4	5
46	1	2	3	4	5
47	5	4	3	2	1

Autonomy	A	B	C	D	E
48	5	4	3	2	1
49	1	2	3	4	5
50	1	2	3	4	5
51	1	2	3	4	5
52	1	2	3	4	5
53	1	2	3	4	5
54	1	2	3	4	5
55	1	2	3	4	5
56	1	2	3	4	5
57	1	2	3	4	5
58	1	2	3	4	5
59	1	2	3	4	5
60	1	2	3	4	5

Potency	A	B	C	D	E
61	5	4	3	2	1
62	5	4	3	2	1
63	5	4	3	2	1
64	1	2	3	4	5
65	1	2	3	4	5
66	5	4	3	2	1
67	5	4	3	2	1
68	5	4	3	2	1
69	5	4	3	2	1
70	1	2	3	4	5
71	5	4	3	2	1
72	5	4	3	2	1
73	5	4	3	2	1
74	5	4	3	2	1
75	1	2	3	4	5

Viscidity	A	B	C	D	E
76	1	2	3	4	5
77	1	2	3	4	5
78	1	2	3	4	5
79	5	4	3	2	1
80	1	2	3	4	5
81	1	2	3	4	5
82	1	2	3	4	5
83	5	4	3	2	1
84	1	2	3	4	5
85	1	2	3	4	5
86	1	2	3	4	5
87	1	2	3	4	5

Polarization	A	B	C	D	E
111	5	4	3	2	1
112	1	2	3	4	5
113	1	2	3	4	5
114	5	4	3	2	1
115	5	4	3	2	1
116	1	2	3	4	5
117	1	2	3	4	5
118	5	4	3	2	1
119	5	4	3	2	1
120	1	2	3	4	5
121	1	2	3	4	5
122	1	2	3	4	5

Permeability	A	B	C	D	E
88	5	4	3	2	1
89	5	4	3	2	1
90	5	4	3	2	1
91	1	2	3	4	5
92	1	2	3	4	5
93	5	4	3	2	1
94	5	4	3	2	1
95	5	4	3	2	1
96	1	2	3	4	5
97	5	4	3	2	1
98	5	4	3	2	1
99	1	2	3	4	5
100	1	2	3	4	5

Flexibility	A	B	C	D	E
123	5	4	3	2	1
124	1	2	3	4	5
125	1	2	3	4	5
126	1	2	3	4	5
127	5	4	3	2	1
128	1	2	3	4	5
129	1	2	3	4	5
130	1	2	3	4	5
131	1	2	3	4	5
132	1	2	3	4	5
133	1	2	3	4	5
134	1	2	3	4	5
135	5	4	3	2	1

Participation	A	B	C	D	E
101	5	4	3	2	1
102	5	4	3	2	1
103	1	2	3	4	5
104	1	2	3	4	5
105	1	2	3	4	5
106	5	4	3	2	1
107	5	4	3	2	1
108	1	2	3	4	5
109	1	2	3	4	5
110	1	2	3	4	5

Homogeneity	A	B	C	D	E
136	5	4	3	2	1
137	1	2	3	4	5
138	1	2	3	4	5
139	1	2	3	4	5
140	1	2	3	4	5
141	5	4	3	2	1
142	1	2	3	4	5
143	1	2	3	4	5
144	1	2	3	4	5
145	5	4	3	2	1
146	1	2	3	4	5
147	1	2	3	4	5
148	1	2	3	4	5
149	1	2	3	4	5
150	1	2	3	4	5

GROUP DIMENSIONS PROFILE AND FACE SHEET

Name _____ Age _____ Date _____

Name of group _____

Length of your membership _____ No. of group members _____

General purpose of the group _____

Dimension		Stanine Score								
		1	2	3	4	5	6	7	8	9
A	Autonomy	.	.	.	.	.	.	.	.	.
B	Control	.	.	.	.	.	.	.	.	.
C	Flexibility	.	.	.	.	.	.	.	.	.
D	Hedonic Tone	.	.	.	.	.	.	.	.	.
E	Homogeneity	.	.	.	.	.	.	.	.	.
F	Intimacy	.	.	.	.	.	.	.	.	.
G	Participation	.	.	.	.	.	.	.	.	.
H	Permeability	.	.	.	.	.	.	.	.	.
I	Polarization	.	.	.	.	.	.	.	.	.
J	Potency	.	.	.	.	.	.	.	.	.
K	Stability	.	.	.	.	.	.	.	.	.
L	Stratification	.	.	.	.	.	.	.	.	.
M	Viscidity	.	.	.	.	.	.	.	.	.

IV.B.2. INDEX: BALES'S INTERACTION PROCESS ANALYSIS

VARIABLE MEASURED: Group interaction.

DESCRIPTION: This index consists of twelve categories—shows solidarity, shows tension release, agrees, gives suggestion, gives opinion, gives orientation, asks for orientation, asks for opinion, asks for suggestion, disagrees, shows tension, shows antagonism. Scoring is made by designating each person in the group with a number. All interaction is analyzed according to the category and marked in the fashion of 1-5 or 1-0 as the interaction takes place. After observation a summary or profile can be constructed and inferences made to describe the underlying workings of the group.

WHERE PUBLISHED: R. F. Bales, *Interaction Process Analysis: A Method for the Study of Small Groups* (Cambridge, Mass.: Addison-Wesley, 1950). Cf. John Madge, *The Origins of Scientific Sociology* (New York: Free Press, 1967), pp. 424-477.

RELIABILITY: With competent and trained observers an inter-observer correlation of between .75 and .95 can be obtained.

VALIDITY: Face validity.

UTILITY: A general purpose, standard set of categories well suited for the observation and analysis of small groups. The chief disadvantage is that the training of observers requires long practice. Frequent retraining is also necessary.

RESEARCH APPLICATIONS:
BORGATTA, EDGAR F. "The Analysis of Patterns of Social Interaction," *Social Forces,* 44 (September, 1965), 27-34.
HARE, PAUL A. *Handbook of Small Group Research.* Glencoe, Ill.: Free Press, 1963.
HARE, PAUL A., BORGATTA, EDGAR F., and BALES, ROBERT F. (eds.). *Small Groups: Studies in Social Interaction.* Rev. ed. New York: Alfred A. Knopf, Inc., 1965. See the bibliography of small group research.
O'ROURKE, JOHN F. "Field and Laboratory: The Decision Making Behavior of Family Groups in Two Experimental Conditions," *Sociometry,* 26 (December, 1963), 422-435.

1	SHOWS SOLIDARITY, raises other's status, gives help, reward:				
2	SHOWS TENSION RELEASE, jokes, laughs, shows satisfaction:				
3	AGREES, shows passive acceptance, understands, concurs, complies:				
4	GIVES SUGGESTION, direction, implying autonomy for other:				
5	GIVES OPINION, evaluation, analysis, expresses feeling, wish:				
6	GIVES ORIENTATION, information, repeats, clarifies, confirms:				
7	ASKS FOR ORIENTATION, information, repetition, confirmation:				
8	ASKS FOR OPINION, evaluation, analysis, expression of feeling:				
9	ASKS FOR SUGGESTION, direction, possible ways of action:				
10	DISAGREES, shows passive rejection, formality, withholds help:				
11	SHOWS TENSION, asks for help, withdraws "Out of Field":				
12	SHOWS ANTAGONISM, deflates other's status, defends or asserts self:				

PERCENT: 0

Prepared for use with
Interaction Process Analysis
by Robert F. Bales
PRINTED IN U.S.A.

INTERACTION SCORING FOR

Published by
ADDISON-WESLEY PRESS, INC.
Cambridge M

Group _____

Date _____

Observer _____

IV.B.3. INDEX: SEASHORE'S GROUP COHESIVENESS INDEX

VARIABLE MEASURED: The index measures group cohesiveness, defined as attraction to the group or resistance to leaving.

DESCRIPTION: The test consists of three questions: "Do you feel that you are really a part of your work group?" "If you had a chance to do the same kind of work for the same pay, in another work group, how would you feel about moving?" and "How does your work group compare with other work groups at Midwest on each of the following points?"—The way the men get along together, the way the men stick together, and the way the men help each other on the job. The first two questions can be answered by five degrees, while the three items of the third question are answered by four degrees.

WHERE PUBLISHED: Stanley E. Seashore, *Group Cohesiveness in the Industrial Work Group* (Ann Arbor: Survey Research Center, Institute for Social Research, University of Michigan, 1954).

RELIABILITY: Intercorrelations among mean scale values for the groups on scales comprising the index of cohesiveness ranged from .15 to .70.

VALIDITY: The variance found between groups on this scale was significant beyond the .001 level.

UTILITY: As the questions are phrased, the index is especially set up for an industrial situation. It can probably, with a few changes, be adapted to almost any situation where an index of group cohesiveness is required. The test takes very little time to administer. The subject should be assured that his replies will be kept confidential.

RESEARCH APPLICATIONS: The study of 228 section-shift groups in a company manufacturing heavy machinery, described in the aforementioned Seashore article.

INDEX OF GROUP COHESIVENESS

"Do you feel that you are really a part of your work group?"

- ☐ Really a part of my work group
- ☐ Included in most ways
- ☐ Included in some ways, but not in others
- ☐ Don't feel I really belong
- ☐ Don't work with any one group of people
    - ☐ Not Ascertained

"If you had a chance to do the same kind of work for the same pay, in another work group, how would you feel about moving?"

- ☐ Would want very much to move
- ☐ Would rather move than stay where I am
- ☐ Would make no difference to me
- ☐ Would rather stay where I am than move
- ☐ Would want very much to stay where I am
    - ☐ Not Ascertained

"How does your work group compare with other work groups at Midwest on each of the following points?"

	Better than most	About the same as most	Not as good as most	Not ascertained
The way the men get along together	☐	☐	☐	☐
The way the men stick together	☐	☐	☐	☐
The way the men help each other on the job	☐	☐	☐	☐

IV.B.4. INDEX: SOCIOMETRY SCALES OF SOCIOMETRIC CHOICE AND SOCIOMETRIC PREFERENCE

VARIABLE MEASURED: The degree to which individuals are accepted in a group, interpersonal relationships that exist among individuals, and structure of the group.

DESCRIPTION: Results are most satisfactory for small cohesive groups. The sociometric technique consists of asking each individual in a group to state with whom among the members of the group he would prefer to associate for specific activities or in particular situations. Criteria (selected areas that should include different aspects of possible association: work, play, visiting) range in number from 1 to 8 or more; and choices, from 1 to as many as desired by the researcher.

WHERE PUBLISHED: J. L. Moreno, *Who Shall Survive?* (Beacon, N.Y.: Beacon House, 1934).

RELIABILITY:

Loeb's correlation between odd-even items	$r = .65$ to $.85$
Loeb's correlation between split-halves	$r = .53$ to $.85$
Mary L. Northway between general criteria	$r = .64$ to $.84$
Mary L. Northway between skill criteria	$r = .37$ to $.50$

Correlations between scores on tests given at different times $r = .74$
Constancy of choice (actual preference on 1st test repeated later on) $r = .69$

VALIDITY: Eugene Byrd comparison of sociometric choice with actual choice and then an 8-week interval retest shows $r = .76, .80, .89$. See Eugene Byrd, "A Study of Validity and Constancy of Choices in a Sociometric Test," *Sociometry*, 9 (1946), 21.

N. Gronlund comparison of judgment of teachers vs. testing shows $r = .59$. See N. Gronlund, *Accuracies of Teachers' Judgments Concerning the Sociometric Status of Sixth Grade Pupils*, Sociometry Monograph No. 25 (Beacon, N.Y.: Beacon House, 1951.)

For discussion of reliability and validity, see Mary L. Northway, *A Primer of Sociometry* (Toronto: University of Toronto, 1952), pp. 16-20. Also cf. Merl E. Bonney, "A Study of Constancy of Sociometric Ranks Among College Students Over a Two-Year Period," *Sociometry*, 18 (December, 1955), 531-542.

STANDARD SCORES: None.

RESEARCH APPLICATIONS:

BRONFENBRENNER, URIE. *The Measurement of Sociometric Status, Structure and Development*, Sociometry Monograph No. 6. Beacon, N.Y.: Beacon House, Inc., 1945.

JACOBS, JOHN H. "The Application of Sociometry to Industry," *Sociometry*, 8 (May, 1945), 181-198.

JENNINGS, HELEN H. *Leadership and Isolation: A Study of Personality in Interpersonal Relations*. 2nd ed. New York: David McKay Company, Inc., 1950.

LUNDBERG, GEORGE A., and DICKSON, LENORE. "Inter-Ethnic Relations in a High School Population," *American Journal of Sociology*, 57 (July, 1952), 1-10.

MASSARIK, FRED, TANNENBAUM, ROBERT, RAHANE, MURRAY, and WESCHLER, IRVING. "Sociometric Choice and Organizational Effectiveness: A Multi-Relational Approach," *Sociometry* (August, 1953), 211-238; or see MASSARIK, FRED, *et al. Leadership and Organization*. New York: McGraw-Hill Book Company, 1961, pp. 346-370.

MORENO, J. L. *Who Shall Survive? A New Approach to the Problem of Human Relationships*. Beacon, N.Y.: Beacon House, Inc., 1934; see also MORENO, J. L. *Sociometry and the Science of Man*. Beacon, N.Y.: Beacon House, Inc., 1956.

WHITE, HARRISON. "Management Conflict and Sociometric Structure," *American Journal of Sociology*, 67 (September, 1961), 185-199.

ZELENY, LESLIE D. "Selection of Compatible Flying Partners," *American Journal of Sociology*, 52 (March, 1947), 424-431.

For an excellent review of the literature on "Measures of Sociometric Structure" see M. Glanzer and R. Glaser, "Techniques for the Study of Group Structure and Behavior: I. Analysis of Structure," *Psychological Bulletin*, 56 (September, 1959), 317-332. Cf. J. L. Moreno, "Contributions of Sociometry to Research Methodology in Sociology," *American Sociological Review*, 12 (June, 1947), 287-292; Jacob L. Moreno, *et al.*, *The Sociometry Reader* (Glencoe, Ill.: Free Press, 1959).

SPONTANEOUS CHOICE TEST

Opposite each name check how you feel about persons in your group.

	Like	Dislike	Indifferent
Mary J.			
James F.			
John J.			
Etc.			

SOCIOMETRIC PREFERENCE TEST

Choose five persons you would most like to work with.* Mark 1st, 2nd, 3rd, 4th, 5th choice.

Mary J.	
James F.	
John J.	
Sam E.	
Etc.	

* Many criteria may be employed. For example, to have in a discussion group, to have in your neighborhood, to play bridge with, to work on a project with, etc.

IV.B.5. INDEX: BOGARDUS SOCIAL DISTANCE SCALE

VARIABLE MEASURED: The social distance or degree of social acceptance that exists between given persons and certain social groups. The scale may be adapted to measure the social distance between two persons or between two or more social groups. The method has been applied to racial distance, regional distance, sex distance, age distance, parent-child distance, educational distance, class distance, occupational distance, religious distance, international distance.

DESCRIPTION: Typically, a group of persons are asked to rank a series of social types with respect to the degrees of social distance on seven attributes starting with *acceptance to close kinship by marriage* and concluding with *would exclude from my country.* One hundred persons acting as judges have identified these seven attributes among 60 as those ordered on a continuant of social distance.

WHERE PUBLISHED: Best source is Emory S. Bogardus, *Social Distance* (Yellow Springs, Ohio: Antioch Press, 1959); Emory S. Bogardus, *Immigration and Race Attitudes* (Boston, Heath, 1928); E. S. Bogardus, "A Social Distance Scale," *Sociology and Social Research,* XVII (January-February, 1933), 265-271. Excellent instructions may be found in William J. Goode and Paul K. Hatt, *Methods in Social Research* (New York: McGraw-Hill, 1952), pp. 26, 245-249.

RELIABILITY: Split-half reliability coefficient reported at .90 or higher in repeated tests by Eugene L. Hartley and Ruth E. Hartley.

VALIDITY: Theodore Newcomb reports high validity if we use "agreement with other scales that in certain particulars are more exact." Application of the known-group method is advocated in determination of validity. This involves finding groups known to be favorable toward some of the ethnic types and unfavorable toward others. If the responses of these groups fit the requisite pattern, evidence for validity may be accepted. For full discussion see E. S. Bogardus, *Social Distance* (Yellow Springs, Ohio: Antioch Press, 1959), pp. 92-95.

SCORING: A variety of scoring methods has been used. A simple method that has been found to be as reliable as the more complex ones is that of counting the numbers of the "nearest column" that is checked. That is, if the racial distance quotient, *RDQ,* of a number of persons is desired, then the arithmetic mean of the total number of the "nearest columns" that are checked by all the subjects for each race is obtained. If the *RDQ* of a person is sought, then the arithmetic mean of the total numbers of the "nearest column" for each race is obtained.

STANDARD SCORES: Racial Distance Quotients Given Racial Groups in 1956 by 2,053 selected persons throughout the United States.

1.	Americans (U.S. White)	1.08
2.	Canadians	1.16
3.	English	1.23
4.	French	1.47
5.	Irish	1.56
6.	Swedish	1.57
7.	Scots	1.60
8.	Germans	1.61
9.	Hollanders	1.63
10.	Norwegians	1.56
11.	Finns	1.80
12.	Italians	1.89
13.	Poles	2.07
14.	Spanish	2.08
15.	Greeks	2.09
16.	Jews	2.15
17.	Czechs	2.22
18.	Armenians	2.33
19.	Japanese Americans	2.34
20.	Indians (American)	2.35
21.	Filipinos	2.46
22.	Mexican Americans	2.51
23.	Turks	2.52
24.	Russians	2.56
25.	Chinese	2.68
26.	Japanese	2.70
27.	Negroes	2.74
28.	Mexicans	2.79
29.	Indians (from India)	2.80
30.	Koreans	2.83

Arithmetic Mean of 61,590 Racial Reactions 2.08.

UTILITY: The Bogardus Scale may be used to estimate the amount of potential and real conflict existing between any cultural groups, anywhere in the industrial, political, racial, religious, and other phases of life. It also helps to determine the extent of the trend toward conflict or toward cooperation between groups. The test is easy to administer and to score. It can be adapted easily to other problems of social distance.

A good illustration of such an adaptation is to be found in the Mock Table for a Scale to Measure the Attractiveness of Different Communities. See William J. Goode and Paul K. Hatt, *Methods in Social Research* (New York: McGraw-Hill, 1952), p. 248. The fullest description of applications is to be found in Emory S. Bogardus, *Social Distance* (Yellow Springs, Ohio: Antioch Press, 1959).

RESEARCH APPLICATIONS:

BARBER, BERNARD. *Social Stratification*. New York: Harcourt, Brace and Company, Inc., 1957.

BARDIS, PANOS D. "Social Distance among Foreign Students," *Sociology and Social Research*, 41, 112-115.

————. "Social Distance in a Greek Metropolitan City," *Social Science*, 37 (April, 1962), 108-111.

BEST, W. H., and SOHNER, C. P. "Social Distance Methodology in the Measurement of Political Attitudes," *Sociology and Social Research*, 40, 266-270.

————. "Social Distance and Politics," *Sociology and Social Research*, 40, 339-342.

BIESANZ, J., and BIESANZ, M. "Social Distance in the Youth Hostel Movement," *Sociology and Social Research*, 25, 237-245.

BINNEWIES, W. G. "A Method of Studying Rural Social Distance," *Sociology and Social Research*, 10, 239-242.

BOGARDUS, EMORY S. *Sociometry*, X, 306-311; *International Journal of Opinion and Attitude Research*, I, 55-62; *American Sociological Review*, 16, 48-53; *Journal of Educational Sociology*, 3, 497-502; *Survey Graphic*, IX, 169-170, 206, 208; *Journal of Applied Sociology*, 9, 216-226; *Sociology and Social Research*, 12, 173-178; 13, 73-81; 13, 171-175; 14, 174-180; 17, 167-173; 17, 265-271; 18, 67-73; 20, 473-477; 22, 462-476; 24, 69-75; 32, 723-727; 32, 798-802; 32, 882-887; 33, 291-295; 36, 40-47; 43, 439-441; *The Urban Community*. Edited by E. W. Burgess. Chicago: The University of Chicago Press, 1927, pp. 48-54.

BRADWAY, JOHN S. "Social Distance Between Lawyers and Social Workers," *Sociology and Social Research*, 14, 516-524.

BRIGGS, ARTHUR E. "Social Distance Between Lawyers and Doctors," *Sociology and Social Research*, 13, 156-163.

BROOKS, LEE M. "Racial Distance as Affected by Education," *Sociology and Social Research*, 21, 128-133.

CAMPBELL, DONALD T. "The Bogardus Social Distance Scale," *Sociology and Social Research*, 36, 322-325.

CATAPUSAN, BENICIO T. "Social Distance in the Philippines," *Sociology and Social Research*, 38, 309-312.

DODD, STUART C. "A Social Distance Test in the Near East," *American Journal of Sociology*, XLI (September, 1935), 194-204.

———, and NEHNEVAJSA, J. "Physical Dimensions of Social Distance," *Sociology and Social Research*, 38, 287-292.

DUNCAN, W. L. "Parent-Child Isolations," *The Family*, 10, 115-118.

DUVALL, EVERETT W. "Child-Parent Social Distance," *Sociology and Social Research*, 21, 458-463.

EISENSTADT, S. N. *From Generation to Generation: Age Groups and the Social Structure*. Glencoe, Ill.: The Free Press, 1956.

ELLEFSEN, J. B. "Social Distance Attitudes of Negro College Students," *Phylon*, 17, 79-83.

ELLIS, ROBERT A. "Social Status and Social Distance," *Sociology and Social Research*, 40, 240-246.

FRANKLIN, CLAY. "The Effect of the Format Upon the Scale Values of the Bogardus Social Distance Scale," *Research Studies of the State College of Washington*, 18, 117-120.

GLEASON, GEORGE. "Social Distance in Russia," *Sociology and Social Research*, 17, 37-43.

GRACE, H. A., and NEUHAUS, J. O. "Information and Social Distance as Predictors of Hostility Toward Nations," *Journal of Abnormal and Social Psychology*, 47 (1952), 540-545.

GREIFER, JULIAN L. "Attitudes to the Stranger," *American Sociological Review*, 10 (December, 1945), 739-745.

GURNEE, H., and BAKER, E. "Social Distances of Some Common Social Relationships," *Journal of Abnormal and Social Psychology*, 33 (1938), 265-269.

HALBWACHS, M. *The Psychology of Social Classes*. Glencoe, Ill.: The Free Press, 1958.

HAMREN, VANDYCE. "Social Farness Between the A.F. of L. and the C.I.O.," *Sociology and Social Research*, 24, 442-452.

———. "Social Nearness Between the A.F. of L. and the C.I.O.," *Sociology and Social Research*, 26, 232-240.

HARTLEY, EUGENE L. *Problems in Prejudice*. New York: Columbia University Press, 1946.

———, and HARTLEY, RUTH E. *Fundamentals of Social Psychology*. New York: Alfred A. Knopf, Inc., 1952. Pp. 431-443.

HUNT, CHESTER L. "Social Distance in the Philippines," *Sociology and Social Research*, 40, 253-260.

HYPES, E. L. "The Social Distance Score Card as a Teaching Device," *Social Forces*, 7 (December, 1928), 234-237.

JAMESON, S. H. "Social Distance between Welfare Organizations," *Sociology and Social Research*, 5, 230-243.

———. "Social Nearness among Welfare Organizations," *Sociology and Social Research*, 15, 322-333.

KAHL, JOSEPH A. *The American Class Structure*. New York: Rinehart & Company, Inc., 1957.

KOCH, H. L. "Study of Some Factors Conditioning the Social Distance between the Sexes," *Journal of Social Psychology*, 20, 79-107.

KROUT, M. H. "Periodic Change in Social Distance; A Study in the Shifting Bases of Perception," *Sociology and Social Research*, 27, 339-351.

LAMBERT, W. E. "Comparison of French and American Modes of Response to the Bogardus Social Distance Scale," *Social Forces*, 31, 155-160.

McDONAGH, EDWARD C. "Social Distance between China and Japan," *Sociology and Social Research*, 22, 131-136.

———. "Asiatic Stereotypes and National Distance," *Sociology and Social Research*, 22, 474-478.

———. "Military Social Distance," *Sociology and Social Research*, 29, 289-296.

McKENZIE, R. D. "Spatial Distance and Community Organization Pattern," *Social Forces*, 5, 623-627.

———. "Spatial Distance," *Sociology and Social Research*, 13, 536-544.

McMATH, ELLA M. "A Girl without a Country," *Journal of Applied Sociology*, 11, 65-71.

MARTIN, R. R. "Sudden Change in Social Distance," *Sociology and Social Research*, 22, 53-56.

MITCHELL, ROY. "An Ethnic Distance Study in Buffalo," *Sociology and Social Research*, 40, 35-40.

MOWRER, E. R. *Domestic Discord*. Chicago: The University of Chicago Press, 1928. Ch. III.

NEPRASH, J. A. "Minority Group Contacts and Social Distance," *Phylon*, 14, 207-212.

NEWCOMB, THEODORE M. *Social Psychology*, rev. ed., New York: Holt, Rinehart & Winston, Inc., 1955. Pp. 154-175.

NIMKOFF, M. F. "Parent-Child Conflict," *Sociology and Social Research*, 12, 446-458.

————. "Parent-Child Conflict," *Sociology and Social Research*, 14, 135-150.

NORTH, C. C. *Social Differentiation*. Chapel Hill: University of North Carolina Press, 1926.

OWEN, JOHN E. "Social Distance in England," *Sociology and Social Research*, 30, 460-465.

PARISH, HELEN R. "Social Nearness between Latin America and the United States," *Sociology and Social Research*, 19, 253-258.

PARK, R. E. "The Concept of Social Distance," *Journal of Applied Sociology*, 8, 339-344.

PETTIGREW, THOMAS F. "Social Distance Attitudes of South African Students," *Social Forces*, 38 (March, 1960), 246-253.

POOLE, W. C. JR. "Distance in Sociology," *American Journal of Sociology*, 33, 99-104.

————. "Social Distance and Social Pathology," *Sociology and Social Research*, 12, 268-272.

————. "Social Distance and Personal Distance," *Journal of Applied Sociology*, 11, 114-120.

————. "The Social Distance Margin Reviewed," *Sociology and Social Research*, 13, 49-54.

————, and POOLE, HARRIET K. "Laws of Social Distance," *Journal of Applied Sociology*, 11, 365-369.

PROTHRO, E. T., and MILES, O. K. "Social Distance in the Deep South as Measured by a Revised Bogardus Scale," *Journal of Social Psychology*, 37, 171-174.

RUNNER, JESSIE R. "Social Distance in Adolescent Relationships," *American Journal of Sociology*, 43, 428-439.

SARTAIN, A. I., and BELL, HAROLD V., JR. "An Evaluation of the Bogardus Scale of Social Distance by the Method of Equal-Appearing Intervals," *Journal of Social Psychology*, 29, 85-91.

SARVIS, GUY W. "Social Distance in Religion," *The Christian Century*, 49, 1331-1333.

SCHENK, Q. F., and ROMNEY, A. K. "Some Differential Attitudes among Adolescent Groups as Revealed by Bogardus' Social Distance Scale," *Sociology and Social Research*, 35, 38-45.

SCHNETZ, ALFRED. "The Stranger," *The American Journal of Sociology*, 49, 499-508.

SCHROFF, RUTH. "Charting Social Distance," *Sociology and Social Research*, 14, 567-570.

SEYMOUR, J. G. "Rural Social Distance of Normal School Students," *Sociology and Social Research*, 14, 238-248.

SHERIF, MUZAFER, and SHERIF, CAROLYN W. *An Outline of Social*

Psychology. New York: Harper & Brothers, Inc., 1956. Pp. 659-678.

SHIDELER, ERNEST. "The Social Distance Margin," *Sociology and Social Research,* 12, 243-252.

SOROKIN, P. *Social Mobiilty.* New York: Harper & Brothers, Inc., 1927. Ch. VI, "Occupational Stratification."

STEPHENSON, C. M., and WILCOX, CAROL G. "Social Distance Variations of College Students," *Sociology and Social Research,* 39, 240-241.

TURBEVILLE, GUS. "A Social Distance Study of Duluth, Minnesota," *Sociology and Social Research,* 18, 420-430.

VAN DER BERGHE, PIERRE L. "Distance Mechanisms of Stratification," *Sociology and Social Research,* 44 (January-February, 1960), 155-164.

WESTIE, F. R. "Negro-White Status Differentials and Social Distance," *American Sociological Review,* 17 (October, 1952), 550-558.

WESTIE, FRANK R., and WESTIE, MARGARET L. "The Social Distance Pyramid: Relationships between Caste and Class," *Ameriacn Journal of Sociology,* 63, 190-196.

————. "Social Distance Scales, a Tool for the Study of Stratification," *Sociology and Social Research,* 43, 251-258.

WOOD, MARGARET MARY. *Paths of Loneliness.* New York: Columbia University Press, 1953.

ZELIGS, ROSE, and HENDRICKSON, G. "Checking the Social Distance Technique through Personal Interviews," *Sociology and Social Research,* 18, 420-430.

ZIEGLER, GEORGE H. "Social Farness between Hindus and Moslems," *Sociology and Social Research,* 33, 188-195.

Interesting adaptations of the social distance scale are found in:

DeFLEUR, M. L., and WESTIE, FRANK R. "Verbal Attitudes and Overt Acts: An Experiment on the Salience of Attitudes," *American Sociological Review,* 23 (December, 1958), 667-673.

JACKSON, ELTON F. "Status Consistency and Symptoms of Stress," *American Sociological Review,* 27 (August, 1962), 469-480.

LONGWORTHY, RUSSELL L. "Community Status and Influence in a High School," *American Sociological Review,* 24 (August, 1959), 537-539.

MARTIN, JAMES G., and WESTIE, FRANK R. "The Tolerant Personality," *American Sociological Review,* 24 (August, 1959), 521-528.

PHOTIADIS, JOHN D., and BIGGAR, JEANNE. "Religiosity, Education, and Ethnic Distance," *American Journal of Sociology,* 67 (May, 1962), 666-673.

PHOTIADIS, JOHN D., and JOHNSON, ARTHUR L. "Orthodoxy, Church Participation, and Authoritarianism," *American Journal of Sociology*, 69 (November, 1963), 244-248.

WESTIE, FRANK R. "A Technique for the Measurement of Race Attitudes," *American Sociological Review*, 18 (February, 1953), 73-78.

BOGARDUS RACIAL DISTANCE SCALE

(Race is defined here largely as a cultural group.)

1. Remember to give your *first feeling reactions* in every case.
2. Give your reactions to each race as a *group*. Do not give your reactions to the best or to the worst members that you have known, but think of the picture or stereotype that you have of the whole race.
3. Put a cross after each race in as many of the seven rows as your feelings dictate.

Category	English	Swedes	Poles	Koreans	Etc.
1. To close kinship by marriage					
2. To my club as personal chums					
3. To my street as neighbors					
4. To employment in my occupation					
5. To citizenship in my country					
6. As visitors only to my country					
7. Would exclude from my country					

SECTION C

Morale and Job Satisfaction

Morale has been viewed as a global concept and also as a set of specific dimensions. The Minnesota (Rundquist-Sletto) Survey of Opinions (General Adjustment and Morale Scales) is a Likert-type scale that was carefully constructed to tap a general variable. Use the Short Form of the Minnesota Scale of General Adjustment and Morale when the problem calls for an overall assessment of morale. Use the Long Form to assess specific attitudes toward personal inferiority, family, law, conservatism, and education, in addition to morale and general adjustment.

Many social scientists believe that morale is a meaningful concept only when the separate dimensions of morale have been identified. Scale analysis has shown repeatedly that morale is composed of many dimensions. The S.R.A. Employee Morale Inventory is a diagnostic tool that was constructed by including dimensions of job morale. This is the most widely used instrument for diagnosis of employee morale problems. Item analysis was used in its construction. Use the S.R.A. Employee Morale Inventory if you are seeking to diagnose morale problems in work organizations. Norms are available that make possible departmental and interorganizational comparisons. This is probably the best standardized of all sociometric scales.

Nancy Morse and associates have constructed a set of subscales to measure intrinsic job satisfaction, pride in performance, company involvement, and financial and job status. Use the Morse Scales if short scales are needed to tap these dimensions.

Guttman type scales insure that the factor in the scale has been demonstrated to be of one dimension only in the respondent population. The military morale scales are of this type, the reproducibility coefficients providing evidence for the response pattern. Use these scales for military or organizational research of any kind by substituting appropriate units in place of Air Force, Air Site, and Air Craft and Warning Stations (A.C.&W.). Check scalability by Guttman methods for your respondents. The probability is high that these items will scale for any respondent sample to which they would logically apply.

The Brayfield and Rothe Index of Job Satisfaction has been constructed by applying Thurstone's Method of Equal-Appearing Intervals and combining Likert's scoring system that gives an intensity measure. This scale fits two important criteria: a continuum of interval measures and an intensity measure. Use the Brayfield and Rothe Index when a precise general measure of job satisfaction is desired.

IV.C.1(a). INDEX: SHORT FORM OF THE MINNESOTA SURVEY OF OPINIONS (GENERAL ADJUSTMENT AND MORALE SCALES)

VARIABLE MEASURED: Individual morale and general adjustment.

DESCRIPTION: This short form is taken from the Minnesota Scale for the Survey of Opinions that consists of 132 items. The short form consists of only 31 of the most discriminating items. These items are taken from the seven scales that make up the Minnesota Scale for the Survey of Opinions. These scales are the morale scale, the general adjustment scale, inferiority scale, family scale, law scale, conservatism, and education scale.

WHERE PUBLISHED: Edward A. Rundquist and Raymond F. Sletto, *Personality in the Depression,* Child Welfare Monograph Series No. 12 (Minneapolis: University of Minnesota). Copyright 1936 by the University of Minnesota.

RELIABILITY: Split-half reliability in the .80s may be expected for the adjustment *score* and the total morale *score*. Split-half reliability coefficients for the general adjustment *scale* range from .686 to .821 with high school seniors as the lowest correlation and an all male group as the highest correlation. The females on the same basis range from .686 to .836. Reliability of actual scores from test to retest was measured over a sixty-day period. The average changes were 4.03 for 68 General College men and 5 03 for 68 General College women. Test-retest *r*'s are .793 for men and .668 for women.

VALIDITY: Validity for the general adjustment scale was determined by two general methods: (1) relating it to those outside variables that imply maladjustment and (2) relating it to scores on the other six scales. An extensive report of validity is included in Rundquist and Sletto, *Personality in the Depression,* pp. 226-241.

UTILITY: This short form is presented to assist those who may wish to obtain a measure of general adjustment and morale without administering the entire survey. It consists of only 31 items in the questionnaire and can be administered in 15 to 20 minutes. There are 16 items in the general adjustment scale and 22 items in the morale scale, both scales included in the 31 item survey. The Long Form of the Survey takes 30 to 40 minutes.

RESEARCH APPLICATIONS:

MILLER, D. C. "Morale of College Trained Adults," *American Sociological Review,* 5 (December, 1940), 880-889.

————. "Economic Factors in the Morale of College Trained Adults," *American Journal of Sociology,* 47 (September, 1941), 139-157.

SCORING INSTRUCTIONS FOR THE SHORT FORM MINNESOTA SCALE FOR THE SURVEY OF OPINIONS

Administration

The survey requires between 15 and 20 minutes for all to complete it. Although the printed directions on the survey are self-explanatory, it is advisable to read the directions aloud while the subjects are reading them silently. To secure frankness and cooperation, it is well to assure the group that their opinions are valued, will be held in complete confidence, and will not affect their grades in any course or their standing with their employers or other persons of responsibility. They may be directed to fill in all the information items (name, age, sex, etc.) or to omit those that the examiner does not require for research or counseling purposes.

Scoring

The five alternative responses to each item are weighted from 1 to 5 in scoring. The sum of the scores in the extreme lefthand column is the adjustment score; the sum of the next column is the score on the acceptable morale items; the sum of the next is the score on the unacceptable morale items. To obtain the total morale score, add the total scores on acceptable and unacceptable items.

Norms

The scoring norms in the table permit conversion of raw scores into standard scores. These norms are based on the scores of 1,000 young people, 500 of each sex. The standardization group included 400 college students, 200 high school seniors, and 400 youth employed and unemployed persons in continuation classes at high school level. The distribution of paternal occupation for the standardization group approximated the census distribution of occupations and indicates that it is composed of a fairly representative sample of young persons between the ages of sixteen and twenty-five years. No significant differences between the scores of high school and college students were found, and the norms are adequate for both groups.

The standard scores given in the table were obtained by the McCall T-Score technique, which expresses scores in tenths of standard deviation units from the mean score for the standardization group. *The mean raw score of the standardization group becomes the standard score of 50.* A standard score of 60 is one standard deviation higher than the mean; a standard score of 40 is one standard deviation below the mean. Response weights to items have been so assigned that a high standard score is unfavorable.

To illustrate the use of the table, suppose an individual makes the same raw scores—say 57—on the morale, economic conservatism, and education scales. We find 57 in the raw score column. Reading to the right, we observe that the individual's standard scores are 50 on the morale scale, 40 on the economic conservatism scale, and 60 on the education scale. These scores indicate that the individual is average, that he is conservative in his economic views (one standard deviation below the mean), and that his estimate of the value of education is relatively unfavorable (one standard deviation above the mean).

Standard Score Equivalents for Raw Scores
(*Based on Standardization Group of 1,000*)

Raw Score	M	I	F	L	EC	E	GA	Raw Score	M	I	F	L	EC	E	GA
110								62	55	46	55	53	45	65	78
109					91			61	54	45	54	52	44	64	77
108					90			60	53	44	53	51	43	63	76
107					89										
106					88			59	52	43	52	50	42	62	74
105					87			58	51	42	51	49	41	61	73
104					86			57	50	41	51	48	40	60	72
103					85			56	49	40	50	47	39	59	70
102			92		84			55	48	39	49	46	38	58	69
101		86	91		83			54	47	37	48	45	37	57	68
100		85	90		82			53	46	36	47	44	36	56	66
								52	45	35	46	43	35	55	65
99		84	89		81			51	43	34	45	42	34	54	64
98		83	88		80			50	42	33	44	41	33	53	62
97		82	87		79										
96		81	86		78			49	41	32	43	39	32	52	61
95	90	80	85		77			48	40	31	42	38	31	51	60
94	89	79	84		76			47	39	30	41	37	30	49	58
93	88	78	84		75			46	38	29	40	36	29	48	57
92	87	77	83		74			45	37	28	40	35	28	47	56
91	86	76	82		73	96		44	36	27	39	34	27	46	54
90	85	75	81	84	72	95		43	35	26	38	33	26	45	53
								42	34	25	37	32	25	44	52
89	83	74	80	82	71	94		41	33	24	36	31	24	43	50
88	82	73	79	81	70	93		40	32	23	35	30	23	42	49
87	81	72	78	80	69	92									
86	80	71	77	79	68	90		39	31	22	34	29	22	41	48
85	79	70	76	78	67	89		38	30	21	33	28	21	40	47
84	78	68	75	77	66	88		37	29	20	32	27	20	39	45
83	77	67	74	76	65	87		36	28	19	31	26	19	38	44
82	76	66	73	75	64	86		35	27	18	30	24	18	37	43
81	75	65	73	74	63	85		34	26	17	29	23	17	36	41
80	74	64	72	73	62	84		33	25	16	29	22	16	35	40
								32	23	15	28	21	15	34	39
79	73	63	71	72	61	83		31	22	14	27	20	14	33	37
78	72	62	70	71	60	82		30	21	13	26	19	13	32	36
77	71	61	69	70	59	81									
76	70	60	68	69	58	80		29	20	12	25	18	12	31	35
75	69	59	67	67	57	79		28	19	11	24	17	11	30	33
74	68	58	66	66	56	78		27	18	10	23	16	10	28	32
73	67	57	65	65	56	77		26	17	9	22	15	9	27	31
72	66	56	64	64	55	76		25						26	29
71	65	55	63	63	54	75		24						25	28
70	63	54	62	62	53	74	89	23						24	27
								22						23	25
69	62	53	62	61	52	73	87	21							24
68	61	52	61	60	51	72	86	20							23
67	60	51	60	59	50	71	85								
66	59	50	59	58	49	69	83	19							21
65	58	49	58	57	48	68	82	18							20
64	57	48	57	56	47	67	81	17							19
63	56	47	56	55	46	66	79	16							17

* M–Morale; I–Inferiority; F–Family; L–Law; EC–Economic Conservatism; GA–General Adjustment.

MINNESOTA SURVEY OF OPINION (SHORT FORM)

E. A. Rundquist and R. F. Sletto, Institute of Child Welfare,
University of Minnesota

Name _____ Age _____ Sex _____ Date _____
       (Last)   (First)

The following pages contain a number of statements about which
there is no general agreement. People differ widely in the way they feel
about each item. There are no right answers. The purpose of the survey
is to see how different groups feel about each item. We should like your
honest opinion on each of these statements.

READ EACH ITEM CAREFULLY AND UNDERLINE QUICKLY
THE PHRASE THAT BEST EXPRESSES YOUR FEELING ABOUT
THE STATEMENT. Wherever possible, let your own personal experience determine your answer. Do not spend much time on any item.
If in doubt, underline the phrase that seems most nearly to express your
present feeling about the statement. WORK RAPIDLY. Be sure to
answer every item.

1. TIMES ARE GETTING BETTER.
   Strongly agree [1] Agree [2] Undecided [3]
   Disagree [4] Strongly disagree [5]

2. ANY MAN WITH ABILITY AND WILLING-
   NESS TO WORK HARD HAS A GOOD
   CHANCE OF BEING SUCCESSFUL.
   Strongly agree [1] Agree [2] Undecided [3]
   Disagree [4] Strongly disagree [5]

3. IT IS DIFFICULT TO SAY THE RIGHT
   THING AT THE RIGHT TIME.
   Strongly agree [5] Agree [4] Undecided [3]
   Disagree [2] Strongly disagree [1]

4. MOST PEOPLE CAN BE TRUSTED.
   Strongly agree [1] Agree [2] Undecided [3]
   Disagree [4] Strongly disagree [5]

5. HIGH SCHOOLS ARE TOO IMPRACTICAL.
   Strongly agree [5]   Agree [4]   Undecided [3]
   Disagree [2]   Strongly disagree [1]

6. A PERSON CAN PLAN HIS FUTURE SO THAT EVERYTHING WILL COME OUT ALL RIGHT IN THE LONG RUN.
   Strongly agree [1]   Agree [2]   Undecided [3]
   Disagree [4]   Strongly disagree [5]

7. NO ONE CARES MUCH WHAT HAPPENS TO YOU.
   Strongly agree [5]   Agree [4]   Undecided [3]
   Disagree [2]   Strongly disagree [1]

8. SUCCESS IS MORE DEPENDENT ON LUCK THAN ON REAL ABILITY.
   Strongly agree [5]   Agree [4]   Undecided [3]
   Disagree [2]   Strongly disagree [1]

9. IF OUR ECONOMIC SYSTEM WERE JUST, THERE WOULD BE MUCH LESS CRIME.
   Strongly agree [5]   Agree [4]   Undecided [3]
   Disagree [2]   Strongly disagree [1]

10. A MAN DOES NOT HAVE TO PRETEND HE IS SMARTER THAN HE REALLY IS TO "GET BY."
    Strongly agree [1]   Agree [2]   Undecided [3]
    Disagree [4]   Strongly disagree [5]

11. LAWS ARE SO OFTEN MADE FOR THE BENEFIT OF SMALL SELFISH GROUPS THAT A MAN CANNOT RESPECT THE LAW.
    Strongly agree [5]   Agree [4]   Undecided [3]
    Disagree [2]   Strongly disagree [1]

12. ONE SELDOM WORRIES SO MUCH AS TO BECOME VERY MISERABLE.
    Strongly agree [1]   Agree [2]   Undecided [3]
    Disagree [4]   Strongly disagree [5]

13. THE FUTURE LOOKS VERY BLACK.
    Strongly agree [5]   Agree [4]   Undecided [3]
    Disagree [2]   Strongly disagree [1]

14. REAL FRIENDS ARE AS EASY TO FIND AS EVER.
Strongly agree [1]   Agree [2]   Undecided [3]
_____   Disagree [4]   Strongly disagree [5]

15. POVERTY IS CHIEFLY A RESULT OF IN-JUSTICE IN THE DISTRIBUTION OF WEALTH.
Strongly agree [5]   Agree [4]   Undecided [3]
_____   Disagree [2]   Strongly disagree [1]

16. IT IS DIFFICULT TO THINK CLEARLY THESE DAYS.
Strongly agree [5]   Agree [4]   Undecided [3]
_____   Disagree [2]   Strongly disagree [1]

17. THERE IS LITTLE CHANCE FOR AD-VANCEMENT IN INDUSTRY AND BUSI-NESS UNLESS A MAN HAS UNFAIR PULL.
Strongly agree [5]   Agree [4]   Undecided [3]
_____   _____   Disagree [2]   Strongly disagree [1]

18. IT DOES NOT TAKE LONG TO GET OVER FEELING GLOOMY.
Strongly agree [1]   Agree [2]   Undecided [3]
_____   Disagree [4]   Strongly disagree [5]

19. THE YOUNG MAN OF TODAY CAN EX-PECT MUCH OF THE FUTURE.
Strongly agree [1]   Agree [2]   Undecided [3]
_____   _____   Disagree [4]   Strongly disagree [5]

20. IT IS GREAT TO BE LIVING IN THESE EXCITING TIMES.
Strongly agree [1]   Agree [2]   Undecided [3]
_____   Disagree [4]   Strongly disagree [5]

21. LIFE IS JUST ONE WORRY AFTER AN-OTHER.
Strongly agree [5]   Agree [4]   Undecided [3]
_____   _____   Disagree [2]   Strongly disagree [1]

22. THE DAY IS NOT LONG ENOUGH TO DO ONE'S WORK WELL AND HAVE ANY TIME FOR FUN.
Strongly agree [5]   Agree [4]   Undecided [3]
_____   Disagree [2]   Strongly disagree [1]

23. A MAN CAN LEARN MORE BY WORKING FOUR YEARS THAN BY GOING TO HIGH SCHOOL.
Strongly agree ^{5} Agree ^{4} Undecided ^{3}
Disagree ^{2} Strongly disagree ^{1}

24. THIS GENERATION WILL PROBABLY NEVER SEE SUCH HARD TIMES AGAIN.
Strongly agree ^{1} Agree ^{2} Undecided ^{3}
Disagree ^{4} Strongly disagree ^{5}

25. ONE CANNOT FIND AS MUCH UNDERSTANDING AT HOME AS ELSEWHERE.
Strongly agree ^{5} Agree ^{4} Undecided ^{3}
Disagree ^{2} Strongly disagree ^{1}

26. THESE DAYS ONE IS INCLINED TO GIVE UP HOPE OF AMOUNTING TO SOMETHING.
Strongly agree ^{5} Agree ^{4} Undecided ^{3}
Disagree ^{2} Strongly disagree ^{1}

27. EDUCATION IS OF NO HELP IN GETTING A JOB TODAY.
Strongly agree ^{5} Agree ^{4} Undecided ^{3}
Disagree ^{2} Strongly disagree ^{1}

28. THERE IS REALLY NO POINT IN LIVING.
Strongly agree ^{5} Agree ^{4} Undecided ^{3}
Disagree ^{2} Strongly disagree ^{1}

29. MOST PEOPLE JUST PRETEND THAT THEY LIKE YOU.
Strongly agree ^{5} Agree ^{4} Undecided ^{3}
Disagree ^{2} Strongly disagree ^{1}

30. THE FUTURE IS TOO UNCERTAIN FOR A PERSON TO PLAN ON MARRYING.
Strongly agree ^{5} Agree ^{4} Undecided ^{3}
Disagree ^{2} Strongly disagree ^{1}

31. LIFE IS JUST A SERIES OF DISAPPOINTMENTS.
Strongly agree ^{5} Agree ^{4} Undecided ^{3}
Disagree ^{2} Strongly disagree ^{1}

GA   Ma   Mu   Ma + Mu = Total Morale Score

IV.C.1.b. Index: Long Form of the Minnesota Survey of Opinions *

DIRECTIONS

READ EACH ITEM CAREFULLY AND UNDERLINE QUICKLY THE PHRASE THAT BEST EXPRESSES YOUR FEELING ABOUT THE STATEMENT. WORK RAPIDLY. BE SURE TO ANSWER EVERY ITEM.

1. THE FUTURE IS TOO UNCERTAIN FOR A PERSON TO PLAN ON MARRYING.
   Strongly agree ^{5} Agree ^{4} Undecided ^{3} Disagree ^{2}
   Strongly disagree ^{1} **(M)**

2. AFTER BEING CAUGHT IN A MISTAKE, IT IS HARD TO DO GOOD WORK FOR A WHILE.
   Strongly agree ^{5} Agree ^{4} Undecided ^{3} Disagree ^{2}
   Strongly disagree ^{1} **(I)**

3. HOME IS THE MOST PLEASANT PLACE IN THE WORLD.
   Strongly agree ^{1} Agree ^{2} Undecided ^{3} Disagree ^{4}
   Strongly disagree ^{5} **(F)**

4. THE LAW PROTECTS PROPERTY RIGHTS AT THE EXPENSE OF HUMAN RIGHTS.
   Strongly agree ^{5} Agree ^{4} Undecided ^{3} Disagree ^{2}
   Strongly disagree ^{1} **(L)**

5. THE GOVERNMENT SHOULD TAKE OVER ALL LARGE INDUSTRIES.
   Strongly agree ^{5} Agree ^{4} Undecided ^{3} Disagree ^{2}
   Strongly disagree ^{1} **(EC)**

6. A MAN CAN LEARN MORE BY WORKING FOUR YEARS THAN BY GOING TO HIGH SCHOOL.
   Strongly agree ^{5} Agree ^{4} Undecided ^{3} Disagree ^{2}
   Strongly disagree ^{1} **(E)**

* Containing the Scales of General Adjustment, Morale, Inferiority, Family, Law, Conservatism, and Education. For scoring, see E. A. Rundquist and R. F. Sletto, as cited, p. 385. Add numbers given by response. Norms are shown above. Items marked *M* are in Morale Scale; *I* items are in Inferiority Scale; *F* items, Family Scale; *L* items, Law Scale; *EC,* Economic Conservatism Scale; *E,* Education Scale.

7. IT IS DIFFICULT TO THINK CLEARLY THESE DAYS.
Strongly agree [5]   Agree [4]   Undecided [3]   Disagree [2]
Strongly disagree [1]   **(M)**

8. IT IS EASY TO EXPRESS ONE'S IDEAS.
Strongly agree [1]   Agree [2]   Undecided [3]   Disagree [4]
Strongly disagree [5]   **(I)**

9. PARENTS EXPECT TOO MUCH FROM THEIR CHILDREN.
Strongly agree [5]   Agree [4]   Undecided [3]   Disagree [2]
Strongly disagree [1]   **(F)**

10. A PERSON SHOULD OBEY ONLY THOSE LAWS THAT SEEM REASONABLE.
Strongly agree [5]   Agree [4]   Undecided [3]   Disagree [2]
Strongly disagree [1]   **(L)**

11. LABOR SHOULD OBEY ONLY THOSE LAWS THAT SEEM REASONABLE.
Strongly agree [5]   Agree [4]   Undecided [3]   Disagree [2]
Strongly disagree [1]   **(EC)**

12. THE MORE EDUCATION A MAN HAS THE BETTER HE IS ABLE TO ENJOY LIFE.
Strongly agree [1]   Agree [2]   Undecided [3]   Disagree [4]
Strongly disagree [5]   **(E)**

13. THE FUTURE LOOKS VERY BLACK.
Strongly agree [5]   Agree [4]   Undecided [3]   Disagree [2]
Strongly disagree [1]   **(M)**

14. IT IS DIFFICULT TO SAY THE RIGHT THING AT THE RIGHT TIME.
Strongly agree [5]   Agree [4]   Undecided [3]   Disagree [2]
Strongly disagree [1]   **(I)**

15. ONE OUGHT TO DISCUSS IMPORTANT PLANS WITH MEMBERS OF HIS FAMILY.
Strongly agree [1]   Agree [2]   Undecided [3]   Disagree [4]
Strongly disagree [5]   **(F)**

16. IT IS ALL RIGHT TO EVADE THE LAW IF YOU DO NOT ACTUALLY VIOLATE IT.
Strongly agree [5]   Agree [4]   Undecided [3]   Disagree [2]
Strongly disagree [1]   **(L)**

17. LEGISLATURES ARE TOO READY TO PASS LAWS TO CURB BUSINESS FREEDOM.
Strongly agree [1]   Agree [2]   Undecided [3]   Disagree [4]
Strongly disagree [5]   **(EC)**

18. EDUCATION HELPS A PERSON TO USE HIS LEISURE
TIME TO BETTER ADVANTAGE.
Strongly agree [1]   Agree [2]   Undecided [3]   Disagree [4]
Strongly disagree [5]   (E)

19. LIFE IS JUST ONE WORRY AFTER ANOTHER.
Strongly agree [5]   Agree [4]   Undecided [3]   Disagree [2]
Strongly disagree [1]   (M)

20. ONE CAN USUALLY KEEP COOL IN IMPORTANT SITU-
ATIONS.
Strongly agree [1]   Agree [2]   Undecided [3]   Disagree [4]
Strongly disagree [5]   (I)

21. IN PLANS FOR THE FUTURE, PARENTS SHOULD BE
GIVEN FIRST CONSIDERATION.
Strongly agree [1]   Agree [2]   Undecided [3]   Disagree [4]
Strongly disagree [5]   (F)

22. THE SENTENCES OF JUDGES IN COURTS ARE DETER-
MINED BY THEIR PREJUDICES.
Strongly agree [5]   Agree [4]   Undecided [3]   Disagree [2]
Strongly disagree [1]   (L)

23. FOR MEN TO DO THEIR BEST, THERE MUST BE THE
POSSIBILITY OF UNLIMITED PROFIT.
Strongly agree [1]   Agree [2]   Undecided [3]   Disagree [4]
Strongly disagree [5]   (EC)

24. A GOOD EDUCATION IS A GREAT COMFORT TO A MAN
OUT OF WORK.
Strongly agree [1]   Agree [2]   Undecided [3]   Disagree [4]
Strongly disagree [5]   (E)

25. MOST PEOPLE CAN BE TRUSTED.
Strongly agree [1]   Agree [2]   Undecided [3]   Disagree [4]
Strongly disagree [5]   (M)

26. IT IS EASY TO GET ONE'S OWN WAY IN MOST SITU-
ATIONS.
Strongly agree [1]   Agree [2]   Undecided [3]   Disagree [4]
Strongly disagree [5]   (I)

27. A MAN SHOULD BE WILLING TO SACRIFICE EVERY-
THING FOR HIS FAMILY.
Strongly agree [1]   Agree [2]   Undecided [3]   Disagree [4]
Strongly disagree [5]   (F)

28. ON THE WHOLE, JUDGES ARE HONEST.
Strongly agree [1]   Agree [2]   Undecided [3]   Disagree [4]
Strongly disagree [5]   (L)

29. POVERTY IS CHIEFLY A RESULT OF INJUSTICE IN THE DISTRIBUTION OF WEALTH.
Strongly agree [5]   Agree [4]   Undecided [3]   Disagree [2]
Strongly disagree [1]   **(EC)**

30. ONLY SUBJECTS LIKE READING, WRITING, AND ARITHMETIC SHOULD BE TAUGHT AT PUBLIC EXPENSE.
Strongly agree [5]   Agree [4]   Undecided [3]   Disagree [2]
Strongly disagree [1]   **(E)**

31. TIMES ARE GETTING BETTER.
Strongly agree [1]   Agree [2]   Undecided [3]   Disagree [4]
Strongly disagree [5]   **(M)**

32. IT IS EASY TO HAVE A GOOD TIME AT A PARTY.
Strongly agree [1]   Agree [2]   Undecided [3]   Disagree [4]
Strongly disagree [5]   **(I)**

33. PARENTS TOO OFTEN EXPECT THEIR GROWN-UP CHILDREN TO OBEY THEM.
Strongly agree [5]   Agree [4]   Undecided [3]   Disagree [2]
Strongly disagree [1]   **(F)**

34. JURIES SELDOM UNDERSTAND A CASE WELL ENOUGH TO MAKE A REALLY JUST DECISION.
Strongly agree [5]   Agree [4]   Undecided [3]   Disagree [2]
Strongly disagree [1]   **(L)**

35. THE GOVERNMENT SHOULD NOT ATTEMPT TO LIMIT PROFITS.
Strongly agree [1]   Agree [2]   Undecided [3]   Disagree [4]
Strongly disagree [5]   **(EC)**

36. EDUCATION IS OF NO HELP IN GETTING A JOB TODAY.
Strongly agree [5]   Agree [4]   Undecided [3]   Disagree [2]
Strongly disagree [1]   **(E)**

37. IT DOES NOT TAKE LONG TO GET OVER FEELING GLOOMY.
Strongly agree [1]   Agree [2]   Undecided [3]   Disagree [4]
Strongly disagree [5]   **(M)**

38. MEETING NEW PEOPLE IS USUALLY EMBARRASSING.
Strongly agree [5]   Agree [4]   Undecided [3]   Disagree [2]
Strongly disagree [1]   **(I)**

39. ONE CANNOT FIND AS MUCH UNDERSTANDING AT HOME AS ELSEWHERE.
Strongly agree [5]   Agree [4]   Undecided [3]   Disagree [2]
Strongly disagree [1]   **(F)**

40. ON THE WHOLE, POLICEMEN ARE HONEST.
    Strongly agree [1] Agree [2] Undecided [3] Disagree [4]
    Strongly disagree [5]   **(L)**

41. THE MORE A MAN LEARNS ABOUT OUR ECONOMIC
    SYSTEM, THE LESS WILLING HE IS TO SEE CHANGES
    MADE.
    Strongly agree [1] Agree [2] Undecided [3] Disagree [4]
    Strongly disagree [5]   **(EC)**

42. MOST YOUNG PEOPLE ARE GETTING TOO MUCH
    EDUCATION.
    Strongly agree [5] Agree [4] Undecided [3] Disagree [2]
    Strongly disagree [1]   **(E)**

43. THE DAY IS NOT LONG ENOUGH TO DO ONE'S WORK
    WELL AND HAVE ANY TIME FOR FUN.
    Strongly agree [5] Agree [4] Undecided [3] Disagree [2]
    Strongly disagree [1]   **(M)**

44. IT IS EASY TO KEEP UP ONE'S COURAGE.
    Strongly agree [1] Agree [2] Undecided [3] Disagree [4]
    Strongly disagree [5]   **(I)**

45. ONE OWES HIS GREATEST OBLIGATION TO HIS FAMILY.
    Strongly agree [1] Agree [2] Undecided [3] Disagree [4]
    Strongly disagree [5]   **(F)**

46. A MAN SHOULD OBEY THE LAWS NO MATTER HOW
    MUCH THEY INTERFERE WITH HIS PERSONAL AM-
    BITIONS.
    Strongly agree [1] Agree [2] Undecided [3] Disagree [4]
    Strongly disagree [5]   **(L)**

47. THE GOVERNMENT OUGHT TO GUARANTEE A LIVING
    TO THOSE WHO CANNOT FIND WORK.
    Strongly agree [5] Agree [4] Undecided [3] Disagree [2]
    Strongly disagree [1]   **(EC)**

48. A HIGH SCHOOL EDUCATION IS WORTH ALL THE TIME
    AND EFFORT IT REQUIRES.
    Strongly agree [1] Agree [2] Undecided [3] Disagree [4]
    Strongly disagree [5]   **(E)**

49. NO ONE CARES MUCH WHAT HAPPENS TO YOU.
    Strongly agree [5] Agree [4] Undecided [3] Disagree [2]
    Strongly disagree [1]   **(M)**

50. IT IS EASY TO IGNORE CRITICISM.
    Strongly agree [1] Agree [2] Undecided [3] Disagree [4]
    Strongly disagree [5]   **(I)**

51. IT IS HARD TO KEEP A PLEASANT DISPOSITION AT HOME.
Strongly agree [5]   Agree [4]   Undecided [3]   Disagree [2]
Strongly disagree [1]   **(F)**

52. COURT DECISIONS ARE ALMOST ALWAYS JUST.
Strongly agree [1]   Agree [2]   Undecided [3]   Disagree [4]
Strongly disagree [5]   **(L)**

53. LARGE INCOMES SHOULD BE TAXED MUCH MORE THAN THEY ARE NOW.
Strongly agree [5]   Agree [4]   Undecided [3]   Disagree [2]
Strongly disagree [1]   **(EC)**

54. OUR SCHOOLS ENCOURAGE AN INDIVIDUAL TO THINK FOR HIMELF.
Strongly agree [1]   Agree [2]   Undecided [3]   Disagree [4]
Strongly disagree [5]   **(E)**

55. ANY MAN WITH ABILITY AND WILLINGNESS TO WORK HARD HAS A GOOD CHANCE OF BEING SUCCESSFUL.
Strongly agree [1]   Agree [2]   Undecided [3]   Disagree [4]
Strongly disagree [5]   **(M)**

56. IT IS EASY TO ACT NATURALLY IN A GROUP.
Strongly agree [1]   Agree [2]   Undecided [3]   Disagree [4]
Strongly disagree [5]   **(I)**

57. PEOPLE IN THE FAMILY CAN BE TRUSTED COMPLETELY.
Strongly agree [1]   Agree [2]   Undecided [3]   Disagree [4]
Strongly disagree [5]   **(F)**

58. IN THE COURTS A POOR MAN WILL RECEIVE AS FAIR TREATMENT AS A MILLIONAIRE.
Strongly agree [1]   Agree [2]   Undecided [3]   Disagree [4]
Strongly disagree [5]   **(L)**

59. MEN WOULD NOT DO THEIR BEST, IF GOVERNMENT OWNED ALL INDUSTRY.
Strongly agree [1]   Agree [2]   Undecided [3]   Disagree [4]
Strongly disagree [5]   **(EC)**

60. THERE ARE TOO MANY FADS AND FRILLS IN MODERN EDUCATION.
Strongly agree [5]   Agree [4]   Undecided [3]   Disagree [2]
Strongly disagree [1]   **(E)**

61. IT IS GREAT TO BE LIVING IN THESE EXCITING TIMES.
Strongly agree [1]   Agree [2]   Undecided [3]   Disagree [4]
Strongly disagree [5]   **(M)**

62. IT IS HARD TO BRING ONESELF TO CONFIDE IN OTHERS.
Strongly agree [1]   Agree [2]   Undecided [3]   Disagree [4]
Strongly disagree [5]   **(I)**

63. ONE BECOMES NERVOUS AT HOME.
Strongly agree [5]   Agree [4]   Undecided [3]   Disagree [2]
Strongly disagree [1]   **(F)**

64. PERSONAL CIRCUMSTANCES SHOULD NEVER BE CON-SIDERED AN EXCUSE FOR LAWBREAKING.
Strongly agree [1]   Agree [2]   Undecided [3]   Disagree [4]
Strongly disagree [5]   **(L)**

65. MOST GREAT FORTUNES ARE MADE HONESTLY.
Strongly agree [1]   Agree [2]   Undecided [3]   Disagree [4]
Strongly disagree [5]   **(EC)**

66. EDUCATION ONLY MAKES A PERSON DISCONTENTED.
Strongly agree [5]   Agree [4]   Undecided [3]   Disagree [2]
Strongly disagree [1]   **(E)**

67. THESE DAYS ONE IS INCLINED TO GIVE UP HOPE OF AMOUNTING TO SOMETHING.
Strongly agree [5]   Agree [4]   Undecided [3]   Disagree [2]
Strongly disagree [1]   **(M)**

68. IT IS HARD TO DO YOUR BEST WHEN PEOPLE ARE WATCHING YOU.
Strongly agree [5]   Agree [4]   Undecided [3]   Disagree [2]
Strongly disagree [1]   **(I)**

69. THE JOYS OF FAMILY LIFE ARE MUCH OVERRATED.
Strongly agree [5]   Agree [4]   Undecided [3]   Disagree [2]
Strongly disagree [1]   **(F)**

70. A MAN SHOULD TELL THE TRUTH IN COURT, REGARD-LESS OF CONSEQUENCES.
Strongly agree [1]   Agree [2]   Undecided [3]   Disagree [4]
Strongly disagree [5]   **(L)**

71. PRIVATE OWNERSHIP OF PROPERTY IS NECESSARY FOR ECONOMIC PROGRESS.
Strongly agree [1]   Agree [2]   Undecided [3]   Disagree [4]
Strongly disagree [5]   **(EC)**

72. SCHOOL TRAINING IS OF LITTLE HELP IN MEETING THE PROBLEMS OF REAL LIFE.
Strongly agree [5]   Agree [4]   Undecided [3]   Disagree [2]
Strongly disagree [1]   **(E)**

73. THERE IS LITTLE CHANCE FOR ADVANCEMENT IN INDUSTRY AND BUSINESS UNLESS A MAN HAS UNFAIR PULL.
Strongly agree [5]   Agree [4]   Undecided [3]   Disagree [2]
Strongly disagree [1]   **(M)**

74. IT IS EASY TO GET ALONG WITH PEOPLE.
Strongly agree [1]   Agree [2]   Undecided [3]   Disagree [4]
Strongly disagree [5]   **(I)**

75. ONE'S PARENTS USUALLY TREAT HIM FAIRLY AND SENSIBLY.
Strongly agree [1]   Agree [2]   Undecided [3]   Disagree [4]
Strongly disagree [5]   **(F)**

76. A PERSON WHO REPORTS MINOR LAW VIOLATIONS IS ONLY A TROUBLEMAKER.
Strongly agree [5]   Agree [4]   Undecided [3]   Disagree [2]
Strongly disagree [1]   **(L)**

77. WITHOUT SWEEPING CHANGES IN OUR ECONOMIC SYSTEM, LITTLE PROGRESS CAN BE MADE IN THE SOLUTION OF SOCIAL PROBLEMS.
Strongly agree [5]   Agree [4]   Undecided [3]   Disagree [2]
Strongly disagree [1]   **(EC)**

78. EDUCATION TENDS TO MAKE AN INDIVIDUAL LESS CONCEITED.
Strongly agree [1]   Agree [2]   Undecided [3]   Disagree [4]
Strongly disagree [5]   **(E)**

79. THE YOUNG MAN OF TODAY CAN EXPECT MUCH OF THE FUTURE.
Strongly agree [1]   Agree [2]   Undecided [3]   Disagree [4]
Strongly disagree [5]   **(M)**

80. IT IS EASY TO FEEL AS THOUGH YOU HAD A WORLD OF SELF-CONFIDENCE.
Strongly agree [1]   Agree [2]   Undecided [3]   Disagree [4]
Strongly disagree [5]   **(I)**

81. ONE SHOULD CONFIDE MORE FULLY IN MEMBERS OF HIS FAMILY.
Strongly agree [1]   Agree [2]   Undecided [3]   Disagree [4]
Strongly disagree [5]   **(F)**

82. A PERSON IS JUSTIFIED IN GIVING FALSE TESTIMONY TO PROTECT A FRIEND ON TRIAL.
Strongly agree [5]   Agree [4]   Undecided [3]   Disagree [2]
Strongly disagree [1]   **(L)**

83. ON THE WHOLE, OUR ECONOMIC SYSTEM IS JUST AND WISE.
Strongly agree [1]   Agree [2]   Undecided [3]   Disagree [4]
Strongly disagree [5]   **(EC)**

84. SOLUTION OF THE WORLD'S PROBLEMS WILL COME THROUGH EDUCATION.
Strongly agree [1]   Agree [2]   Undecided [3]   Disagree [4]
Strongly disagree [5]   **(E)**

85. THIS GENERATION WILL PROBABLY NEVER SEE SUCH HARD TIMES AGAIN.
Strongly agree [1]   Agree [2]   Undecided [3]   Disagree [4]
Strongly disagree [5]   **(M)**

86. MOST PEOPLE JUST PRETEND THAT THEY LIKE YOU.
Strongly agree [5]   Agree [4]   Undecided [3]   Disagree [2]
Strongly disagree [1]   **(I)**

87. ONE FEELS MOST CONTENTED AT HOME.
Strongly agree [1]   Agree [2]   Undecided [3]   Disagree [4]
Strongly disagree [5]   **(F)**

88. A HUNGRY MAN HAS A RIGHT TO STEAL.
Strongly agree [5]   Agree [4]   Undecided [3]   Disagree [2]
Strongly disagree [1]   **(L)**

89. LABOR DOES NOT GET ITS FAIR SHARE OF WHAT IT PRODUCES.
Strongly agree [5]   Agree [4]   Undecided [3]   Disagree [2]
Strongly disagree [1]   **(EC)**

90. HIGH SCHOOL COURSES ARE TOO IMPRACTICAL.
Strongly agree [5]   Agree [4]   Undecided [3]   Disagree [2]
Strongly disagree [1]   **(E)**

91. REAL FRIENDS ARE AS EASY TO FIND AS EVER.
Strongly agree [1]   Agree [2]   Undecided [3]   Disagree [4]
Strongly disagree [5]   **(M)**

92. SO MANY PEOPLE DO THINGS WELL THAT IT IS EASY TO BECOME DISCOURAGED.
Strongly agree [5]   Agree [4]   Undecided [3]   Disagree [2]
Strongly disagree [1]   **(I)**

93. FAMILY TIES ARE STRENGTHENED WHEN TIMES ARE HARD.
Strongly agree [1]   Agree [2]   Undecided [3]   Disagree [4]
Strongly disagree [5]   **(F)**

94. ALL LAWS SHOULD BE STRICTLY OBEYED BECAUSE THEY *ARE* LAWS.
Strongly agree [1]   Agree [2]   Undecided [3]   Disagree [4]
Strongly disagree [5]   **(L)**

95. WHEN A RICH MAN DIES, MOST OF HIS PROPERTY SHOULD GO TO THE STATE.
Strongly agree [5]   Agree [4]   Undecided [3]   Disagree [2]
Strongly disagree [1]   **(EC)**

96. A MAN IS FOOLISH TO KEEP ON GOING TO SCHOOL IF HE CAN GET A JOB.
Strongly agree [5]   Agree [4]   Undecided [3]   Disagree [2]
Strongly disagree [1]   **(E)**

97. LIFE IS JUST A SERIES OF DISAPPOINTMENTS.
Strongly agree [5]   Agree [4]   Undecided [3]   Disagree [2]
Strongly disagree [1]   **(M)**

98. IT IS HARD NOT TO BE SELF-CONSCIOUS.
Strongly agree [5]   Agree [4]   Undecided [3]   Disagree [2]
Strongly disagree [1]   **(I)**

99. PARENTS ARE INCLINED TO BE TOO OLD-FASHIONED IN THEIR IDEAS.
Strongly agree [5]   Agree [4]   Undecided [3]   Disagree [2]
Strongly disagree [1]   **(F)**

100. LAWS ARE SO OFTEN MADE FOR THE BENEFIT OF SMALL SELFISH GROUPS THAT A MAN CANNOT RESPECT THE LAW.
Strongly agree [5]   Agree [4]   Undecided [3]   Disagree [2]
Strongly disagree [1]   **(L)**

101. IF OUR ECONOMIC SYSTEM WERE JUST, THERE WOULD BE MUCH LESS CRIME.
Strongly agree [5]   Agree [4]   Undecided [3]   Disagree [2]
Strongly disagree [1]   **(EC)**

102. SAVINGS SPENT ON EDUCATION ARE WISELY INVESTED.
Strongly agree [1]   Agree [2]   Undecided [3]   Disagree [4]
Strongly disagree [5]   **(E)**

103. ONE SELDOM WORRIES SO MUCH AS TO BECOME VERY MISERABLE.
Strongly agree ^{1} Agree ^{2} Undecided ^{3} Disagree ^{4}
Strongly disagree ^{5} **(M)**

104. IT IS NO TRICK TO BE THE LIFE OF THE PARTY.
Strongly agree ^{1} Agree ^{2} Undecided ^{3} Disagree ^{4}
Strongly disagree ^{5} **(I)**

105. MEMBERS OF THE FAMILY ARE TOO CURIOUS ABOUT ONE'S PERSONAL AFFAIRS.
Strongly agree ^{5} Agree ^{4} Undecided ^{3} Disagree ^{2}
Strongly disagree ^{1} **(F)**

106. ALMOST ANYTHING CAN BE FIXED UP IN THE COURTS IF YOU HAVE ENOUGH MONEY.
Strongly agree ^{5} Agree ^{4} Undecided ^{3} Disagree ^{2}
Strongly disagree ^{1} **(L)**

107. THE INCOMES OF MOST PEOPLE ARE A FAIR MEASURE OF THEIR CONTRIBUTION TO HUMAN WELFARE.
Strongly agree ^{1} Agree ^{2} Undecided ^{3} Disagree ^{4}
Strongly disagree ^{5} **(EC)**

108. AN EDUCATED MAN CAN ADVANCE MORE RAPIDLY IN BUSINESS AND INDUSTRY.
Strongly agree ^{1} Agree ^{2} Undecided ^{3} Disagree ^{4}
Strongly disagree ^{5} **(E)**

109. A MAN DOES NOT HAVE TO PRETEND HE IS SMARTER THAN HE REALLY IS TO "GET BY."
Strongly agree ^{1} Agree ^{2} Undecided ^{3} Disagree ^{4}
Strongly disagree ^{5} **(M)**

110. IT IS EASY TO KEEP PEOPLE FROM TAKING ADVANTAGE OF YOU.
Strongly agree ^{1} Agree ^{2} Undecided ^{3} Disagree ^{4}
Strongly disagree ^{5} **(I)**

111. PARENTS KEEP FAITH IN THEIR CHILDREN EVEN THOUGH THEY CANNOT FIND WORK.
Strongly agree ^{1} Agree ^{2} Undecided ^{3} Disagree ^{4}
Strongly disagree ^{5} **(F)**

112. IT IS DIFFICULT TO BREAK THE LAW AND KEEP ONE'S SELF RESPECT.
Strongly agree ^{1} Agree ^{2} Undecided ^{3} Disagree ^{4}
Strongly disagree ^{5} **(L)**

113. A MAN SHOULD STRIKE IN ORDER TO SECURE GREATER RETURNS TO LABOR.
Strongly agree ^{5} Agree ^{4} Undecided ^{3} Disagree ^{2}
Strongly disagree ^{1} **(EC)**

114. PARENTS SHOULD NOT BE COMPELLED TO SEND THEIR CHILDREN TO SCHOOL.
Strongly agree ^{5} Agree ^{4} Undecided ^{3} Disagree ^{2}
Strongly disagree ^{1} **(E)**

115. SUCCESS IS MORE DEPENDENT ON LUCK THAN ON REAL ABILITY.
Strongly agree ^{5} Agree ^{4} Undecided ^{3} Disagree ^{2}
Strongly disagree ^{1} **(M)**

116. MOST PEOPLE ARE TOO CRITICAL OF ONE'S BEHAVIOR.
Strongly agree ^{5} Agree ^{4} Undecided ^{3} Disagree ^{2}
Strongly disagree ^{1} **(I)**

117. PARENTS ARE TOO PARTICULAR ABOUT THE KIND OF COMPANY ONE KEEPS.
Strongly agree ^{5} Agree ^{4} Undecided ^{3} Disagree ^{2}
Strongly disagree ^{1} **(F)**

118. ON THE WHOLE, LAWYERS ARE HONEST.
Strongly agree ^{1} Agree ^{2} Undecided ^{3} Disagree ^{4}
Strongly disagree ^{5} **(L)**

119. A MAN SHOULD BE ALLOWED TO KEEP AS LARGE AN INCOME AS HE CAN GET.
Strongly agree ^{1} Agree ^{2} Undecided ^{3} Disagree ^{4}
Strongly disagree ^{5} **(EC)**

120. EDUCATION IS MORE VALUABLE THAN MOST PEOPLE THINK.
Strongly agree ^{1} Agree ^{2} Undecided ^{3} Disagree ^{4}
Strongly disagree ^{5} **(E)**

121. A PERSON CAN PLAN HIS FUTURE SO THAT EVERY-THING WILL COME OUT ALL RIGHT IN THE LONG RUN.
Strongly agree ^{1} Agree ^{2} Undecided ^{3} Disagree ^{4}
Strongly disagree ^{5} **(M)**

122. FEAR OF SOCIAL BLUNDERS KEEPS ONE FROM HAVING A GOOD TIME AT A PARTY.
Strongly agree ^{5} Agree ^{4} Undecided ^{3} Disagree ^{2}
Strongly disagree ^{1} **(I)**

123. OBLIGATIONS TO ONE'S FAMILY ARE A GREAT HANDI-CAP TO A YOUNG MAN TODAY.
Strongly agree [5]   Agree [4]   Undecided [3]   Disagree [2]
Strongly disagree [1]   **(F)**

124. VIOLATORS OF THE LAW ARE NEARLY ALWAYS DE-TECTED AND PUNISHED.
Strongly agree [1]   Agree [2]   Undecided [3]   Disagree [4]
Strongly disagree [5]   **(L)**

125. MONEY SHOULD BE TAKEN FROM THE RICH AND GIVEN TO THE POOR DURING HARD TIMES.
Strongly agree [5]   Agree [4]   Undecided [3]   Disagree [2]
Strongly disagree [1]   **(EC)**

126. A HIGH SCHOOL EDUCATION MAKES A MAN A BETTER CITIZEN.
Strongly agree [1]   Agree [2]   Undecided [3]   Disagree [4]
Strongly disagree [5]   **(E)**

127. THERE IS REALLY NO POINT IN LIVING.
Strongly agree [5]   Agree [4]   Undecided [3]   Disagree [2]
Strongly disagree [1]   **(M)**

128. IT IS EASY TO LOSE CONFIDENCE IN ONESELF.
Strongly agree [5]   Agree [4]   Undecided [3]   Disagree [2]
Strongly disagree [1]   **(I)**

129. SO FAR AS IDEAS ARE CONCERNED, PARENTS AND CHILDREN LIVE IN DIFFERENT WORLDS.
Strongly agree [5]   Agree [4]   Undecided [3]   Disagree [2]
Strongly disagree [1]   **(F)**

130. IT IS ALL RIGHT FOR A PERSON TO BREAK THE LAW IF HE DOESN'T GET CAUGHT.
Strongly agree [5]   Agree [4]   Undecided [3]   Disagree [2]
Strongly disagree [1]   **(L)**

131. OUR ECONOMIC SYSTEM IS CRITICIZED TOO MUCH.
Strongly agree [1]   Agree [2]   Undecided [3]   Disagree [4]
Strongly disagree [5]   **(EC)**

132. PUBLIC MONEY SPENT ON EDUCATION FOR THE PAST FEW YEARS COULD HAVE BEEN USED MORE WISELY FOR OTHER PURPOSES.
Strongly agree [5]   Agree [4]   Undecided [3]   Disagree [2]
Strongly disagree [1]   **(E)**

IV.C.2. INDEX: THE SCIENCE RESEARCH ASSOCIATES
EMPLOYEE INVENTORY

VARIABLE MEASURED: The SRA Employee Inventory provides a measure of employee attitudes toward the work environment. It is a diagnostic instrument identifying attitudinal levels for individuals and groups in such areas as job demands, working conditions, pay, employee benefits, friendliness and cooperation of fellow employees, supervisor-employee interpersonal relations, confidence in management, technical competence of supervision, effectiveness of administration, adequacy of communication, security of job and work relations, status and recognition, identification with the company, opportunity for growth and advancement, and finally reactions to the inventory itself.

DESCRIPTION: The inventory is not just an opinion survey. It is a kind of "morale audit" for work organizations that provides standard scores in each category based upon more than one million employees in a wide variety of business firms. Practical uses include assessing the general level of morale in an organization, locating the problem departments in the organization, determining satisfactions and dissatisfactions among employees, evaluating supervisory and executive training needs, and providing material for supervisory training programs.

WHERE PUBLISHED: Science Research Associates, Inc., 259 East Erie Street, Chicago, Illinois. Copyright, 1952, by the Industrial Relations Center of the University of Chicago. All rights reserved. Authors of the inventory include Robert K. Burns, L. L. Thurstone, David G. Moore, and Melony E. Baehr.

RELIABILITY: Both individual and group reliability have been determined by the test-retest method with an interval of one week between the test administrations. A sample of 134 employees shows a product moment correlation of .89. Group reliabilities range from .96 to .99 with reliability greater for groups of 50 or more employees.

VALIDITY: Good correspondence was found to exist between the inventory results and the considered judgments of experienced observers. In three of the companies surveyed, validity was established by conducting nondirective interviews among a cross-section of the employees.

STANDARD SCORES: Well standardized scores are available for comparative analysis of attitude levels in similar business firms and within similar departments.

SRA EMPLOYEE INVENTORY

Form A

Instructions

Purpose of the Inventory

Your company would like to know what you think about your job, your pay, your boss, and the company in general. This Inventory is designed to help you tell us your ideas and opinions quickly and easily without signing your name. This booklet contains a number of statements. All you have to do is to mark a cross by each statement to show how you feel. It is easy to do and you can be completely frank in your answers.

How to fill in the Inventory

Read each statement carefully and decide how you feel about it. You will agree with some statements, and you will disagree with others. You may be undecided about some. To help you express your opinion, three possible answers have been placed beside each statement:

	AGREE	?	DISAGREE
I would rather work in a large city than in a small town.	☐	☐	☐

Choose the answer most like your own opinion and mark a cross in the box under it.

For example:

This person feels he wants to work in a large city:

	AGREE	?	DISAGREE
I would rather work in a large city than in a small town.	☒	☐	☐

This person wants to work in a small town:

	AGREE	?	DISAGREE
I would rather work in a large city than in a small town.	☐	☐	☒

This person can't decide between a large city and a small town:

	AGREE	?	DISAGREE
I would rather work in a large city than in a small town.	☐	☒	☐

This is not a test

There are no "right" answers and no "wrong" answers. It is your own, honest opinion that we want.

Work rapidly but answer all statements

Do *not* spend too much time on any one statement. If you cannot decide about a statement, mark the "?" box, and go on to the next statement. If you make a mistake, erase your mark, or fill in the box completely. Then mark a cross in the correct box.

General information

Do *not* sign your name on the booklet. Be *sure* to fill in the blanks for general information on page 2 and page 4 of this booklet. This information will be used only to make the results more meaningful. It will not be used to identify you in any way.

When you have finished

When you have finished filling out the questionnaire, check to see that you have marked every statement. Then turn to page 2 where you will find the space to write your comments. In this space we would like you to write anything about your job or the company that is important to you. If something is irritating or trying for you, please comment on it. If something is pleasing or satisfying, please comment on that also. Or if you have a suggestion to help your job or the company, write that also.

	AGREE	?	DISAG
1. The hours of work here are O.K...........................	☐	☐	☐
2. Management does everything possible to prevent accidents in our work..	☐	☐	☐
3. Management is doing its best to give us good working conditions..	☐	☐	☐
4. In my opinion, the pay here is lower than in other companies..	☐	☐	☐
5. They should do a better job of handling pay matters here...	☐	☐	☐
6. I understand what the company benefit program provides for employees..	☐	☐	☐
7. The people I work with help each other out when someone falls behind or gets in a tight spot.............................	☐	☐	☐
8. My boss is too interested in his own success to care about the needs of employees...	☐	☐	☐
9. My boss is always breathing down our necks; he watches us too closely...	☐	☐	☐
10. My boss gives us credit and praise for work well done..........	☐	☐	☐
11. Management here does everything it can to see that employees get a fair break on the job........................	☐	☐	☐
12. If I have a complaint to make, I feel free to talk to someone up-the-line.......................................	☐	☐	☐
13. My boss sees that employees are properly trained for their jobs..	☐	☐	☐
14. My boss see that we have the things we need to do our jobs..	☐	☐	☐
15. Management here is really trying to build the organization and make it successful.....................................	☐	☐	☐
16. Management here sees to it that there is cooperation between departments......................................	☐	☐	☐
17. Management tells employees about company plans and developments...	☐	☐	☐
18. They encourage us to make suggestions for improvements here..	☐	☐	☐
19. I am often bothered by sudden speedups or unexpected slack periods in my work.......................................	☐	☐	☐
20. Changes are made here with little regard for the welfare of employees..	☐	☐	☐
21. Compared with other employees, we get very little attention from management................................	☐	☐	☐
22. Sometimes I feel that my job counts for very little in this organization...	☐	☐	☐

3. The longer you work for this company the more you feel you belong.. AGREE ? DISAGREE ☐ ☐ ☐

4. I have a great deal of interest in this company and its future.. AGREE ? DISAGREE ☐ ☐ ☐

5. I have little opportunity to use my abilities in this organization... AGREE ? DISAGREE ☐ ☐ ☐

6. There are plenty of good jobs here for those who want to get ahead.. AGREE ? DISAGREE ☐ ☐ ☐

7. I often feel worn out and tired on my job.................... AGREE ? DISAGREE ☐ ☐ ☐

8. They expect too much work from us around here.............. AGREE ? DISAGREE ☐ ☐ ☐

9. Poor working conditions keep me from doing my best in my work... AGREE ? DISAGREE ☐ ☐ ☐

0. For my kind of job, the working conditions are O.K........... AGREE ? DISAGREE ☐ ☐ ☐

1. I'm paid fairly compared with other employees................ AGREE ? DISAGREE ☐ ☐ ☐

2. Compared with other companies, employee benefits here are good... AGREE ? DISAGREE ☐ ☐ ☐

3. A few of the people I work with think they run the place....... AGREE ? DISAGREE ☐ ☐ ☐

4. The people I work with get along well together................ AGREE ? DISAGREE ☐ ☐ ☐

5. My boss has always been fair in his dealings with me.......... AGREE ? DISAGREE ☐ ☐ ☐

6. My boss gets employees to work together as a team........... AGREE ? DISAGREE ☐ ☐ ☐

7. I have confidence in the fairness and honesty of management... AGREE ? DISAGREE ☐ ☐ ☐

8. Management here is really interested in the welfare of employees... AGREE ? DISAGREE ☐ ☐ ☐

9. Most of the higher-ups are friendly toward employees.......... AGREE ? DISAGREE ☐ ☐ ☐

0. My boss keeps putting things off; he just lets things ride........ AGREE ? DISAGREE ☐ ☐ ☐

1. My boss lets us know exactly what is expected of us............ AGREE ? DISAGREE ☐ ☐ ☐

2. Management fails to give clear-cut orders and instructions... AGREE ? DISAGREE ☐ ☐ ☐

3. I know how my job fits in with other work in this organization... AGREE ? DISAGREE ☐ ☐ ☐

4. Management keeps us in the dark about things we ought to know... AGREE ? DISAGREE ☐ ☐ ☐

257

	AGREE	?	DISAGREE
45. Long service really means something in this organization........	☐	☐	☐
46. You can get fired around here without much cause..............	☐	☐	☐
47. I can be sure of my job as long as I do good work.............	☐	☐	☐
48. I have plenty of freedom on the job to use my own judgment...	☐	☐	☐
49. Everybody in this organization tries to boss us around..........	☐	☐	☐
50. I really feel part of this organization........................	☐	☐	☐
51. The people who get promotions around here usually deserve them..	☐	☐	☐
52. I can learn a great deal on my present job....................	☐	☐	☐
53. My job is often dull and monotonous........................	☐	☐	☐
54. There is too much pressure on my job........................	☐	☐	☐
55. Some of the working conditions here are annoying.............	☐	☐	☐
56. I have the right equipment to do my work....................	☐	☐	☐
57. My pay is enough to live on comfortably.....................	☐	☐	☐
58. I'm satisfied with the way employee benefits are handled here..	☐	☐	☐
59. The company's employee benefit program is O.K..............	☐	☐	☐
60. The people I work with are very friendly.....................	☐	☐	☐
61. My boss really tries to get our ideas about things.............	☐	☐	☐
62. My boss ought to be friendlier toward employees..............	☐	☐	☐
63. My boss lives up to his promises............................	☐	☐	☐
64. Management here has a very good personnel policy.............	☐	☐	☐
65. Management ignores our suggestions and complaints...........	☐	☐	☐
66. My boss knows very little about his job......................	☐	☐	☐

	AGREE	?	DISAGREE
57. My boss has the work well organized............................	☐	☐	☐
58. This company operates efficiently and smoothly................	☐	☐	☐
59. Management really knows its job..............................	☐	☐	☐
60. They have a poor way of handling employee complaints here..	☐	☐	☐
61. You can say what you think around here......................	☐	☐	☐
62. You always know where you stand with this company..........	☐	☐	☐
63. When layoffs are necessary, they are handled fairly............	☐	☐	☐
64. I am very much underpaid for the work that I do.............	☐	☐	☐
65. I'm really doing something worthwhile in my job..............	☐	☐	☐
66. I'm proud to work for this company..........................	☐	☐	☐
67. Filling in this Inventory is a good way to let management know what employees think.....................	☐	☐	☐
68. I think some good may come out of filling in an Inventory like this one..................................	☐	☐	☐

#	AGREE ? DISAGREE	#	AGREE ? DISAGREE	#	AGREE ? DISAGREE
79.	☐ ☐ ☐	86.	☐ ☐ ☐	93.	☐ ☐ ☐
80.	☐ ☐ ☐	87.	☐ ☐ ☐	94.	☐ ☐ ☐
81.	☐ ☐ ☐	88.	☐ ☐ ☐	95.	☐ ☐ ☐
82.	☐ ☐ ☐	89.	☐ ☐ ☐	96.	☐ ☐ ☐
83.	☐ ☐ ☐	90.	☐ ☐ ☐	97.	☐ ☐ ☐
84.	☐ ☐ ☐	91.	☐ ☐ ☐	98.	☐ ☐ ☐
85.	☐ ☐ ☐	92.	☐ ☐ ☐	99.	☐ ☐ ☐

General information

1	2	3
4	5	6

Please write your comments here

```
┌─────────────────────────────────────────────────────────┐
│                                                           │
│                                                           │
│                                                           │
│                                                           │
│                                                           │
│                                                           │
│                                                           │
│                                                           │
│                                                           │
│                                                           │
│                                                           │
│                                                           │
│                                                           │
│                                                           │
└─────────────────────────────────────────────────────────┘
```

General information

1	2	3
4	5	6

UTILITY: Inexpensive, easily interpreted, quickly scored, and permits use in all kinds of work organizations. Comparative analysis is facilitated by available standard scores.

RESEARCH APPLICATIONS:

MOORE, DAVID G., and BURNS, ROBERT K. "How Good is Good Morale?" *Factory* (February, 1956), 130-136.

The *SRA Employee Inventory* was prepared by the Employee Attitude Research Group of the Industrial Relations Center, University of Chicago. This group has members from both the University and industry. Thus, both the theoretical and practical aspects are well represented in all development work. Further details are given in the *Manual*.

The *SRA Employee Inventory* is published by SCIENCE RESEARCH ASSOCIATES, INC., 259 East Erie Street, Chicago, Illinois. It is copyrighted 1951 by the Industrial Relations Center of the University of Chicago.

Please use number 7-1591 when reordering this booklet.

IV.C.3. INDEX: MORSE INDEXES OF EMPLOYEE SATISFACTION

VARIABLE MEASURED: The degree of satisfaction that individuals obtain from the various roles they play in an organization; specifically (1) satisfaction with doing the actual content of the work, (2) satisfaction with being in the work group, (3) satisfaction with working in the company, (4) satisfaction with pay and job status.

DESCRIPTION: These are indexes of employee satisfaction, each of which contains four items developed through a combined logical and empirical method. The items were initially selected from an employee interview on the basis of the definitions of each area of employee satisfaction. Intercorrelations were then computed among all items that logically appeared to belong in each area. Items that showed very low correlations were removed. The items making up each index were not differentially weighed, but were added with unit weights to give a single measure of each type of employee satisfaction. The four indexes are called *intrinsic job satisfaction, company involvement, financial and job status satisfaction,* and *pride in group performance.* Each index has four items that are answered on a five-point scale ranging from strong like to strong dislike. This gives a range of scores from 4-20 on each index.

WHERE PUBLISHED: Nancy C. Morse, *Satisfactions in the White Collar Job* (Ann Arbor: University of Michigan, Institute for Social Research, 1953).

RELIABILITY: No split half or test-retest reliabilities are reported. Internal consistency of the scales is attested by the average intercorrelations of items:

Intrinsic job satisfaction	$r = .50$
Company involvement	$r = .45$
Financial and job status satisfaction	$r = .52$
Pride in group performance	$r = .39$

VALIDITY: The intrinsic job satisfaction, company involvement, and financial job status indexes, both from the intercorrelations of the total index scores and from the item analysis, appear to be significantly interrelated (intercorrelations ranging from $r = .35$ to $r = .43$). These three areas can be used to represent a general morale factor. This factor predicts the individual's desire to stay in the company rather than his productivity.

Pride in group performance (and its subitems) is, with few exceptions, not significantly related to the items of the other indexes or to the indexes themselves. It must be treated as an independent factor. This index was related to the amount of voluntary help given by members to one another, friendliness in interpersonal relations, and the absence of antiproductivity group norms. It was also correlated with supervisor's identification with employees.

STANDARD SCORES:

		Range	*N*
Intrinsic Job Satisfaction	High Group	04-07	(717)
	Medium Group	08-11	(222)
	Low Group	12-20	(181)
Financial and Job Status Satisfaction	High Group	04-08	(160)
	Medium Group	09-12	(227)
	Low Group	13-20	(248)
Company Involvement	High Group	04-08	(250)
	Medium Group	09-12	(255)
	Low Group	13-20	(165)
Pride in Group Performance	High Group	04-08	(227)
	Medium Group	09-10	(264)
	Low Group	11-20	(251)

UTILITY: The indexes consist of easily administered questionnaire items. The time required is about 10 minutes for the administration of all four indexes.

RESEARCH APPLICATIONS: Morse reports relationships between the indexes and various supervisory practices, working conditions, and various background factors such as sex, age, length of service, and education. See *Satisfactions in the White Collar Job* previously cited.

Company Involvement Index

1. "How do you like working here?"
   code: Five-point scale ranging from strong like, complete satisfaction to strong dislike.
2. "Would you advise a friend to come to work for the Company?"
   code: Three-point scale including: yes, pro-con, and no.
3. An overall coder rating of the employee's feelings about the fairness of the company, based on answers to questions throughout the interview.
   code: Three-point scale including: feels company fair and generous, feels company fair but very exacting, feels company unfair.
4. An overall coder rating of the employee's degree of identification with the company based on answers to questions throughout the interview.
   code: Three-point scale including: strong identification, some identification, and no identification.

Financial and Job Status Index

1. "How well satisfied are you with your salary?"
   code: Five-point scale ranging from very well satisfied to very dissatisfied.
2. "How satisfied are you with your chances of getting more pay?"
   code: Five-point scale ranging from very satisfied to very dissatisfied.
3. "How about your own case, how satisfied are you with the way things have been working out for you?" (This question was preceded by two questions on "getting ahead here at the Company" and was answered in that context.)
   code: Five-point scale ranging from very satisfied to very dissatisfied.
4. Coder overall rating of degree of frustration evidenced by respondent in advancing in his job or in his main vocational objectives. Answers to questions throughout the interview were used to measure the degree to which employee felt his vocational desires were blocked.
   code: Five-point scale ranging from strong frustration to high adjustment, no frustration.

Intrinsic Job Satisfaction Index

1. "How well do you like the sort of work you are doing?"
   code: Five-point scale varying from strong like to strong dislike.
2. "Does your job give you a chance to do the things you feel you do best?"
   code: Five-point scale varying from yes (strong) to no (strong).
3. "Do you get any feeling of accomplishment from the work you are doing?"
   code: Five-point scale varying from strong sense of task completion to no sense of task completion.
4. "How do you feel about your work, does it rate as an important job with you?"
   code: Five-point scale varying from very important to of no importance.

Pride-in-Group-Performance Index

1. "How well do you think your section compares with other sections in the Company in getting a job done?"
   code: Five-point scale ranging from very good, one of best in company, to very poor, one of worst in company.
2. Answers to the section comparison question were also coded on the degree of emotional identification with the section that employee showed. (The use of "we" as opposed to "it" or "they" was one of the indications to the coder of identification.)
   code: Three-point scale: strong identification, mild identification, indifference or lack of identification.
3. "How well do you think your division compares with other divisions in the Company in getting a job done?"
   code: Five-point scale ranging from very good, one of best in company, to very poor, one of worst in company.
4. Answers to the division comparison question were also coded on degree of emotional identification with the division the employee showed.
   code: Three-point scale: strong identification, mild identification, indifference or lack of identification.

IV.C.4. INDEX: GUTTMAN SCALES OF MILITARY BASE MORALE

VARIABLE MEASURED: Satisfaction with Air Force, satisfaction with Air Site, satisfaction with the job, personal commitment to Aircraft Control and Warning Mission.

WHERE PUBLISHED: Delbert C. Miller and Nahum Z. Medalia, "Efficiency, Leadership, and Morale in Small Military Organizations," *The Sociological Review*, 3 (July, 1955), 93-107.

RELIABILITY: Scalability shown by reproducibility coefficients.

Satisfaction with Air Force	$R = .93$
Satisfaction with the Air Site	$R = .90$
Satisfaction with the job	$R = .90$
Personal commitment to AC&W Mission	$R = .94$

VALIDITY: Correlation between ratings made by outside military inspectors of site morale and satisfaction with Air Site scale in 50 squadrons show Spearman Rank Correlation of $r_s = .52$.

UTILITY: Scales are short and unidimensional. They may be easily converted for use in other organizations by substituting appropriate unit names. However, as in all Guttman Scales reproducibility varies with respondent samples and must be recomputed.

RESEARCH APPLICATIONS:

GROSS, EDWARD, and MILLER, DELBERT C. "The Impact of Isolation on Worker Adjustment in Military Installations of the United States and Japan," *Estudios de Sociologia* (Buenos Aires), 1 (Fall, 1961), 70-86.

McCANN, GLENN C. *Morale and Human Relations Problems in A C & W Sites*. Air Force Personnel and Training Research Center Technical Memorandum CRL-TM-56-5, April, 1956.

MEDALIA, NAHUM Z. "Unit Size and Leadership Perception," *Sociometry*, 17 (February, 1954), 64-67.

———. "Authoritarianism, Leader Acceptance, and Group Cohesion," *Journal of Abnormal and Social Psychology*, 51 (September, 1955), 207-213.

———, and MILLER, DELBERT C. "Human Relations Leadership and the Association of Morale and the Effectiveness of Work Groups," *Social Forces*, 33 (May, 1955), 348-352.

MILLER, DELBERT C., and MEDALIA, N. Z. "Efficiency, Leadership, and Morale in Small Military Organizations," *The Sociological Review*, 3, No. 1 (July, 1955), 93-107.

MILLER, DELBERT C., MEDALIA, NAHUM Z., McCANN, GLENN C and others. "Morale and Human Relations Leadership as Factor in Organizational Effectiveness," in *Studies in Organizational Effectiveness*. Edited by R. V. Bowers. Washington, D.C.: Air Force Office of Scientific Research, 1962.

MORALE SCALES FOR MILITARY ORGANIZATIONS

Satisfaction with Air Force (All items answered by Strongly Agree Agree, Undecided, Disagree, Strongly Disagree.)

1. I have a poor opinion of the Air Force most of the time.
2. Most of the time the Air Force is not run very well.
3. I am usually dissatisfied with the Air Force.
4. The Air Force is better than any of the other Services.
5. If I remain in military service I would prefer to stay in the Air Force.

Satisfaction with the Air Site

1. In general this Air Site is run very well.
2. This Air Site is the best in the whole Division.
3. I am usually dissatisfied with this Air Site.
4. I would rather be stationed at this Air Site than any I know about.
5. I would like to stay at this Air Site.

Satisfaction with the Job

1. I would be more satisfied with some other job in AC&W than I am with my usual job.
2. My Air Force job is usually interesting to me.
3. I believe the Air Force has placed me in a job that suits me very well.
4. I believe my Air Force job is usually worthwhile.
5. If I have a chance, I will change to some other job at this Site

Personal Commitment to Aircraft Control and Warning Mission

1. Under present world conditions, I would advise many of my civilian friends to get into AC&W if they should ask my advice on joining the service. (*a*) No, I would advise them to stay out of AC&W. (*b*) I would tell them it makes no difference what you join. (*c*) Yes, I would advise them to join AC&W.

2. Under present world conditions, I feel that I can do more for my country as a member of AC&W than as a civilian. (*a*) No, I would be more valuable as a civilian. (*b*) I am undecided about this. (*c*) Yes, I am more valuable in AC&W.
3. Under present world conditions I feel that I can do more for my country as a member of some other part of the armed services, rather than as a member of AC&W. (*a*) Yes, I could be of more value elsewhere in the armed services. (*b*) It is a toss-up where I could contribute the most. (*c*) No, I am of more value in AC&W.
4. Under present world conditions I feel I can do more for my country as a member of AC&W than some other part of the Air Force. (*a*) No, I would be of more value elsewhere in the Air Force. (*b*) I am about of equal value any place in the Air Force. (*c*) Yes, I am definitely more valuable in AC&W.
5. If present world conditions continue to be about the same, I would want to continue to be a member of AC&W as long as I remain in military service. (*a*) No, I would want to transfer from AC&W. (*b*) It doesn't matter whether I am in AC&W or not. (*c*) Yes, I would definitely want to remain in AC&W.
6. If the U.S. should enter a third world war and if I should remain in military service, I would want to stay in AC&W. (*a*) No, I prefer to be in some other part of the service. (*b*) It wouldn't make much difference where I serve. (*c*) Yes, I would prefer to remain in AC&W. (All of the aforementioned items are interspersed when they are administered.)

V.C.5. INDEX: BRAYFIELD AND ROTHE'S INDEX OF JOB SATISFACTION

VARIABLE MEASURED: General measure of job satisfaction.

WHERE PUBLISHED: Arthur H. Brayfield and Harold F. Rothe, "An Index of Job Satisfaction," *Journal of Applied Psychology,* 35 (October, 1951), 307-311.

CONSTRUCTION: As a working approach for this study it was assumed that job satisfaction could be inferred from the individual's attitude toward his work. This approach dictated the methodology of attitude scaling. The following requirements were formulated as desirable attributes of an attitude scale designed to provide a useful index of job satisfaction: (1) it should give an index of "overall" job satisfaction rather than specific aspects of job satisfaction; (2) it should be applicable to a wide variety of jobs; (3) it should be sensitive to variations in attitude; (4) the items should be of such a nature (interesting, realistic, and varied) that the scale would evoke cooperation from both management and employees; (5) it should yield a reliable index; (6) it should yield a valid index; (7) it should be brief and easily scored.

The construction of this scale was made a class project in Personnel Psychology for members of an Army Specialized Training Program in personnel psychology at the University of Minnesota in the summer and fall of 1943. Seventy-seven men cooperated. Items referring to specific aspects of a job were eliminated since an "overall" attitudinal factor was desired.

The present index contains 18 items with Thurstone scale values ranging from 1.2 to 10.0 with approximately .5 step intervals. The items are not arranged in the order of magnitude of scale values. The Likert scoring system consisting of five categories of agreement-disagreement was applied to each item, and the Thurstone scoring system of five categories is applied to the items. The Thurstone scale value gives the direction of scoring method so that a low total score would represent the dissatisfied end of the scale and a high total score the satisfied end. The items are selected so that the satisfied end of the scale was indicated by *Strongly Agree* and *Agree,* and *Disagree* and *Strongly Disagree* for the other half. The neutral response is *Undecided.* The Likert scoring weights for each item range from 1 to 5 and the range of possible total scores is 18 to 90 with 54 (Undecided) the neutral point.

RELIABILITY: The revised scale (which is the present one) was administered as part of a study of 231 female office employees. The blanks were signed along with other tests. One of the investigators personally administered the tests to employees in small groups. The range of job satisfaction scores for this sample was 35-87. The mean score was 63.8 with an S. D. of 9.4. The odd-even product moment reliability coefficient computed for this sample was .77, which was corrected by the Spearman-Brown formula to a reliability coefficient of .87.

VALIDITY: Evidence for the high validity of the blank rests upon the nature of the items, the method of construction, and its differentiating power when applied to two groups that could reasonably be assumed to differ in job satisfaction. The nature of the individual items is partial, although not crucial, evidence for the validity of the scale. This is an appeal to "face" validity. Additional evidence is furnished by the method of construction. The attitude variable of job satisfaction is inferred from verbal reactions to a job expressed along a favorable-unfavorable continuum.

The job satisfaction blank was administered to 91 adult night school students in classes in Personnel Psychology at the University of Minnesota during 1945 and 1946. The range of job satisfaction scores for this sample was 29-89. The mean score was 70.4 with an S. D. of 13.2. The assumption was made that those persons employed in occupations appropriate to their expressed interest should, on the average, be more satisfied with their jobs than those members of the class employed in occupations inappropriate to their expressed interest in personnel work. The 91 persons accordingly were divided into two groups (Personnel and Nonpersonnel) with respect to their employment in a position identified by payroll title as a personnel function. The mean of the Personnel group was 76.9 with an S. D. of 8.6 as compared to a mean of 65.4 with an S. D. of 14.02 for the Nonpersonnel group. This difference of 11.5 points is significant at the 1 per cent level; the difference between the variances also is significant at the 1 per cent level. It might also be mentioned that scores on this index correlated .92 with scores on the Hoppock job satisfaction scale.

RESEARCH APPLICATIONS:

BRAYFIELD, ARTHUR H., WELLS, RICHARD V., and STRATE, MARVIN W. "Interrelationships Among Measures of Job Satisfaction and General Satisfaction," *Journal of Applied Psychology,* 41 (August, 1957), 201-205.

AN INDEX OF JOB SATISFACTION * †

Some jobs are more interesting and satisfying than others. We want to know how people feel about different jobs. This blank contains 18 statements about jobs. You are to cross out the phrase below each statement that has best described how you feel about your present job. There are no right or wrong answers. We should like your honest opinion on each one of the statements. Work out the sample item numbered (o).

o. There are some conditions concerning my job that could be improved.
    Strongly agree, agree, undecided, disagree, strongly disagree.

1. My job is like a hobby to me.
    Strongly agree, agree, undecided, disagree, strongly disagree.

2. My job is usually interesting enough to keep me from getting bored.
    Strongly agree, agree, undecided, disagree, strongly disagree.

3. It seems that my friends are more interested in their jobs.
    Strongly agree, agree, undecided, disagree, strongly disagree.

4. I consider my job rather unpleasant.
    Strongly agree, agree, undecided, disagree, strongly disagree.

5. I enjoy my work more than my leisure time.
    Strongly agree, agree, undecided, disagree, strongly disagree.

6. I am often bored with my job.
    Strongly agree, agree, undecided, disagree, strongly disagree.

7. I feel fairly well satisfied with my job.
    Strongly agree, agree, undecided, disagree, strongly disagree.

8. Most of the time I have to force myself to go to work.
    Strongly agree, agree, undecided, disagree, strongly disagree.

9. I am satisfied with my job for the time being.
    Strongly agree, agree, undecided, disagree, strongly disagree.

10. I feel that my job is no more interesting than others I could get.
    Strongly agree, agree, undecided, disagree, strongly disagree.

11. I definitely dislike my work.
    Strongly agree, agree, undecided, disagree, strongly disagree.

12. I feel that I am happier in my work than most other people.
    Strongly agree, agree, undecided, disagree, strongly disagree.

13. Most days I am enthusiastic about my work.
    Strongly agree, agree, undecided, disagree, strongly disagree.

14. Each day of work seems like it will never end.
    Strongly agree, agree, undecided, disagree, strongly disagree.

15. I like my job better than the average worker does.
    Strongly agree, agree, undecided, disagree, strongly disagree.

16. My job is pretty uninteresting.
    Strongly agree, agree, undecided, disagree, strongly disagree.

17. I find real enjoyment in my work.
    Strongly agree, agree, undecided, disagree, strongly disagree.

18. I am disappointed that I ever took this job.
    Strongly agree, agree, undecided, disagree, strongly disagree.

* Arthur H. Brayfield and Harold F. Rothe, *Journal of Applied Psychology*, 35, No. 5 (October, 1951), 307-311.

† This blank containing 18 items with Thurstone scale values ranging from 1.2 to 10.0 with approximately .5 step intervals is not arranged in order of magnitude of scale values. The Likert scoring system of five categories is applied to each item. Thurstone scale values give the direction of scoring method. Likert scoring weights range for each item 1 to 5. The range of possible total scores became 18 to 90 with the undecided or neutral point at 54.

Community

Measures of community variables are scarce. One of the first attempts to secure measures of the "goodness" of a city was made by E. L. Thorndike. His research monograph, *Our City* (New York: Harcourt, Brace, 1939), provided the first careful attempt to evaluate the quality of American cities. Ratings of 310 American cities over 30,000 population were made. In his *144 Smaller Cities,* Thorndike applied his "goodness" rating to cities between 20,000 and 30,000 population. The method requires the gathering of statistics on factors not too easily obtained. Paul B. Gillen in his *The Distribution of Occupations as a City Yardstick* (New York: Columbia University, 1951) presents a shorter technique based on the occupational distribution of the city. These indexes are recommended if a comparative rating of cities is desired.

The scales chosen for this section are chosen for more diagnostic research within a given community. Bosworth's *Community Attitude Scale* is designed to assess the degree of progressive attitude evidenced by members of a community. Fessler's *Community Solidarity Index* purports to measure community member solidarity. This scale is useful in determining relationships between community progress and solidarity. The *Community Rating Schedule* is a useful rating device in ascertaining the different views of such groups as businessmen, labor leaders, ministers, teachers, welfare workers etc. *The Scorecard for Community Services Activity* can be used to assess participation in the community services activity of the community. The relationship of community member progressiveness and community service activity might be fruitfully explored. Each scale opens possibilities of studying the relation of such background factors as occupation, social class, education, age, sex, and marital status upon community participation and progress.

IV.D.1. INDEX: COMMUNITY ATTITUDE SCALE

VARIABLE MEASURED: The degree of progressive attitude evidenced on such areas of community life as (1) general community improvement, (2) living conditions, (3) business and industry, (4) health and recreation, (5) education, (6) religion, (7) youth programs, (8) utilities, and (9) communications.

DESCRIPTION: A cross section of a wide range of groups in various communities defined the meaning of progress by submitting a number of statements that they designated as progressive and unprogressive. These statements provided 364 items that were placed in a five point Likert-type format. A representative panel of leaders independently designated each item as progressive or unprogressive. Various tests showed that 60 items were most discriminating. These 60 items were compiled into three subscales with 20 items each. These scales are identified as Community Integration, Community Services, and Civic Responsibilities.

WHERE PUBLISHED: A Ph.D. dissertation by Claud A. Bosworth, submitted to the University of Michigan, 1954.

RELIABILITY: 60 item scale, $r = .56$.

VALIDITY: Total mean scores discriminated significantly between a progressive and an unprogressive group at the .025 level. It was also found that those citizens who positively endorsed the scale items designed to measure attitudes toward other phases of community progress also voted for the sewer extension plan.

UTILITY: The scale is easily administered either in an interview or by questionnaire. Approximate time required is 20 minutes.

COMMUNITY ATTITUDE SCALE

Claud A. Bosworth

	St. Agree	Agree	?	Disagree	St. Dis.
(Community Services Subscale)					
1. The school should stick to the 3 R's and forget about most of the other courses being offered today.	—	—	—	—	—
2. Most communities are good enough as they are without starting any new community improvement programs.	—	—	—	—	—
3. Every community should encourage more music and lecture programs.	—	—	—	—	—
4. This used to be a better community to live in.	—	—	—	—	—
5. Long term progress is more important than immediate benefits.	—	—	—	—	—
6. We have too many organizations for doing good in the community.	—	—	—	—	—
7. The home and the church should have all the responsibility for preparing young people for marriage and parenthood.	—	—	—	—	—
8. The responsibility for older people should be confined to themselves and their families instead of the community.	—	—	—	—	—
9. Communities have too many youth programs.	—	—	—	—	—
10. Schools are good enough as they are in most communities.	—	—	—	—	—
11. Too much time is usually spent on the planning phases of community projects.	—	—	—	—	—
12. Adult education should be an essential part of the local school program.	—	—	—	—	—
13. Only the doctors should have the responsibility for the health program in the community.	—	—	—	—	—
14. Mental illness is not a responsibility of the whole community.	—	—	—	—	—
15. A modern community should have the services of social agencies.	—	—	—	—	—

COMMUNITY ATTITUDE SCALE—(Continued)

(Community Services Subscale)	St. Agree	Agree	?	Disagree	St. Dis.

16. The spiritual needs of the citizens are adequately met by the churches.

17. In order to grow, a community must provide additional recreation facilities.

18. In general, church members are better citizens.

19. The social needs of the citizens are the responsibility of themselves and their families and not of the community.

20. Churches should be expanded and located in accordance with population growth.

(Community Integration Subscale)

21. No community improvement program should be carried on that is injurious to a business.

22. Industrial development should include the interest in assisting local industry.

23. The first and major responsibility of each citizen should be to earn dollars for his own pocket.

24. More industry in town lowers the living standards.

25. The responsibility of citizens who are not actively participating in a community improvement program is to criticize those who are active.

26. What is good for the community is good for me.

27. Each one should handle his own business as he pleases and let the other businessmen handle theirs as they please.

28. A strong Chamber of Commerce is beneficial to any community.

29. Leaders of the Chamber of Commerce are against the welfare of the majority of the citizens in the community.

COMMUNITY ATTITUDE SCALE—(Continued)

(Community Integration Subscale)	St. Agree	Agree	?	Disagree	St. Dis.
30. A community would get along better if each one would mind his own business and others take care of theirs.	—	—	—	—	—
31. Members of any community organization should be expected to attend only those meetings that affect him personally.	—	—	—	—	—
32. Each of us can make real progress only when the group as a whole makes progress.	—	—	—	—	—
33. The person who pays no attention to the complaints of the persons working for him is a poor citizen.	—	—	—	—	—
34. It would be better if we would have the farmer look after his own business and we look after ours.	—	—	—	—	—
35. All unions are full of Communists.	—	—	—	—	—
36. The good citizens encourage the widespread circulation of all news including that which may be unfavorable to them and their organizations.	—	—	—	—	—
37. The good citizen should help minority groups with their problems.	—	—	—	—	—
38. The farmer has too prominent a place in our society.	—	—	—	—	—
39. A citizen should join only those organizations that will promote his own interests.	—	—	—	—	—
40. Everyone is out for himself at the expense of everyone else.	—	—	—	—	—

(Civic Responsibilities Subscale)

	St. Agree	Agree	?	Disagree	St. Dis.
41. Busy people should not have the responsibility for civic programs.	—	—	—	—	—
42. The main responsibility for keeping the community clean is up to the city officials.	—	—	—	—	—
43. Community improvements are fine if they don't increase taxes.	—	—	—	—	—

COMMUNITY ATTITUDE SCALE—(Continued)

(Civic Responsibilities Subscale)

	St. Agree	Agree	?	Disagree	St. Dis.
44. The younger element have too much to say about our community affairs.					
45. A progressive community must provide adequate parking facilities.					
46. Government officials should get public sentiment before acting on major municipal projects.					
47. A good citizen should be willing to assume leadership in a civic improvement organization.					
48. Progress can best be accomplished by having only a few people involved.					
49. Community improvement should be the concern of only a few leaders in the community.					
50. A community would be better if less people would spend time on community improvement projects.					
51. Only those who have the most time should assume the responsibility for civic programs.					
52. Living conditions in a community should be improved.					
53. A good citizen should sign petitions for community improvement.					
54. Improving slum areas is a waste of money.					
55. The police force should be especially strict with outsiders.					
56. The paved streets and roads in most communities are good enough.					
57. The sewage system of a community must be expanded as it grows even though it is necessary to increase taxes.					
58. Some people just want to live in slum areas.					
59. The main problem we face is high taxes.					
60. Modern methods and equipment should be provided for all phases of city government.					

IV.D.2. INDEX: COMMUNITY SOLIDARITY INDEX

VARIABLE MEASURED: Amount of consensus among members o primary rural communities (250-2,000 pop.).

DESCRIPTION: Eight major areas of community behavior are ex amined:

1. community spirit
2. interpersonal relations
3. family responsibility toward the community
4. schools
5. churches
6. economic behavior
7. local government
8. tension areas

These eight areas are covered in a series of 40 statements that are rated by the respondent on a five-item scale according to his judgment of how the statements apply to his community. The items range from "very true" to "definitely untrue" with scores ranging from 5 for the "very true" response to 1 for the "definitely untrue" response. The standard deviation of the scores of all the schedules for the community is taken as a measure of the degree of consensus and, there fore, of solidarity in the community. The smaller the S, the greater the solidarity is assumed to be. The mean of the total score is con sidered to be an index of the members' opinion of the quality of the community. For comparison with other communities an octagona profile may be used.

WHERE PUBLISHED: Donald R. Fessler, "The Development of a Scale for Measuring Community Solidarity," *Rural Sociology*, 1 (1952), 144-152.

RELIABILITY: Split-half r was described as being high but not given

VALIDITY: Face validity.

UTILITY: This index measures an important community variable When relationships are examined between community action pro grams and community solidarity, this measure may be highly pre dictive of the success or failure of community efforts.

ESEARCH APPLICATIONS: Other scales and efforts to measure community attachment and identification include:

ANDERSON, C. ARNOLD. "Community Chest Campaigns as an Index of Community Integration," *Social Forces*, 33 (October, 1954), 76-81.

FANELLI, A. ALEXANDER. "Extensiveness of Communication Contacts and Perceptions of the Community," *American Sociological Review*, 21 (August, 1956), 439-445.

WILENSKY, HAROLD L. "Mass Society and Mass Culture: Interdependence or Independence?" *American Sociological Review*, 29 (April, 1964), 173-197.

COMMUNITY SOLIDARITY INDEX SCHEDULE

Name _____ Community _____

Occupation _____ Married _____ Single _____

If married, number of children in school, if any _____

boys _____ girls _____, number of children out of school _____

Number of years resident in community _____. Location of residenc

in town _____ outside of town _____ how far _____ miles?

Think of each of the statements below as relating to the people
this entire community both in town and on neighboring farms. If y
think the statement fits this community very well, after the stateme
circle *vt* (for very true); if it applies only partially, circle *t* (for true
if you cannot see how it relates one way or another to this particul
community, circle *nd* (for not decided); if you think it is not tru
circle *u* (for untrue); and if it definitely is not true, circle *du* (f
definitely untrue). PLEASE RECORD THE IMPRESSION THA
FIRST OCCURS TO YOU. Do not go back and change your answer

1. Real friends are hard to find in this community. *vt t nd u*
   (2) *

2. Our schools do a poor job of preparing young people for lif
   vt t nd u du (4)

3. Local concerns deal fairly and squarely with everyone. *vt t*
   u du (6)

4. The community is very peaceful and orderly. *vt t nd u du* (8

5. A lot of people here think they are too nice for you. *vt t nd u*
   (1)

6. Families in this community keep their children under contro
   vt t nd u du (3)

7. The different churches here cooperate well with one anothe
   vt t nd u du (5)

* The number in parentheses indicates the area to which the statement belong

8. Some people here "get by with murder" while others take the rap for any little misdeed. *vt t nd u du* (7)

9. Almost everyone is polite and courteous to you. *vt t nd u du* (2)

10. Our schools do a good job of preparing students for college. *vt t nd u du* (4)

11. Everyone here tries to take advantage of you. *vt t nd u du* (6)

12. People around here show good judgment. *vt t nd u du* (8)

13. People won't work together to get things done for the community. *vt t nd u du* (1)

14. Parents teach their children to respect other people's rights and property. *vt t nd u du* (3)

15. Most of our church people forget the meaning of the word brotherhood when they get out of church. *vt t nd u du* (5)

16. This community lacks real leaders. *vt t nd u du* (7)

17. People give you a bad name if you insist on being different. *vt t nd u du* (2)

18. Our high-school graduates take an active interest in making their community a better place in which to live. *vt t nd u du* (4)

19. A few people here make all the dough. *vt t nd u du* (6)

20. Too many young people get into sex difficulties. *vt t nd u du* (8)

21. The community tries hard to help its young people along. *vt t nd u du* (1)

22. Folks are unconcerned about what their kids do so long as they keep out of trouble. *vt t nd u du* (3)

23. The churches are a constructive factor for better community life. *vt t nd u du* (5)

24. The mayor and councilmen run the town to suit themselves. *vt t nd u du* (7)

25. I feel very much that I belong here. *vt t nd u du* (2)

26. Many young people in the community do not finish high school. *vt t nd u du* (4)

27. The people here are all penny pinchers. *vt t nd u du* (6)

28. You must spend lots of money to be accepted here. *vt t nd u du* (8)

29. The people as a whole mind their own business. *vt t nd u du* (1)

30. Most people get their families to Sunday School or church on Sunday. *vt t nd u du* (3)

31. Every church wants to be the biggest and the most impressive. *vt t nd u du* (5)

32. A few have the town politics well sewed up. *vt t nd u du* (7)

33. Most of the students here learn to read and write well. *vt t nd u du* (4)

34. People are generally critical of others. *vt t nd u du* (2)

35. Local concerns expect their help to live on low wages. *vt t nd u du* (6)

36. You are out of luck here if you happen to be of the wrong nationality. *vt t nd u du* (8)

37. No one seems to care much how the community looks. *vt t nd u du* (1)

38. If their children keep out of the way, parents are satisfied to let them do whatever they want to do. *vt t nd u du* (3)

39. Most of our churchgoers do not practice what they preach. *vt t nd u du* (5)

40. The town council gets very little done. *vt t nd u du* (7)

IV.D.3. INDEX: COMMUNITY RATING SCHEDULE

VARIABLE MEASURED: The quality of community life, of "goodness" of the community, is assessed.

DESCRIPTION: Ten institutional areas of community life are rated as good, fair, or poor. The areas selected include education, housing and planning, religion, equality of opportunity, economic development, cultural opportunities, recreation, health and welfare, government, and community organization. Scores range from 0-100.

WHERE PUBLISHED: New York State Citizen's Council, *Adult Leadership*, Vol. 1, No. 5 (October, 1952), 19.

RELIABILITY: Not known.

VALIDITY: Rests upon face validity.

STANDARD SCORES:

> Good communities = 90-100
> Fair communities = 70-89
> Poor communities = 0-69

UTILITY: The schedule is easy to administer; the time required is about 10 minutes. Raters often have difficulty in making a general judgment and express qualifications. These should be expected. The special advantage of this index is that it permits analysis of individual raters. Individual raters from business, labor, welfare, education, and religion often differ widely in their assessments of the same community.

RESEARCH APPLICATIONS: No reported studies. However, the index opens possibilities of examining the patterns of new industrial locations with quality of the community. The relationship of leadership to community quality is an important area that should be explored.

COMMUNITY RATING SCHEDULE *

Ask respondent to rate community as good, fair, or poor as judged by similar communities in the United States.

	Good	Fair	Poor
Standard No. 1 Education Modern education available for every child, youth and adult. Uncrowded, properly equipped schools in good physical conditions. Highly qualified, well paid teachers.			
Standard No. 2 Housing and Planning Every family decently housed. Continuous planning for improvement of residential areas, parks, highways, and other community essentials. Parking, traffic, and transportation problems under control.			
Standard No. 3 Religion Full opportunity for religious expression accorded to every individual—churches strong and well supported.			
Standard No. 4 Equality of Opportunity People of different races, religions, and nationalities have full chance for employment and for taking part in community life. Dangerous tensions kept at minimum by avoidance of discrimination and injustices.			
Standard No. 5 Economic Development Good jobs available. Labor, industry, agriculture, and government work together to insure sound economic growth.			
Standard No. 6 Cultural Opportunities Citizens' lives strengthened by ample occasion to enjoy music, art, and dramatics. A professionally administered library service benefits people of all ages. Newspapers and radio carefully review community affairs.			

* Prepared by New York State Citizen's Council; Reprinted in *Adult Leadership*, Vol. 1, No. 5 (October, 1952), 19.

COMMUNITY RATING SCHEDULE—(Continued)

Good Fair Poor

Standard No. 7   Recreation

Enough supervised playgrounds and facilities for outdoor activities. Full opportunity to take part in arts and crafts, photography, and other hobbies.

Standard No. 8   Health and Welfare

Positive approach to improving health of entire community. Medical care and hospitalization readily available. Provision made for under-privileged children, the aged, and the handi-capped. Families in trouble can secure needed assistance.

Standard No. 9   Government

Capable citizens seek public office. Officials concerned above all with community betterment. Controversy stems from honest differences of opinion, not from squabbles over privilege.

Standard No. 10   Community Organization

An organization-community forum, citizen's council, or community federation-representative of entire town is working for advancement of the whole community. Citizens have opportunity to learn about and take part in local affairs. There is an organized, community-wide discussion program. Specialized organizations give vigorous attention to each important civic need.

	Good ____ 10 points for each item ____
Total Score for your Town	Fair ____ 5 points for each item ____
	Poor ____ no points
	Total ____

IV.D.4. INDEX: SCORECARD FOR COMMUNITY SERVICES ACTIVITY

VARIABLE MEASURED: Individual participation in community services.

DESCRIPTION: The scorecard is an arbitrary index to assess individual participation in community services. Fifteen possible behavioral items are presented as those that compose bulk of community service activity. Scores of 0-15 may be recorded as each item participation is given a weight of one.

WHERE PUBLISHED: Unpublished.

RELIABILITY: No tests have been made.

VALIDITY: Rests on face validity.

STANDARD SCORES:

> 10-15 outstanding community member
> 6-9   an average member
> 0-5   low participating member

Cutting points were based upon a random sample of 100 adults in a middle class community.

UTILITY: Administration of the scorecard takes less than four minutes. It provides for both individual and group assessment.

RESEARCH APPLICATIONS: None reported. However, the index opens possibilities of exploring important facets of citizenship including the importance of background factors such as age, sex, education, race, and social class. The relation between community service activity, community solidarity, and community rating is a challenging research endeavor.

SCORECARD FOR COMMUNITY SERVICES ACTIVITY

Constructed by Delbert C. Miller

(* Score one point for each "yes")

FINANCIAL SUPPORT—Did you, in the past year,

_____ Contribute money to a community chest campaign?

_____ Contribute money to a church?

_____ Contribute money for other charitable purposes?

GENERAL ACTIVITY—Did you, in the past year,

_____ Serve on any board responsible for civic programs?

_____ Serve on any committee working to improve civic life?

_____ Assume leadership of any civic action program?

COMMUNITY ISSUES AND PROBLEMS—Did you, in the past year,

_____ Inform yourself about civic issues and problems?

_____ Discuss civic problems frequently with more than one person?

_____ Persuade others to take a particular position?

_____ Get advice from others?

_____ Speak to key leaders about problems?

_____ Visit community organizations or board meetings to inform yourself?

_____ Write letters, or circulate literature, or hold home meetings?

GROUP ACTION—Did you, in the past year,

_____ Belong to one or more organizations that takes stands on community issues and problems?

_____ Make group visits or invite visits of community officials to your organization?

_____ Total Score

> * 10-15 points—An outstanding community member
> 6-9 points—An average member
> 0-5 points—A low participating member

FOR THE ADVANCED STUDENT

1. Consult Jack P. Gibbs (ed.), *Urban Research Methods* (Princeton, N.J.: Van Nostrand, 1961).
2. Robert C. Angell, "Moral Integration of Cities," *American Journal of Sociology*, 57, Pt. 2 (July, 1951).
3. Eshref Shevky and Wendell Bell, *Social Area Analysis* (Stanford: Stanford University, 1955). Contains indexes of social rank, urbanization, and segregation. Cf. Robert C. Tryon, *Identification Of Social Areas by Cluster Analysis* (Berkeley: University of California, 1955).
4. Christian T. Jonassen, *The Measurement of Community Dimensions and Elements* (Columbus: Center for Educational Administration, Ohio State University, 1959). Cf. his "Functional Unities in Eighty-eight Community Systems," *American Sociological Review*, 26 (June, 1961), 399-407.
5. For measurement of occupational, ethnic, and social class segregation, see the work of Karl E. Taeuber and Alma F. Taeuber, *Negroes in Cities* (Chicago: Aldine, 1965), pp. 195-245. Cf. also Donald O. Cowgill, "Segregation Scores for Metropolitan Areas," *American Sociological Review*, 27 (June, 1962), 400-402; Otis D. Duncan and Beverly Duncan, "Measuring Segregation," *American Sociological Review*, 28 (February, 1963), 133; Julius Jahn and Calvin F. Schmid, "The Measurement of Ecological Segregation," *American Sociological Review*, 12 (June, 1947), 293-303; and Theodore R. Anderson and Lee L. Bean, "The Shevky-Bell Social Areas: Confirmation of Results and a Reinterpretation," *Social Forces*, 40 (December, 1961), 119-124.

Social Participation

This section includes *Chapin's Social Participation Scale*. It is a general scale of participation in voluntary organizations of all kinds —professional, civic, and social. It is used when the total participation pattern is an important variable. The *Leisure Participation and Enjoyment Scale* enables the researcher to get a detailed picture of leisure patterns and also to get a score for each respondent on both participation and enjoyment.

A measure of neighborhood participation is included. *Wallin Women's Neighborliness Scale* is a Guttman-type scale that has exhibited unidimensionality on the samples of respondents that have been tested. It is designed to be answered by women respondents only.

The *Citizen Political Action Schedule* is a scorecard for political behavior reported by a community resident. If the respondent reports accurately, the scale can reveal the behavioral acts in the political sphere.

IV.E.1. INDEX: CHAPIN'S SOCIAL PARTICIPATION SCALE, 1952 EDITION

VARIABLE MEASURED: Degree of a person's or family's participation in community groups and institutions.

DESCRIPTION: This is a Guttman-type scale with reproducibility coefficients of .92 to .97 for groups of leaders. High scores of 18 and over represent titular leader achievement. The five components are (1) Member, (2) Attendance, (3) Financial contributions, (4) Member of Committees, (5) Offices held. These components measure different dimensions: intensity of participation by Nos. 2, 3, 4, and 5; extensity by No. 1. Also, rejection-acceptance in formal groups is measured by Nos. 1, 4, and 5, for which the intercorrelations are found to be of the order of $r_{14} = .53$ to .58; $r_{15} = .36$ to .40; $r_{45} = .36$ to .40. Social participation is measured by Nos. 2 and 3 with intercorrelations of $r_{23} = .80$ to .89. Other intercorrelations among the components have been found to be of the order of $r_{12} = .88$; $r_{13} = .89$; $r_{24} = .60$; $r_{34} = .40$; $r_{35} = .35$; and $r_{45} = .50$ to .58.

WHERE PUBLISHED: F. Stuart Chapin, *Experimental Designs in Sociological Research* (New York: Harper, 1955), Appendix B, pp. 275-278.

RELIABILITY: $r = .89$ to .95.

VALIDITY:

With Chapin's social status scale scores	$r = .62$ to .66
With income class	$r = .52$
With occupational groups	$r = .63$
With years of formal education	$r = .54$
Between husband and wife	$r = .76$

STANDARD SCORES: Mean scores for occupational groups are as follows:

    I. Professional, 20.
    II. Managerial and Proprietary, 20.
   III. Clerical, 16.
   IV. Skilled, 12.
    V. Semiskilled, 8.
   VI. Unskilled, 4.

UTILITY: One sheet is used for entries on each group affiliation of subject recorded in five entries under five columns by the visitor in reply to questions answered by the subject. It takes 10 to 15 minutes to fill in the subject's answers.
    The scale may also be self-administered.

RESEARCH APPLICATIONS:
    CHAPIN, F. S. "The Effects of Slum Clearance on Family and Community Relationships in Minneapolis in 1935-1936," *American Journal of Sociology*, 43 (March, 1938), 744-763.
    ————. "Social Participation and Social Intelligence," *American Sociological Review*, 4 (April, 1939), 157-166.
    ERBE, WILLIAM M. "Social Involvement and Political Activity: A Replication and Elaboration," *American Sociological Review*, 29 (April, 1964), 198-215.
    EVAN, WILLIAM M. "Dimensions of Participation on Voluntary Associations," *Social Forces*, 35 (December, 1957), 148-153.
    LUNDBERG, G. A., and LANSING, MARGARET. "The Sociography of Some Community Relations," *American Sociological Review*, 2 (June, 1937), 318-328.
    MARTIN, WALTER T. "A Consideration of Differences in the Extent and Location of the Formal Associational Activities of Rural-Urban Fringe Residents," *American Sociological Review*, 17 (December, 1952), 687-694.

NELSON, JOEL I. "Participation and Integration: The Case of the Small Businessman," *American Sociological Review,* 33 (June, 1968), 427-438.

SOCIAL PARTICIPATION SCALE, 1952 EDITION *

F. Stuart Chapin, University of Minnesota

DIRECTIONS

1. List by name the organizations with which the husband and wife are affiliated (at the present time) as indicated by the five types of participation No. 1 to No. 5 across the top of the schedule.

   It is not necessary to enter the date at which the person became a member of the organization. It is important to enter *L* if the membership is in a purely local group, and to enter *N* if the membership is in a local unit of some state or national organization.

2. An organization means some active and organized grouping, usually but not necessarily in the community or neighborhood of residence, such as club, lodge, business or political or professional or religious organization, labor union, etc.; subgroups of a church or other institution are to be included separately *provided they are organized* as more or less independent entities.

3. Record under attendance the mere fact of attendance or non-attendance without regard to the number of meetings attended (corrections for the number attended *have not* been found to influence the final score sufficiently to justify such labor).

4. Record under contributions the mere fact of financial contributions or absence of contributions, and *not the amount* (corrections for amount of contributions *have not* been found to influence the final score sufficiently to justify such labor).

5. Previous memberships, committee work, offices held, etc., should *not be* counted or recorded or used in computing the final score.

6. Final score is computed by counting each membership as 1, each attended as 2, each contributed to as 3, each committee membership as 4, and each office held as 5. If both parents are living regularly in the home, add their total scores and divide the sum by two. The result is the mean social participation score of the family. In case only one parent lives in the home, as widow, widower, etc., the sum of that one person's participations is the score for the family (unless it is desired to obtain scores on children also).

SOCIAL PARTICIPATION SCALE

Case No. _____

Husband

Address _____

Age _____ Education _____ Race or Nationality _____

Occupation _____ Income _____

Name of Organization	1. Member *	2. Attend-ance	3. Financial Contributions	4. Member of Committees (Not Name)	5. Offices Held
1.					
2.					
3.					
4.					
5.					
6.					
7.					
8.					
9.					
10.					
Totals _____					

Wife

Age _____ Education _____ Race or Nationality _____

Occupation _____ Income _____

Name of Organization	1. Member *	2. Attendance	3. Financial Contributions	4. Member of Committees (Not Name)	5. Offices Held
1. _____					
2. _____					
3. _____					
4. _____					
5. _____					
6. _____					
7. _____					
8. _____					
9. _____					
10. _____					
Totals _____					

Date _____ Investigator _____

* Enter L if purely local group; enter N if a local unit of a state or national organization.
Distribution of total scores from a representative sample of an urban population, a J-curve; skewed to higher scores of 100 and over; mode at 0 to 11 points.

IV.E.2. INDEX: LEISURE PARTICIPATION AND ENJOYMENT

VARIABLE MEASURED: The customary use of and degree of enjoyment of leisure time.

DESCRIPTION: The scale includes 47 items that are activities in which one might be expected to participate. Each item is ranked on two five-point scales. Leisure participation is scaled according to frequency of participation (1. Never, 2. Rarely, 3. Occasionally, 4. Fairly Often, 5. Frequently), and leisure enjoyment is scaled according to likes (1. Dislike very much, 2. Dislike, 3. Indifferent, 4. Like, 5. Like very much). The appropriate degree on each scale is circled for each item. No ranking on the like-dislike scale is given for those items in which the individual never participates.

WHERE PUBLISHED: C. R. Pace, *They Went to College* (Minneapolis: University of Minnesota, 1941). Copyright 1941 by the University of Minnesota.

RELIABILITY: Not known.

VALIDITY:
Leisure participation

with income	$r = .019$
with sociocivic activities scale	$r = .40$
with cultural status	$r = .039$

STANDARD SCORES: A summary of responses to the questionnaire on the Minnesota study is included on pages 142-145 of the Pace book.

	1924-25		*1928-29*	
	Grads.	*Non-grads.*	*Grads.*	*Non-grads.*
Median leisure participation for men	125.00	123.24	132.29	131.72
Median leisure enjoyment for men	169.83	167.53	171.67	170.65
Median leisure participation for women	139.80	137.90	137.50	133.97
Median leisure enjoyment for women	177.73	178.75	180.38	176.87

UTILITY: This scale is easily administered and may be self-adminis-tered. It is equally easy to score. It takes little time to administer. Both leisure participation and leisure enjoyment scores are derived and can be compared.

RESEARCH APPLICATIONS: Comparative study of 951 graduates and nongraduates of the University of Minnesota (C. R. Pace, *They Went to College*).

YOUR LEISURE-TIME ACTIVITIES

The use of leisure time is supposed to be an increasingly important social problem. We want to know how people usually spend their leisure time. Here is a list of activities. On the left side of the page put a circle around the number that tells how often you do these things now, using the key at the top of the column. On the right side of the page put a circle around the number that tells how well you like these things, using the key at the top of the column. If you never do the activity mentioned, circle number one in the left column to indicate no participation, and circle no number on the right side of the page. Try not to skip any item.

How Often Do You Do These Things	How Well Do You Like These Things
1. Never	1. Dislike very much
2. Rarely	2. Dislike
3. Occasionally	3. Indifferent
4. Fairly often	4. Like
5. Frequently	5. Like very much

1 2 3 4 5	1. Amateur dramatics	1 2 3 4 5
1 2 3 4 5	2. Amusement parks and halls	1 2 3 4 5
1 2 3 4 5	3. Art work (individual)	1 2 3 4 5
1 2 3 4 5	4. Attending large social functions (balls, benefit bridge, etc.)	1 2 3 4 5
1 2 3 4 5	5. Attending small social entertainments (dinner parties, etc.)	1 2 3 4 5
1 2 3 4 5	6. Book reading for pleasure	1 2 3 4 5
1 2 3 4 5	7. Conventions	1 2 3 4 5
1 2 3 4 5	8. Conversation with family	1 2 3 4 5
1 2 3 4 5	9. Card playing	1 2 3 4 5
1 2 3 4 5	10. Church and related organizations	1 2 3 4 5
1 2 3 4 5	11. Dancing	1 2 3 4 5
1 2 3 4 5	12. Dates	1 2 3 4 5

Continued on page 296.

How Often Do You Do	How Well Do You Like
These Things	These Things
1. Never	1. Dislike very much
2. Rarely	2. Dislike
3. Occasionally	3. Indifferent
4. Fairly often	4. Like
5. Frequently	5. Like very much

1 2 3 4 5   13. Entertaining at home   1 2 3 4 5

1 2 3 4 5   14. Fairs, exhibitions, etc.   1 2 3 4 5

1 2 3 4 5   15. Informal contacts with friends   1 2 3 4 5

1 2 3 4 5   16. Informal discussions, e.g., "bull sessions"   1 2 3 4 5

1 2 3 4 5   17. Indoor team recreation or sports—basketball, volleyball   1 2 3 4 5

1 2 3 4 5   18. Indoor individual recreation or sports—bowling, gym,
            pool, billiards, handball   1 2 3 4 5

1 2 3 4 5   19. Knitting, sewing, crocheting, etc.   1 2 3 4 5

1 2 3 4 5   20. Lectures (not class)   1 2 3 4 5

1 2 3 4 5   21. Listening to radio or TV   1 2 3 4 5

1 2 3 4 5   22. Literary writing—poetry, essays, stories, etc.   1 2 3 4 5

1 2 3 4 5   23. Magazine reading (for pleasure)   1 2 3 4 5

1 2 3 4 5   24. Movies   1 2 3 4 5

1 2 3 4 5   25. Newspaper reading   1 2 3 4 5

1 2 3 4 5   26. Odd jobs at home   1 2 3 4 5

1 2 3 4 5   27. Organizations or club meetings as a member   1 2 3 4 5

1 2 3 4 5   28. Organizations or club meetings as a leader (as for
            younger groups)   1 2 3 4 5

1 2 3 4 5   29. Outdoor individual sports—golf, riding, skating, hiking,
            tennis   1 2 3 4 5

1 2 3 4 5   30. Outdoor team sports—hockey, baseball, etc.   1 2 3 4 5

1 2 3 4 5   31. Picnics   1 2 3 4 5

1 2 3 4 5   32. Playing musical instrument or singing   1 2 3 4 5

1 2 3 4 5   33. Shopping   1 2 3 4 5

1 2 3 4 5   34. Sitting and thinking   1 2 3 4 5

1 2 3 4 5   35. Spectator of sports   1 2 3 4 5

1 2 3 4 5   36. Symphony or concerts   1 2 3 4 5

1 2 3 4 5   37. Telephone visiting   1 2 3 4 5

1 2 3 4 5   38. Theater attendance   1 2 3 4 5

1 2 3 4 5   39. Traveling or touring   1 2 3 4 5

1 2 3 4 5   40. Using public library   1 2 3 4 5

How Often Do You Do These Things	How Well Do You Like These Things
1. Never	1. Dislike very much
2. Rarely	2. Dislike
3. Occasionally	3. Indifferent
4. Fairly often	4. Like
5. Frequently	5. Like very much

1 2 3 4 5   41. Visiting museums, art galleries, etc.   1 2 3 4 5

1 2 3 4 5   42. Volunteer work—social service, etc.   1 2 3 4 5

1 2 3 4 5   43. Writing personal letters   1 2 3 4 5

1 2 3 4 5   44. Special hobbies—stamps, photography, shop work, gardening, and others not included above   1 2 3 4 5

1 2 3 4 5   45. Fishing or hunting   1 2 3 4 5

1 2 3 4 5   46. Camping   1 2 3 4 5

1 2 3 4 5   47. Developing and printing pictures   1 2 3 4 5

IV.E.3. INDEX: A GUTTMAN SCALE FOR MEASURING WOMEN'S NEIGHBORLINESS

VARIABLE MEASURED: The neighborliness of women under sixty years.

DESCRIPTION: This instrument is a unidimensional Guttman scale consisting of twelve items. The scale items can be simply scored for any sample by counting each *GN* (greater neighborliness) answer as 1 and each *LN* (lesser neighborliness) as 0. The possible range of scores is 12 to 0.

WHERE PUBLISHED: Paul Wallin, "A Guttman Scale for Measuring Women's Neighborliness," *The American Journal of Sociology*, 59 (1953), 243-246. Copyright 1953 by the University of Chicago.

RELIABILITY: The coefficient of reproducibility of the scale from two samples of women was .920 and .924.

VALIDITY: Face validity.

UTILITY: A short, easy-to-administer scale that may be used for investigating factors accounting for individual differences in neighborliness. The scale also can be used for testing hypotheses as to intracommunity and intercommunity difference in neighborliness.

RESEARCH APPLICATIONS:
EDELSTEIN, ALEX S., and LARSEN, OTTO N. "The Weekly Press's Contribution to a Sense of Urban Community," *Journalism Quarterly* (Autumn, 1960), 489-498.

FAVA, SYLVA F. "Suburbanism as a Way of Life," *American Sociological Review*, 21 (1956), 34-37.

GREER, SCOTT. "Urbanism Reconsidered: A Comparative Study of Local Areas in a Metropolis," *American Sociological Review*, 21 (1956), 19-25.

LARSEN, OTTO N., and EDELSTEIN, ALEX S. "Communication, Consensus and the Community Involvement of Urban Husbands and Wives," *Acta Sociologia* (Copenhagen), 5 (1960), 15-30.

For some recent research on neighborhood satisfaction and integration see:

FELLIN, PHILLIP, and LITWAK, EUGENE. "Neighborhood Cohesion under Conditions of Mobility," *American Sociological Review*, 28 (June, 1963), 364-376.

LITWAK, EUGENE. "Voluntary Associations and Neighborhood Cohesion," *American Sociological Review*, 26 (April, 1961), 258-271.

STUCKERT, ROBERT P. "Occupational Mobility and Family Relationships," *Social Forces*, 41 (March, 1963), 301-307.

SWINEHART, JAMES W. "Socio-Economic Level, Status Aspiration, and Maternal Role," *American Sociological Review*, 28 (June, 1963), 391-399.

A GUTTMAN SCALE FOR MEASURING WOMEN'S NEIGHBORLINESS

Paul Wallin

1. How many of your best friends who live in your neighborhood did you get to know since you or they moved into the neighborhood? Two or more (*GN*); one or none (*LN*).
2. Do you and any of your neighbors go to movies, picnics, or other things like that together? Often or sometimes (*GN*); rarely or never (*LN*).
3. Do you and your neighbors entertain one another? Often or sometimes (*GN*); rarely or never (*LN*).
4. If you were holding a party or tea for an out-of-town visitor, how many of your neighbors would you invite? Two or more (*GN*); one or none (*LN*).
5. How many of your neighbors have ever talked to you about their problems when they were worried or asked you for advice or help? One or more (*GN*); none (*LN*).
6. How many of your neighbors' homes have you ever been in? Four or more (*GN*); three or less (*LN*).
7. Do you and your neighbors exchange or borrow things from one another such as books, magazines, dishes, tools, recipes, preserves, or garden vegetables? Often, sometimes, or rarely (*GN*); none (*LN*).
8. About how many of the people in your neighborhood would you recognize by sight if you saw them in a large crowd? About half or more (*GN*); a few or none (*LN*).
9. With how many of your neighbors do you have a friendly talk fairly frequently? Two or more (*GN*); one or none (*LN*).
10. About how many of the people in your neighborhood do you say "Hello" or "Good morning" to when you meet on the street? Six or more (*GN*); five or less (*LN*).

11. How many of the names of the families in your neighborhood do you know? Four or more (2); one to three (1); none (0).
12. How often do you have a talk with any of your neighbors? Often or sometimes (*GN*); rarely or never (*LN*).

IV.E.4. INDEX: CITIZEN POLITICAL ACTION SCHEDULE

VARIABLE MEASURED: Individual participation in citizen political action.

DESCRIPTION: This is an arbitrary index to assess individual participation in community services. Twelve possible behavioral items are presented as those that compose bulk of citizen political activity. Scores of 0-12 may be recorded as each item participation is given a weight of one.

WHERE PUBLISHED: League of Women Voters of Pennsylvania, Publication No. 101, Philadelphia, Pa.

RELIABILITY: No tests have been made.

VALIDITY: Face validity.

STANDARD SCORES:

> 10-12 an outstanding citizen!
> 6-9 an average citizen.
> 0-5 a citizen?

UTILITY: May be administered in less than four minutes. It provides a measure suitable for both individual and group assessment.

RESEARCH APPLICATION: None reported. However, index opens possibilities of exploring important facets of political behavior including the importance of background factors of age, sex, education, race, and social class. For selection of alternate scales and related research, see John P. Robinson, *et. al., Measures of Political Attitudes* (Ann Arbor, Mich.: Institute of Social Research, University of Michigan, 1968), pp. 427-435.

SCORE CARD FOR CITIZEN POLITICAL ACTION

*Published by the League of Women Voters of Pennsylvania,
Publication No. 101*

(* Score one point for each "yes")

VOTING—Did you vote

—Once in the last four years? ____

—Two to five times? ____

—Six or more times? ____

PUBLIC ISSUES—Do you

—Inform yourself from more than one source on public issues? ____

—Discuss public issues frequently with more than one person? ____

INDIVIDUAL ACTION ON PUBLIC ISSUES—Did you

—Write or talk to your Congressman or any other public official —local, state or national—to express your views once in the past year? ____

—Two or more times? ____

GROUP ACTION ON PUBLIC ISSUES—Do you

—Belong to one or more organizations that take stands on public issues? ____

PRIMARY ELECTION ACTIVITY— Did you

—Discuss the qualifications needed for the offices on the ballot? ____

—Work for the nomination of a candidate before the primary election once in the last four years? ____

GENERAL OR MUNICIPAL ELECTION ACTIVITY—Did you

—Work for the election of a candidate once in the last four years? ____

FINANCIAL SUPPORT—Did you

—Contribute money to a party or candidate once in the last four years? ____

TOTAL SCORE ____

* 10-12 points—An outstanding citizen!
6-9 points—An average citizen.
5-0 points—a citizen?

301

Leadership in the Work Organization

This section contains two leadership scales that may be widely used in work organizations. The first scale, the *Leadership Opinion Questionnaire,* is designed to find answers to the question, "What *should you* as a supervisor do?" The second scale, the *Supervisory Behavior Description,* is designed to find answers to the question, "What does *your own supervisor* actually do?" Note that these two scales make it possible to get measures of two levels of leadership in an organization. The relation of a supervisor to his immediate superior has been shown to be a very important one. The use of both questionnaires makes it possible to secure a comparison between the two levels. However, each scale may be used for the specific purpose for which it was designed. Use the *Leadership Opinion Questionnaire* whenever a measure of a leader's personal orientation is desired. Use the *Supervisory Behavior Description* when it is desirable to get the perceptions of a supervisor by those who report to him. This scale can be given to employees or any group of supervisors or managers. These two scales have been subjected to repeated refinement and may be considered highly reliable and valid in terms of present progress in scale construction.

The *Work Patterns Profile* is an analysis form, which permits a description of work activity patterns. This schedule has its greatest worth as a diagnostic instrument. The relation of the work patterns profile to the leadership orientation of initiation and consideration offer interesting research problems.

Many measures of organizational analyses might be included. Space prevents their addition, but the following measures are annotated for the consideration of the organizational researcher:

    1. Executive Position Description

This description contains 191 items to determine the basic charcteristics of executive positions in business and industry. Part I overs Position Activities; Part II, Position Responsibilities; Part II, Position Demands and Restrictions; Part IV, Position Characeristics. See John K. Hemphill, *Dimensions of Executive Positions* Columbus: Ohio State University Bureau of Business Research, 960).

2. Responsibility, Authority, and Delegation Scales
These scales were designed to measure different degrees of pereived responsibility, authority, and delegation as exhibited by individuals who occupy administrative or supervisory positions. See .alph M. Stogdill and Carroll L. Shartle, *Methods in the Study of dministrative Leadership* (Columbus: Ohio State University Bueau of Business Research, 1955), pp. 33-43.

3. Multirelational Sociometric Survey
This survey measures interpersonal variables surrounding work ctivities. Five dimensions are included: the prescribed, the pereived, the actual, the desired, and the rejected. See Robert Tannenaum, Irving W. Weschler, and Fred Massarik, *Leadership and 'rganization: A Behavioral Science Approach* (New York: McGraw-[ill, 1961), pp. 346-370.

4. A Method for the Analysis of the Structure of Complex 'rganizations
This is an application of sociometric analysis based on work conacts. The method enables the researcher to depict the organization oordination structure as established through the activities of liaison ersons and the existence of the contacts between groups. See Robert . Weiss and Eugene Jacobson, "A Method for the Analysis of the tructure of Complex Organizations," *American Sociological Reiew*, 20 (December, 1955), 661-668. Cf. with Ralph M. Stogdill and arroll L. Shartle, *Methods in the Study of Administrative Leaderuip* (Columbus: Ohio State University Bureau of Business Research,)55), pp. 18-32.

IV.F.1. INDEX: LEADERSHIP OPINION QUESTIONNAIRE

ARIABLE MEASURED: The questionnaire measures leader's orientation around two major factors, *Structure* and *Consideration*.

Structure (S): Reflects the extent to which an individual is likel; to define and structure his own role and those of his subordinate toward goal attainment. A high score on this dimension characterize individuals who play a more active role in directing group activitie through planning, communicating information, scheduling, trying ou new ideas, etc.

Consideration (C): Reflects the extent to which an individual i likely to have job relationships characterized by mutual trust, respec for subordinate's ideas, and consideration of their feelings. A hig score is indicative of a climate of good rapport and two-way com munication. A low score indicates the superior is likely to be mor impersonal in his relations with group members.

DESCRIPTION: This is a forty-item questionnaire divided into th two factors, *Structure* and *Consideration*. Each factor is tested by 2 items. The items are presented with a five-point continuum with scor ing weights of zero to four depending on item's orientation to tota dimension.

WHERE PUBLISHED: Copyright © 1960, Science Research Assoc ates, Inc., Chicago, Illinois. Scale is sold as Leadership Opinion Que: tionaire by Edwin A. Fleishman. It was first presented to soci; scientists in Ralph M. Stogdill and Alvin E. Coons (eds.), *Lead Behavior: Its Description and Measurement* (Columbus: Ohio Sta University Bureau of Business Research, 1957), pp. 120-133.

RELIABILITY: Test-retest coefficients *for 31 foremen* after a 3-mont interval show

$r = .80$ on Consideration,
$r = .74$ on Initiating Structure;

for 24 Air Force NCO's

$r = .77$ on Consideration,
$r = .67$ on Initiating Structure.

Split-half reliability estimates for the Consideration and Initiatin Structure were found to be .69 and .73, respectively.

VALIDITY: Validity was evaluated through correlations with inde pendent leadership measures, such as merit rating by supervisors, pee ratings, forced choice performance reports by management, and lead erless group situation tests. Relatively low validities were found fc the particular criteria employed, although a few statistically significar correlations were found. Correlations with other measures reveale that scores on the *Leadership Opinion Questionnaire* were independer of the "intelligence" of the supervisor, an advantage not achieved by other available leadership attitude questionnaires.

The questionnaire scores have been found to be sensitive for discriminating reliably between leadership attitudes in different situations as well as for evaluating the effects of leadership training.

Science Research Associates has compiled evidence for validity from recent studies in many different organizational settings. It has been used in a test battery to ascertain effectiveness of sales supervisors. It has been administered to foremen in a large wholesale pharmaceutical company, to first line supervisors in a large petrochemical refinery, to department managers in a large shoe manufacturing company, and to bank managers. In all instances, significant correlations between the questionnaire and proficiency have been shown. The Leadership Opinion Questionnaire has also shown that leadership patterns are directly related to organizational stress and effectiveness in three hospitals.

STANDARDIZED SCORES (Published in Edwin A. Fleishman, "The Measurement of Leadership Attitudes in Industry," *Journal of Applied Psychology* (June, 1953), 156.)

Dimension	Level in Organization	Mean	S.D.
Consideration	Superintendents (N = 13)	52.6	8.1
	General Foremen (N = 30)	53.2	7.1
	Foremen (N = 122)	53.9	7.2
	Workers (N = 394)	57.0	5.5
Structure	Superintendents (N = 13)	55.5	5.7
	General Foremen (N = 30)	53.6	6.9
	Foremen (N = 122)	53.3	7.8
	Workers (N = 394)	44.2	3.9

UTILITY: Easily administered and scored. Time of administration, 10-15 minutes. See Edwin A. Fleishman, *A Manual for Administering the Leadership Opinion Questionnaire* (Chicago: Science Research Associates, 1960).

RESEARCH APPLICATIONS:

BASS, B. M. "Leadership Opinions as Forecasters of Supervisory Success," *Journal of Applied Psychology* (1956), 345-346.

FLEISHMAN, E. A. *Leadership Climate and Supervisory Behavior* (Columbus: Ohio State University Personnel Research Board, 1951).

————. "The Measurement of Leadership Attitudes in Industry," *Journal of Applied Psychology* (June, 1953), 153-158.

————. "Leadership Climate, Human Relations Training, and Supervisory Behavior," *Personnel Psychology*, 6 (1953), 205-222.

————, HARRIS, E. F., and BURTT, H. E. *Leadership and Supervision in Industry* (Columbus: Ohio State University, Bureau of Educational Research).

HEMPHILL, J. K. *Leader Behavior Description* (Columbus: Personnel Research Board, Ohio State University, 1950).

SEEMAN, MELVIN. "Social Mobility and Administrative Behavior," *American Sociological Review,* 23 (December, 1958), 633-642.

LEADERSHIP OPINION QUESTIONNAIRE *

This questionnaire contains forty items when presented as a complete scale. The items that follow exemplify the type found in the longer questionnaire. They are presented here so that the researcher may evaluate them for his possible use of the complete scale.

Structure

ASSIGN PEOPLE IN THE WORK GROUP TO PARTICULAR TASKS.

1. Always   2. Often   3. Occasionally   4. Seldom   5. Never

STRESS BEING AHEAD OF COMPETING WORK GROUPS.

1. A great deal   2. Fairly much   3. To some degree
4. Comparatively little   5. Not at all

CRITICIZE POOR WORK

1. Always   2. Often   3. Occasionally   4. Seldom   5. Never

EMPHASIZE MEETING OF DEADLINES.

1. A great deal   2. Fairly much   3. To some degree
4. Comparatively little   5. Not at all

Consideration

PUT SUGGESTIONS MADE BY PEOPLE IN THE WORK GROUP INTO OPERATION.

    1. Always   2. Often   3. Occasionally   4. Seldom   5. Never

HELP PEOPLE IN THE WORK GROUP WITH THEIR PERSONAL PROBLEMS

    1. Often   2. Fairly often   3. Occasionally   4. Once in a while
    5. Seldom

GET THE APPROVAL OF THE WORK GROUP ON IMPORTANT MATTERS BEFORE GOING AHEAD.

    1. Always   2. Often   3. Occasionally   4. Seldom   5. Never

IV.F.2. INDEX: SUPERVISORY BEHAVIOR DESCRIPTION

VARIABLE MEASURED: Perceptions of subordinates of the leadership behavior demonstrated by their immediate superior. Factor analysis revealed that "Initiating Structure" and "Consideration" items are the most significant factors in distinguishing leadership performance. "Initiating Structure" reflects the extent to which the supervisor facilitates group interaction toward goal attainment; "Consideration" reflects the extent to which the supervisor is considerate of the feelings of those under him. All questions are worded in terms of "What does your own supervisor actually do?"

DESCRIPTION: This is a 48-item questionnaire divided into two independent areas of leadership called "Initiating Structure" and "Consideration." The first area includes 20 items and the second is made up of 28 items. The items were presented with a five-point continuum answer scale that has scoring weights of zero to four depending on the item orientation to the total dimension. Highest possible score was 112 on "Consideration" and 80 for "Initiation."

WHERE PUBLISHED: Edwin A. Fleishman, "A Leader Behavior Description for Industry," in Ralph M. Stogdill and Alvin E. Coons (eds.), *Leader Behavior: Its Description and Measurement* (Columbus: Ohio State University Bureau of Business Research, 1957), pp. 103-119.

RELIABILITY: Test-retest reliability coefficients based on numerous samples range from .46 to .87.

		Dimension	
	Time Between		*Initiating*
Sample	*Administration*	*Consideration*	*Structure*
		r	*r*
Workers describing 18 foremen	11 months	.87	.75
Workers describing 59 foremen	11 months	.58	.46
Workers describing 31 foremen	3 weeks	.56	.53

Split-half reliabilities are reported for samples as between .68 to .98.

VALIDITY: The correlation between "Consideration" and "Initiating Structure" was found to be —.02 when based on replies of 122 foremen. The intercorrelation was shown to be —.33 when administered to 394 workers who described the 122 foremen. The correlation between the two scales was shown to be —.05 when administered to 176 Air Force and Army ROTC students who described their superior officers. The independence of the two factors appears to be confirmed.

Correlations have been obtained between descriptions of foreman behavior and independent indexes of accident rates, absenteeism, grievances, and turnover among the foreman's own work groups. In production departments, high scores on the "Consideration" scale were predictive of low ratings of proficiency by the foreman's supervisor, but low absenteeism among the workers. A high score on "Initiating Structure" was predictive of a high proficiency rating, but high absenteeism and labor grievances as well.

Among nonproduction departments, a foreman with a high score on "Consideration" was predictive of low accident rates with a trend toward low absenteeism as well. A high score on "Initiating Structure" was related to high labor turnover in nonproduction departments.

STANDARD SCORES:

MEANS AND STANDARD DEVIATIONS OF SUPERVISORY BEHAVIOR DESCRIPTION SCORES

	Dimension			
	Consideration		*Initiating Structure*	
Sample	*M*	*SD*	*M*	*SD*
Descriptions of 122 foremen	79.8	14.5	41.5	7.6
Descriptions of 31 foremen	71.5	13.2	37.5	6.3
Descriptions of 31 foremen	73.0	12.7	40.7	7.3
Descriptions of 8 Civil Service Supervisors	75.1	17.6	37.3	9.6
Descriptions of 60 General Foremen	82.3	15.5	51.5	8.8

UTILITY: The questionnaire may be administered in a 10-15 minute period. When used in group applications, it is very efficient. By using this questionnaire in conjunction with the Leader Behavior Description, it is possible to get a view of how a supervisor thinks he should lead and compare this view with an assessment by his subordinates of his actual leadership performance.

RESEARCH APPLICATIONS: The best summary of research is found in the monograph cited in the aforementioned. Other references may be found in the publications cited under the Leadership Opinion Questionnaire. Most of the research has been done by E. A. Fleishman in the plants of the International Harvester Company.

Items Selected for the Revised Form of the Supervisory Behavior Description

Item Number	Item *

Consideration: Revised Key

1. He refuses to give in when people disagree with him.
2. He does personal favors for the foremen under him.
3. He expresses appreciation when one of us does a good job.
4. He is easy to understand.
5. He demands more than we can do.
6. He helps his foremen with their personal problems.
7. He criticizes his foremen in front of others.
8. He stands up for his foremen even though it makes him unpopular.
9. He insists that everything be done his way.
10. He sees that a foreman is rewarded for a job well done.
11. He rejects suggestions for changes.
12. He changes the duties of people under him without first talking it over with them.
13. He treats people under him without considering their feelings.
14. He tries to keep the foremen under him in good standing with those in higher authority.
15. He resists changes in ways of doing things.
16. He "rides" the foreman who makes a mistake.
17. He refuses to explain his actions.
18. He acts without consulting his foreman first.
19. He stresses the importance of high morale among those under him.

* Most items were answered as: 1. always; 2. often; 3. occasionally; 4. seldom; 5. never.

ITEMS SELECTED FOR THE REVISED FORM OF THE
SUPERVISORY BEHAVIOR DESCRIPTION—*Continued*

Item
Number   *Item*

Consideration: Revised Key

20. He backs up his foremen in their actions.
21. He is slow to accept new ideas.
22. He treats all his foremen as his equal.
23. He criticizes a specific act rather than a particular individual.
24. He is willing to make changes.
25. He makes those under him feel at ease when talking with him.
26. He is friendly and can be easily approached.
27. He puts suggestions that are made by foremen under him into operation.
28. He gets the approval of his foremen on important matters before going ahead.

Initiating Structure: Revised Key

1. He encourages overtime work.
2. He tries out his new ideas.
3. He rules with an iron hand.
4. He criticizes poor work.
5. He talks about how much should be done.
6. He encourages slow-working foremen to greater effort.
7. He waits for his foremen to push new ideas before he does.
8. He assigns people under him to particular tasks.
9. He asks for sacrifices from his foremen for the good of the entire department.
10. He insists that his foremen follow standard ways of doing things in every detail.
11. He sees to it that people under him are working up to their limits.
12. He offers new approaches to problems.
13. He insists that he be informed on decisions made by foremen under him.
14. He lets others do their work the way they think best.
15. He stresses being ahead of competing work groups.
16. He "needles" foremen under him for greater effort.
17. He decides in detail what shall be done and how it shall be done.
18. He emphasizes meeting of deadlines.
19. He asks foremen who have slow groups to get more out of their groups.
20. He emphasizes the quantity of work.

IV.F.3. INDEX: WORK PATTERNS PROFILE

VARIABLE MEASURED: The roles in the organization as composed of certain activities.

DESCRIPTION: The profile includes fourteen descriptions of leadership functions that have been found within leadership jobs. These include inspection of the organization; investigation and research; planning; preparation of procedures and methods; coordination; evaluation; interpretation of plans and procedures; supervision of technical operations; personnel activities; public relations; professional consultation; negotiations; scheduling, routing, and dispatching; technical and professional operations. By using questionnaire and interview methods, each person studied in the organization indicates the proportion of time spent on each activity.

WHERE PUBLISHED: Ralph M. Stogdill and Carroll L. Shartle, *Methods in the Study of Administrative Leadership* (Columbus: Ohio State University Bureau of Business Research, 1955), pp. 44-53; also Carroll L. Shartle, *Executive Performance and Leadership* (Englewood Cliffs, N.J.: Prentice-Hall, 1956), pp. 81-93.

RELIABILITY: Forms were administered to 32 officers in a Naval District Command Staff. One month later, the forms were administered again to the same officers. Test-retest coefficients are shown for the fourteen major responsibilities.

Inspection	.51
Research	.59
Planning	.49
Preparing Procedures	.55
Coordination	.60
Evaluation	.58
Interpretation	.18
Supervision	.03
Personal Functions	.46
Professional Consultation	.61
Public Relations	.83
Negotiations	.83
Scheduling	.38
Technical and Professional Performance	.59

VALIDITY: In a study of a Naval Air Station, 34 officers kept a log of work performance for a period of three days. Results suggest that there is a fairly high degree of correspondence between logged time and estimated time for objectively observable performances. More subjective, less observable performances, such as planning and reflection, are not estimated in terms that correspond highly with time recorded on the log. A number of officers expressed the feeling that their estimates of time spent in planning were more accurate than the log, for the reason that they were not always aware at the moment that what they were doing constituted planning.

STANDARD SCORES: The fourteen activities are plotted in percent of time spent in the activities. No standard scores have been developed since many roles must first be analyzed.

UTILITY: This instrument will make it possible to compare patterns of performance. Therefore, executive selection may be made more appropriately in relation to the role as defined in the organization.

RESEARCH APPLICATIONS:

STOGDILL, RALPH M., SHARTLE, CARROLL L., COONS, ALVIN E., and JANES, WILLIAM E. *A Predictive Study of Administrative Work Patterns*. (Columbus: Ohio State University Bureau of Business Research, 1956).

STOGDILL, RALPH M., SHARTLE, CARROLL L., and others. *Patterns of Administrative Performance*. (Columbus: Ohio State University Bureau of Business Research, 1956). Chap. IV.

WORK PATTERNS PROFILE

The Ohio State University Personnel Research Board

The purpose of this analysis is to determine the relative proportion of your time devoted to major administrative and operative responsibilities, disregarding the methods of accomplishment.

Please consider your entire range of responsibilities from day to day. Attempt to account as accurately as possible for the relative percentage of time devoted to various administrative and technical functions.

Before each item below, please write the approximate percentage of time spent in the responsibility described.

(%)   1. *Inspection of the Organization*—Direct observation and personal inspection of installations, buildings, equipment, facilities, operations, services or personnel—for the purpose of determining conditions and keeping informed.

(%)   2. *Investigation and Research*—Acts involving the accumulation and preparation of information and data. (Usually prepared and presented in the form of written reports.)

(%)   3. *Planning*—Preparing for and making decisions that will affect the aims or future activities of the organization as to volume or quality of business or service. (Including thinking, reflection, and reading, as well as consultations and conferences with persons relative to short-term and long-range plans.)

(%)   4. *Preparation of Procedures and Methods*—Acts involving the mapping of procedures and methods for putting new plans into effect, as well as devising new methods for the performance of operations under existing plans.

(%)   5. *Coordination*—Acts and decisions designed to integrate and coordinate the activities of units within the organization or of persons within units, so as to achieve the maximal overall efficiency, economy, and control of operations.

(%)   6. *Evaluation*—Acts involving the consideration and evaluation of reports, correspondence, data, plans, divisions, or performances in relation to the aims, policies, and standards of the organization.

(%)   7. *Interpretation of Plans and Procedures*—Acts involving the interpretation and clarification for assistants and other personnel of directives, regulations, practices, and procedures.

(%)   8. *Supervision of Technical Operations*—Acts involving the direct supervision of personnel in the performance of duties.

(%)   9. *Personnel Activities*—Acts involving the selection, training, evaluation, motivation or disciplining of individuals, as well as acts designed to affect the morale, motivation, loyalty, or harmonious cooperation of personnel.

(%) 10. *Public Relations*—Acts designed to inform outside persons, regarding the program and functions of the organization, to obtain information regarding public sentiment, or to create a favorable attitude toward the organization.

(%) 11. *Professional Consultation*—Giving professional advice and specialized assistance on problems of a specific or technical nature to persons within or outside the organization. (Other than technical supervision and guidance of own staff personnel.)

(%) 12. *Negotiations*—Purchasing, selling, negotiating contracts or agreements, settling claims, etc.

(%) 13. *Scheduling, Routing, and Dispatching*—Initiating action and determining the time, place, and sequence of operations.

(%) 14. *Technical and Professional Operations*—The performance of duties specific to a specialized profession (e.g., practice of medicine, conducting religious services, classroom teaching, auditing records, operating machines, or equipment).

(100%) Total time spent in major responsibilities.

Scales of Attitudes, Values, and Norms

This section includes some attitude scales that revolve around problems of current interest and concern. The most common is concern with alienation and three scales are included which assess various dimensions. These are the Neal and Seeman Powerlessness Scale, the Srole Anomia Scale, and the Dean Alienation Scale.

Achievement orientation has commanded considerable attention and Kahl's scale is shown.

The measurement of international patterns and norms relates to the growing interest in comparative study. Miller's Battery of Rating Scales are included for such measurements.

Innumerable attitude scales are in existence. Some important sources of other scales are:

BONJEAN, CHARLES M., HILL, RICHARD J., and LENMORE, S. DALE M. *Sociological Measurement, An Inventory of Scales and Indices.* San Francisco: Chandler, 1967.

REMMERS, H. H., and SILANCE, E. F. "Generalized Attitude Scales," *Journal of Social Psychology,* 5, 298-312.

RILEY, MATILDA W., RILEY, J. W., JR., and TOBY, JACKSON. *Sociological Studies in Scale Analysis: Applications, Theory, Procedures.* New Brunswick, N.J.: Rutgers University Press, 1954.

ROBINSON, JOHN P., RUSK, JERROLD G., and HEAD, KENDRA B. *Measures of Political Attitudes.* Ann Arbor, Mich.: Institute for Social Research, University of Michigan, 1968.

SHAW, MARVIN E., and WRIGHT, JACK M. *Scales for the Measurement of Attitudes.* New York: McGraw-Hill Book Company, 1968.

THURSTONE, L. L., and CHAVE, E. J. *The Measurement of Attitude, A Psychophysical Method.* Chicago: University of Chicago Press, 1929.

Interest in the measurement of *values* is growing. Some important sources of information on this topic are:

ALLPORT, G. W., and VERNON, P. E. "A Test for Personal Values," *Journal of Abnormal and Social Psychology,* 26, 231-248.

ALMOND, GABRIEL A., and VERBA, SIDNEY. *The Civic Culture.* Boston: Little, Brown and Company, 1963.

CANTRIL, HADLEY. *The Pattern of Human Concerns.* New Brunswick, N.J.: Rutgers University Press, 1965.

CARTER, ROY E. "An Experiment in Value Measurement," *American Sociological Review,* 21 (April, 1956), 156-163.

DODD, STUART C. "Ascertaining National Goals: Project Aimscales," *The American Behavioral Scientist,* 4 (March, 1961), 11-15.

FALLDING, HAROLD. "A Proposal for the Empirical Study of Values," *American Sociological Review,* 30 (April, 1965), 223-233.

HALLER, ARCHIBALD O., and MILLER, IRWIN W. *The Occupational Aspiration Scale: Theory, Structure, and Correlates,* Technical Bulletin 288. East Lansing: Michigan State University, Agricultural Experiment Station, 1963.

NEAL, SISTER MARIE AUGUSTA. *Values and Interest in Social Change.* Englewood Cliffs, N.J.: Prentice-Hall, Inc., 1965.

SCOTT, WILLIAM A. "Empirical Assessment of Values and Ideologies," *American Sociological Review,* 24 (June, 1959), 299-310.

THURSTONE, L. L. *The Measurement of Values.* Chicago: University of Chicago Press, 1959.

WILSON, WILLIAM J., and NYE, F. IVAN. *Some Methodological Problems in the Empirical Study of Values,* Washington Agricultural Experiment Station Bulletin No. 672. Pullman: Washington State University, July 1966.

THE MEASUREMENT OF ALIENATION AND ANOMIE

The concepts of alienation and anomie have enjoyed a new popularity as social events have demonstrated a weakening of personal and social identities to traditional groups and institutions. The "rediscovery of alienation," as Daniel Bell puts it, has only recently encouraged scientists to develop scales to measure these phenomena.[1] The research has been demonstrating that a number of independent

[1] See for example, Allan H. Roberts and Milton Rokeach, "Anomie, Authoritarianism, and Prejudice: A Replication," *American Journal of Sociology,* 61 (January, 1956), 355-358; Gwynn Nettler, "A Measure of Alienation," *American Sociological Review,* 22 (December, 1957), 670-677; and Leo Srole, "Social Integration and Certain Corollaries: An Exploratory Study," *American Sociological Review,* 21 (December, 1956), 709-716.

factors may be identified. In 1959 Melvin Seeman set forth a five-fold classification: powerlessness, meaninglessness, normlessness, isolation, and self-estrangement.[2]

The scales which have been produced have sought to isolate such factors and measure them. The first element, powerlessness, was suggested by Hegel, Marx, and Weber in their discussions of the workers' "separation" from effective control over their economic destiny; of their helplessness; of their being used for purposes other than their own. Weber argued that in the industrial society, the scientist, the civil servant, the professor is likewise "separated from control over his work."

The first scale presented is the Neal and Seeman Powerlessness Scale. It is especially useful for the measurement of worker alienation.[3] Other applications in the hospital, reformatory, and ghetto are cited in Research Applications of the scale.

The second scale taps anomie or normlessness, a concept attributed to Durkheim. The loss or absence of social norms is seen to bring personal insecurity, the loss of intrinsic values that might give purpose or direction to life. Leo Srole has sought to isolate this variable by measuring self-to-others sense of belonging. Note the extensive applications shown in the cited research.

Dwight Dean has developed three subscales to measure powerlessness, normlessness, and social isolation. He combined the three subscales to make up an alienation scale. He believes that the pattern of intercorrelations demonstrates that alienation may be treated as a composite concept but "there appears to be enough independence among the subscales to warrant treating them as independent variables." Neal and Rettig using factor analysis have found empirical evidence for the structural independence of powerlessness, normlessness, and Srole's Anomia Scale. At this time, the subscales should be utilized when the greatest precision is desired. There is great variety in the scales being used and consensus is low. The scales presented are those most widely used.

However, the researcher may wish to examine other scales not exhibited in this handbook:

[2] Melvin Seeman, "On the Meaning of Alienation," *American Sociological Review*, 24 (December, 1959), 783-791.

[3] Arthur G. Neal and Solomon Rettig, "Dimensions of Alienation among Manual and Non-Manual Workers," *American Sociological Review*, 26 (August, 1963), 599-608.

McCLOSKY, HERBERT, and SCHAAR, JOHN H. "Psychological Dimensions of Anomy," *American Sociological Review*, 30 (February 1965), 14-40.

MIDDLETON, RUSSELL. "Alienation, Race, and Education," *American Sociological Review*, 28 (December, 1963), 973-977.

NETTLER, GWYNN. "A Measure of Alienation," *American Sociologica. Review*, 22 (December, 1957), 670-677.

IV.G.1. INDEX: NEAL AND SEEMAN POWERLESSNESS SCALE

VARIABLE MEASURED: The authors define powerlessness as "low expectancies for control of events" as lack of control over the political system, the industrial economy, and international affairs. Basically measures the subjectively held probabilities that the outcome of political and economic events cannot be adequately controlled by oneself or collectively by persons like oneself.

DESCRIPTION: This instrument is a unidimensional 7-item scale that presents a choice between mastery and powerlessness.

This scale, as most of the powerlessness scales, is an adaptation of the forced-choice instrument developed by the late Professor Shephard Liverant and his colleagues at the Ohio State University. For further description of this method see Julian B. Rotter, Melvin Seeman, and Shephard Liverant, "Internal vs. External Control of Reinforcements: A Major Variable in Behavior Theory," in Norman F. Washburne (ed.), *Decisions, Values and Groups*, Vol. 2 (London: Pergamon, 1962), pp. 473-516.

WHERE PUBLISHED: Arthur G. Neal and Melvin Seeman, "Organizations and Powerlessness: A Test of the Mediation Hypothesis," *American Sociological Review*, 29 (April, 1964), 216-226.

RELIABILITY: The seven items yielded a reproducibility coefficient of .87 on the sample used by Neal and Seeman. An early version of the scale shows that the split-half reliability coefficient was .70. See Melvin Seeman and John Evans, "Alienation in a Hospital Setting," *American Sociological Review*, 27, 772-782.

VALIDITY: The mean difference of alienation scores of organized and unorganized workers is significant at the .01 level. The difference of means for mobility oriented and non-mobility oriented non-manual workers is significant at the .001 level. Correlation between anomie and powerlessness $r = .33$. M. Seeman and J. Evans found a negative relation between powerlessness and objective information concerning nature of illness among patients in hospital settings.

M. Seeman and J. Evans, "On the Personal Consequences of Alienation in Work," *American Sociological Review,* 32 (April, 1967), 273-285 report the following correlation between powerlessness and anomie for non-manual workers and manual workers in Sweden:

	Manual Workers	Non-Manual Workers
Anomie	.37 P < .01	.39 P < .01
Expert Orientation	.13 P < .05	.29 P < .01
Mobility Attitude	.15 P < .05	.14
Prejudice	.24 P < .01	.29 P < .01

Each of the seven items is scored dichotomously and the scores are summed. The powerlessness response is scored as "1" and the alternate response is scored as "0." A reproducibility coefficient of .87 (Guttman Scalogram Technique) was obtained for a community-wide sample (Columbus, Ohio) of 604 respondents.

RESEARCH APPLICATIONS:

BULLOUGH, BONNIE. "Alienation in the Ghetto," *American Journal of Sociology,* 72 (March, 1967), 469.

GROAT, THEODORE, and NEAL, ARTHUR G. "Social Psychological Correlates of Urban Fertility," *American Sociological Review,* 32 (December, 1967), 945-949.

NEAL, ARTHUR G. *Stratification Concomitants of Powerlessness and Normlessness: A Study of Political and Economic Alienation.* Unpublished Ph.D. dissertation, Ohio State University, Columbus, 1959.

————, and RETTIG, SOLOMON. "Dimensions of Alienation Among Manual and Non-Manual Workers," *American Sociological Review,* 28 (August, 1963), 599-608.

SEEMAN, MELVIN. "On the Personal Consequences of Alienation in Work," *American Sociological Review,* 32 (April, 1967), 273-285.

————. "Alienation and Social Learning in a Reformatory," *American Journal of Sociology,* 69 (November, 1963), 270-284.

————, and EVANS, JOHN. "Alienation and Learning in a Hospital Setting," *American Sociological Review,* 27 (December, 1962), 772-782.

THE POWERLESSNESS SCALE *

(Respondent chooses between the 7 pairs of statements)

1. _____ I think we have adequate means for preventing run-away inflation.

   _____ There's very little we can do to keep prices from going higher.

2. _____ Persons like myself have little chance of protecting our personal interests when they conflict with those of strong pressure groups.

   _____ I feel that we have adequate ways of coping with pressure groups.

3. _____ A lasting world peace can be achieved by those of us who work toward it.

   _____ There's very little we can do to bring about a permanent world peace.

4. _____ There's very little persons like myself can do to improve world opinion of the United States.

   _____ I think each of us can do a great deal to improve world opinion of the U.S.

5. _____ This world is run by the few people in power, and there is not much the little guy can do about it.

   _____ The average citizen can have an influence on government decisions.

6. _____ It is only wishful thinking to believe that one can really influence what happens in society at large.

   _____ People like me can change the course of world events if we make ourselves heard.

7. _____ More and more, I feel helpless in the face of what's happening in the world today.

   _____ I sometimes feel personally to blame for the sad state of affairs in our government.

IV.G.2. INDEX: SROLE'S ANOMIA SCALE

VARIABLE MEASURED: According to Srole, this scale refers to the individual eunomia-anomia continuum representing "the individual's generalized pervasive sense of self-to-others belongingness at one extreme compared with self-to-others distance and self-to-others alienation at the other pole of the continuum."

---

* These seven items were derived from a larger "internal-external control" scale by Neal and Seeman; cf. J. B. Rotter, "Generalized Expectancies for Internal vs. External Control of Reinforcements," *Psychological Monographs*, 80, No. 1 (Whole #609, 1966), 1-28.

DESCRIPTION: Srole's Anomia Scale contains five items with which the respondent may either agree or disagree. Each item was scored o or 1 according to whether the subject disagrees or agrees. Thus, respondent scores fall in a range from o to 5; the higher the score, the greater anomie manifested by the respondent.

WHERE PUBLISHED: Leo Srole, "Social Integration and Certain Corollaries: An Exploratory Study," *American Sociological Review,* 21 (December, 1956), 709-716. See p. 713.

RELIABILITY: The coefficient of reproducibility when used as a Guttman scale = .90 in L. Killian and C. Grigg, "Urbanism, Race, and Anomia," *American Journal of Sociology,* 67 (May, 1962), 661-665; and .90 in Dorothy L. Meier and Wendell Bell, "Anomia and Differential Access to the Achievement of Life Goals," *American Sociological Review,* 24 (April, 1959), 189-202. See correction, 24: 566.

VALIDITY: Relationships with Anomia.

$$\begin{array}{ll} \text{Authoritarianism F} & r = .47 \\ \text{Attitudes toward minorities} & r = .43 \\ \text{Socioeconomic status} & r = .30 \end{array}$$

in Srole, *op. cit.*

SROLE'S ANOMIA SCALE

(5-item scale)

1) In spite of what some people say, the lot of the average man is getting worse.
2) It's hardly fair to bring children into the world with the way things look for the future.
3) Nowadays a person has to live pretty much for today and let tomorrow take care of itself.
4) These days a person doesn't really know who he can count on.
5) There's little use writing to public officials because often they aren't really interested in the problems of the average man.

RESEARCH APPLICATIONS:

ANGELL, ROBERT C. "Preferences for Moral Norms in Three Problem Areas," *American Journal of Sociology,* 67 (May, 1962), 650-660. See pp. 650-651.

BELL, WENDELL. "Anomie, Social Isolation, and the Class Structure," *Sociometry,* 20 (June, 1957), 105-116. See pp. 106-107.

BLALOCK, H. M., JR. "Making Causal Inferences for Unmeasured Variables from Correlations among Indicators," *American Journal of Sociology,* 69 (July, 1963), 53-62. See p. 56.

CARTER, ROY E., JR., and CLARKE, PETER. "Public Affairs Opinion Leadership among Educational Television Viewers," *American Sociological Review*, 27 (December, 1962), 792-799. See p. 795.

EHRLICH, HOWARD J. "Instrument Error and the Study of Prejudice," *Social Forces*, 43 (December, 1964), 197-206. See p. 200.

FREEMAN, HOWARD E., and SIMMONS, OZZIE G. "Wives, Mothers, and the Posthospital Performance of Mental Patients," *Social Forces*, 37 (December, 1958), 153-159. See p. 156.

KILLIAN, LEWIS M., and GRIGG, CHARLES M. "Urbanism, Race, and Anomia," *American Journal of Sociology*, 67 (May, 1962), 661-665. See p. 661.

LENSKI, GERHARD E., and LEGGETT, JOHN C. "Caste, Class, and Deference in the Research Interview," *American Journal of Sociology*, 65 (March, 1960), 463-467. See pp. 464-465.

LIPMAN, AARON, and HAVENS, A. EUGENE. "The Columbia Violence: An Ex Post Facto Experiment," *Social Forces*, 44 (December, 1965), 238-245. See p. 240.

LOWENTHAL, MARJORIE FISKE. "Social Integration and Mental Illness in Old Age," *American Sociological Review*, 29 (February, 1964), 54-70. See p. 63.

McDILL, EDWARD L. "Anomie, Authoritarianism, Prejudice, and Socio-Economic Status: An Attempt at Clarification," *Social Forces*, 39 (March, 1961), 239-245. See pp. 239-240.

————, and RIDLEY, JEANNE CLARE. "Status, Anomia, Political Alienation, and Political Participation," *American Journal of Sociology*, 67 (September, 1962), 205-213. See p. 208.

MEIER, DOROTHY L., and BELL, WENDELL. "Anomia and Differential Access to the Achievement of Life Goals," *American Sociological Review*, 24 (April, 1959), 189-202. See p. 190.

MIZRUCHI, EPHRAIM H. "Social Structure and Anomia in a Small City," *American Sociological Review*, 25 (October, 1960), 645-654. See p. 647.

PHOTIADIS, JOHN D., and BIGGAR, JEANNE. "Religiosity, Education, and Ethnic Distance," *American Journal of Sociology*, 67 (May, 1962), 666-672. See p. 669.

————, and JOHNSON, ARTHUR L. "Orthodoxy, Church Participation, and Authoritarianism," *American Journal of Sociology*, 69 (November, 1963), 244-248. See p. 244.

RHODES, LEWIS. "Anomia, Aspiration, and Status," *Social Forces*, 42 (May, 1964), 433-440. See p. 436.

ROBERTS, A. H., and ROKEACH, MILTON. "Anomie, Authoritarianism, and Prejudice: A Replication," *American Journal of Sociology*, 61 (January, 1956), 355-358. See p. 357.

ROSE, ARNOLD M. "Alienation and Participation: A Comparison of

Group Leaders and the 'Mass,' " *American Sociological Review*, 27 (December, 1962), 834-838. See p. 836.

———. "Attitudinal Correlates of Social Participation," *Social Forces*, 37 (March, 1959), 202-206. See pp. 203-204.

SEEMAN, MELVIN. "On the Personal Consequences of Alienation in Work," *American Sociological Review*, 32 (April, 1967), 273-285.

WEINSTEIN, EUGENE A., and GEISEL, PAUL N. "Family Decision Making over Desegregation," *Sociometry*, 25 (March, 1962), 21-29. See p. 25.

IV.G.3. INDEX: DEAN'S ALIENATION SCALE

VARIABLE MEASURED: The variable measured is considered as having three major components: powerlessness, normlessness, and social isolation.

DESCRIPTION: The scale consists of nine powerlessness items, six normlessness items, and nine social isolation items. The three sub-scales are combined to make up the alienation scale, which thus consists of 24 items.

WHERE PUBLISHED: Dwight G. Dean, "Alienation: Its Meaning and Measurement," *American Sociological Review*, 26 (October, 1961), 753-758.

RELIABILITY: The powerlessness scale, tested by the "split-half" technique, was .78 (N = 378). When corrected by the Spearman-Brown prophecy formula, the normlessness reliability was .73. The social isolation reliability when corrected for attenuation was .84. The total alienation scale had a reliability of .78 when corrected.

VALIDITY: Correlation coefficients between alienation and five background factors (N = 384).

Components:	Education	Occupation	Income	Age	Community
Powerlessness	—.20**	—.22**	—.26**	.14**	—.10*
Normlessness	—.21**	—.18**	—.14**	.13**	—.10*
Social Isolation	—.07	—.11*	—.13**	—.03	—.06
Alienation	—.19**	—.21**	—.23**	.12**	—.10*

* Significant at the .05 level of confidence.
** Significant at the .01 level of confidence.

The correlation coefficients between the various components of alienation and Adorno "F" scale (for a college sample pretest of 73 respondents) were as follows:

Powerlessness $r = .37$
Normlessness $r = .33$
Social Isolation $r = .23$
Total Alienation $r = .26$

STANDARD SCORES (Alienation Scores on Dean Scale for Six Samples):

	(1) *	(2) †	(3) ‡	(4) §	(5) ‖	(6) ¶
POWERLESSNESS:						
Mean	13.65			12.73	10.90	
Standard Deviation	6.1					
NORMLESSNESS:						
Mean	7.62	8.63	3.77	7.63	3.55	see
Standard Deviation	4.7	3.26	3.50			below
SOCIAL ISOLATION:						
Mean	11.76			14.85	15.16	
Standard Deviation	4.6					
(TOTAL) ALIENATION:						
Mean	36.64			36.25	30.16	
Standard Deviation	13.5					

* Columbus, Ohio, N = 384 (men), stratified sample, 1955. (See D. Dean, "Alienation: Its Meaning and Measurement," *op. cit.*)

† Protestant liberal arts college, N = 135 (women), random sample, 1960.

‡ Catholic women's college, N = 121 (women), random sample, 1960.

§ Protestant liberal arts college, N = 75 (women), random sample, 1955.

‖ Catholic women's college, N = 65 (women), random sample, 1955. This and sample number three are identical except for date. (Samples 4 and 5 are described in Dwight G. Dean and Jon A. Reeves, "Anomie: A Comparison of a Catholic and a Protestant Sample," *Sociometry,* 25 [June, 1962], 209-212.)

¶ A state university, Midwest, normlessness scores were: Catholics 12.84, S.D. 3.51; Protestants 14.40, S.D. 3.13. Questionnaires sent to a sample of 245, about 55 percent return.

RESEARCH APPLICATIONS: Alienation (Dean) (Subscales: powerlessness, normlessness, social isolation)

BONJEAN, CHARLES M. "Mass, Class, and the Industrial Community: A Comparative Analysis of Managers, Businessmen, and Workers," *American Journal of Sociology,* 71 (September, 1966), 149-162.

DEAN, DWIGHT G. "Alienation and Political Apathy," *Social Forces,* 38 (March, 1960), 185-189. See p. 188.

———. "Alienation: Its Meaning and Measurement," *American Sociological Review,* 26 (October, 1961), 753-758. See p. 757.

———, and REEVES, JON A. "Anomie: A Comparison of a Catholic and Protestant Sample," *Sociometry,* 25 (June, 1962), 209-212. See p. 210 (only the normlessness subscale is used here).

ERBE, WILLIAM. "Social Involvement and Political Activity: A Replication and Elaboration," *American Sociological Review,* 29 (April, 1964), 198-215. See pp. 205-206.

DEAN SCALE FOR MEASURING ALIENATION

Below is a keyed copy of the alienation scale. The letter to the left of each item indicates whether it belongs to the powerlessness, normlessness or isolation subscale. When scoring, it is helpful to cut a "stencil" from a manila folder for each subscale.

PUBLIC OPINION QUESTIONNAIRE *

Below are some statements regarding public issues, with which some people agree and others disagree. Please give us your own opinion about these items, i.e., whether you agree or disagree with the items as they stand.

Please check in the appropriate blank, as follows:

    _____A   (Strongly Agree)
    _____a   (Agree)
    _____U   (Uncertain)
    _____d   (Disagree)
    _____D   (Strongly Disagree)

I   1. Sometimes I feel all alone in the world.
      _4_ A   _3_ a   _2_ U   _1_ d   _0_ D

P   2. I worry about the future facing today's children.
      _4_ A   ___ a   ___ U   ___ d   ___ D

I   3. I don't get invited out by friends as often as I'd really like.
      _4_ A   ___ a   ___ U   ___ d   ___ D

N   4. The end often justifies the means.
      _4_ A   ___ a   ___ U   ___ d   ___ D

I   5. Most people today seldom feel lonely.
      _0_ A   _1_ a   _2_ U   _3_ d   _4_ D

P   6. Sometimes I have the feeling that other people are using me.
      _4_ A   ___ a   ___ U   ___ d   ___ D

N   7. People's ideas change so much that I wonder if we'll ever have anything to depend on.
      _4_ A   ___ a   ___ U   ___ d   ___ D

I   8. Real friends are as easy as ever to find.
      _0_ A   ___ a   ___ U   ___ d   ___ D

P   9. It is frightening to be responsible for the development of a little child.
      _4_ A   ___ a   ___ U   ___ d   ___ D

* Obviously, scores would be omitted when administered.

N 10. Everything is relative, and there just aren't any definite rules to live by.

<u>4 </u>A _____ a _____U _____ d _____D

I 11. One can always find friends if he shows himself friendly.

<u>o </u>A _____ a _____U _____ d _____D

N 12. I often wonder what the meaning of life really is.

<u>4 </u>A _____ a _____U _____ d _____D

P 13. There is little or nothing I can do towards preventing a major "shooting" war.

<u>4 </u>A _____ a _____U _____ d _____D

I 14. The world in which we live is basically a friendly place.

<u>o </u>A _____ a _____U _____ d _____D

P 15. There are so many decisions that have to be made today that sometimes I could just "blow up."

<u>4 </u>A _____ a _____U _____ d _____D

N 16. The only thing one can be sure of today is that he can be sure of nothing.

<u>4 </u>A _____ a _____U _____ d _____D

I 17. There are few dependable ties between people any more.

<u>4 </u>A _____ a _____U _____ d _____D

P 18. There is little chance for promotion on the job unless a man gets a break.

<u>4 </u>A _____ a _____U _____ d _____D

N 19. With so many religions abroad, one doesn't really know which to believe.

<u>4 </u>A _____ a _____U _____ d _____D

P 20. We're so regimented today that there's not much room for choice even in personal matters.

<u>4 </u>A _____ a _____U _____ d _____D

P 21. We are just so many cogs in the machinery of life.

<u>4 </u>A _____ a _____U _____ d _____D

I 22. People are just naturally friendly and helpful.

<u>o </u>A _____ a _____U _____ d _____D

P 23. The future looks very dismal.

<u>4 </u>A _____ a _____U _____ d _____D

I 24. I don't get to visit friends as often as I'd really like.

<u>4 </u>A _____ a _____U _____ d _____D

IV.G.4. KAHL'S ACHIEVEMENT ORIENTATION SCALE

VARIABLE MEASURED: "It is an index of a generalized motivation to do well, to excel in a variety of tasks."

DESCRIPTION: It is composed of four scales derived through the use of factor analysis from a series of studies in the United States, Mexico, and Brazil. The four scales were: (1) Occupational primacy, "occupational success [is placed] ahead of alternative possibilities." In Mexico and Brazil this scale was used with three items. (2) Trust, "belief in the stability of life and the trustworthiness of people." Composed of six items. (3) Activism, "emphasizes planning for a controllable future." Composed of seven items. (4) Integration with relatives, "loyalty to parents instead of to self or to career." Composed of three items.

WHERE PUBLISHED: Joseph A. Kahl, "Some Measurements of Achievement Orientation," *American Journal of Sociology,* 70 (May, 1965), 669-681 and his book, *The Measurement of Modernism: A Study of Values in Brazil and Mexico* (Austin, Texas: University of Texas Press, 1968).

RELIABILITY: Not known from the original study, but inferred from Michael A. LaSorte's Ph.D. dissertation which used similar scales. Applying the Spearman-Brown prophecy formula for correction, the reliability coefficients were occupational primacy, .81, trust, .94, mastery (activism), .94, and familism (which departs significantly from the integration with relatives), .86.

VALIDITY: Trust, activism, and independence from family scales are positively correlated with an index of socioeconomic status (based on occupation, education, and self-identification); occupational primacy is negatively correlated with the others and with status: [1]

	Brazil	*Mexico*
Trust	.30	.26
Activism	.42	.49
Occupational (primacy)	—.20	—.09
Integration with relatives	—.30	—.46

RESEARCH APPLICATIONS:

Cox, HENRIETTA. "Study of Social Class Variations in Value Orientations in Selected Areas of Mother-Child Behavior." Unpublished Ph.D. dissertation, Washington University, St. Louis, 1964.

[1] Kahl, *op. cit.,* p. 674.

KAHL'S INDEX OF ACHIEVEMENT ORIENTATION
(Scale Items Show Factor Loadings)

TRUST

Mexico Brazil

−.66 −.78 It is not good to let your relatives know everything about your life, for they might take advantage of you.

−.71 −.74 It is not good to let your friends know everything about your life, for they might take advantage of you.

−.67 −.55 Most people will repay your kindness with ingratitude.

+.38 Most people are fair and do not try to get away with something.

−.62 People help persons who have helped them not so much because it is right but because it is good business.

−.40 You can only trust people whom you know well.

ACTIVISM

Mexico Brazil

−.63 −.74 Making plans only brings unhappiness because the plans are hard to fulfil.

−.58 −.65 It doesn't make much difference if the people elect one or another candidate for nothing will change.

−.67 −.63 With things as they are today an intelligent person ought to think only about the present, without worrying about what is going to happen tomorrow.

−.54 −.57 We Brazilians (Mexicans) dream big dreams, but in reality we are inefficient with modern industry.

−.61 −.47 The secret of happiness is not expecting too much out of life, and

ACTIVISM (*continued*)

Mexico Brazil

being content with what comes your way.

+.46 It is important to make plans for one's life and not just accept what comes.

+.41 How important is it to know clearly in advance your plans for the future? (*Very important* is coded positively.)

OCCUPATIONAL PRIMACY

Mexico Brazil

+.59 +.69 The job should come first, even if it means sacrificing time from recreation.

+.64 +.59 The best way to judge a man is by his success in his occupation.

+.80 +.62 The most important qualities of a real man are determination and driving ambition.

+.46 The most important thing for a parent to do is to help his children get further ahead in the world than he did.

INTEGRATION WITH RELATIVES

Mexico Brazil

+.73 +.76 When looking for a job, a person ought to find a position in a place located near his parents, even if that means losing a good opportunity elsewhere.

+.78 +.75 When you are in trouble, only a relative can be depended upon to help you out.

+.65 +.64 If you have the chance to hire an assistant in your work, it is always better to hire a relative than a stranger.

KAHL, JOSEPH A. "Urbanizacão e Mudancas Occupacionais no Brasil," *America Latina,* V (October, 1962), 21-30.

———. "Some Measurements of Achievement Orientation," *American Journal of Sociology,* 70 (May, 1965), 669-681.

LASORTE, MICHAEL ANTONIO. "Achievement Orientation and Community of Orientation." Unpublished Ph.D. dissertation, Indiana University, Bloomington, 1967.

SCANZONI, JOHN. "Socialization, Achievement, and Achievement Values," *American Sociological Review,* 32 (June, 1967), 449-456.

The serious student should read the communication between Wallace D. Loh, Harry J. Crockett, Jr., Clyde Z. Nunn, and John Scanzoni over the relation of socialization practices and occupational achievement values. See *American Sociological Review,* 33 (April, 1968), 284-291.

For another important scale that incorporates occupational aspiration see David Horton Smith and Alex Inkeles, "The OM Scale: A Comparative Socio-Psychological Measure of Individual Modernity," *Sociometry,* 29 (December, 1966), 353-377.

IV.G.5. INDEX: MILLER'S SCALE BATTERY OF INTERNATIONAL PATTERNS AND NORMS

VARIABLE MEASURED: Norms and patterns of national cultures.

DESCRIPTION: It consists of a scale battery of twenty rating scales to ascertain important norms and patterns within national cultures: (1) social acceptance; (2) standards of personal and community health; (3) concern for and trust of others; (4) confidence in personal security and protection of property; (5) family solidarity; (6) independence of the child; (7) moral code and role definitions of men and women; (8) definition of religion and moral conduct; (9) class structure and class consciousness; (10) consensus on general philosophy and objectives of the society; (11) labor's orientation to the prevailing economic and social system; (12) belief in democratic political system; (13) definition of work and individual achievement; (14) civic participation and voluntary activity; (15) definition of the role of private and public ownership of property. Five more scales are under development with tests in United States, England, and Spain already completed. All rating scales have six positions ranging between two contrasting poles.

WHERE PUBLISHED: Delbert C. Miller, "The Measurement of International Patterns and Norms: A Tool for Comparative Research,"

Southwestern Social Science Quarterly, 48 (March, 1968), 531-54
See also D. C. Miller, *International Community Power Structure
Comparative Studies of Four World Cities* (Bloomington: Indian
University, 1970).

RELIABILITY: Test-retest correlations for the fifteen scales rang
from .74 to .97 as tested in the United States and Peru. Most scale
have reliabilities of .90 and above.

VALIDITY: Three criteria for validity have been met. These are: (1
the mean difference on each rating scale is 2.00 or more when th
United States and Peru are rated and compared; (2) average devia
tion of each scale shows a dispersion less than 1.00 when United State
and Peru are rated; (3) judges' rankings permit a structuring of sig
nificant variations in the social patterning of the United States an
Peru. Extended research in Argentina, Spain, England, and the Unite
States reinforces these tests of validity.

UTILITY: Scales are rated by qualified judges who have experience i
two or more national cultures. The rating requires approximately 3
minutes. The scales may be applied to numerous problems of cross
cultural research including the impact of a foreign culture on th
stranger. The use of foreign and native judges rating the same tw
national cultures in which they have both had extensive experienc
reveals the significance of cross-cultural differences. Ratings can b
made of national cultures by raters who have had no previous exper
ence to examine stereotyping. The relation of the class position of th
respondent offers the possibility of revealing international difference
when viewed from varying class or racial positions occupied by th
respondent in the national society.

COMPARATIVE SCORES: The mean scores shown for the ratin
scales on the seven samples may be used for comparative study.

RESEARCH APPLICATIONS: Delbert C. Miller, "The Measuremen
of International Patterns and Norms: A Tool for Comparative Re
search," as cited above. This article reports on a test of the hypothesi
that respondent exposure to two or more Latin American cultures wi
demonstrate that any two countries in Latin America are more alik
in cultural patterning than any Latin American country compare
with the United States. Tests were made using the fifteen rating scale
in Peru, Argentina, and the United States with panels of judges bot
foreign and native in the three countries. Studies have been made als
with American university students who go abroad to study. Before an
after ratings of their own country and the host country have bee
secured.

Scale of International Patterns and Norms	U.S.[a] (1966) N = 21	U.S.[b] (1968) N = 32	Spain[c] (1968) N = 17	Argen- tina[d] (1967) N = 15	Peru[e] (1966) N = 21	England[f] (1968) N = 15	Colom- bia[g] (1969) N = 10
Social Acceptance	1.7	1.6	3.1	3.2	4.5	4.0	4.2
Personal and Community Health	1.4	1.9	3.2	2.9	4.7	3.1	4.4
Concern and Trust of Others	1.8	2.7	4.1	3.3	4.9	2.0	4.3
Personal Security and Protection of Property	2.3	3.7	2.2	3.5	5.0	2.1	5.7
Family Solidarity	5.4	4.0	2.3	2.7	1.9	2.9	1.8
Independence of the Child	1.3	2.1	4.5	2.8	4.4	2.1	4.4
Moral Code and Role Definition	2.0	2.3	4.6	2.8	4.9	3.4	4.9
Religion and Moral Conduct	4.6	4.3	2.6	3.7	2.1	4.6	2.6
Class Structure and Consciousness	5.0	4.9	2.1	3.1	1.4	3.1	1.8
Societal Consensus	1.6	2.1	5.0	3.9	4.6	2.1	3.9
Labor's Orientation	5.3	5.4	2.3	2.7	3.1	4.0	2.7
Democratic Belief	1.4	1.8	4.6	2.8	3.7	2.1	3.8
Work and Achievement	1.5	2.1	4.0	3.1	4.8	3.1	4.2
Civic Participation	1.2	1.9	4.8	3.6	4.8	3.1	4.2
Role of Property	1.2	1.7	3.1	3.6	3.3	3.3	2.7
Honesty of Government Officials		1.8	3.5			1.3	
Political Influence of Foreign Enterprise		5.2	3.8			5.3	
Encouragement of Foreign Enterprise		2.2	2.5			2.3	
Nepotism in Organizations		4.8	1.5			4.0	
Reciprocity of Favors		3.9	1.5			5.0	

[a] American raters.
[b] American raters.
[c] Spanish raters in Madrid, Barcelona, and Seville.
[d] Argentine raters. (Data gathered by Judson Yearwood.)
[e] American raters living in Peru.
[f] Englishmen living in London, Liverpool, and Bristol, England.
[g] Colombian raters. (Data gathered by Dr. Teresa Camacho de Pinto.)

Research by the writer has been completed in Spain and England (1968) to ascertain significance of differences in norms and patterns in Ibero-Latin American civilization compared with Anglo-Saxon civilization. Dr. Harry M. Makler is making a study using the scales with panels of Americans and Portuguese in Portugal. Dr. Francisco Suarez is conducting research in Uruguay; Dr. Teresa Pinto is carrying out research in Colombia. Mexico, Chile, and Venezuela are being added to the international samples.

New scales are now being tested to include: (1) degree of honesty and integrity in government; (2) degree of nepotism in business, governmental, and organizational life generally; (3) degree of expected reciprocity in favors and rewards; (4) encouragement of foreign enterprise; (5) degree to which foreign enterprise is believed to influence the host government. The scales and scores are shown for the United States and Spain in the following test battery.

Applying Scales: Instructions to the Judge

(A qualified judge is a college graduate, especially trained to appraise his own country and with six months or more consecutive experience with the host country. He must be able to read and speak the language of the host country.)

Each characteristic has been placed on a scale of six points. The descriptions defining the scale are shown at 1 and 2, 3 and 4, and 5 and 6. Thus, the first characteristic, social acceptance, attributes highest social acceptance to number 1 position and lowest social acceptance to the number 6 position. The range between represents a continuum of different degrees of the characteristic.

Task 1. Establish anchor points for each scale by selecting countries from anywhere in the world that reflect the extreme positions of the scale for social acceptance. These countries may or may not be known to you personally. In making a selection *think of the way the pattern appears on the average throughout the country and as it is experienced by a person in the middle sector of society*—i.e., omitting the very rich and the very poor. When the selection has been made, write the names of the countries in the answer sheets. Proceed to select countries representing the extremes of all 19 remaining characteristics —i.e., standards of health, standards of personal and community health, etc. Write the names on the answer sheets.

Task 2. Now place the two countries in their proper positions on all 20 characteristics. Again, think of the pattern as it appears on the average throughout the country and as it is experienced by a person in the middle sector of society—i.e., omitting the very rich and the very poor. Write answers on answer sheet.

Task 3. Place a third country on the scale if you have lived six months or more within it. Write answers on answer sheet.

Miller's Scale Battery of International Patterns and Norms

Delbert C. Miller
Indiana University

Respondent: Kindly check if you are male or female and indicate years lived in native country and in other countries. Sign your name and give your address if you wish a final report. Read the accompanying directions carefully before you begin. Thank you.

Check: Male_____ Female_____
Years lived in:
Native Country _____
Other Countries _____

(Optional)
Name: _____
Address: _____

1. SOCIAL ACCEPTANCE

1	2	3	4	5	6
High social acceptance. Social contacts open and non-restrictive. Introductions not needed for social contacts. Short acquaintance provides entry into the home and social organizations.		Medium social acceptance. Ready acceptance in neighborhood and in community organizations but not in family and social life. Friendly in business and other public contacts.		Low social acceptance. Acceptance in specifically designated groups in which membership has been validated. Sponsored introduction is needed for social contacts in all parts of community life.	

2. STANDARDS OF PERSONAL AND COMMUNITY HEALTH

1	2	3	4	5	6
High standards of personal and community hygiene. Hygienic habits valued in all parts of society.		Varied. High community standards for water and sewage. Personal habits and community standards for cleanliness and hygiene vary widely across the community.		Personal and community standards of hygiene are not valued highly.	

3. CONCERN FOR AND TRUST OF OTHERS

1	2	3	4	5	6
High concern for others. Respect for the motives and integrity of others. Mutual trust prevails.		Moderate or uneven pattern of concern for and trust of others.		Lack of concern for others and lack of trust.	

333

4. CONFIDENCE IN PERSONAL SECURITY AND PROTECTION OF PROPERTY

1	2	3	4	5	6
	High confidence in personal security. Free movement, night and day, for both sexes. High sense of security of property. Locking of homes is optional.		Moderate confidence in personal security. Confidence of men is high in personal security but women are warned to take precautions. Movements of women restricted to daytime. Simple property precautions essential.		Low confidence in both personal security and protection of property. Men and women restrict all movement at night to predetermined precautions. Many property precautions obligatory. Extensive use of locks, dogs, and guards.

5. FAMILY SOLIDARITY

1	2	3	4	5	6
	High solidarity with many obligations of kinship relations within large, extended family system.		Relations of solidarity within a limited kinship circle with specified obligations only.		Small, loosely integrated, independent family with highly specific individual relations.

6. INDEPENDENCE OF THE CHILD

1	2	3	4	5	6
	Child is raised to be self-reliant and independent in both thought and action.		Child is given specified areas of independence only.		Child is raised to be highly dependent and docile.

7. MORAL CODE AND ROLE DEFINITIONS OF MEN AND WOMEN

1	2	3	4	5	6
	Single code of morality prevails for men and women. Separate occupational and social roles are not defined for men and women. Similar amounts and standards of education prevail.		Variations between moral definitions for men and women exist for certain specified behaviors. Occupational and social role definitions vary in degree. Varying educational provisions for the sexes.		Double code of morality prevails. Separate occupational and social roles for men and women exist and are sharply defined. Amount and standards of education vary widely between the sexes.

334

8. DEFINITION OF RELIGION AND MORAL CONDUCT

1	2	3	4	5	6
Belief in the sacred interpretation of life as primary explanation of purpose of life and role of death. Emphasis is placed on importance of worshiper role in fulfilling spiritual obligations and duties.		Belief in supreme being a sacred purpose for life. Emphasis is placed on secular interpretation of moral values and importance of applying them to daily conduct.		Belief in secular interpretation of life. Emphasis on importance of achieving the good society for achieving the good life. Moral values prescribed by social and scientific definitions of human well being in the society. Emphasis on social conduct as moral conduct.	

9. CLASS STRUCTURE AND CLASS CONSCIOUSNESS

1	2	3	4	5	6
Highly conscious of class differences. Extensive use of status symbols. Social classes and social circles rigidly defined. Very small upward class movement. Contacts between classes limited by social distinctions. Private schools predominate for upper social groups.		Class consciousness prevails moderately. Upward class movement occurs but definite characteristics mark off and limit contact between classes.		Class consciousness low. Class differences devalued. Minimal use of status symbols. Considerable upward class movement. Relatively free social contacts between social classes. Public schools dominate for all social classes.	

10. CONSENSUS OVER GENERAL PHILOSOPHY AND OBJECTIVES OF THE SOCIETY

1	2	3	4	5	6
High consensus over philosophy and objectives of the society as achieved either through evolution or revolution. Competition and conflict between parties takes place within generally accepted goals of the society. Stable governments usually prevail.		Consensus is partial. Differing ideological systems conflict. Stable government may be maintained but under threat of overthrow.		Absence of consensus (or very low) over philosophy and objectives of the society. Conflicting and splinter parties may represent the divergent ideologies and cleavages. Unstable governments prevail.	

335

11. LABOR'S ORIENTATION TO THE PREVAILING ECONOMIC AND SOCIAL SYSTEM

1	2	3	4	5	6
Highly alienated. Ideologically opposed to the prevailing economic and social system. Revolutionary in orientation.		Antagonistic. Partly alienated with some unions ideologically in support and some in opposition to prevailing economic and social system.		Highly assimilated. Ideologically in agreement with prevailing economic and social system. Labor disputes over distribution shares of goods and services to working people but accepts on-going system.	

12. BELIEF IN DEMOCRATIC POLITICAL SYSTEM

1	2	3	4	5	6
Strongly committed. Deep and persistent belief in the democratic processes regardless of problems or crisis.		Reserved commitment. Belief in democracy as process requiring careful control against mass abuse. Accepts necessity of dictatorial intervention in crisis situations or special safeguard such as one-party systems, relinquishing freedoms in internal crises, etc.		Lack of belief in democracy as political system. Regarded as weak and ineffectual in the solving of problems and improving the lot of the average man. Generally regarded as dangerous because it exposes government to mob psychology.	

13. DEFINITION OF WORK AND INDIVIDUAL ACHIEVEMENT

1	2	3	4	5	6
A belief in hard work as obligation to self, employer, and God. Efficiency values accepted. Individual is expected to progress in his work life.		Work is important to the advancement of self and family. Efficiency values accepted. Achievement expectations vary.		Lack of belief in hard work. Work is regarded as necessary, but involves no obligation beyond delivery of minimum services. Efficiency values rejected. Individual is expected only to maintain family status at his inherited level.	

14. CIVIC PARTICIPATION AND VOLUNTARY ACTIVITY

1	2	3	4	5	6
High civic activity. People work together to get things done for the community. High identity with volunteer groups. Civic participation and volunteer activity in groups is an important source of social prestige. Moral and altruistic motives are important sources of motivation.		Moderate activity in special areas. Organized participation exists for economic or political self-interest but often is lacking for a general community need.		Low civic activity, often deliberately avoided with no social sanctions. Low identity with volunteer groups. Civic participation is not an important source of prestige. Mistrust of motives is common since self-interest is generally assumed as the principal motivation for all persons.	

15. DEFINITION OF THE ROLE OF PRIVATE AND PUBLIC OWNERSHIP OF PROPERTY

1	2	3	4	5	6
Strong belief in the right of private property for all persons in all types of goods. Private ownership and control of means of production is accepted for all industries and services except for a few natural monopolies (i.e. water, post office, etc.).		Belief in the wide mixture of private ownership and public ownership in all industries and services. Public ownership of large basic industries (steel, coal, electricity, etc.) and services (transport and communication) is especially common.		Strong belief in the public ownership and governmental controls of all industries and services except for small enterprises. Private ownership accepted in the ownership of personal goods.	

16. STANDARDS OF HONESTY AND INTEGRITY OF GOVERNMENT OFFICIALS

1	2	3	4	5	6
Government officials at all levels have a high standard of honesty and integrity. Violations are prosecuted vigorously and punished with appropriate penalties.		Government officials are generally honest but there are differences in the honesty of officials at different levels. Violations do occur and are prosecuted. The certainty of detection and the severity of penalty varies according to differing practices.		Government officials at all levels commonly engage in various kinds of corrupt practices. Most violations are seldom prosecuted. Occasionally token prosecutions are made when abuse becomes excessive.	

337

17. POLITICAL INFLUENCE OF FOREIGN ENTERPRISE ON HOST GOVERNMENT

1	2	3	4	5	6
	Foreign enterprise has marked political influence on major economic and political policies of the nation. It can resist attempted nationalization of its own enterprises and enforce favorable trade and political relations.		Foreign enterprise does have significant political influence over certain economic conditions of its special concern, but it has no real influence over political policy and process within the host country.		Foreign enterprise has no real influence over national policies—economic or political. Host government may enforce strict control over all foreign enterprise but often permits foreign enterprise to operate within same set of guidelines as domestic firms.

18. ENCOURAGEMENT OF FOREIGN ENTERPRISE

1	2	3	4	5	6
	All foreign enterprise is strongly encouraged to invest and operate businesses of all kinds throughout the country.		Selected forms of foreign investment are encouraged. Use of foreign management personnel may be discouraged.		Foreign investment and operation of enterprise is discouraged by official and unofficial means.

19. DEGREE OF NEPOTISM IN ORGANIZATIONAL LIFE

1	2	3	4	5	6
	Family members of owners, managers, clerical, and manual workers are given preferential and sometimes privileged opportunities for employment in all types of organizations.		Family members of owners, managers, and professionals are given priority within organizations owned or managed by their relatives.		Merit and training is the sole basis for selection of all persons in all types of organizations.

20. DEGREE OF EXPECTED RECIPROCITY IN FAVORS AND REWARDS

1	2	3	4	5	6
	Pattern of expected reciprocity in favors prevails in regard to economic or political support given to individual or group. Personal basis of contact is encouraged and reciprocity is expected by a returned favor (or gift) in near future.		Reciprocity is expected only in specific situations when both parties have a written or oral agreement to exchange political and social support for services rendered.		No pattern of expected reciprocity prevails in economic or political life. Favors or special gifts for service and business rendered is regarded as self-serving and "wrong."

Family and Marriage

The *Marriage-Prediction Schedule* and the *Marriage-Adjustment Schedule* are products of intensive research efforts led by Ernest W. Burgess and his associates and aided by many social researchers who have been seeking factors associated with success or failure in marriage.

The *Marriage-Prediction Schedule* is used in assessing the probabilities of engaged couples to be able to establish happy marital adjustment if they should marry.

The *Marriage-Adjustment Schedule* is for married couples. It can be used as a diagnostic instrument to help the marriage counselor detect the social areas where difficulties exist. The researcher may use it to assess new relationships such as the role of parent-child relations and marital adjustment.

IV.H.1. INDEX: MARRIAGE-PREDICTION SCHEDULE AND MARRIAGE ADJUSTMENT SCHEDULE

VARIABLE MEASURED: The marital prediction schedule predicts the statistical probabilities of success in marriage; the marriage adjustment schedule is predictive of adjustment in marriage.

DESCRIPTION: The marital adjustment schedule was the first schedule developed. Five hundred twenty-six Illinois couples who had been married one to six years were studied. Marital adjustment was defined as (1) Agreement between husband and wife upon matters that might be made critical issues; (2) Common interests and joint activities; (3) Frequent overt demonstrations of affection and mutual confidence; (4) Few complaints; (5) Few reports of feeling lonely, miserable, irritable, etc. Items classified under these five headings serve as indicators of marital adjustment. Each of the items shows a measurable relationship to the ratings given by the couples to their expressed happiness rating of their marriage. For the development of the marital adjustment schedule see E. W. Burgess and Leonard S. Cottrell, *Predicting Success or Failure in Marriage* (Englewood Cliffs, N.J.: Prentice-Hall, 1939). Cf. Nathan Hurvitz, "The Measurement of Marital Strain," *American Journal of Sociology,* 65 (May, 1960), 610-615.

The marital prediction schedule was developed by seeking items predictive of marriage adjustment among 1,000 engaged couples. Selected background items significantly associated with marital adjustment were combined into an expectancy table for premarital prediction of success in marriage. For the development of the marital prediction schedule see Ernest W. Burgess and Paul Wallin, *Engagement and Marriage* (Philadelphia: Lippincott, 1953).

WHERE PUBLISHED: Ernest W. Burgess and Harvey J. Locke, *The Family* (2nd ed.; New York: American Book, 1960), pp. 693-716. (Contains the refined version of the schedules based upon approximately 25 years of research.)

RELIABILITY: Husband-wife adjustment scores correlated with $r = .88$. ($N = 526$ couples)

VALIDITY:

Happiness ratings and adjustment scores correlated .92. ($n = 526$ couples).

Second sample of 63 cases showed correlation between happiness ratings and adjustment scores of .95.

Correlation between happiness ratings and absence of marital disorganization, divorce, separation, and contemplation of divorce or separation. $r = .89$.

Harvey Locke computed Burgess-Cottrell Adjustment scores for divorced men, divorced women, happily married men, and happily married women. Correlations between scores attained in this way and scores from the 29 questions in his test were respectively, .83, .87, .85, and .88.

Burgess and Wallin gave an adjustment test to 1,000 engaged couples, and then, three years after marriage, gave a marital adjustment test to as many couples as could be contacted. Correlation between adjustment scores of engaged couples was .57; three years after marriage, marital adjustment scores of 505 husbands and wives correlated .41. See Lewis M. Terman and Paul Wallin, "The Validity of Marriage Prediction and Marital Adjustment Tests," *American Sociological Review,* 14 (August, 1949), 497-504; Harvey J. Locke and Robert G. Williamson, "Marriage Adjustment: A Factor Analysis Study," *American Sociological Review*, 23 (October, 1958), 562-569.

Scoring the Marriage-Prediction and Marriage-Adjustment Schedules

The narrow columns at the right side of each page of the *Marriage-Prediction Schedule* and the *Marriage-Adjustment Schedule* are provided for scoring the replies to the questions. The score values assigned are arbitrary in the sense that usually each gradation in reply differs by one point. Although arbitrary, the score values are in general conformity with the findings of the studies in this field, particularly those of E. W. Burgess and L. S. Cottrell, *Predicting Success or Failure in Marriage;* L. M. Terman and Others, *Psychological Factors in Marital Happiness;* E. W. Burgess and Paul Wallin, *Engagement and Marriage;* and Harvey J. Locke, *Predicting Adjustment in Marriage: A Comparison of a Divorced and a Happily Married Group.*

The two-digit numbers after each subdivision of the questions provide the code for scoring the replies. The score value of each response is obtained simply by adding together the two digits in the number that is a subscript under the last letter of the final word of the response that has been checked. For example, if you have checked a response numbered 42, your score for that item is $4 + 2 = 6$. To obtain your total score, follow these steps:

1. For each item, enter in Column 1 at the right-hand side of each page the two-digit number that appears as a subscript under the last letter of the final word of the answers to each question. An example is: What is your present state of health? chronic ill-health (13)____; temporary ill-health (23)____; average health (15)____; healthy (25)____; very healthy (17)____. If your answer to this question is "average health," then write 15 in Column 1.

   In Part Two of the Marriage-Prediction Schedule, put only the score of your fiancé(e) in the blank on the right-hand margin.

2. Enter in Column 2 the sum of the two digits appearing in Column 1 for each item. For each part of the questionnaire, compute the total of the values appearing in Column 2, and enter that figure in the space provided at the end of that section.

3. In scoring Part Two of the Marriage-Adjustment Schedule, multiply the total number of check marks in each of the four columns as follows:

Column A by 6	Column C by 4
Column B by 5	Column D by 6

Add together the four figures obtained in the four columns. This sum equals your total score for Part Two.

4. Enter the total score for each part in the spaces provided at the end of the questionnaire. Your total score on the inventory equals the sum of the total scores of the separate parts and is your marriage-adjustment score.

STANDARD SCORES

A. *Marriage-Prediction Schedule*

High scores on the Marriage-Prediction Schedule, those above 630, are favorable for marital adjustment, as indicated by research findings that approximately 75 percent of persons with these scores in the engagement period are well adjusted in their marriages. Low scores, or those below 567, are much less favorable for happiness in marriage, as shown by the probability that only 25 percent of persons with these scores will be well adjusted in married life. Scores between 567 and 630 indicate that there is about a 50 percent chance for marital success and about a 50 percent chance for marital failure.

The prediction score of a person and his corresponding matrimonial-risk-group assignment should be interpreted with extreme caution. The following points should be kept in mind:

1. The prediction does not apply directly to the individual. It states the statistical probabilities of marital success for a group of persons of which the individual is one. If he belongs to the lower risk group, in which 75 percent of the marriages turn out unhappily, there is no way of telling by this statistical prediction whether he falls in the 25 percent of the marriages with varying degrees of happiness or in the 75 percent of unhappy unions.

2. The prediction is for an individual's general matrimonial risk irrespective of the particular person to whom he is engaged. The individual's specific matrimonial risk for marriage to a given person is much more valuable but also more complicated, and therefore not suited for self-scoring.

3. In the majority of cases the specific matrimonial risk of a couple may be roughly estimated from the two general matrimonial-risk groups to which the two persons are assigned. An average of the two scores will generally be close to what may be expected from a specific matrimonial-risk-group assignment.

4. With the aforementioned reservations in mind, a low prediction score should not be taken as indicating lack of suitability for marriage. It should, however, be helpful to the person in stimu-

lating him to secure adequate preparation for marriage, to be more careful in the selection of a marriage partner, and to give attention to the solving of any difficulties in the relation before, rather than after, the marriage.

B. *Marriage-Adjustment Schedule*

In evaluating the total score secured on the Marriage-Adjustment Schedule, see the following table:

MARRIAGE-ADJUSTMENT SCORES AS INDICATIVE OF
ADJUSTMENT IN MARRIAGE

Marital-Adjustment Scores	Adjustment in Marriage
720 and over	Extremely well adjusted
700 to 719	Decidedly well adjusted
680 to 699	Fairly adjusted
660 to 679	Somewhat adjusted
640 to 659	Indifferently adjusted
620 to 639	Somewhat unadjusted
600 to 619	Unadjusted
580 to 599	Decidedly unadjusted
579 and under	Extremely unadjusted

UTILITY: Each form may be filled out in approximately 30 minutes. The measure may be used for both research and counseling purposes. Short marital-adjustment and prediction tests are now available. It is claimed that "with the short tests, measurement or prediction can be accomplished with approximately the same accuracy in a few minutes as ordinarily would require an hour or more with the longer ones." Harvey J. Locke and Karl M. Wallace, "Short Marital-Adjustment and Prediction Tests: Their Reliability and Validity," *Marriage and Family Living*, 21 (August, 1959), 251-255.

RESEARCH APPLICATIONS:

BOWERMAN, CHARLES. "Adjustment in Marriage, Overall and in Specific Areas," *Sociology and Social Research*, 41 (March-April, 1957), 257-263.

BURGESS, E. W., and WALLIN, PAUL. "Predicting Adjustment in Marriage from Adjustment in Engagement," *American Journal of Sociology*, 49 (1944), 324-330.

HURVITZ, NATHAN. "The Measurement of Marital Strain," *American Journal of Sociology,* 65 (May, 1960), 610-615.

KARLSSON, GEORG. *Adaptability and Communication in Marriage: A Swedish Predictive Study of Marital Satisfaction.* Uppsala, Sweden: Almquist and Wiksell, 1951.

KING, CHARLES. "The Burgess-Cottrell Method of Measuring Marital Adjustment Applied to a Non-White Southern Urban Population," *Marriage and Family Living,* XIV (November, 1952), 280-285.

LOCKE, HARVEY J. *Predicting Adjustment in Marriage: A Comparison of a Divorced and a Happily Married Group.* New York: Henry Holt and Company, 1951.

————, and KARLSSON, GEORG. "Marital Adjustment and Prediction in Sweden and the United States," *American Sociological Review,* 17 (February, 1952), 10-17.

————, and KLAUSNER, WILLIAM J. "Marital Adjustment of Divorced Persons in Subsequent Marriages," *Sociology and Social Research,* 33 (1948), 97-101.

————, and MACKEPRANG, MURIEL. "Marital Adjustment and the Employed Wife," *American Journal of Sociology,* 54 (1949), 536-538.

————, and SNOWBARGER, VERNON A. "Marital Adjustment and Predictors in Sweden," *American Journal of Sociology,* 60 (July, 1954), 51-53.

————, and WILLIAMSON, ROBERT C. "Marital Adjustment: A Factor Analysis Study," *American Sociological Review,* 23 (October, 1958), 562-569.

LUCKEY, ELEANORE BRAUN. "Marital Satisfaction and Congruent Self-Spouse Concepts," *Social Forces,* 39 (December, 1960), 153-157.

NIMKOFF, MEYER F., and GRIGG, C. M. "Values and Marital Adjustment of Nurses," *Social Forces,* 37 (October, 1958), 67-70.

SCHNEPP, GERALD J. "Do Religious Factors Have Predictive Value?" *Marriage and Family Living,* 14 (1952), 301-304.

WILLIAMSON, ROBERT C. "Socio-Economic Factors and Marital Adjustment in an Urban Setting," *American Sociological Review,* 19 (April, 1954), 213-216.

WINCH, ROBERT F. "Personality Characteristics of Engaged and Married Couples," *American Journal of Sociology,* 46 (1941), 686-697.

SCHEDULES FOR THE PREDICTION AND MEASUREMENT OF MARRIAGE ADJUSTMENT

I. Marriage-Prediction Schedule *

Please Read Carefully Before and After Filling Out Schedule.

This schedule is prepared for persons who are seriously considering marriage. Although designed for couples who are engaged or who have a private understanding to be married, it can also be filled out by other persons who would like to know their probability of success in marriage. The value of the findings of the schedule depends upon your frankness in answering the questions.

The following points should be kept in mind in filling out the schedule:

1. Be sure to answer every question.
2. Do not leave a blank to mean a "no" answer.
3. The word "fiancé(e)" will be used to refer to the person to whom you are engaged or are considering as a possible marriage partner.
4. Do not confer with your fiancé(e) on any of these questions.

* Reproduced by permission of Ernest W. Burgess, Leonard S. Cottrell, Paul Wallin, and Harvey J. Locke.

Part One

1. What is your present state of health? chronic ill-health (13)____; temporary ill-health (23)____; average health (15)____; healthy (25)____; very healthy (17)____

2. Give your present marital status: single (35)____; widowed (43) ____; separated (41)____; divorced (31)____

3. Total number of years of schooling completed at present time:

   Grades (22)   High School (32)   College (15) ·
   1__2__3__4__5__6__7__8__; 1__2__3__4; 1__2__3__4__;
   graduate of college (25); number of years beyond college in graduate work or professional training (35)____

4. Work record: regularly employed (17)____; worked only during vacations and/or only part time while in school (34)____; none because in school or at home (24)____; always employed but continually changing jobs (32)____; irregularly employed (13)____

5. Are you a church member? yes (16)____; no (23)____
   Your activity in church: never attend (40)____; attend less than once a month (23)____; once or twice a month (33)____; three times a month (16)____; four times a month (26)____

6. At what age did you stop attending Sunday school or other religious school for children and young people? never attended (31)____; before 10 years old (23)____; 11-18 years (42) ____; 19 and over (16)____; still attending (35)____

7. How many organizations do you belong to or attend regularly, such as church club, athletic club, social club, luncheon club (like the Rotary, Kiwanis, Lions), fraternal order, college fraternity, college sorority, civic organization, music society, patriotic organization, Y.W.C.A., Y.M.C.A., C.Y.O., Y.M.H.A.? none (22) ____; one (32)____; two (15)____; three or more (25)____

8. What do you consider to have been the economic status of your parents during your adolescence? well-to-do (34)____; wealthy (43)____; comfortable (15)____; meager (32)____; poor (40)____

9. What do you consider to be the social status of your parents in their own community? one of the leading families (26)____; upper class (16)____; upper-middle class (42)____; middle class (32)____; lower-middle class (40)____; lower class (21)____; no status as they are dead (33)____

10. Marital status of your parents: married (both living) (24)____; separated (41)____; divorced (31)____; both dead (15)____; one dead (specify which one) (33)____

11. Your appraisal of the happiness of your parents' marriage; very happy (56)____; happy (16)____; average (24)____; unhappy (41)____; very unhappy (31)____

12. Indicate your attitudes toward your parents on the following scales:

    (1) Your attitude toward your father when you were a child; very strong attachment (35)____; considerable attachment (25)____; mild attachment (41)____; mild hostility (13) ____; considerable hostility (30)____; very strong hostility (21)____

    (2) Your present attitude toward your father: very strong attachment (44)____; considerable attachment (16)____; mild attachment (23)____; mild hostility (22)____; considerable hostility (12)____; very strong hostility (21) ____; no attitude as he is dead (24)____

    (3) Your attitude toward your mother when you were a child: very strong attachment (26)____; considerable attachment (34)____; mild attachment (14)____mild hostility (31)____; considerable hostility (30)____; very strong hostility (12)____

    (4) Your present attitude toward your mother: very strong attachment (17)____; considerable attachment (43)____; mild attachment (32)____; mild hostility (13)____; considerable hostility (21)____; very strong hostility (30) ____; no attitude as she is dead (15)____

13. Rate your parents' appraisal of the happiness of their marriage. Write M for mother's rating; F for father's rating; extraordinarily happy (27)____; decidedly happy (25)____; happy (41) ____; somewhat happy (30)____; average (30)____; somewhat unhappy (12)____; unhappy (21)____; decidedly unhappy (30)____; extremely unhappy (12)____

14. Outside your family and kin, how many separated and divorced people do you know personally? none (26)____; one (43) ____; two (23)____; three (40)____; four (30)____; five (12)____; six or more (21)____

15. How do you rate your first information about sex? wholesome (16)____; unwholesome (23)____
Where did you get your first information about sex? from parent (35)____; from wholesome reading (16)____; brother (41) ____; sister (41)____; other relative (41)____; other adult or teacher (24)____; other children (31)____; from pernicious reading (12)____; other (specify) (15)____

Do you consider your present knowledge of sex adequate for marriage? yes (34)____; no (14)____; doubtful (42)____

16. Do you smoke? not at all (26)____; rarely (15)____; occasionally (32)____; often (22)____

17. Do you drink? not at all (35)____; rarely (42)____; occasionally (33)____; often (31)____

The table on the right margin includes rows labeled M, F, and T.

347

Rate the following personality traits of yourself, your fiancé(e), your father, your mother. Write *F* for father, *M* for mother, *S* for fiancé(e), and *Y* for yourself. If either of your parents is dead, rate as remembered. Be sure to rate your father, your mother, your fiancé(e), and yourself on each trait.

Trait	Very much so	Con- siderably	Some- what	A little	Not at all	I	2
Willingly takes responsibility	26	16	6	23	13		
Dominating	13	23	33	16	44		
Irritable	40	14	24	25	17		
Punctual	35	25	15	14	13		
Moody	22	41	51	43	35		
Angers easily	40	50	60	34	26		
Ambitious	13	23	33	25	44		
Jealous	31	41	15	16	26		
Sympathetic	17	16	24	32	4		
Easygoing	44	43	42	14	22		
Stubborn	22	14	24	25	17		
Sense of duty	26	25	15	41	31		
Sense of humor	35	34	24	23	22		
Easily hurt	31	23	51	52	35		
Self-confident	44	16	15	14	13		
Selfish	22	23	33	43	44		
Nervous	22	23	24	25	35		
Likes belonging to organizations	26	16	33	41	13		
Impractical	40	14	6	34	17		
Easily depressed	13	5	42	16	26		
Easily excited	31	32	24	7	44		
						T	

I	2

Part Three

1. What is the attitude of your closest friend or friends to your fiancé(e)? approve highly (25)_____; approve with qualification (15)_____; are resigned (32)_____; disapprove mildly (13) _____; disapprove seriously (31)_____

2. How many of your present men and women friends are also friends of your fiancé(e)? all (17)_____; most of them (25) _____; a few (23)_____; none (13)_____

3. How would you rate the physical appearance of your fiancé(e)? very good looking (35)_____; good looking (25)_____; fairly good looking (41)_____; plain looking (22)_____; very plain looking (31)_____

4. Do you think your fiancé(e) is spending a disproportionate amount of present income on any of the following (check only one)? clothes (or other personal ornamentation) (13)_____; recreation (41)_____; hobbies (22)_____; food (24)_____; rent (33)_____; education (16)_____; do not think so (35)_____

5. With how many of the opposite sex, other than your fiancé(e), have you gone steadily? none (25)_____; one (42)_____; two (24)_____; three or more (15)_____

6. Defining friends as something more than mere acquaintances but not necessarily as always having been boon companions, give an estimate of the number of your men friends before going steadily with your fiancé(e): none (31)_____; few (14)_____; several (24)_____; many (34)_____; (in round numbers, how many? _____)

7. Estimate the number of your women friends before going steadily with your fiancé(e): none (4)_____; few (32)_____; several (33)_____; many (16)_____; (in round numbers, how many? _____)

8. Have you ever been engaged before (or had any previous informal understanding that you were to be married)? never (35)_____; once (42)_____; twice (14)_____; three or more times (31)_____

9. Give the attitude of your father and mother toward your marriage: both approve (26)_____; both disapprove (31)_____; one disapproves: (your father (22)_____, your mother (31) _____)

10. What is your attitude toward your future father-in-law? like him very much (25)_____; like him considerably (15)_____; like him mildly (32)_____; mild dislike (40)_____; considerable dislike (12)_____; very strong dislike (30)_____; no attitude, as he is dead (42)_____
mother-in-law: like her very much (34)_____; like her considerably (24)_____; like her mildly (41)_____; mild dislike (22) _____; considerable dislike (21)_____; very strong dislike (12) _____; no attitude, as she is dead (24)_____

11. How long have you been keeping company with your fiancé(e)? less than 3 months (13)_____; 3 to 5 months (32)_____; 6 to 11 months (24)_____; 12 to 17 months (25)_____; 18 to 23 months (35)_____; 24 to 35 months (17)_____; 36 months or more (44)_____

12. How many months will elapse between your engagement (or time at which you both had a definite understanding that you were to be married) and the date selected for your marriage? less than 3 months (40)_____; 3 to 5 months (14)_____; 6 to 11 months (33)_____; 12 to 17 months (25)_____; 18 to 23 months (35)_____; 24 or more months (44)_____

Part Four

1. Do you and your fiancé(e) engage in interests and activities together? all of them (43)_____; most of them (15)_____; some of them (23)_____; a few of them (31)_____; none of them (22)_____

2. Is there any interest vital to you in which your fiancé(e) does not engage? yes (31)__; no (43)_____

3. Do you confide in your fiancé(e)? about everything (36)_____; about most things (16)_____; about some things (23)_____; about a few things (22)_____; about nothing (30)_____

4. Does your fiancé(e) confide in you? about everything (27) _____; about most things (25)_____; about some things (41) _____; about a few things (31)_____; about nothing (12)_____

5. What is the frequency of demonstrations of affection you show your fiancé(e) (kissing, embracing, etc.)? occupies practically all of the time you are alone together (18)_____; very frequent (26)_____; occasional (14)_____; rare (31)_____; almost never (12)_____

6. Who generally takes the initiative in the demonstration of affection? mutual (26)_____; you (23)_____; your fiancé(e) (41) _____

7. Are you satisfied with the amount of demonstration of affection? yes (35)_____; (no: desire less (30)_____; desire more (12) _____)

8. Is your fiancé(e) satisfied with the amount of demonstration of affection? yes (44)_____; (no: desires less (3)_____; desires more (30)_____)

9. In leisure-time activities: we both prefer to stay at home (26) _____; we both prefer to be "on the go" (14)_____; one prefers to stay at home and the other to be "on the go" (40)_____

10. State the present approximate agreement or disagreement with your fiancé(e) on the following items. Please place a check in the proper column opposite every item.

T

350

Check one column for each item below	Always agree (35)	Almost always agree (16)	Occasionally disagree (42)	Frequently disagree (14)	Almost always disagree (22)	Always disagree (30)	Never discussed (15)	1	2
Money matters									
Matters of recreation									
Religious matters									
Demonstrations of affection									
Friends									
Table manners									
Matters of conventionality									
Philosophy of life									
Ways of dealing with your families									
Arrangements for your marriage									
Dates with one another									

11. When disagreements arise between you and your fiancé(e) they usually result in: agreement by mutual give and take (53)_____; your giving in (16)_____; your fiancé(e) giving in (30)_____; neither giving in (21)_____

12. Do you ever wish you had not become engaged? never (44) _____; once (14)_____; occasionally (13)_____; frequently (40) _____

13. Have you ever contemplated breaking your engagement? never (35)_____; once (41)_____; occasionally (31)_____; frequently (40)_____

14. Has your steady relationship with your fiancé(e) ever been broken off temporarily? never (61)_____; once (23)_____; twice (40)_____; three or more times (13)_____

15. How confident are you that your marriage will be a happy one? very confident (25)_____; confident (33)_____; a little uncertain (14)_____; very uncertain (40)_____

	T	

Part Five

1. Where do you plan to be married? at church (35)_____; at home (16)_____; elsewhere (32)_____

2. By whom do you plan to be married? minister, priest, or rabbi (16)_____; other person (14)_____

3. Where do you plan to live after marriage? private house (26) _____; small apartment building (52)_____; large apartment building (15)_____; apartment hotel (41)_____; hotel (22)_____; rooming house (30)_____

4. Have bought a home (44)_____; plan to buy a home (25)_____; plan to rent a home (14)_____

5. Population of city or town where you plan to live: open country (27)_____; 2,500 or under (35)_____; 2,500 to 10,000 (16) _____; 10,000 to 50,000 (42)_____; 50,000 to 100,000 (32)_____; 100,000 to 500,000 (4)_____; over 500,000 (30)_____; suburb (17)_____

6. After marriage where do you plan to live? in own home (53) _____; with your parents (13)_____; with parents-in-law (30) _____; with other relatives (21)_____; with relatives-in-law (3)_____; with other persons (12)_____

7. What is your attitude toward having children? desire children very much (25)_____; mildly desire them (41)_____; mild objection to them (31)_____; object very much to having them (13)_____

8. How many children would you like to have? four or more (17) _____; three (52)_____; two (33)_____; one (41)_____ none (13)_____

9. What is your fiancé(e)'s attitude toward having children? desires children very much (43)_____; mildly desires them (14) _____; mild objection to them (40)_____; objects very much to having them (31)_____

I	2
T	

Part I_____, Part II_____, Part III_____, Part IV_____, Part V_____, Total___ _

352

II. Marriage-Adjustment Schedule *

To Be Filled Out by Married Persons

This schedule may be filled out by either the husband or the wife. Frank and sincere replies are of the highest importance if the findings are to be of value to the person filling it out or for research purposes. There are no right or wrong answers.

The following points are to be kept in mind in filling out the schedule:

1. Be sure to answer all questions.
2. Do not leave any blanks, as is sometimes done, to signify a "no" reply.
3. The word spouse is used to refer to your husband or wife.
4. Do not confer with your spouse in answering these questions or show your answers to your spouse.

Your Present Marital Status

1. Are you now (check): married_____? divorced_____? separated _____? widowed_____?
2. If divorced or separated, how long have you been separated? months_____
   (If you are divorced or separated, answer the questions as of the time of your separation.)

* Reproduced by permission of Ernest W. Burgess, Leonard S. Cottrell, Paul Wallin, and Harvey J. Locke.

Part One

1. Present occupation of husband (be as specific as possible)_____
   _____ If unemployed, check here_____
   How satisfied are you, on the whole, with present occupation of
   husband? If unemployed, answer this question about his usual
   occupation: extremely satisfied (26)_____; very much satisfied
   (34)_____; satisfied (14)_____; somewhat satisfied (40)_____;
   somewhat dissatisfied (3)_____; dissatisfied (21)_____; very
   much dissatisfied (30)_____; extremely dissatisfied (12)_____

2. To what extent were you in love with your spouse before marriage? "head over heels" (17)_____; very much (25)_____;
   somewhat (32)_____; a little (22)_____; not at all (13)_____

3. To what extent was your spouse in love with you before your
   marriage? "head over heels" (26)_____; very much (43)_____;
   somewhat (23)_____; a little (40)_____; not at all (22)_____

4. How much conflict (arguments, etc.) was there between you
   before your marriage? none at all (35)_____; a little (43)_____;
   some (5)_____; considerable (31)_____; very much (13)_____

5. To what extent do you think you knew your spouse's faults and
   weak points before your marriage? not at all (44)_____; a little
   (52)_____; somewhat (32)_____; considerably (40)_____; very
   much (4)_____

6. To what extent do you think your spouse knew your faults and
   weaknesses before your marriage? not at all (17)_____; a little
   (43)_____; somewhat (41)_____; considerably (22)_____; very
   much (13)_____

7. What is your attitude toward your father-in-law? like him very
   much (61)_____; considerably (15)_____; somewhat (50)_____;
   a little (4)_____; dislike him a little (30)_____; dislike him
   somewhat (12)_____; dislike him considerably (3)_____; dislike
   him very much (21)_____; no attitude, as he is dead (24)_____

8. What is your attitude toward your mother-in-law? like her very
   much (25)_____; like her considerably (42)_____; like her somewhat (32)_____; like her a little (22)_____; dislike her a little
   (12)_____; dislike her somewhat (30)_____; dislike her considerably (3)_____; dislike her very much (21)_____; no attitude, as she is dead (51)_____

9. What is your attitude to having children? desire children very
   much (16)_____; desire children a good deal (62)_____; desire
   children somewhat (33)_____; desire children a little (5)_____;
   desire no children (31)_____

10. If children have been born to you, what effect have they had on
    your happiness? added to it very much (27)_____; added to it
    considerably (61)_____; added to it somewhat (14)_____;
    added to it a little (40)_____; have had no effect (30)_____;
    have decreased it a little (12)_____; have decreased it somewhat
    (21)_____; have decreased it considerably (3)_____; have de-
    creased it very much (30)_____; no children (24)_____

11. In leisure-time activities: we both prefer to stay at home (26) _____; we both prefer to be "on the go" (41)_____; one prefers to be "on the go" and the other to stay at home (22)_____

12. Do you and your spouse engage in outside interests together? all of them (44)_____; most of them (51)_____; some of them (14)_____; a few of them (40)_____; none of them (22)_____

13. Do you kiss your spouse? every day (62)_____; almost every day (70)_____; quite frequently (24)_____; occasionally (32) _____; rarely (13)_____; almost never (40)_____

14. Do you confide in your spouse? about everything (17)_____; about most things (52)_____; about some things (5)_____; about a few things (13)_____; about nothing (40)_____

15. Does your spouse confide in you? about everything (26)_____; about most things (52); about some things (41)_____; about a few things (4)_____; about nothing (31)_____

16. Are you satisfied with the amount of demonstration of affection in your marriage? yes (25)_____; no: (desire less (22)_____; desire more (13) _____)

17. Is your spouse satisfied with the amount of demonstration of affection? yes (16)_____; no: (desires less (40)_____; desires more (31)_____)

18. How frequently do you "humor" your spouse? frequently (4) _____; occasionally (32)_____; rarely (51)_____; never (16) _____

19. Has your spouse ever failed to tell you the truth? often (22) _____; a few times (14)_____; once (33)_____; never (25)_____

20. If until now your marriage has been at all unhappy, how confident are you that it will work out all right in the future? very confident (32)_____; confident (13)_____; somewhat uncertain (21)_____; very uncertain (30)_____; marriage has not been at all unhappy (15)_____

21. Everything considered, how happy has your marriage been for you? extraordinarily happy (45)_____; decidedly happy (16) _____; happy (50)_____; somewhat happy (13)_____; average (31)_____; somewhat unhappy (3)_____; unhappy (12)_____; decidedly unhappy (30)_____; extremely unhappy (21)_____

22. If your marriage is now at all unhappy, how long has it been so (in months)? less than 3 (23)_____; 3 to 11 (31)_____; 12 or more (12)_____; marriage has not been at all unhappy (33) _____

23. Everything considered, how happy has your marriage been for your spouse? extraordinarily happy (36)_____; decidedly happy (43)_____; happy (32)_____; somewhat happy (4)_____; average (21)_____; somewhat unhappy (30)_____; unhappy (12) _____; decidedly unhappy (3)_____; extremely unhappy (21)

24. Indicate your approximate agreement or disagreement with your spouse on the following things. Do this for each item by putting a check in the column that shows extent of your agreement or disagreement.

Check one column for each item below	Always agree (35)	Almost always agree (16)	Occasionally disagree (42)	Frequently disagree (23)	Almost always disagree (22)	Always disagree (12)
Handling family finances						
Matters of recreation						
Religious matters						
Demonstration of affection						
Friends						
Table manners						
Matters of conventionality						
Philosophy of life						
Ways of dealing with your families						
Wife's working						
Intimate relations						
Caring for the baby						
Sharing of household tasks						
Politics						

25. When disagreements arise between you and your spouse they usually result in: agreement by mutual give and take (44)_____; your giving in (52)_____; your spouse giving in (33)_____; neither giving in (40)_____ .

26. Have you ever considered either separating from or divorcing your spouse? have never considered it (26)_____; not seriously (61)_____; somewhat seriously (40)_____; seriously (22)_____

27. How many serious quarrels or arguments have you had with your spouse in the past twelve months; none (27)_____; one (42)_____; two (32)_____; three (13)_____; four or more (30)_____

28. Indicate to what extent you are in love with your spouse by placing a check in one square on the boxed line below, which ranges from extraordinarily in love to somewhat in love:

Extraor-dinarily in love	A	B	C	D	E	F	G	H	I	J	Somewhat in love
	36	17	25	43	15	33	23	41	40	13	

Indicate by a cross in the above scale the extent to which you think your spouse is in love with you.

29. How does your present love for your spouse compare with your love before marriage? very much stronger (27)_____; considerably stronger (52)_____; somewhat stronger (24)_____; a little stronger (14)_____; a little weaker (30)_____; somewhat weaker (12)_____; considerably weaker (3)_____; very much weaker (21)_____

30. If you had your life to live over, what do you think you would do? marry the same person: (certainly (35)_____; possibly (41)_____;) marry a different person (22)_____; not marry at all (31)_____

31. If your spouse could do it over again, do you think your spouse would marry you? (certainly (44)_____; possibly (50)_____); marry a different person (13)_____; not marry at all (40)_____

32. How satisfied, on the whole, are you with your marriage; entirely satisfied (18)_____; very much satisfied (52)_____; satisfied (23)_____; somewhat satisfied (31)_____; somewhat dissatisfied (3)_____; dissatisfied (12)_____; very much dissatisfied (30)_____; entirely dissatisfied (21)_____

33. How satisfied, on the whole, is your spouse with your marriage? entirely satisfied (45)_____; very much satisfied (34)_____; satisfied (41)_____; somewhat satisfied (22)_____somewhat dissatisfied (21)_____; dissatisfied (30)_____; very much dissatisfied (12)_____; entirely dissatisfied (3)_____

34. Have you ever been ashamed of your spouse? never (44)_____; once (14)_____; a few times (31)_____; often (40)_____

35. Even if satisfied with your spouse, have you ever felt that you might have been at all happier if married to another type of person? never (26)_____; rarely (41)_____; occasionally (22)_____; frequently (13)_____

36. Do you ever regret your marriage? never (17)_____; rarely (50)_____; occasionally (13)_____; frequently (40)_____

1	2
T	

357

In responding to the following items, place a check in the appropriate column to the right of each item below.

Check Column A to indicate the things that have occurred in your marriage but have not interfered with your happiness.

Check Column B to indicate those things that have made your marriage less happy than it should have been.

Check Column C to indicate those things that have done most to make your marriage unhappy.

Check Column D if the item was not present in your marriage.

For the husband or wife to fill out	A 24	B 32	C 13	D 33
Insufficient income				
Poor management of income				
Lack of freedom due to marriage				
Spouse considerably older than I				
Spouse considerably younger than I				
Matters relating to in-laws				
My spouse and I differ in:				
Education				
Intellectual interests				
Religious beliefs				
Choice of friends				
Preferences for amusements and recreation				
Attitude toward drinking				
Tastes in food				
Respect for conventions				
My spouse:				
is argumentative				
For the husband to fill out				
My wife:				
is slovenly in appearance				
has had much poor health				
is interested in other men				
is nervous or emotional				
neglects the children				

For the husband or wife to fill out	A 24	B 32	C 13	D
My spouse:				
is not affectionate				
is narrow-minded				
is not faithful to me				
complains too much				
is lazy				
is quick-tempered				
criticizes me				
spoils the children				
is untruthful				
is conceited				
is easily influenced by others				
is jealous				
is selfish and inconsiderate				
is too talkative				
smokes				
drinks				
swears				
For the husband to fill out				
My wife:				
wants to visit or entertain a lot				
does not have meals ready on time				
interferes if I discipline the children				
tries to improve me				

<table>
<tr><td colspan="1"></td><td>A</td><td>B</td><td>C</td><td>D</td></tr>
</table>

the husband to fill out (cont.)	A 24	B 32	C 13	D 33
wife:				
poor housekeeper				
ot interested in my business				
xtravagant				
her feelings be hurt too asily				
oo interested in social affairs				
annoying habits and nannerisms				
poor cook				
erferes with my business				
the wife to fill out				
husband:				
vs attention to other women				
nervous or impatient				
es no interest in the children				
untidy				
always wrapped up in his business				
mbles				
touchy				
not interested in the home				
vulgar habits				
likes to go out with me evenings				
ate to meals				
harsh with the children				
poor table manners				

For the husband to fill out (cont.)	A 24	B 32	C 13	D 33
My wife:				
is a social climber				
is too interested in clothes				
is insincere				
gossips indiscreetly				
nags me				
interferes with my hobbies				
works outside the home				
is fussy about keeping the house neat				
For the wife to fill out				
My husband:				
is tight with money				
has no backbone				
does not talk things over freely				
is rude				
is bored if I tell him of the things that happen in my everyday life				
is unsuccessful in his business				
does not show his affection for me				
gets angry easily				
drinks too much				
has friends I do not approve of				
is constantly nagging and bickering				
lacks ambition				
T				

Part I_____, Part II_____, Total_____

Personality Measurements

Of the hundreds of personality inventories only two are selected for presentation. These two measures are probably the most widely used personality measures in research today. The *Minnesota Multiphasic Personality Inventory* is described but not reproduced. It is a battery of scales containing 550 statements. It is thorough and so well constructed that it has generally won the confidence of researchers as the best scale to probe the personality. The research applications included in the description of the instrument attest to its use.

The *California F-Scale* to measure the authoritarian personality has won high acceptance and has stimulated wide research application.

Of all the personality measures, it was believed the social researcher might find these two scales to be the most useful for his purpose. For a compilation of other measures of personality the following might be consulted:

ANDERSON, HAROLD H., and ANDERSON, GLADYS L. *An Introduction to Projective Techniques and Other Devices for Understanding the Dynamics of Human Behavior.* Englewood Cliffs, N.J.: Prentice-Hall, Inc., 1951.

CATTEL, R. B. *Personality and Motivation Structure and Measurement.* New York: World Book, 1957.

GREENE, EDWARD B. *Measurements of Human Behavior.* Rev. ed. New York: The Odyssey Press, Inc., 1952.

KRECH, DAVID, CRUTCHFIELD, RICHARD S., and BALACHEY, EGERTON L. *Individual in Society.* New York: McGraw-Hill, 1962.

The Psychological Corporation has a catalog of personality and other psychological tests. This organization distributes such widely used tests as the *Minnesota Multiphasic Personality Inventory*, Edward's *Personal Preference Schedule, Bernreuter Personality Inventory,* Allport, Vernon, and Lindzey's *Study of Values, Rorschach Technique,* and Murray's *Thematic Apperception Test.* For a catalog of the Test Division, write The Psychological Corporation, 304 East 45 Street, New York, N.Y., 10017.

IV.I.1. INDEX: MINNESOTA MULTIPHASIC PERSONALITY INVENTORY (*MMPI*)

VARIABLE MEASURED: Measures twenty-six areas of personality traits and attitudes.

DESCRIPTION: The *MMPI* is primarily designed to provide, in a single test, scores on all the more clinically important phases of personality. The instrument itself comprises 550 statements covering a wide range of subject matter, from the physical condition of the individual being tested to his morale and social attitude. For administration of the inventory the subject is asked to respond to all statements, which are in the first person, as True, False, or Cannot Say. The *MMPI* yields scores on nine scales of personality characteristics indicative of clinical syndromes.

WHERE PUBLISHED: Starke R. Hathaway, *The Minnesota Multiphasic Personality Inventory* (Minneapolis: University of Minnesota, 1942); Starke R. Hathaway and J. Charnley McKinley, *Manual for the Minnesota Multiphasic Personality Inventory* (rev. ed.; New York: Psychological Corporation, 1951); W. Grant Dahlstrom and George Schlager Welsh, *An MMPI Handbook: A Guide to Use in Clinical Practice and Research* (Minneapolis: University of Minnesota, 1960).

RELIABILITY: $r = .71$ to .83. See Starke R. Hathaway and J. Charnley McKinley, *Manual for the Minnesota Multiphasic Personality Inventory* (rev. ed.; New York: The Psychological Corporation, 1951).
   See also: Harrison G. Gough, "Simulated Patterns on the Minnesota Multiphasic Personality Inventory," *The Journal of Abnormal and Social Psychology,* 42 (April, 1947), 215-225; Charles A. Weisgerber, "The Predictive Value of the Minnesota Multiphasic Personality Inventory with Student Nurses," *The Journal of Social Psychology,* 33 (February, 1951), 3-11.

VALIDITY: Hathaway and McKinley maintain, "... the chief criterion of excellence has been the valid prediction of clinical cases against the neuro-psychiatric staff diagnosis, rather than statistical measures of reliability and validity." Starke R. Hathaway and J. Charnley McKinley, *Manual for the Minnesota Multiphasic Personality Inventory* (rev. ed.; New York: The Psychological Corporation, 1951). See also:

ALTUS, W. D., and TAFEJIAN, T. T. "MMPI Correlates of the California E-F Scale," *The Journal of Social Psychology*, 38 (August, 1953), 145-149.

BENTON, A. L., and PROBST, K. A. "A Comparison of Psychiatric Ratings with Minnesota Multiphasic Personality Inventory Scores," *The Journal of Abnormal and Social Psychology*, 41 (January, 1946), 75-78.

ELLIS, A. "The Validity of Personality Questionnaires," *The Psychological Bulletin*, 43 (September, 1946), 385-440.

LOUGH, ORPHA M., and GREEN, MARY E. "Comparison of the Minnesota Multiphasic Personality Inventory and the Washburne S-A Inventory as Measures of Personality of College Women," *The Journal of Social Psychology*, 32 (August, 1950), 23-30.

MEEHL, PAUL E., and HATHAWAY, STARKE R. "The K Factor as a Suppressor Variable in the Minnesota Multiphasic Personality Inventory," *Journal of Applied Psychology*, 30 (1946), 525-564.

UTILITY: The inventory is easily administered. The time required varies from 30 to 90 minutes. No supervision is needed beyond that required for the subject to understand clearly the nature of his task and to assure his optimal cooperation.

RESEARCH APPLICATIONS:

ALTUS, WILLIAM D. "A College Achiever and Non-Achiever Scale for the Minnesota Multiphasic Personality Inventory," *Journal of Applied Psychology*, 32 (August, 1948), 385-397.

————, and TAFEJIAN, T. T. "MMPI Correlates of the California E-F Scale," *The Journal of Social Psychology*, 38 (August, 1953), 145-149.

BENTON, ARTHUR L., and PROBST, KATHRYN A. "A Comparison of Psychiatric Ratings with Minnesota Multiphasic Personality Inventory Scores," *The Journal of Abnormal and Social Psychology*, 41 (January, 1946), 75-78.

BROWER, DANIEL. "The Relation Between Intelligence and Minnesota Multiphasic Personality Inventory Scores," *The Journal of Social Psychology*, 25 (May, 1947), 243-245.

————. "The Relations Between Minnesota Multiphasic Personality Inventory Scores and Cardio-Vascular Measures Before and After Experimentally Induced Visuo-Motor Conflict," *The Journal of Social Psychology*, 26 (August, 1947), 55-60.

BURTON, ARTHUR. "The Use of the Masculinity-Femininity Scale of the Minnesota Multiphasic Personality Inventory as an Aid in the Diagnosis of Sexual Inversion," *The Journal of Psychology*, 24 (July, 1947), 161-164.

CARP, ABRAHAM. "MMPI Performance and Insulin Shock Therapy," *Journal of Abnormal and Social Psychology*, 45 (October, 1950), 721-726.

CARPENTER, LEWIS G., JR. "An Experimental Test of an Hypothesis for Predicting Outcome with Electroshock Therapy," *The Journal of Psychology*, 36 (July, 1953), 131-135.

CLARK, JERRY H. "Application of the *MMPI* in Differentiating A.W.O.L. Recidivists from Non-Recidivists," *The Journal of Psychology*, 26 (July, 1948), 229-234.

CLARK, J. H. "Grade Achievement of Female College Students in Relation to Non-Intellective Factors: MMPI Items," *The Journal of Social Psychology*, 37 (May, 1953), 275-281.

COFER, C. N., CHANCE, JUNE, and JUDSON, A. J. "A Study of Malingering on the Minnesota Multiphasic Personality Inventory," *The Journal of Psychology*, 27 (April, 1949), 491-499.

COOK, ELLSWORTH B., and WHERRY, ROBERT J. "A Factor Analysis of MMPI and Aptitude Test Data," *Journal of Applied Psychology*, 34 (August, 1950), 260-266.

COTTLE, WILLIAM C. "Card Versus Booklet Forms of the MMPI," *Journal of Applied Psychology*, 34 (August, 1950), 255-259.

DANIELS, E. E., and HUNTER, W. A. "MMPI Personality Patterns for Various Occupations," *Journal of Applied Psychology*, 33 (December, 1949), 559-565.

DRAKE, LEWIS E. "A Social *I.E.* Scale for the Minnesota Multiphasic Personality Inventory," *Journal of Applied Psychology*, 30 (1946), 51-54.

———. "Differential Sex Responses to Items of the MMPI," *Journal of Applied Psychology*, 37 (February, 1953), 46.

ENGELHARDT, OLGA E. DE C., and ORBISON, WILLIAM D. "Comparison of the Terman-Miles M-F Test and the Mf Scale of the MMPI," *Journal of Applied Psychology*, 34 (October, 1950), 338-342.

FRY, FRANKLIN D. "A Normative Study of the Reactions Manifested by College Students and by State Prison Inmates in Response to the Minnesota Multiphasic Personality Inventory, the Rozenzweig Picture-Frustration Study, and the Thematic Apperception Test," *The Journal of Psychology*, 34 (July, 1952), 27-30.

———. "A Study of the Personality Traits of College Students and of State Prison Inmates as Measured by the Minnesota Multiphasic Personality Inventory," *The Journal of Psychology*, 28 (October, 1949), 439-449.

GOUGH, HARRISON. "A New Dimension of Status: I. The Development of a Personality Scale," *American Sociological Review,* 13 (August, 1948), 401-409.

————. "A New Dimension of Status: II. Relationship of the *St* Scale to Other Variables," *American Sociological Review,* 13 (October, 1948), 534-537.

————. "A New Dimension of Status: III. Discrepancies Between the *St* Scale and 'Objective' Status," *American Sociological Review,* 14 (April, 1949), 275-281.

————. "Simulated Patterns on the Minnesota Multiphasic Personality Inventory," *Journal of Abnormal and Social Psychology,* 42 (April, 1947), 215-225.

GREENBERG, PAUL, and GILLILAND, A. R. "The Relationship Between Basal Metabolism and Personality," *The Journal of Social Psychology,* 35 (February, 1952), 3-7.

GUTHRIE, GEORGE M. "Six MMPI Diagnostic Profile Patterns," *The Journal of Psychology,* 30 (October, 1950), 317-323.

HAMPTON, PETER J. "The Minnesota Multiphasic Personality Inventory as a Psychometric Tool for Diagnosing Personality Disorders among College Students," *The Journal of Social Psychology,* 26 (August, 1947), 99-108.

HARMON, LINDSEY R., and WIENER, DANIEL N. "Use of the Minnesota Multiphasic Personality Inventory in Vocational Advisement," *Journal of Applied Psychology,* 29 (April, 1945), 132-141.

HATHAWAY, STARKE R., and MONACHESI, ELIO D. *Analyzing and Predicting Juvenile Delinquency with the MMPI.* Minneapolis: University of Minnesota Press, 1953.

————. "The Minnesota Multiphasic Personality Inventory in the Study of Juvenile Delinquents," *American Sociological Review,* 17 (December, 1952), 704-710.

LOUGH, ORPHA M. "Teachers College Students and the Minnesota Multiphasic Personality Inventory," *Journal of Applied Psychology,* 30 (June, 1946), 241-247.

————. "Women Students in Liberal Arts, Nursing, and Teacher Training Curricula and the Minnesota Multiphasic Personality Inventory," *Journal of Applied Psychology,* 31 (August, 1947), 437-445.

————, and GREEN, MARY E. "Comparison of the Minnesota Multiphasic Personality Inventory and the Washburne S-A Inventory as Measures of Personality of College Women," *The Journal of Social Psychology,* 32 (August, 1950), 23-30.

MAC LEAN, A. G., *et al.* "F Minus K Index on the MMPI," *Journal of Applied Psychology,* 37 (August, 1953), 315-316.

MASLOW, A. H., *et al.* "A Clinically Derived Test for Measuring Psychological Security-Insecurity," *Journal of General Psychology*, 33 (1945), 21-41.

MEEHL, PAUL E., and HATHAWAY, STARKE R. "The *K* Factor as a Suppressor Variable in the Minnesota Multiphasic Personality Inventory," *Journal of Applied Psychology*, 30 (1946), 525-564.

MICHAELIS, JOHN U., and TYLER, FRED T. "MMPI and Student Teaching," *Journal of Applied Psychology*, 35 (April, 1951), 122-124.

MONACHESI, ELIO D. "Some Personality Characteristics of Delinquents and Non-Delinquents," *Journal of Criminal Law and Criminology*, 37 (January-February, 1948), 487-500.

NORMAN, RALPH D., and REDLO, MIRIAM. "MMPI Personality Patterns for Various College Major Groups," *Journal of Applied Psychology*, 36 (December, 1952), 404-409.

SCHMIDT, HERMANN O. "Test Profiles as a Diagnostic Aid: The Minnesota Multiphasic Inventory," *Journal of Applied Psychology*, 29 (April, 1945), 115-131.

SCHOFIELD, WILLIAM. "A Further Study of the Effects of Therapies on MMPI Responses," *Journal of Abnormal and Social Psychology*, 48 (January, 1953), 67-77.

————. "A Study of Medical Students with the MMPI: I. Scale Norms and Profile Patterns," *The Journal of Psychology*, 36 (July, 1953), 59-65.

————. "A Study of Medical Students with the MMPI: II. Group and Individual Changes after Two Years," *The Journal of Psychology*, 36 (July, 1953), 137-141.

————. "A Study of Medical Students with the MMPI: III. Personality and Academic Success," *Journal of Applied Psychology*, 37 (February, 1953), 47-52.

SOPCHACK, ANDREW L. "Parental 'Identification' and 'Tendency Toward Disorders' as Measured by the Minnesota Multiphasic Personality Inventory," *Journal of Abnormal and Social Psychology*, 47 (April, 1952), 159-165.

TYDLASKA, M., and MENGEL, R. "Scale for Measuring Work Attitude for the MMPI," *Journal of Applied Psychology*, 37 (December, 1953), 474-477.

TYLER, FRED T., and MICHAELIS, JOHN U. "Comparison of Manual and College Norms for the MMPI," *Journal of Applied Psychology*, 37 (August, 1953), 273-275.

VERNIAUD, WILLIE MAUDE. "Occupational Differences in the Minnesota Multiphasic Personality Inventory," *Journal of Applied Psychology*, 30 (December, 1946), 604-613.

WEISGERBER, CHARLES A. "The Predictive Value of the Minnesot Multiphasic Personality Inventory with Student Nurses," *TI Journal of Social Psychology,* 33 (February, 1951), 3-11.

WINFIELD, DON L. "The Relationship Between IQ Scores and Minne sota Multiphasic Personality Inventory Scores," *The Journal Social Psychology,* 38 (November, 1953), 299-300.

Content of Minnesota Multiphasic Personality Inventory (MMPI) *

1. General health (9 items)
2. General neurologic (19 items)
3. Cranial nerves (11 items)
4. Motility and coordination (6 items)
5. Sensibility (5 items)
6. Vasomotor, trophic, speech, secretory (10 items)
7. Cardio-respiratory system (5 items)
8. Gastro-intestinal system (11 items)
9. Genito-urinary system (5 items)
10. Habits (19 items)
11. Family and marital (26 items)
12. Occupational (18 items)
13. Educational (12 items)
14. Sexual attitudes (16 items)
15. Religious attitudes (19 items)
16. Political attitudes—law and order (46 items)
17. Social attitudes (72 items)
18. Affect, depressive (32 items)
19. Affect, manic (24 items)
20. Obsessive and compulsive states (15 items)
21. Delusions, hallucinations, illusions, ideas of reference (31 items
22. Phobias (29 items)
23. Sadistic, masochistic trends (7 items)
24. Morale (33 items)
25. Item primarily related to masculinity-femininity (55 items)
26. Items to indicate whether the individual is trying to place himsel in an acceptable light (15 items)

IV.I.2. INDEX: AUTHORITARIAN PERSONALITY (F) SCALE, FORMS 45 AND 40

VARIABLE MEASURED: "Authoritarianism" or antidemocratic po tential.

* By permission of Hathaway and McKinley and the University of Minnesot Press.

DESCRIPTION: The scale consists of thirty items grouped into nine attitudinal categories considered as variables in a personality syndrome. The items are rated on a seven-point scale, from $+3$ to -3, according to the subjects' agreement or disagreement with the statement.

WHERE PUBLISHED: T. W. Adorno, Else Frenkel-Brunswik, D. J. Levinson, and R. N. Sanford, *The Authoritarian Personality* (New York: Harper, 1950).

RELIABILITY: Authors' report on studies—mean $r = .90$, range .81 to .97.

Correlation with Ethnocentrism Scale—mean $r = .75$ with a range from $r = .59$ to $r = .87$.

Using Fisher's Z_r, each item was correlated with every other item—mean $r = .13$ and the range was from $r = -.05$ to $r = .44$.

In addition, each item was correlated with the remainder of the scale, the mean r being .33, the range .15 to .52.

See also:

CHRISTIE, RICHARD, HAVEL, JOAN, SEIDENBERG, BERNARD. "Is the F Scale Irreversible?" *Journal of Abnormal and Social Psychology,* 56 (1958), 143-159.

————, and JAHODA, MARIE (eds.). *Studies in the Scope and Method of "The Authoritarian Personality."* Glencoe, Ill.: The Free Press, 1954.

VALIDITY: The authors used the case study method to validate the scale. The scale has been correlated with the Campbell Xenophobia: $r = .60$.

See also:

BASS, BERNARD M. "Authoritarianism or Acquiescence?" *Journal of Abnormal and Social Psychology,* 51 (November, 1955), 616-623.

CAMILLERI, SANTO F. "A Factor Analysis of the F-Scale," *Social Forces,* 37 (May, 1959), 316-323.

CHRISTIE, RICHARD, and JAHODA, MARIE (eds.). *Studies in the Scope and Method of "The Authoritarian Personality."* Glencoe, Ill.: The Free Press, 1954.

HIMMELHOCH, JEROME. "Tolerance and Personality Needs: A Study of the Liberalization of Ethnic Attitudes among Minority Group College Students," *American Sociological Review,* 15 (February, 1950), 79-88.

PROTHRO, E. TERRY, and MELIKIAN, LEVON. "The California Public Opinion Scale in an Authoritarian Culture," *Public Opinion Quarterly,* 17 (1953), 115-135.

UTILITY: The test may be administered either in interviews or by questionnaire.

RESEARCH APPLICATIONS:

ADELSON, JOSEPH. "A Study of Minority Group Authoritarianism," *Journal of Abnormal and Social Psychology*, 48 (October, 1953), 477-485.

BASS, BERNARD M. "Authoritarianism or Acquiescence?" *Journal of Abnormal and Social Psychology*, 51 (November, 1955), 616-623.

BROWN, ROGER W. "A Determinant of the Relationship Between Rigidity and Authoritarianism," *Journal of Abnormal and Social Psychology*, 48 (October, 1953), 469-476.

CAMILLERI, SANTO F. "A Factor Analysis of the *F*-Scale," *Social Forces*, 37 (May, 1959), 316-323.

CAMPBELL, DONALD T., and McCORMACK, THELMA H. "Military Experience and Attitudes Toward Authority," *American Journal of Sociology*, 62 (March, 1957), 482-490.

CHRISTIE, RICHARD. "Changes in Authoritarianism as Related to Situational Factors," *American Psychologist*, 8 (1952), 307-308.

———, and COOK, PEGGY. "Guide to Published Literature Relating to the Authoritarian Personality," *Journal of Psychology*, 45 (1958), 171-199 (bibliography).

———, and GARCIA, JOHN. "Subcultural Variation in Authoritarian Personality," *Journal of Abnormal and Social Psychology*, 46 (October, 1951), 457-469.

———, HAVEL, JOAN, and SEIDENBERG, BERNARD. "Is the *F*-Scale Irreversible?" *Journal of Abnormal and Social Psychology*, 56 (1958), 143-159.

———, and JAHODA, MARIE (eds.). *Studies in the Scope and Method of "The Authoritarian Personality."* Glencoe, Ill.: The Free Press, 1954.

DAVIDS, ANTHONY. "Some Personality and Intellectual Correlates of Intolerance of Ambiguity," *Journal of Abnormal and Social Psychology*, 51 (November, 1955), 415-420.

GELBMANN, FREDERICK JOHN. *Authoritarianism and Temperament.* Washington, D.C.: The Catholic University of America Press, 1958.

GOUGH, HARRISON G. "Studies of Social Intolerance: I. Some Psychological and Sociological Correlates of Anti-Semitism," *Journal of Social Psychology*, 33 (May, 1951), 237-246.

———. "Studies of Social Intolerance: II. A Personality Scale for Anti-Semitism," *Journal of Social Psychology*, 33 (May, 1951), 247-255.

————. "Studies of Social Intolerance: III. Relationship of the *Pr* Scale to Other Variables," *Journal of Social Psychology*, 33 (May, 1951), 257-262.

GREENBERG, HERBERT, and HUTTO, DOLORES. "The Attitudes of West Texas College Students Toward School Integration," *Journal of Applied Psychology*, 42 (October, 1958), 301-304.

HAYTHORN, WILLIAM, COUCH, ARTHUR, FAEFNER, DONALD, LANGHAM, PETER, and CARTER, LAUNOR F. "The Behavior of Authoritarian and Equalitarian Personalities in Groups," *Human Relations*, 9 (February, 1956), 57-73.

HIMMELHOCH, JEROME. "Tolerance and Personality Needs: A Study of the Liberalization of Ethnic Attitudes among Minority Group College Students," *American Sociological Review*, 15 (February, 1950), 79-88.

JONES, EDWARD E. "Authoritarianism as a Determinant of First-Impression Formation," *Journal of Personality*, 23 (September, 1954), 107-127.

KATES, SOLIS L. "First-Impression Formation and Authoritarianism," *Human Relations*, 12 (August, 1959), 277-285.

————, and DIAB, LUFTY N. "Authoritarian Ideology and Attitudes on Parent-Child Relationships," *Journal of Abnormal and Social Psychology*, 51 (July, 1955), 13-16.

KAUFMAN, WALTER C. "Status, Authoritarianism, and Anti-Semitism," *American Journal of Sociology*, 62 (January, 1957), 379-382.

MACKINNON, WILLIAM J., and CENTERS, RICHARD. "Authoritarianism and Urban Stratification," *American Journal of Sociology*, 61 (May, 1956), 610-620.

MARTIN, JAMES G., and WESTIE, FRANK R. "The Tolerant Personality," *American Sociological Review*, 24 (August, 1959), 521-528.

MEER, SAMUEL J. "Authoritarianism Attitudes and Dreams," *Journal of Abnormal and Social Psychology*, 51 (July, 1955), 74-78.

MISHLER, ELLIOT G. "Personality Characteristics and the Resolution of Role Conflicts," *Public Opinion Quarterly*, 17, No. 1 (1953), 115-135.

O'NEIL, WILLIAM M., and LEVINSON, DANIEL J. "A Factorial Exploration of Authoritarianism and Some of Its Ideological Concomitants," *Journal of Personality*, 22 (June, 1954), 449-463.

PROTHRO, E. TERRY, and MELIKIAN, LEVON. "The California Public Opinion Scale in an Authoritarian Culture," *Public Opinion Quarterly*, 17, No. 3 (1953), 353-362.

ROBERTS, ALAN H., and ROKEACH, MILTON. "Anomie, Authoritarianism, and Prejudice: A Replication," *American Journal of Sociology*, 61 (January, 1956), 355-358.

SANFORD, NEVITT. "Recent Developments in Connection with the

Investigation of the Authoritarian Personality," *Sociological Review*, 2 (July, 1954), 11-33.

SCODEL, ALVIN, and MUSSEN, PAUL. "Social Perceptions of Authoritarians and Nonauthoritarians," *Journal of Abnormal and Social Psychology*, 48 (April, 1953), 181-184.

SMITH, CHARLES U., and PROTHRO, JAMES W. "Ethnic Differences in Authoritarian Personality," *Social Forces*, 35 (May, 1957), 334-338.

SROLE, LEO. "Social Integration and Certain Corollaries: An Exploratory Study," *American Sociological Review*, 21 (December, 1956), 709-716.

THIBAUT, JOHN W., and RIECKEN, HENRY W. "Authoritarianism, Status, and the Communication of Aggression," *Human Relations*, 8 (May, 1955), 95-120.

F-SCALE CLUSTERS: FORMS 45 AND 40 *

A. Conventionalism: Rigid adherence to conventional, middle-class values.

   1. Obedience and respect for authority are the most important virtues children should learn.

   12. A person who has bad manners, habits, and breeding can hardly expect to get along with decent people.

   37. If people would talk less and work more, everybody would be better off.

   41. The businessman and the manufacturer are much more important to society than the artist and the professor.

B. Authoritarian Submission: Submissive, uncritical attitude toward idealized moral authorities of the ingroup.

   1. Obedience and respect for authority are the most important virtues children should learn.

   4. Science has its place, but there are many important things that can never possibly be understood by the human mind.

   8. Every person should have complete faith in some supernatural power whose decisions he obeys without question.

   21. Young people sometimes get rebellious ideas, but as they grow up they ought to get over them and settle down.

   23. What this country needs most, more than laws and political programs, is a few courageous, tireless, devoted leaders in whom the people can put their faith.

* From T. W. Adorno *et. al.*, "F-Scale Clusters: Forms 45 and 40," *The Authoritarian Personality* (New York: Harper, 1950).

42. No sane, normal, decent person could ever think of hurting a close friend or relative.

44. Nobody ever learned anything really important except through suffering.

C. Authoritarian Aggression: Tendency to be on the lookout for, and to condemn, reject, and punish, people who violate conventional values.

12. A person who has bad manners, habits, and breeding can hardly expect to get along with decent people.

13. What youth needs most is strict discipline, rugged determination, and the will to work and fight for family and country.

19. An insult to our honor should always be punished.

25. Sex crimes, such as rape and attacks on children, deserve more than mere imprisonment; such criminals ought to be publicly whipped, or worse.

27. There is hardly anything lower than a person who does not feel a great love, gratitude, and respect for his parents.

34. Most of our social problems would be solved if we could somehow get rid of the immoral, crooked, and feebleminded people.

37. If people would talk less and work more, everybody would be better off.

39. Homosexuals are hardly better than criminals and ought to be severely punished.

D. Anti-intraception: Opposition to the subjective, the imaginative, the tender-minded.

9. When a person has a problem or worry, it is best for him not to think about it, but to keep busy with more cheerful things.

31. Nowadays more and more people are prying into matters that should remain personal and private.

37. If people would talk less and work more, everybody would be better off.

41. The businessman and the manufacturer are much more important to society than the artist and the professor.

E. Superstition and Stereotypy: The belief in mystical determinants of the individual's fate; the disposition to think in rigid categories.

4. Science has its place, but there are many important things that can never possibly be understood by the human mind.

8. Every person should have complete faith in some supernatural power whose decisions he obeys without question.

16. Some people are born with an urge to jump from high places.

26. People can be divided into two distinct classes: the weak and the strong.

29. Some day it will probably be shown that astrology can explain a lot of things.
33. Wars and social troubles may someday be ended by an earthquake or flood that will destroy the whole world.

F. Power and "Toughness": Preoccupation with the dominance-submission, strong-weak, leader-follower dimension; identification with power figures; overemphasis upon the conventionalized attributes of the ego; exaggerated assertion of strength and toughness.
   2. No weakness or difficulty can hold us back if we have enough willpower.
   13. What youth needs most is strict discipline, rugged determination, and the will to work and fight for family and country.
   19. An insult to our honor should always be punished.
   22. It is best to use some prewar authorities in Germany to keep order and prevent chaos.
   23. What this country needs most, more than laws and political programs, is a few courageous, tireless, devoted leaders in whom the people can put their faith.
   26. People can be divided into two distinct classes: the weak and the strong.
   38. Most people don't realize how much our lives are controlled by the plots hatched in secret places.

G. Destructiveness and Cynicism: Generalized hostility, vilification of the human.
   6. Human nature being what it is, there will always be war and conflict.
   43. Familiarity breeds contempt.

H. Projectivity: The disposition to believe that wild and dangerous things go on in the world; the projection outwards of unconscious emotional impulses.
   18. Nowadays when so many different kinds of people move around and mix together so much, a person has to protect himself especially carefully against catching an infection or disease from them.
   31. Nowadays more and more people are prying into matters that should remain personal and private.
   33. Wars and social troubles may someday be ended by an earthquake or flood that will destroy the whole world.
   35. The wild sex life of the old Greeks and Romans was tame compared to some of the goings-on in this country, even in places where people might least expect it.

38. Most people don't realize how much our lives are controlled by plots hatched in secret places.

I. Sex: Exaggerated concern with sexual "goings-on."

25. Sex crimes, such as rape and attacks on children, deserve more than mere imprisonment; such criminals ought to be publicly whipped, or worse.

35. The wild sex life of the old Greeks and Romans was tame compared to some of the goings-on in this country, even in places where people might least expect it.

39. Homosexuals are hardly better than criminals and ought to be severely punished.

A Comprehensive Inventory of Sociometric and Attitude Scales

IV.J.1. AN INVENTORY OF MEASURES UTILIZED IN THE *AMERICAN SOCIOLOGICAL REVIEW, 1965-1968* *

Instructions for Use of Inventory:

A researcher who has not found scales in the handbook to fit his particular problem should carry out the following search:

First, consult the reference book by Charles M. Bonjean, Richard J. Hill, and S. Dale McLemore, *Sociological Measurement: An Inventory of Scales and Indices* (San Francisco: Chandler, 1967). This is the book referred to in the beginning of Part IV. It is now the best compilation available and includes references to related research.

Second, review the inventory of the *American Sociological Review, 1965-1968,* to check on new scales or related research for previous scales. (The Bonjean, Hill, McLemore book terminates with work published in 1965.) In the inventory below, skim the right-hand column and identify similar areas of research interest. The left-hand column contains the scale or indexes used by the researchers. Go to the *American Sociological Review* for the published source of the instrument. For current work see the *Review* as published. A cumulative index is available for all published volumes through Vol. 30 (1965).

Third, if you need an attitude scale, check the list of attitude scales in Marvin E. Shaw and Jack M. Wright, *Scales for the Measurement of Attitudes* (New York: McGraw-Hill, 1967). This list is appended in the latter part of this section for the researcher seeking a particular attitude scale in which he may be interested.

* Assembled by Francisco Suarez and Delbert C. Miller.

Scales for Measuring Social Status

Duncan's Index of Socioeconomic Status (see note under Hatt-North Prestige Scale, (pp. 177-178)	Bruce K. Eckland, "Academic Ability, Higher Education and Occupational Mobility," 30 (October, 1965), 735-746.
	Ira L. Reiss, "Social Class and Premarital Sexual Permissiveness: A Reconsideration," 30 (October, 1965), 747-756.
	Edward O. Laumann and Louis Guttman, "The Relative Associational Contiguity of Occupations in an Urban Setting," 31 (April, 1966), 169-178.
	Peter M. Blau, "The Flow of Occupational Supply and Recruitment," 30 (August, 1965), 475-490.
	Carolyn Cummings Perrucci, "Social Origins, Mobility Patterns and Fertility," 32 (August, 1967), 615-625.
	Margaret A. Parman and Jack Sawyer, "Dimensions of Ethnic Intermarriage in Hawaii," 32 (August, 1967), 593-607.
Occupational Prestige Scores; 1964 Study by National Opinion Research Center	Robert Hodge and Donald J. Treiman, "Social Participation and Social Status," 33 (October, 1968), 722-740.
Ellis and Lane Index of Class Position for College Populations	Robert Ellis and W. Clayton Lane, "Social Mobility and Social Isolation: A Test of Sorokin's Dissociate Hypotheses," 32 (April, 1967), 237-253.
Hollingshead Two-Factor Index of Social Position (see note on p. 196)	R. Jay Turner and Morton O. Wagenfeld, "Occupational Mobility and Schizophrenia: An Assessment of the Social Causation and Social Selection Hypothesis," 32 (February, 1967), 104-112.

Author Constructed Index, Which Includes Measure of Father's Educational Level, Mother's Educational Level, an Estimate of the Funds the Family Could Provide if the Student Were to Attend College, the Degree of Sacrifice This Would Entail for the Family, and the Approximate Wealth and Income Status of Student's Family

William H. Sewell and Michel Armer, "Neighborhood Context and College Plans," 31 (April, 1966), 159-168.

Census "Index of Socioeconomic Status"

Charles B. Nam and Mary G. Powers, "Variations in Socioeconomic Structure By Race, Residence, and the Life Cycle," 30 (February, 1965), 81-96.

Scales for Measuring Group Structures and Dynamics

Intergroup Hostility Scale For Measuring Hostility Toward Negroes, Americans, Estonians, Jews, and Gypsies. Based on Bogardus-Type Social Distance Scale

Melvin Seeman, "On the Personal Consequences of Alienation in Work," 32 (April, 1967), 273-285.

Social Distance Scale for Measuring the Willingness to Accept Ex-Mental-Hospital-Patient; Author Constructed

Bruce P. Dohrenwend and Edwin Chin-Song, "Social Status and Attitudes Toward Psychological Disorder: The Problem of Tolerance of Deviance," (June, 1967), 417-433.

Degree of Bureaucratization Scale Measuring Six Dimensions: Hierarchy of Authority, Division of Labor, Rules, Procedures, Impersonality, Technical Competence; Author Constructed Scale, Likert-Type

Richard Hall, "Professionalization and Bureaucratization," 33 (February, 1968), 92-104.

Social Distance Scale For Measuring Reactions To Physical Handicaps; Author Constructed

Victor Matthews and Charles Westie, "A Preferred Method For Obtaining Rankings Reactions to Physical Handicaps," 31 (December, 1966), 851-854.

Scales for Measuring Community Factors

Rancorous Conflict Index	William Gamson, "Rancorous Conflict in Community Politics," 31 (February, 1966), 71-81.
Index of Occupational Community Involvement of Professional Workers; Author Constructed Index	Harold Wilensky and Jack Ladinsky, "From Religious Community to Occupational Group: Structural Assimilation Among Professors, Lawyers, and Engineers," 32 (August, 1967), 541.

Scales for Measuring Social Participation and Alienation

Kuznets Index of Inequality for Measuring the Distribution of Material Rewards Within Nations	Phillips Cutright, "Inequality: A Cross-National Analysis," 32 (August, 1967), 562.
Index of Religious Community Involvement of Professional Worker; Author Constructed Index	Harold Wilensky and Jack Ladinsky, "From Religious Community to Occupational Group: Structural Assimilation Among Professors, Lawyers, and Engineers," 32 (August, 1967), 451.
Glock's Index of Religiosity Which Measures Several Dimensions of Religious Involvement	Gary T. Marx, "Religion: Opiate or Inspiration of Civil Rights Militancy Among Negroes," 37 (February, 1967), 64-72.
Powerlessness Scale, Based on Arthur G. Neal and Salomon Rettig Scale	Theodore Groat and Arthur G. Neal, "Social Psychological Correlates of Urban Fertility," 32 (December, 1967), 945-959.
Social Isolation Scale; Modified Version of Dwight Dean Scale	Theodore Groat and Arthur G. Neal, "Social Psychological Correlates of Urban Fertility," 32 (December, 1967), 945-959.
Anomie Scale to Measure Feelings of Normlessness, Author Constructed	Herbert McClosky and John H. Scharr, "Psychological Dimensions of Anomy," 30 (February, 1965), 14-40. See application by Robert C. Atchley and M. Patrick McCabe, "Socialization in Correctional Communities: A Replication," 35 (October, 1968), 784.

Work Alienation Scale (Gutt-man-Type) of Five Items; Three Were Developed by the Author and Two by N. Morse

George Miller, "Professionals in Bureaucracy: Alienation Among Industrial Scientists and Engineers," 32 (October, 1967), 755-768.

Author Constructed Index of Alienation from Work and from Expressive Relations; Based on a Selection from Thirteen Items of the Neal Gross, M. Mason, and H. McEachern Scales

Michael Aiken and Jerald Hage, "Organizational Alienation: A Comparative Analysis," 31 (August, 1966), 497-507.

L. Pearlin's Alienation from Work Scale, Guttman-Type

Louis A. Zurcher, Jr., Arnold Meadow, and Susan Lee Zurcher, "Value Orientation, Role Conflict and Alienation From Work: A Cross-Cultural Study," 30 (August, 1965), 539-548.

Marcus R-Scale for Measurement of Union Homogeneity (Guttman-Type)

Philip M. Marcus, "Union Conventions and Executive Boards: A Formal Analysis of Organizational Structure," 31 (February, 1966), 61-70.

Author Constructed Index of Hierarchy of Authority and of Participation in Decision Making as measure of organizational centralization

Michael Aiken and Jerald Hage, "Organizational Alienation: A Comparative Analysis," 31 (August, 1966), 497-507.

Srole's Anomia Scale; Swedish Translated

Melvin Seeman, "On the Personal Consequences of Alienation in Work," 32 (April, 1967), 273-285.

Neal and Seeman Powerlessness Scale

Melvin Seeman, "On the Personal Consequences of Alienation in Work," 32 (April, 1967), 273-285.

Meaninglessness Scale, Author Constructed

Theodore Groat and Arthur G. Neal, "Social Psychological Correlates of Urban Fertility," 32 (December, 1967), 945-959.

Normlessness Scale, Author Constructed

Theodore Groat and Arthur G. Neal, "Social Psychological Correlates of Urban Fertility," 32 (December, 1967), 945-959.

Index of Work Alienation, Based on Blauner's Index

Melvin Seeman, "On The Personal Consequences of Alienation in Work," 32 (April, 1967), 273-285.

Scales to Measure Leadership

Scale of Supervisory Responsibility, Author Constructed

Carolyn Cummings Perrucci, "Social Origins, Mobility Patterns and Fertility," 32 (August, 1967), 615-625.

Measure of Political Involvement and Political Cleavages

Robert R. Alford and Harry M. Scoble, "Community Leadership, Education, and Political Behavior," 33 (April, 1968), 259-271.

Technical Responsibility Scale, Author Constructed

Carolyn Cummings Perrucci, "Social Origins, Mobility Patterns and Fertility," 32 (August, 1967), 615-625.

Scales to Measure Attitudes and Values

Racial Attitude Scale, Author Constructed

James M. Fendrich, "Perceived Reference Group Support: Racial Attitudes and Overt Behavior," 32 (December, 1967), 960-970.

Degree of Professionalization Scale Measuring Four Additional Dimensions: Belief in Self-Regulation, Belief in Service to Public, Sense of Calling to Field and Reference; Author Constructed Scale; Likert-Type

Richard Hall, "Professionalization and Bureaucratization," 33 (February, 1968), 92-104.

Mobility Orientation Scale For Measuring the Degree to Which the Respondent Placed the Value of Occupational Mobility Above Other Values in His Hierarchy of Goals.

Melvin Seeman, "On the Personal Consequences of Alienation in Work," 32 (April, 1967), 273-285.

University Student Political Attitudes and Behavior, Student Voice Factor Score

David Nasatir, "A Note on Contextual Effects and the Political Orientations of University Students," 33 (April, 1968), 210-219.

Peer Value Teen-Age Index, Author Constructed

Paul Lerman, "Individual Values, Peer Values, and Sub-Cultural Delinquency," 33 (April, 1968), 219-235.

Four Teen-Age Non-Conformity Scales: Ratfink, Ace-in-the-Hole, Sociability, and Deviance

LaMar T. Empey and Steven G. Lubeck, "Conformity and Deviance in the 'Situation of Company,' " 33 (October, 1968), 760-774.

Measure of Political Attitude Toward the Cuban Revolution

Maurice Zeitlin, "Economic Insecurity and the Political Attitudes of Cuban Workers," 31 (February, 1966), 35-51.

Rosenberg Attitudes Toward Work Scale for Measuring the Degree of Orientation Toward "Professional" or "Acquisitive" Values

John F. Marsh, Jr., and Frank P. Stafford, "The Effects of Values on Pecuniary Behavior: The Case of Academicians," 32 (October, 1967), 740-754.

Orientation Toward Feminine Role Behavior, Author Constructed Scale, Guttman-Type

Kenneth C. Kammeyer, "Birth Order and the Feminine Sex Role Among College Women," 31 (August, 1966), 508-515.

Measure of Political Liberalism: This Scale Includes Four Dimensions: Civil Rights, Civil Liberties, Internationalism, and Welfare, Each of Which Was Measured by a Guttman Scale Constructed by the Authors

K. Dennis Kelly and William J. Chambliss, "Status Consistency and Political Attitudes," 31 (June, 1966), 375-382.

Pro-Integration Sentiments Scale Based on Favorable (Pro-Negro) Responses to Items Referring Largely to Interracial Contact, Author Constructed, Guttman-Type

Robert W. Hodge and Donald J. Treiman, "Occupational Mobility and Attitudes Toward Negroes," 31 (February, 1966), 93-102.

Conformity Scale to Measure Attitudes Toward Conforming Behavior; The Scale Items Are From Four Sources: F. Baron, R. S. Crutchfield, M. L. Hoffman and T. F. Pettigrew.

Howard E. Freeman, J. Michael Ross, David J. Armor and Thomas F. Pettigrew, "Color Gradation and Attitudes Among Middle Income Negroes," 31 (June, 1966), 365-374.

Right-Wing Extremism Scale, Likert-Type, Author Constructed

Gary B. Rush, "Status Consistency and Right-Wing Extremism," 32 (February, 1967), 86-92.

Anti-White Scale to Measure Resentment Against Caucasians; A Combination of Items From R. Johnson and G. A. Stedeler Scales

Howard Freeman, J. Michael Ross, David Armor and Thomas F. Pettigrew, "Color Gradation and Attitudes Among Middle Income Negroes," 31 (June, 1966), 365-374.

Career Orientation Anchorage Scale, Author Constructed

Curt Tausky and Robert Dubin, "Career Anchorage: Managerial Mobility Motivations," 30 (October, 1965), 725-735.

Male and Female Premarital Sexual Permissiveness Scales, Author Constructed

Ira L. Reiss, "Social Class and Premarital Sexual Permissiveness: A Re-Examination," 30 (October, 1965), 747-756.

Mysticism Scale for Measuring Belief in Such Things as Spiritualism, Necromancy, and Astrology, Author Constructed

Herbert McClosky and John H. Scharr, "Psychological Dimensions of Anomy," 30 (February, 1965), 14-40.

Scales Measuring Family and Marriage Factors

Index of Extended Familism Which Measures Four Dimensions: Intensity, Extensity, Interaction, and Verba Cross-Cultural Study

Robert F. Winch, Scott Greer, and Rae L. Blumberg, "Ethnicity Familism in an Upper-Middle-Class Suburb," 32 (April, 1967), 265-272.

Index of Parent-Youth Relations, Author Constructed Index Based on Items of Almond and Verba Cross-Cultural Study

Glen H. Elder, Jr., "Family Structure and Educational Attainment: A Cross-National Analysis," 30 (February, 1965), 81-96.

Developmental Scale of Wife Independence, Author Constructed

Robert K. Leik and Merlyn Matthews, "A Scale for Developmental Processes," 33 (February, 1968), 62-75.

Student Perception of Parental Encouragement Toward Attending College, Author Constructed Scale

William H. Sewell and Vimal P. Shah, "Parents, Education, and Children's Educational Aspirations and Achievements," 33 (April, 1968), 191-209.

| Index of Intermarriage Distance, Author Constructed | Margaret A. Parkman and Jack Sawyer, "Dimensions of Ethnic Intermarriage in Hawaii," 32 (August, 1967), 593-607. |

Measures of Personality Factors

Minnesota Multiphasic Personality Inventory	Bernard E. Segal, Robert J. Weiss, and Robert Sokol, "Emotional Adjustment, Social Organization and Psychiatric Treatment Rates," 30 (August, 1965), 548-556.
Minnesota Multiphasic Personality Inventory Reports	Omer R. Galle and Karl E. Taeuber, "Metropolitan Migration and Intervening Opportunities," 31 (February, 1966), 5-34.
United States Army Neuropsychiatric Screening Adjunct	Omer R. Galle and Karl E. Taeuber, "Metropolitan Migration and Intervening Opportunities," 31 (February, 1966), 5-34.
Beliefs About Female Personality Traits, Author Constructed Scale; Likert-Type	Kenneth Kammeyer, "Birth Order and the Feminine Sex Role Among College Women," 31 (August, 1966), 508-515.
Inflexibility Index, Author Constructed	Herbert McClosky and John H. Scharr, "Psychological Dimensions of Anomy," 30 (February, 1965), 14-40.
Subjective Victimization Scale, Perceived Effects on Self of Racial Restrictions, A Reformulation of G. W. Allport and B. M. Kramer Scale	Howard Freeman, J. Michael Ross, David Armor, and Thomas F. Pettigrew, "Color Gradation and Attitudes Among Middle Income Negroes," 31 (June, 1966), 365-374.
Authoritarianism Scale, The Authoritarian Personality Syndrome	Howard Freeman, J. Michael Ross, David Armor, and Thomas F. Pettigrew, "Color Gradations and Attitudes Amond Middle Income Negroes," 31 (June, 1966), 365-374.

Measures of Intelligence and Achievement

| American Council on Education Psychological Examination | Bruce K. Eckland, "Academic Ability, Higher Education, and Occupational Mobility, 30 (October, 1965), 735-746. |

Hennon-Nelson Test of Mental Ability

William H. Sewell and Michael Armor, "Neighborhood Context and College Plans," 31 (April, 1966), 159-168.

Measures of Identification

Peer-Value Index for Measuring Identification With Peer Groups, Author Constructed

Paul Lerman, "Argot, Symbolic Deviance and Subcultural Delinquency," 32 (April, 1967), 209-224.

Index of Religious Identification of Professional Workers, Author Constructed

Harold Wilensky and Jack Ladinsky, "From Religious Community To Occupational Group: Structural Assimilation Among Professors, Lawyers and Engineers," 32 (August, 1967), 541-561.

Wilensky Index of Professional Identification

Harold Wilensky and Jack Ladinsky, "From Religious Community To Occupational Group: Structural Assimilation Among Professors, Lawyers and Engineers," 32 (August, 1967), 541-561.

Miscellaneous Scales

Index of Professional Incentives, Author Constructed

George Miller, "Professionals in Bureaucracy: Alienation Among Industrial Scientists and Engineers," 32 (October, 1967), 755-768.

Acquiescence Scale for Measuring the Consistency-Logicality Dimension of Cognitive Function, Author Constructed

Herbert McClosky and John H. Scharr, "Psychological Dimensions of Anomy," 30 (February, 1965), 14-40.

Reference Group Support Scale, Author Constructed

James M. Fendrich, "Perceived Reference Group Support: Racial Attitudes and Overt Behavior," 32 (December, 1967), 960-970.

Index of Militancy, Measuring Several Dimensions of Racial Protest, Author Constructed

Gary T. Marx, "Religion: Opiate or Inspiration of Civil Rights Militancy Among Negroes," 32 (February, 1967), 64-72.

Index of Perceived Legitimate Educational and Occupational Opportunities, Author Constructed	James F. Short, Jr., Ramon Rivera, and Ray A. Tennyson, "Perceived Opportunities, Gang Membership and Delinquency," 30 (February, 1965), 56-67.
Stouffer-Toby Conflict Scale	Louis A. Zurcher, Jr., Arnold Meadow, and Susan Lee Zurcher, "Value Orientation, Role Conflict, and Alienation from Work: A Cross-Cultural Study," 30 (August, 1965), 539-548.
Political Awareness Test For Measuring Degree of Information on Political Affairs, Author Constructed	Melvin Seeman, "On the Personal Consequences of Alienation in Work," 32 (April, 1967), 273-285.

Social Indicators

Index of Political Representativeness for Measuring Degree of Political Organization and Constitutionalization, Author Constructed	Phillips Cutright, "Inequality: A Cross-National Analysis," 32 (August, 1967), 562-578.
Index of Argot for Measuring Symbolic Deviance, Author Constructed	Paul Lerman, "Argot, Symbolic Deviance and Subcultural Delinquency," 32 (April, 1967), 209-224.
Author Constructed Scale to Measure the Degree of Coercive vs. Persuasive Sanctions Toward Hospital Patients	Joseph Julian, "Compliance Patterns and Communication Blocks in Complex Organizations," 31 (June, 1966), 382-389.
Index of Economic Development Based on Data From B. Russett, *et. al.*, *World Handbook of Political and Social Indicators*	Phillips Cutright, "Inequality: A Cross-National Analysis," 32 (August, 1967), 562-578.
Index of Democratic Political Enlightenment (Use of Moscos' items)	Arvin W. Murch, "Political Integration as an Alternative to Independence in the French Antilles," 33 (August, 1968), 544-561.

Index of Governmental Reformism, Author Constructed

Terry N. Clark, "Community Structure, Decision Making, Budget Expenditures, and Urban Renewal in 51 American Communities," 33 (August, 1968), 576-593.

IV.J.2. SCALES FOR THE MEASUREMENT OF ATTITUDES

The following list of 175 attitude inventories and scales have been classified so that the researcher may examine such common areas of interest as: Family and Child, Education, Work and Occupations, Economics, Religion, Welfare, Politics and Law, Nationalism and Internationalism, War, Mass Media, Race and Ethnicity, Health and Medicine, and Personal Interaction and Customary Behavior. All of the scales may be examined in Marvin E. Shaw and Jack M. Wright, *Scales for the Measurement of Attitudes* (New York: McGraw-Hill, 1967).

FAMILY AND CHILD

A Survey of Opinions Regarding the Bringing Up of Children (Itkin, 1952)

A Survey of Opinions Regarding the Discipline of Children (Itkin, 1952)

Attitude Toward Discipline Exercised by Parents (Itkin, 1952)

Attitude Toward the Freedom of Children (Koch, Dentler, Dysart, and Streit, 1934)

Attitude Toward Parental Control of Children's Activities (Stott, 1940)

Attitude Toward Self-Reliance (Ojemann, 1934)

Attitude Toward the Use of Fear as a Means of Controlling the Behavior of Children (Ackerley, 1934)

Attitude Toward Parents Giving Sex Information to Children Between the Ages of Six and Twelve (Ackerley, 1934)

Attitude Toward Older Children Telling Lies (Ackerley, 1934)

The Traditional Family Ideology (TFI) Scale (Levinson and Huffman, 1955)

Familism Scale (Bardis, 1959)

The Family Scale (Rundquist and Sletto, 1936)

Attitudes Toward Parents (Form F) (Itkin, 1952)

Parents' Judgment Regarding a Particular Child (Itkin, 1952)
Attitudes Toward Feminism Belief Patterns Scale (Kirkpatrick, 1936)
The Open Subordination of Women (OSW) Scale (Nadler and Morrow, 1959)
Attitude Toward Divorce (Thurstone, 1929-1934)
A Divorce Opinionnaire (Hardy, 1957)
Attitude Toward Birth Control (Wang and Thurstone, 1931)
Birth Control (Scale BC) Scale (Wilke, 1934)
[Panos D. Bardis has constructed "A Pill Scale: A Technique for the Measurement of Attitudes Toward Oral Contraception," *Social Science* (January, 1969), pp. 35-42.]

EDUCATION

Attitude Toward Teaching (F. D. Miller, 1934)
Attitude Toward Teaching as a Career (Merwin and DiVesta, 1960)
Attitude Toward Physical Education as a Career for Women (Drinkwater, 1960)
Attitude Toward Education (Mitchell, 1941)
Opinionnaire on Attitudes Toward Education (Lindgren and Patton, 1958)
Education Scale (Kerlinger and Kaya, 1959)
Attitude Toward Intensive Competition in Team Games (McCue, 1953)
Attitude Toward Intensive Competition for High School Girls (McGee, 1956)
The Education Scale (Rundquist and Sletto, 1936)
Attitude Toward Education (Glassey, 1945)
Attitudes Toward Mathematics (Gladstone, Deal and Drevdahl, 1960)
Revised Math Attitude Scale (Aiken and Dreger, 1961)
Physical Education Attitude Scale (Wear, 1955)
Counseling Attitude Scale (Form, 1955)
Problem-Solving Attitude Scale (Carey, 1958)
High School Attitude Scale (Remmers, 1960)
Knowledge About Psychology (KAP) Test (Costin, 1963)
An Attitude Scale for Measuring Attitude Toward Any Teacher (Hoshaw, 1935)
Attitude Toward Any School Subject (Silance and Remmers, 1934)
A Scale to Study Attitudes Toward College Courses (Hand, 1953)
Attitudes Toward School Integration (IA) Scale Form 1 (Greenberg, Chase, and Cannon, 1957)
Faculty Morale Scale for Institutional Improvement (AAUP, 1963)
Attitude Toward College Fraternities (Banta, 1961)

WORK AND OCCUPATION

Attitude Toward Labor Scale (Newcomb, 1939)
IRC (Industrial Relations Center) Union Attitude Questionnaire (Uphoff and Dunnette, 1956)
Scale for Management Attitude Toward Union (Stagner, Chalmers, and Derber, 1958)
About Your Company (Storey, 1955)
Scales to Measure Attitudes Toward the Company, Its Policies, and Its Community Contributions (Riland, 1959)
Attitude Toward Earning a Living (Hinckley and Hinckley, 1939)
Attitude Toward Work Relief as a Solution to the Financial Depression (Hinckley and Hinckley, 1939)
Attitude Toward Farming (Myster, 1944)
Attitude Toward Any Practice (Bues, 1934)
Attitude Toward Any Home-Making Activity (Kellar, 1934)
Attitude Toward Any Occupation (H. E. Miller, 1934)
Attitude Toward the Supervisor (AS) Scale (Schmid, Morsh, and Detter, 1956)
The Superior-Subordinate (SS) Scale (Chapman and Campbell, 1957)
Attitude Toward the Supervisor (Nagle, 1953)
Attitude Toward Employment of Older People (Kirchner, Lindbom, and Patterson, 1952)
The (Work Related) Change Scale (Trumbo, 1961)
Attitudes Toward Dependability: Attitude Scale for Clerical Workers (Dudycha, 1941)
Attitudes Toward Legal Agencies (Chapman, 1953)
Older Workers Questionnaire (Tuckman and Lorge, 1952)

ECONOMIC

Attitude Toward the Tariff (Thurstone, 1929-1934)
Distribution of the Wealth (DW) Scale (Wilke, 1934)

RELIGION

Religionism Scale: Scale I (Ferguson, 1944)
Belief Pattern Scale; Attitude of Religiosity (Kirkpatrick, 1949)
Religious Ideology Scale (Putney and Middleton, 1961)
The Religious Attitude Inventory (Ausubel and Schpoont, 1957)
The Religion Scale (Bardis, 1961)

Religious Belief Scale (Martin and Nichols, 1962)

A Survey of Attitudes Toward Religion and Philosophy of Life (Funk, 1958)

The Existence of God Scale (Scale G) (Wilke, 1934)

Attitude Toward God: The Reality of God (Chave and Thurstone, 1931)

Attitude Toward God: Influence on Conduct (Chave and Thurstone, 1931)

Attitude Toward the Church (Thurstone, 1931)

Attitudes and Beliefs of LDS Church Members Toward Their Church and Religion (Hardy, 1949)

Attitude Toward Sunday Observance (Thurstone, 1929-1934)

An Attitude Scale Toward Church and Religious Practices (Dynes, 1955)

Relation Between Religion and Psychiatry Scale (Webb and Kobler, 1961)

Attitudes Toward Evolution (Thurstone, 1931)

Death Attitudes Scale (Kalish, 1963)

WELFARE

Attitude Toward Recieving Relief (Hinckley and Hinckley, 1939)

Humanitarianism Scale: Scale II (Ferguson, 1944)

Belief Pattern Scale; Attitude of Humanitarianism (Kirkpatrick, 1949)

Attitudes Toward Any Proposed Social Action (Remmers, 1934)

POLITICS AND LAW

The Conservatism-Radicalism (C-R) Opinionnaire (Lentz, 1935)

The Florida Scale of Civic Beliefs (Kimbrough and Hines, 1963)

The Economic Conservatism Scale (Rundquist and Sletto, 1936)

Questionnaire on Politico-Economic Attitudes (Sanai, 1950)

Conservatism-Radicalism (C-R) Battery (Centers, 1949; Case, 1963)

Tulane Factors of Liberalism-Conservatism Attitude Value Profile (Kerr, 1946)

The Social Attitudes Scale (Kerlinger, 1965)

Political and Economic Progressivism (PAP) Scale (Newcomb, 1943)

Public Opinion Questionnaire (Edwards, 1941)

Attitude Toward the Law (Katz and Thurstone, 1931)

The Law Scale (Rundquist and Sletto, 1936)

The Ideological and Law-Abidingness Scales (Gregory, 1939)

Attitudes Toward Law and Justice (Watt and Maher, 1958)

Attitude Toward the Constitution of the United States (Rosander and Thurstone, 1931)
Attitude Toward Capital Punishment (Balogh and Mueller, 1960)
Attitude Toward Capital Punishment (Thurstone, 1932)
Attitude Toward Punishment of Criminals (Wang and Thurstone, 1931)
Attitude Toward the Police (Chapman, 1953)
Attitude Toward Probation Officers (Chapman, 1953)
Juvenile Delinquency Attitude (JDA) Scale (Alberts, 1962)
The Academic Freedom Survey (Academic Freedom Committee, American Civil Liberties Union, 1954)

NATIONALISM AND INTERNATIONALISM

Internationalism Scale (Likert, 1932)
Nationalism Scale: Scale III (Ferguson, 1942)
A Survey of Opinions and Beliefs about International Relations (Helfant, 1952)
The Internationalism-Nationalism (IN) Scale (Levinson, 1957)
The Worldmindedness Scale (Sampson and Smith, 1957)
The Patriotism (NP) Scale (Christiansen, 1959)
Attitude Toward Patriotism Scale (Thurstone, 1929-1934)
Attitude Toward Communism Scale (Thurstone, 1929-1934)

WAR

The Peterson War Scale (Thurstone, 1929-1934)
A Scale of Militarism-Pacifism (Droba, 1931)
Attitude Toward Defensive, Cooperative, and Aggressive War (Day and Quackenbush, 1942)
Attitude Toward War (Scale W) (Wilke, 1934)
A Scale for Measuring Attitude Toward War (Stagner, 1942)
The M-P Opinion Scale (Gristle, 1940)

MASS MEDIA

Attitude Toward Newspapers (Rogers, 1955)
Attitude Toward Freedom of Information (Rogers, 1955)
Attitude Toward Movies (Thurstone, 1930)
Semantic Distance Questionnaire (Weaver, 1959)

RACE AND ETHNICITY

Attitude Toward the Negro (Hinckley, 1932)
Attitude Toward Segregation Scale (Rosenbaum and Zimmerman, 1959)
The Segregation Scale (Peak, Morrison, Spivak, and Zinnes, 1956)
The Desegregation Scale (Kelly, Ferson, and Holtzman, 1958)
Attitude Toward Accepting Negro Students in College (Grafton, 1964)
Attitude Toward Negroes (Thurstone, 1931)
Attitude Toward the Negro Scale (Likert, 1932)
The Anti-Negro Scale (Steckler, 1957)
Negro Behavior Attitude Scale (Rosander, 1937)
Experiences with Negroes (Ford, 1941)
The Social Situations Questionnaire (Kogan and Downey, 1956)
The Anti-Semitism (A-S) Scale (Levinson and Sanford, 1944)
Attitude Toward Jews Scale (Harlan, 1942)
Opinions on the Jews (Eysenck and Crown, 1949)
The Anti-White Scale (Steckler, 1957)
Attitude Toward the German People (Thurstone, 1931)
Attitude Toward the Chinese (Thurstone, 1931)
A Survey of Opinions and Beliefs about Russia: The Soviet Union
  (Smith, 1946)
Ethnocentrism Scale (Levinson, 1949)
Intolerant-Tolerant (IT) Scale (Prentice, 1956)
The Social Distance Scale (Bogardus, 1925)
Scale to Measure Attitudes Toward Defined Groups (Grice, 1935)

HEALTH AND MEDICINE

Attitudes Toward Physical Fitness and Exercise (Richardson, 1960)
Opinions About Mental Illness (Cohen and Struening, 1959)
The Socialized Medicine Attitude Scale (Mahler, 1953)
Attitude Toward Censorship Scale (Rosander and Thurstone, 1931)
Attitudes Toward Mentally Retarded People (Bartlett, Quay, and
  Wrightsman, 1960)
The Custodial Mental Illness Ideology (CMI) Scale (Gilbert and Levin-
  son, 1956)
The Psychotherapy-Sociotherapy Ideology (PSI) Scale (Sharaf and
  Levinson, 1957)
Medication Attitudes (Gorham and Sherman, 1961)
Attitude to Blindness Scale (Cowen, Underberg, and Verrillo, 1958)
Attitude Toward Disabled People (ATDP) Scale (Yuker, Block, and
  Campbell, 1960)

Medical Information Test (Perricone, 1964)
Attitude Toward Menstruation (McHugh and Wasser, 1959)
The Vivisection Questionnaire (Molnar, 1955)
Attitudes Toward Mental Hospitals (Souelem, 1955)
Attitudes Relating to the State Hospital (Pratt, Giannitrapani, and
  Khanna, 1960)

PERSONAL INTERACTION AND CUSTOMARY BEHAVIOR

The Self-Others Questionnaire (Phillips, 1951)
Acceptance of Self and Others (Berger, 1952)
People in General (Banta, 1961)
An Intimacy Permissiveness Scale (Christensen and Carpenter, 1962)
Old People (OP) Scale (Kogan, 1961)
The "CI" Attitude Scale (Khanna, Pratt, Gardiner, 1962)
The Chivalry (C) Scale (Nadler and Morrow, 1959)
Attitudes Toward Old People (Tuckman and Lorge, 1953)
Attitude Toward Any Institution (Kelley, 1934)
Attitude Toward the Aesthetic Value (Cohen, 1941)
The Competitive Attitude (CA) Scale (Lakie, 1964)
The "Value Inventory" (Jarrett and Sherriffs, 1953)
Attitude Toward Safe Driving: Siebrecht Attitude Scale (Siebrecht,
  1941)

PART V

Research Funding, Costing, and Reporting

The end product of research designing is a proposal. The graduate student setting forth on his first independent research or the professional with a lifetime of research achievement both face the same requirement. They must produce an acceptable proposal. Other professionals will critically examine the proposal and decide if it is acceptable. The planning and submission of proposals may take up to a year or more—always longer than expected. The competition for funds is often intense. More proposals are generally rejected than accepted because of the quality of the proposal or the limitation of funds. The researcher must know where the money is and develop the skill of research negotiation.

Section A., *Research Funding,* lists various guides to research agencies. A.1 is a list of major financing agencies of social science research. A.2 describes programs of particular relevance including predoctoral and postdoctoral research offered by the National Science Foundation and the National Institute of Mental Health. These two agencies provide the major source of competitive fellowships in the social sciences outside of the universities themselves.

Section B. *Research Costing* is introduced because this task is difficult. Most researchers have never had training in this aspect of research and they acquire their knowledge by trial and error. Most researchers drastically underestimate the time and effort that will be required to complete their own proposal. There are many unforeseen handicaps and delays.

The *Guide to Research Costing,* B.1, requires detailed cost data before it can be used. The researcher must secure the going wage rate for interviewers, the cost of transportation, the rate for machine calculation, etc. These can not be provided here since they vary by time and place. However, the guide will alert the social scientist to the factors he must take into account in planning the cost of the research. It should be remembered that overhead costs are not shown. Universities usually demand substantial overhead costs ranging from thirty to fifty percent of the total contract.

Section C. *Research Reporting.* Finally, plans for the report must be made. This is the "payoff" for the reseacher. *Specifications for Sociological Report Rating,* C.1, indicates the criteria that judges will commonly use in appraising the publishing possibilities of the report. The *Form for Sociological Report Rating,* C.2, will provide a final check on the research design at the point where it counts— transmission to the profession.

Generally, two or three professional examiners will be using similar criteria in determining upon their recommendation for acceptance or rejection of the research report. Recently the editors of the five journals sponsored by the American Sociological Association reported an average acceptance of fifteen percent. Learning how to handle rejection, the most common experience, is never taught to the researcher. It is probably one of the most significant adjustments he must make. He must learn to utilize the criticism of his work and try to meet objections if possible. Often what is needed is better writing. The best advice for all researchers is to rewrite and resubmit. There are scores of journals. Try to get in the best, but above all, try to get published. John Pease and Joan Rytina have recently compiled a list of world sociological journals that they believe is "complete, accurate, and current." This is the *Guide to Sociological Journals,* C.3.

C.4 is a guide to the journals sponsored by the American Psychological Association. There are many others in psychology, but the list includes only those of major relevance. C.5 is a guide to major journals in political science. There are hundreds of journals in anthropology, economics, education, law, business, social work, etc. Directories of world journals include:

INTERNATIONAL COMMITTEE FOR SOCIAL SCIENCES. *Documentation in the Social Sciences: World List of Social Science Periodicals.* 3rd ed. Paris: UNESCO, 1966.
The Standard Periodical Directory. 2nd ed. New York: Oxbridge Publishing Company, 1967.

C.6 is a calendar of annual meetings of various sociological societies and some related societies in the social sciences. Although these meetings change officers and meeting places each year, the national offices can supply current information. Reporting of research at annual meetings is an opportunity to exchange ideas and to improve the research report before submission to a journal.

C.8 is a select bibliography for fellowships and grants.

Research Funding

V.A.1. MAJOR FINANCING AGENCIES OF SOCIAL SCIENCE RESEARCH

1. U.S. Department of Health, Education, and Welfare

   National Institute of Mental Health
   5454 Wisconsin Avenue
   Chevy Chase, Maryland 20203

   U.S. Office of Education
   Bureau of Research
   Washington, D.C. 20201

   Social Security Administration
   Office of Research and Statistics
   330 Independence Avenue
   Washington, D.C. 20201

2. National Science Foundation
   The Fellowship Office
   National Research Council
   2101 Constitution Avenue, N.W.
   Washington, D.C. 20418

3. U.S. Department of Labor
   Office of Manpower Policy, Education, and Research
   Washington, D.C. 20201

4. Social Science Research Council
   230 Park Avenue
   New York, N.Y. 10017

5. Ford Foundation
   320 East 43 Street
   New York, N.Y. 10017

6. Rockefeller Foundation
   111 West 50th Street
   New York, N.Y. 10020

7. Carnegie Foundation
   589 Fifth Avenue
   New York, N.Y. 10017

8. Russell Sage Foundation
   230 Park Avenue
   New York, N.Y. 10017

V.A.2. PROGRAMS OF PARTICULAR RELEVANCE INCLUDING PREDOCTORAL AND POSTDOCTORAL FELLOWSHIPS

DEPARTMENT OF HEALTH, EDUCATION, AND WELFARE PUBLIC HEALTH SERVICE
National Institute of Mental Health, 5454 Wisconsin Avenue, Chevy Chase, Maryland 20203

Programs of particular relevance to sociologists include:

BEHAVIORAL SCIENCES RESEARCH BRANCH, SOCIAL SCIENCES SECTION, Mrs. Lorraine B. Torres, Acting Chief. Stimulates and supports research in the behavioral sciences relevant to an understanding of behavior and mental health. Areas of support include culture and personality, cross-cultural factors, social perception and attitudes, socialization, social structure and dynamics, social change, sociolinguistics, and group behavior.

BEHAVIORAL SCIENCES TRAINING BRANCH, SOCIAL SCIENCES SECTION, Bert E. Boothe, Ph.D., Chief. Provides program support to more than 70 *university programs* and approximately 575 trainees for pre- and postdoctoral training in the social sciences in mental health related fields. An individual desiring this type of support should apply directly to an institution holding a Social Science Research Training Grant from the NIMH.

BEHAVIORAL SCIENCES TRAINING BRANCH, RESEARCH FELLOWSHIPS PROGRAM, Edith Huddleston, Ph.D., Executive Secretary. Provides support to individuals who wish to further their research competencies. Predoctoral research fellowship, postdoctoral research fellowship, special research fellowship, and research career development awards are offered.

Programs of sociological import and of focused interest within the institute include:

NATIONAL CENTER FOR PREVENTION AND CONTROL OF ALCOHOLISM, Jack H. Mendelson, M.D., Chief. The center is the focal point for all research, training, and demonstration acitvities within the Public Health Service relating to alcoholism and other alcohol problems.

CENTER FOR STUDIES OF NARCOTICS AND DRUG ABUSE, Roger E. Meyer, M.D., Acting Chief. Research, training, and demonstration grants are supported in problems related to narcotic and drug abuse.

CENTER FOR STUDIES OF SUICIDE PREVENTION, Edwin S. Shneidman, Ph.D., Chief. Research, training, and demonstration activities are supported in the fields of suicide, suicide prevention, and self-destructive phenomena.

CENTER FOR STUDIES OF MENTAL HEALTH AND SOCIAL PROBLEMS, APPLIED RESEARCH BRANCH, Lewis Long, Ph.D., Chief. Supports applied research in such areas as poverty, race relations, mass violence, and family disorganization.

CENTER FOR STUDIES OF METROPOLITAN AND REGIONAL MENTAL HEALTH PROBLEMS, Harry Cain, M.A., Chief. Research, training, and demonstration grants are supported in mental health programs relevant to urban development.

Applicants are urged to communicate directly with the institute about these and other programs that may be of interest.

ANNOUNCEMENT OF PUBLIC HEALTH SERVICE
PREDOCTORAL RESEARCH FELLOWSHIPS

The Public Health Service awards approximately 2,000 fellowships annually to support training at the predoctoral level for research in health-related areas. Among the fields supported are: accident prevention, air pollution,[1] anatomy, anthropology, behavioral sciences, biochemistry, biomedical engineering, biophysical sciences, biostatistics, botany, dental health, developmental biology, endocrinology, entomology, genetics, health information specialties, health services financing and organization, history of life sciences, medicinal chemistry, microbiology, nursing, nutrition, health-related organic chemistry, parasitology, pathology, pharmacology, physiology, psychology, sociology, toxicology, and zoology.

Fellowships are not awarded for study leading to the M.D., D.D.S., D.V.M., or other applied science degrees.

Eligibility Requirements

Applicants must be citizens or noncitizen nationals of the United States,[2] or have been lawfully admitted to the United States for permanent residence, and as of the beginning date of their fellowship have received a baccalaureate degree or have experience equivalent to that represented by such a degree. Thus a college senior is eligible to apply.

Prior to formal application, an applicant must arrange for admission to an appropriate graduate degree granting institution and acceptance by a sponsor who will supervise his training. A college senior may apply without having been formally accepted by a sponsor or graduate school. In such a case, the Facilities and Commitment Statement (Form PHS 416-2, contained in the application kit), signed by the Dean of the Graduate School, the Chairman of the Admissions Committee, or another responsible institutional official, must be submitted. In no case will an individual be informed of the disposition of his application until the Public Health Service has been notified that he has been admitted to the institution.

Predoctoral fellowships are rarely awarded for study in foreign countries; any such proposal must provide evidence that the desired training cannot be obtained in the United States.

Documents To Be Submitted

An applicant must submit an application (Form PHS 416-1) and copies of undergraduate and graduate transcripts. In addition, the applicant must arrange for the submission of supporting documents on his behalf (letters of reference, statement from his sponsor, etc.). Instructions for filing are contained in the application kit.

A noncitizen must request the Immigration and Naturalization Service to inform the Public Health Service that he has been lawfully admitted to the United States for permanent residence.

Application Material

Applications may be obtained from the Career Development Review Branch, Division of Research Grants, National Institutes of Health, Bethesda, Md., 20014.

Deadlines for Receipt of Applications

Applications received by	Results announced by the following
Jan. 2	September
Apr. 1	June
Oct. 1	February

Applications arriving too late for one review are considered at the following review.

Review of Applications

Applicants are evaluated on the basis of their potential for research, as evidenced by their academic record, letters of reference, proposal for research training, and other available information.

Applications are reviewed initially by committees of consultants in the appropriate scientific fields from the academic community who evaluate the scientific merit of the proposed training situation, i.e., the applicant, the sponsor, the research proposal, and the training institution. The recommendations of the committees are then utilized by the awarding unit (Institute or Division) of the Public Health Service as the primary criterion in the selection of awardees. Program interest is also considered in the final award process.

Notification of Final Action

An applicant is notified of final action on his application by letter from the awarding unit.

Activation Date

An awardee may acitivate his fellowship at any time during the 12-month period following the date of the award letter.

NOTES

1. The facts in this announcement are not in every case applicable to fellowships in air pollution. There are differences in stipends, eligibility requirements, deadlines, etc. Information on this program can be obtained from the National Center for Air Pollution Control, 8120 Woodmont Avenue, Bethesda, Md., 20014.

2. Cuban refugees are exempted from the U. S. citizenship requirement.

OTHER RESEARCH TRAINING PROGRAMS OF THE PUBLIC HEALTH SERVICE

Postdoctoral Fellowships

Applications may be submitted by individuals having a Ph.D., M.D., D.D.S., D.V.M., Sc.D., D. Eng., D.O., or equivalent domestic or foreign degree. Stipends are $6,000, $6,500, or $7,000 per year, depending upon prior education and experience. An allowance of $500 per year is made available for each eligible dependent. In addition a $1,000 supply allowance per year is made available to the institution on behalf of the fellow. An allowance of 8 cents per mile is provided for travel from a fellow's residence to a domestic institution (round trip for a foreign institution) if the distance exceeds 50 miles.

Special Fellowships

Applications may be submitted by individuals who:

1. have a doctorate or equivalent degree and at least three subsequent years of relevant research or professional experience, or
2. have completed residency requirements in a medical specialty, or
3. have otherwise demonstrated to the PHS sufficient competence in their field to pursue the proposed training program.

Stipends are determined on an individual basis. In addition a $1,000 supply allowance per year is made available to the institution on behalf of the fellow. An allowance of 8 cents per mile is provided for travel from a fellow's residence to a domestic institution (round trip for a foreign institution) if the distance exceeds 50 miles.

Training Grants

These are awarded to institutions to establish, expand or improve research training programs in the bio-sciences and other health-related fields and to provide support for graduate and postdoctoral students who are interested in careers in research, teaching or administration. An individual desiring this type of support should apply directly to an institution having a PHS Training Grant. These institutions are listed in "Public Health Service Grants and Awards, Part II."

Research Career Development Awards

Awards are made to institutions to increase the number of stable fulltime career opportunities for scientists of superior potential and capability in the sciences related to health. Institutions may apply for awards on behalf of individuals who have had three or more years of relevant postdoctoral research or professional experience and who are in need of further research career development.

For additional information on the above programs write: Career Development Review Branch, Division of Research Grants, National Institutes of Health, Bethesda, Maryland, 20014.

U.S. DEPARTMENT OF HEALTH, EDUCATION, AND WELFARE OFFICE OF EDUCATION—BUREAU OF RESEARCH WASHINGTON, D.C.

The U.S. Office of Education administers funds for the support of educational research and development through its Bureau of Research. The Bureau is made up of five divisions which deal with elementary education, secondary and vocational education, higher education, information technology and dissemination, and research centers and regional laboratories. Each of the first four divisions handles basic research projects as well as those focused on the development of curricula, methods of teaching and learning, and organizational and administrative procedures in education.

The general purpose of basic research projects is to develop new knowledge about the educational process, thus providing a foundation for further developmental work. The content of basic studies draws primarily on the fields of psychology, for more information about learning and motivation; sociology and anthropology, to examine social and cultural factors related to education; and physiology, to explore the relationships between physical and mental functions.

The Bureau of Research identifies, develops, and programs funds for priority areas, but it is always in a position to receive unsolicited proposals, and funds are reserved for this purpose. Also, "guideline" statements pertaining to particular areas are sometimes made available to stimulate their development, and occasional requests for proposals are issued in selected areas. It is always useful for those interested in specific projects to contact appropriate members of the Bureau staff before actually drafting a proposal in order to become acquainted with current directions as a guide to proposal development.

Persons interested in participating in the Office of Education research and development program should request a copy of the pamphlet "Support for Research and Related Activities" from the Bureau of Research, U.S. Office of Education, Washington, D.C. 20202. Those concerned with a project requiring less than $10,000 in Federal funds should request information on the "Small Project" program. This program is operated in each of the nine H.E.W. Regional Offices by an educational research advisor who may be contacted directly for information about possibilities for small projects in his region. (Regional offices are listed in the pamphlet mentioned above.)

The Bureau also operates the Educational Resources Information Center (ERIC) which provides direct access to research literature in behavioral sciences and education. Monthly issues of *Research in Education* (available from the Government Printing Office) abstract and index over 700 documents—the latter available from the ERIC Document Reproduction Service, National Cash Register Company, 4936 Fairmont Avenue, Bethesda, Maryland 20014.

GRANTS FOR RESEARCH IN SOCIAL WELFARE AND SOCIAL SECURITY

Under the Cooperative Research Grants Program, serving the interests of both agencies, grants are awarded for research on a wide range of questions related to the income maintenance, medical care, and social service programs under the Social Security Act. Particular emphasis is placed on research closely related to important program and policy issues. For example:

1. Studies of alternative income maintenance proposals aimed at preventing poverty and providing equitable earnings replacement for those unable to work.
2. Studies of the effectiveness and efficiency of social welfare programs, such as work incentive-work training programs.
3. Effects of Medicare and Medicaid programs on the costs of health care and the level and type of health services provided.
4. Analyses of the factors affecting the timing of retirement and the adequacy of retirement income.
5. Estimates of needs for income, rehabilitation services, and health care for disabled persons and their families.

Grants may be made only to nonprofit organizations and may not be made to individuals; grantee organizations must pay part of the total cost of the research. Applications are reviewed by an Advisory Panel of non-Federal specialists which recommends applications for approval. Important factors considered in evaluating applications are the potential value and national significance of the knowledge to be gained, soundness of the research design, adequacy of resources to conduct the project, and the relationship of the research to similar work.

If in doubt whether a research proposal is within the scope of the Cooperative Research Program, potential applicants are encouraged to submit a draft of the proposal for review by agency staff. Application deadlines are January 1, June 1, and October 1 for projects that may begin no earlier than June 15, November 1, and March 1 respectively.

Application forms and additional information may be obtained from:

Cooperative Research Branch
Office of Research and Demonstrations
Social and Rehabilitation Service

or

Research Grants Staff
Office of Research and Statistics
Social Security Administration

U.S. Department of Health, Education, and Welfare
330 Independence Avenue, Washington, D.C., 20201

NATIONAL SCIENCE FOUNDATION
WASHINGTON, D.C. 20550

Information may be obtained by writing to the foundation, and informal communication with the foundation's staff is encouraged prior to formal submission of a proposal. Among a variety of forms of foundation support, the activities of greatest interest to sociologists are:

1. Grants for *basic scientific research,* or for related activities, such as research conferences, construction of specialized research facilities, and travel to selected meetings of international scientific organizations of major importance. In addition, social science dissertation research grants provide funds for research expenses (not stipends) in order to improve the quality and significance of dissertations and reduce the time required for their completion. All of these programs seek basic scientific understanding of behavioral and social processes and improved research methods. Support is provided for research which seeks to discover and test scientific generalizations.

2. Programs in *science education.* Sociologists are eligible for support in fellowship programs ranging from graduate through senior postdoctoral. In addition, departments of sociology may apply for graduate traineeships for award to their full-time students. Various programs designed to identify and train promising scientists from secondary school students to senior scientists include institutes for retraining school or college teachers, science course content improvement efforts, and participation in research by students and teachers. All grants and fellowships are awarded on the basis of merit without quotas for any field of science, institution, or geographic area.

3. *Institutional programs.* NSF programs which assist universities and colleges in upgrading their science competence include University Science Development, Graduate Science Facilities, Departmental Science Development, and College Science Improvement.

4. *Computing activities* in education and research. Innovative uses of computers by sociologists in instruction and research are supported by the Office of Computing activities.

5. In the area of *science policy and management,* the foundation contracts for studies or surveys of certain topics, such as communication among scientists, funding of U.S. science, and science manpower resources.

Detailed information on all the foundation's programs is available in the NSF publication *Guide to Programs,* NSF 68-6 (February, 1968) which is available through your college business or research office. It may also be obtained for fifty cents from the Superintendent of Documents, U.S. Government Printing Office, Washington, D.C. 20402.

NATIONAL SCIENCE FOUNDATION
DIVISION OF SOCIAL SCIENCES
SOCIOLOGY AND SOCIAL PSYCHOLOGY PROGRAM

The Division of Social Sciences supports basic research and related activities in anthropology, economic and social geography, economics, the history and philosophy of science, linguistics, political science, social psychology, and sociology.

Included in the sociology and social psychology program are: sociology, social psychology, demography, psycholinguistics, and basic studies of research methodology applicable to these fields.

Research in physiological and experimental psychology and in animal behavior is supported by the foundation's Psychobiology Program, Division of Biological and Medical Sciences. Application procedures are similar for both programs. The foundation does not provide support for research in clinical psychology.

GRANTS FOR SCIENTIFIC RESEARCH

Application Procedures

Formal application blanks are not used in the research grants program. The foundation's guide for the submission of research proposals contains suggestions for the preparation of proposals. Each proposal should contain the following information:

1. Name and address of institution.
2. Name, address (if different), and department of principal investigator(s). Telephone numbers are helpful.
3. Title of proposed research project.
4. Desired starting date (the earliest date on which funds would be required.)
5. Time period for which support is requested.
6. Abstract of description of proposed research project.
7. Description of proposed research project, including objectives and research design.
8. Bibliography of related research.
9. Description of facilities available for the research.
10. Biographical information for senior personnel, and for junior personnel when appropriate, including bibliographies.
11. Budget.
12. Statement of current support and pending applications for this and other research by the principal investigator(s).

Please use this as a check list when submitting an application. Twenty complete copies of the proposal should be submitted. One copy should be signed by the principal investigator, by the department head, and by an official authorized to sign for the institution.

Other Related Research Activities

Includes support for research conferences, construction of specialized research facilities, special projects such as data banks, and travel to selected international scientific meetings.

Submission Dates

Proposals may be submitted at any time. Processing requires three to six months. To allow time for adequate planning, the following schedule is offered as a guide:

Proposals Should Arrive In (or Before):	For Funds Needed In
January	June-July
April	September-October
September	January-February

For further information on the research grants program, write to:

Program Director for
Sociology and Social Psychology
Division of Social Sciences
National Science Foundation
Washington, D.C. 20550

FELLOWSHIPS AND OTHER NSF PROGRAMS OF INTEREST TO SOCIAL SCIENTISTS

Programs in Science Education

Social scientists are eligible to apply for all science education activities. Of particular interest may be the fellowship programs which encompass all levels of advanced study from predoctoral through senior postdoctoral.

1. *Predoctoral,* for students studying for masters or doctorates.
2. *Regular Postdoctoral,* doctoral degrees or equivalent required.
3. *Senior Postdoctoral,* intended primarily for senior scientists five years or more past the doctoral degree or with equivalent experience and training.
4. *Science Faculty,* for college and university teachers who have three years college teaching experience and who plan to continue teaching.

For detailed information on closing dates and application materials, write the Fellowships Program, Division of Graduate Education, National Science Foundation.

Other support for training activities includes summer and academic year institutes for teachers, course content improvement efforts, research participation by students and teachers, advanced science seminars, etc.

Construction or Renovation of Graduate-Level Training and Research Facilities

The foundation may support up to half of the cost of facilities for research and training of graduate students and postdoctoral personnel. Facilities may include any kind of space for research and training, except classrooms. Funds may also be requested for half the cost of movable and general-purpose laboratory apparatus, provided the cost does not exceed 15 percent of the total grant. For further information, write the Division of Institutional Programs, National Science Foundation.

For information about other special programs, write directly to the appropriate program office or to the Division of Social Sciences, which will forward your inquiry to the proper office.

For additional information see bibliography of fellowships and grants C.V.8.

Research Costing

V.B.1. GUIDE TO RESEARCH COSTING

GUIDE TO RESEARCH COSTING * †

Activity	Total	Week Ending ___	Week Ending ___	Week Ending ___	___

1. Total
  a) Man-hours
  b) Cost ($)
  c) % of total completed					

2. Planning
  a) Man-hours
  b) Cost
  c) % completed					

3. Pilot Study and Pretests
  a) Man-hours
  b) Cost
  c) % completed					

4. Drawing Sample
  a) Man-hours
  b) Cost
  c) % completed					

5. Preparing Observational Materials
  a) Man-hours
  b) Cost
  c) % completed					

6. Selection and Training
  a) Man-hours
  b) Cost
  c) % completed					

7. Trial Run
  a) Man-hours
  b) Cost
  c) % completed					

8. Revising Plans
  a) Man-hours
  b) Cost
  c) % completed					

9. Collecting Data
  a) Man-hours
  b) Cost
  c) % completed					

10. Processing Data
  a) Man-hours
  b) Cost
  c) % completed					

11. Preparing Final Report
  a) Man-hours
  b) Cost
  c) % completed					

* Source: Russell K. Ackoff, *Design for Social Research* (Chicago: University of Chicago, 1953), p. 347. By permission of the University of Chicago Press. Copyright 1953 by the University of Chicago.

† Suggested form for budget-time schedule summary. (There is nothing necessary or sufficient about this listing of activities, nor is the order absolute in any sense.)

SECTION C

Research Reporting

V.C.1. SPECIFICATIONS FOR SOCIOLOGICAL REPORT RATING

SPECIFICATIONS FOR SOCIOLOGICAL REPORT RATING *

	Defective	Substandard	Standard	Superior
Statement of Problem:				
1. Clarity of Statement	Statement is ambiguous, unclear, biased, inconsistent, or irrelevant to the research.	Problem must be inferred from incomplete or unclear statement.	Statement is unambiguous and includes precise description of research objectives.	Statement is unambiguous and includes formal propositions, and specifications for testing them.
2. Significance of Problem	No problem stated, or problem is meaningless, unsolvable, or trivial.	Solution of the problem would be of interest to a few specialists.	Solution of the problem would be of interest to many sociologists.	Solution of the problem would be of interest to most sociologists.
3. Documentation	No documentation to earlier work, or documentation is incorrect.	Documentation to earlier work is incomplete or contains errors of citation or interpretation.	Documentation to earlier work is reasonably complete.	Documentation shows in detail the evolution of the research problem from previous research findings.
Description of Method:				
4. Appropriateness of Method	Problem cannot be solved by this method.	Only a partial or tentative solution can be obtained by this method.	Solution of the problem by this method is possible, but uncertain.	Problem is definitely solvable by this method.
5. Adequacy of Sample or Field	Sample is too small, or not suitable, or biased, or of unknown sampling characteristics.	The cases studied are meaningful, but findings can not be projected.	Findings are projectable, but with errors of considerable, or of unknown, magnitude.	Results are projectable with known small errors, or the entire universe has been enumerated.
6. Replicability	Not replicable.	Replicable in substance, but not in detail.	Replicable in detail with additional information from the author(s).	Replicable in detail from the information given.

Presentation of Results:

7. Completeness **8. Comprehensibility**	Results are incomprehensible, or enigmatic.	Comprehension of results requires special knowledge or skills.	Relevant results are presented, partly in detail, partly in summary form.	Relevant details are presented in detail.
9. Yield	No contribution to solution of problem.	Useful hints or suggestions toward solution of problem.	Tentative solution of problem.	Definitive solution of problem.
Interpretation: **10. Accuracy**	Errors of calculation, transcription, dictation, logic, or fact detected.	Errors likely with the procedures used. No major errors detected.	Errors unlikely with the procedures used. No errors detected.	Positive checks of accuracy included in the procedures.
11. Bias	Evident bias in presentation of results and in interpretation.	Some bias in interpretation, but not in presentation of results.	No evidence of bias.	Positive precautions against bias included in procedures.
12. Usefulness	Not useful.	Possible influence on some future work in this area.	Possible influence on some future work in this area.	Probable influence on all future work in this area.

* Source: Theodore Caplow designed this form. It was tested by the Committee on Research, American Sociological Society. See "Official Reports and Proceedings," *American Sociological Review* (December, 1958), 704-711. Cf. Stuart C. Dodd and Louis N. Gray, "Scient-Scales for Measuring Methodology," Institute for Sociological Research, University of Washington, Seattle, 1962 (Mimeograph copies available on request).

V.C.2. FORM FOR SOCIOLOGICAL REPORT RATING *

Author _____

Title _____

Publication Reference _____

Rater _____

Date _____

Check (√) Appropriate Columns	Defective 0	Substandard 1	Standard 2	Superior 3
STATEMENT OF PROBLEM:				
1. Clarity of Statement				
2. Significance of Problem				
3. Documentation				
DESCRIPTION OF METHOD:				
4. Appropriateness of Method				
5. Adequacy of Sample or Field				
6. Replicability				
PRESENTATION OF RESULTS:				
7. Completeness				
8. Comprehensibility				
9. Yield				
INTERPRETATION:				
10. Accuracy				
11. Bias				
12. Usefulness				

Enter number of checks in each column in appropriate blanks; weight as indicated, and add for Total Rating

$\_\_ \times 0 = 0$ $\_\_ \times 1 = \_\_$ $\_\_ \times 2 = \_\_$ $\_\_ \times 3 = \_\_$

[*Total Rating*   ]
[   ]

* Theodore Caplow designed this rating form. Test reliabilities appear in "Official Reports and Proceedings," *American Sociological Review*, 23 (December, 1958), 704-711. See also the reports of the Educational Testing Service, Princeton, N.J., for ingenious rating scales on a large variety of subjects.

V.C.3. GUIDE TO SOCIOLOGICAL JOURNALS *

Acta Sociologica (Scandinavian Review of Sociology), Munksgaard, A. S., 47 Prags Boulevard, Copenhagen S., Denmark.
    1955. Quarterly. Book reviews. Cumulative index for volumes I-V. Text in English, French, German, and the Scandinavian languages.

The American Journal of Sociology, The University of Chicago Press, 5750 Ellis Avenue, Chicago, Ill. 60637.
    1895. Bimonthly. Abstracts. Book reviews. Annual index. Cumulative index for volumes I-LXX.

American Sociological Review, American Sociological Association, 1001 Connecticut Avenue, N.W., Washington, D.C. 20036.
    1936. Bimonthly. Abstracts. Book reviews. Annual index. Cumulative index for volumes I-XXV and volumes XXVI-XXX. Official journal of the American Sociological Association and distributed free to members.

The American Sociologist, American Sociological Association, 1001 Connecticut Avenue, N.W., Washington, D.C. 20036.
    1965. Quarterly. Devoted primarily to discussion of professional concerns and includes employment bulletins and announcements of professional meetings. Official journal of the American Sociological Association and distributed free to members.

Archives Européens de Sociologie (European Journal of Sociology), Musée de l'Homme, Palais de Chaillot, F.-75, Paris XVI, France.
    1960. Semiannually. Annual index. Text in English, French, and German.

The Australian and New Zealand Journal of Sociology, Department of Social Studies, University of Melbourne, Parkville, N. 2, Victoria, Australia.
    1965. Semiannually. Abstracts. Book reviews. Annual index. Official journal of the Sociological Association of Australia and New Zealand.

Berkeley Journal of Sociology, 410 Barrows Hall, University of California, Berkeley, Calif. 94720.
    1955-1958, volumes I-IV published as *Berkeley Publications in Society and Institutions;* 1959. Annually. Cumulative index for volumes I-XI. Official publication of the Graduate Sociology Club of the University of California at Berkeley.

The British Journal of Sociology, Routledge and Kegan Paul, Ltd., Broadway House, 68-74 Carter Lane, London E. C. 4, England.

---

* This guide was assembled by John Pease, University of Maryland. An earlier work was first presented by John Pease and Joan Rytina, "Sociological Journals," *The American Sociologist,* 3 (February, 1968), 41-45.

1950. Quarterly. Book review. Annual index. Cumulative index for volumes I-X.

Case Western Reserve Journal of Sociology, Department of Sociology, Case Western Reserve University, Cleveland, Ohio 44106.

1967. Annually. Book reviews.

Catalyst, Box G, Norton Union, State University of New York, Buffalo, N.Y. 14214.

1965. Semiannually. Book reviews. Official publication of the Sociology Club of the State University of New York at Buffalo.

Contributions to Indian Sociology, Mouton and Company, Herderstraat 5, The Hague, Netherlands.

1957. Irregularly. Book reviews. Annual index.

Current Sociology, Mouton and Company, 45 rue de Lille, Paris 7e, France.

1952. Triannually. Each issue contains an analysis of trends in, and an annotated bibliography on, some aspect of sociology.

Et Al., Post Office Box 77951, Los Angeles, Calif. 90007.

1967. Triannually. Each issue is primarily about a single topic.

G. S. S. Journal, Columbia University Graduate Sociology Club, Department of Sociology, Columbia University, 605 West 115th Street, New York, N.Y. 10025.

1961. Triannually. Official journal of the Columbia University Graduate Sociology Club and distributed free to members.

Ghana Journal of Sociology, Department of Sociology, University of Ghana, Legon, Ghana, West Africa.

1963. Semiannually. Book reviews. Official publication of the Ghana Sociological Association.

Graduate Sociology Journal, The Graduate Sociology Club, The University of Pennsylvania, Philadelphia, Pa. 19104.

1960. Annually. Official publication of the Graduate Sociology Club of the University of Pennsylvania and distributed free to members.

Indian Sociological Bulletin, Rakesh Marg, Pili Kothi, G. T. Road, Ghaziabad, U. P., India.

1963. Quarterly. Book reviews. Annual index.

International Journal of Comparative Sociology, E. J. Brill, Leiden, Netherlands.

1960. Semiannually. Book reviews. Annual index.

The Jewish Journal of Sociology, 55 New Cavendish Street, London, W. 1, England.

1959. Semiannually. Book reviews. Annual index.

Journal of Health and Social Behavior, American Sociological Association, 1001 Connecticut Avenue N.W., Washington, D.C. 20036.

1960-1966, volumes I-VII published as *The Journal of Health and*

Human Behavior: 1967. Quarterly. Book reviews. Annual index. Official publication of the American Sociological Association.

The Kansas Journal of Sociology, Department of Sociology, The University of Kansas, Lawrence, Kans. 66045.

1964. Quarterly.

The Pacific Sociological Review, Department of Sociology, University of Oregon, Eugene, Ore., 97403.

1958. Semiannually. Annual index. Cumulative index for volumes I-X. Official journal of the Pacific Sociological Association and distributed free to members.

Philippine Sociological Review, Philippine Sociological Society, Post Office Box 154, Manila, Philippines.

1953. Quarterly. Cumulative index for volumes I-XII. Official journal of the Philippine Sociological Society and distributed free to members.

The Polish Sociological Bulletin, RUCH Export and Import Enterprise, Post Office Box 154, Warsaw 1, Poland.

1961. Semiannually. Official publication of the Polish Sociological Association.

Revista Mexicana de Sociología, Facultad de Ciencias Políticas y Sociales, Ciudad Universitaria, Mexico 20, D.F.

1938. Quarterly.

Revista de Sociología, Departamento de Sociología de la Universidad Nacional Mayor de San Marcos de Lima, Lima, Peru.

1963. Biannually.

Romanian Journal of Sociology, Publishing House of the Romanian People's Republic, Cartimex, Str. 13 Decemvrie 3-5, Post Office Box 134-135, Bucharest, Romania.

1962, volume I published as *Rumanian Journal of Sociology;* 1963. Annually. Book reviews. Text in English, French, and Romanian.

Rural Sociology, Department of Rural Sociology, South Dakota State University, Brookings, S.D. 57006.

1936. Quarterly. Abstracts. Book reviews. Annual index. Cumulative indexes for volumes I-XX and volumes XXI-XXX. Official journal of the Rural Sociological Society and distributed free to members.

Social Forces, University of North Carolina Press, Post Office Box 510, Chapel Hill, N.C. 27514.

1922-1925, volumes I-III published as the *Journal of Social Forces;* 1925. Quarterly. Abstracts. Book reviews. Annual index.

Social Problems, Post Office Box 190, Kalamazoo, Mich. 49005.

1953. Quarterly. Book reviews. Annual index. Official journal of the Society for the Study of Social Problems and distributed free to members.

Sociologia, Fundacão Escola de Sociologia e Política, Rua General Jardin, 522 São Paulo, SP, Brazil.

    1939. Quarterly. Abstracts. Book reviews. Annual index. Text in English and Portuguese.

Sociologia Internationalis, Verlagsbuchhandlung, Duncker and Humblot, 1000 Berlin 41 (Steglitz), Dietrich-Schäfer-Weg 9, Postfach 330, Germany.

    1963. Semiannually. Book reviews. Text in English, French, German, and Spanish.

Sociologia Neerlandica, Royal VanGorcum, Limited, Assen, Netherlands.

    1962. Semiannually. Book reviews. Official publication of the Netherlands Sociological Society.

Sociologia Ruralis, Royal VanGorcum, Limited, Assen, Netherlands.

    1960. Quarterly. Abstracts. Book reviews. Annual index. Text in English, French, and German. Official journal of the European Society for Rural Sociology and distributed to members free.

Sociological Analysis, The American Catholic Sociological Society, 1403 North St. Mary's Street, San Antonio, Tex. 78215.

    1940-1963, volumes I-XXIV published as *American Catholic Sociological Review;* 1964. Quarterly. Abstracts. Book reviews. Annual index. Official journal of the American Catholic Sociological Society and distributed free to members.

Sociological Bulletin, Indian Sociological Society, Department of Sociology, Delhi School of Economics, University of Delhi, Delhi-7, India.

    1952. Semiannually. Official publication of the Indian Sociological Society.

Sociological Focus, Department of Sociology, University of Akron, 302 E. Buchtel Ave., Akron, Ohio 44304.

    1967. Quarterly. Official journal of the Ohio Valley Sociological Society and distributed free to members.

Sociological Inquiry, Department of Sociology and Anthropology, Haverford College, Haverford, Pa. 19041.

    1930-1960, volumes I-XXX published as *Alpha Kappa Deltan;* 1961. Semiannually. Annual index. Each issue devoted to a single topic. Official journal of Alpha Kappa Delta and distributed free to members for the first two years.

The Sociological Quarterly, Central Publications, Southern Illinois University, Edwardsville, Ill. 62025.

    1960. Quarterly. Book reviews. Annual index. Official journal of the Midwest Sociological Society and distributed free to members.

Sociological Review Monographs, University of Keele, Keele, Staffordshire, England.

    1958. Annually. Each issue is devoted to a single topic.

The Sociological Review: New Series, University of Keele, Keele, Staffordshire, England.

　1953. Triannually. Book reviews. Annual index.

Sociological Studies, Cambridge University Press, 32 East 57 Street, New York, N.Y. 10022.

　1968. Annually. Each issue is devoted to a single topic.

Sociological Symposium, Department of Sociology and Anthropology, Western Kentucky University, Bowling Green, Ky. 42101.

　1968. Semiannually. Each issue is devoted to a single topic.

Sociologiske Meddelelser, Sociological Institute, University of Copenhagen, Rosenborggrade 15, Copenhagen K, Denmark.

　1952. Semiannually. Book reviews. Annual index. Cumulative index for volumes I-X. Text in Danish (and occassionally in other Scandinavian languages) and English.

Sociologus: New Series, Duncker and Humblot, Dietrich-Schäfer-Weg 9, Berlin 41, Germany.

　1951. Semiannually. Abstracts. Book reviews. Text in English and German.

Sociology, British Sociological Association, 13 Endsleigh Street, London, W.C. 1, England.

　1967. Triannually. Official publication of the British Sociological Association.

Sociology and Social Research, University of Southern California, 703 West 34 Street, Los Angeles, Calif. 90007.

　1916-1921, volumes I-V published as *Studies in Sociology;* 1921-1927, volumes VI-XI published as *Journal of Applied Sociology;* 1927. Quarterly. Abstracts. Book reviews. Annual index. Cumulative index for volumes I-XXX.

Sociology of Education, American Sociological Association, 1001 Connecticut Avenue, N.W., Washington, D.C. 20036.

　1927-1962, volumes I-XXXVI published as *The Journal of Educational Sociology;* 1963. Quarterly. Abstracts. Annual index. Official publication of the American Sociological Association.

Sociometry, American Sociological Association, 1001 Connecticut Avenue, N.W., Washington, D.C. 20036.

　1937. Quarterly. Abstracts. Annual index. Official publication of the American Sociological Association.

Soviet Sociology, International Arts and Sciences Press, 108 Grand Street, White Plains, N.Y. 10601.

　1962. Quarterly. Book reviews. Annual index. A journal of translations.

Summation, Department of Sociology, Michigan State University, East Lansing, Mich. 48823.

　1968. Semiannually. Abstracts. Book reviews. Official journal of the

Michigan State University Sociological Association and distributed free to members.

The Wisconsin Sociologist: New Series, Department of Sociology, University of Wisconsin-Milwaukee, Milwaukee, Wis. 53211.

1962. Quarterly. Book reviews. Official journal of the Wisconsin Sociological Association and distributed free to members.

V.C.4. GUIDE TO THE JOURNALS SPONSORED BY THE AMERICAN PSYCHOLOGICAL ASSOCIATION, 1200 SEVENTEENTH STREET, N.W., WASHINGTON, D.C. 20036

American Psychologist

The *American Psychologist* is the official journal of the American Psychological Association, publishing both the official papers of the association and substantive articles on psychology. The May issue contains the highlights of the annual convention to be held the following September and the December issue contains a list of all the papers presented at the convention. In addition, once each year the *American Psychologist* devotes an entire issue (normally the November issue) to the extensive coverage and analysis of a single topic of current concern to the social sciences. Some of the topics covered in these special issues: psychological testing and public policy towards testing (1965); scientific communication—behavior of scientists and technologists in information subsystems (1966); recognition by Congress, individual legislators, and opinion leaders of the contribution, and shortcomings, of the social sciences to the pursuit of long-term social goals (1967).

The broad scope of this publication makes it of interest to a wide and varied audience.

Published monthly.

Contemporary Psychology

A journal of reviews—critical reviews—of books, films, and other material in the field of psychology. Material reviewed is selected by the editorial staff to represent a world-wide cross-section of psychological works. The reviews are prepared by those who have competence in specialized fields in psychology, but are written for a broad and varied audience. It provides a means by which the reader may keep abreast of current psychological thought and opinion. Reviews of approximately 380 books are published annually.

Published monthly.

Journal of Abnormal Psychology

The *Journal of Abnormal Psychology* is devoted to basic research and theory in the broad area of abnormal behavior. To cite a few illustrative examples, case histories, studies of therapy and behavior change, experimental studies and analyses of abnormal behavior and motivation, and theories of personality or emotional abnormality all are areas which would fall within the field of interest of this journal. Approximately 450 pages containing an average of 100 articles are published annually.

Published bimonthly.

Journal of Applied Psychology

This journal gives primary consideration to original quantitative investigations of value to those people interested in the following broad areas: personnel research; industrial working conditions; research on opinion and morale factors; job analysis and classification research; marketing and advertising research; and vocational and educational prognosis, diagnosis, and guidance at the secondary and college levels. Approximately 450 pages containing an average of 80 articles are published annually. Several monograph supplements may be added.

Published bimonthly.

Journal of Comparative and Physiological Psychology

This journal publishes original research reports in the field of comparative and physiological psychology, including animal learning, conditioning, and sensory processes. Editorial policies favor articles reporting studies of substantial scope, usually involving series of related experiments. A section of Supplementary Reports provides for short articles describing replications of or advances in techniques used in previously published researches. Approximately 1,100 pages containing over 200 articles are published annually. In addition, several monograph supplements may be published.

Published bimonthly, 2 vols. per year.

Journal of Consulting and Clinical Psychology

This publication is devoted to the area of clinical psychology, both child and adult. Its range of content reflects the many facets of this area, including such topics as personality assessment and diagnosis, theories and techniques of behavior modification, community mental health concepts and techniques, etiology of behavior, structure and dynamics of personality, and clinical psychopathology. The journal publishes original research papers, major formulations of clinical theory or concepts, and significant applications of psychological principles to clinical practice. Approximately 600 pages containing over 100 articles are published annually. There may be, in addition, several monograph supplements.

Published bimonthly.

Journal of Educational Psychology

The *Journal of Educational Psychology* publishes original investigations and theoretical papers dealing with problems of learning and teaching, and with the psychological development, relationships, and adjustment of the individual. Preference is given to studies of the more complex types of learning and behavior, especially in or relating to educational settings. Journal articles pertain to all levels of education and to all age groups. Approximately 400 pages containing 50 articles are published annually.

Published bimonthly.

Journal of Experimental Psychology

The journal publishes original experimental investigations which are intended to contribute to the development of psychology as an experimental science. Studies with normal human subjects involving abnormal or animal subjects, except when the latter are specifically oriented toward the extension of general psychological theory. The objective of this publication is the concise exposition of both data and conclusions from substantial segments of current research effort. Approximately 1,800 pages containing 175 prime articles and 25 supplementary reports are published. In addition, as many as six monograph supplements may be published.

Published monthly, 3 vols. per year.

Psychological Abstracts

Psychological Abstracts publishes concise abstracts of the world's literature in psychology and pertinent allied subjects. All titles and abstracts of foreign material are translated into English. During the past year steps were taken to extend the international coverage of material on a systematic basis. Abstracts of research literature are non-evaluative and informative, giving the problem, methods and subjects used, and the principal results and conclusions. Abstracts of discussion papers describe topics and principal points of view. Each monthly issue contains 1,200 to 1,500 abstracts, grouped by subject area, and an author and subject index. In addition there is a separate annual cumulative subject author index which is included as part of the subscription.

The rapid growth of the literature and the increased coverage of both domestic and foreign material has greatly increased the number of abstracts published annually—13,622 in 1966, 17,202 in 1967 and a projected 20,000 in 1968—and has necessitated a major reorganization of the abstracting services, including the adoption of new techniques for producing, compiling and publishing abstracts. As a result, the time between the appearance of the printed article and the appearance of the printed abstract has been reduced to *no more than 3 months,* in most cases.

Published monthly.

Psychological Bulletin

The *Psychological Bulletin* is concerned with research reviews and methodological contributions in the field of psychology. One of the principal functions of this journal is to publish critical, evaluative summaries of research. The methodological articles are directed toward people who might or do make practical use of such information, and are intended to bridge the gap between the technical statistician and the typical research psychologist. Articles feature the application of new methodology as well as the creative application of more familiar methodology. Approximately 900 pages containing 60 prime articles and 10 brief reports are published annually.

Published monthly, 2 vols. per year.

Journal of Counseling Psychology

The *Journal of Counseling Psychology* serves as a primary publication medium for research on counseling theory and practice. Topical reviews of research and other systematic surveys may be included periodically as well as measurement studies which directly relate to counseling. The journal is designed to be of interest to psychologists and counselors in schools, colleges and universities, public and private agencies, business and industry, and military agencies. Approximately 600 pages containing over 90 articles are published annually. There may be, in addition, several monograph supplements.

Published bimonthly.

Psychological Review

The *Psychological Review* is the major psychological journal for articles of theoretical significance to any area of scientific endeavor in psychology. It contains original articles which propose theoretical ideas and developments, and offers critical discussions of theoretical issues. Recent issues have contained papers on such topics as memory, drive and incentive, speech perception, conceptual behavior, pastural sets, electroconvulsive shock, food intake, depth perception, learning sets, and cognitive interactions. Approximately 500 pages containing 25 prime articles and 15 short articles are published annually.

Published bimonthly.

Journal of Personality and Social Psychology

This journal is devoted to basic research and theory in the broad areas of social interaction and group processes, Specifically, it deals with (a) interpersonal perception and attitude change, (b) the psychological aspects of formal social systems and less structured collective phenomena, (c) the socialization process at both the child and adult levels, (d) social motivation and personality dynamics, (e) the structure of personality, and (f) the relation of personality to group process and social systems. Approximately 1,600 pages containing 125 prime articles and 125 brief reports are published. In addition, as many as six monograph supplements may be published.

Published monthly, 3 vols. per year.

V.C.5. GUIDE TO MAJOR JOURNALS IN POLITICAL SCIENCE

American Political Science Review, American Political Science Association, 1726 Massachusetts Avenue, N.W., Washington, D.C. 20036.

Official journal of the American Political Science Association. Offers scientific studies, essays, bibliographies, and news and notes on contemporary matters in the profession. Founded 1903. Circulation 13,000.

Political Science Quarterly, Academy of Political Science, Fayerweather Hall, Columbia University, New York, N.Y. 10027.

Studies in the field of political science and economics of interest to scholars and laymen. Founded 1886. Circulation 9,000.

Annals of the American Academy of Political and Social Science, 3397 Chestnut Street, Philadelphia, Pa. 19104.

Founded 1890. Circulation 17,000.

Journal of Politics, Southern Political Science Association, University of Florida, Gainesville, Fla. 32601.

Interpretative articles covering all of the various subfields of political science by leading United States and foreign scholars. Scholarly review of new publications. Founded 1938.

Midwest Journal of Political Science, Wayne State University Press, 5980 Cass Avenue, Detroit, Mich. 48202.

Scholarly publication of Midwest Conference of Political Science. Founded 1957. Circulation 800.

The Review of Politics, University of Notre Dame, Notre Dame, Ind. 46556.

Political theory, contemporary social movements, international relations, cultural developments, and politics. Founded 1939. Circulation 2,500.

Foreign Affairs, Council on Foreign Relations, Inc., 58 East 68th Street, New York, N.Y. 10021.

A nonpartisan review of current ideas and policies affecting United States relations in all parts of the world, including international, political, commercial, and business communities. Founded 1922. Circulation 58,000.

Social Research, Graduate Faculty of New School for Social Research, 66 West 12th Street, New York, N.Y. 10011.

International quarterly of political and social science. Founded 1934. Circulation 1,700.

World Politics, Center of International Studies, Princeton University, Crown Hall, Princeton, N.J. 08540.

Problems of international relations of a general and theoretical nature, emphasizing social change and employing multidisciplinary methods and concepts. Founded 1948. Circulation 2,300.

Other journals to which political scientists contribute and read are the *Western Political Quarterly, Public Interest,* and *Commentary.* A great number of specialized journals exist.

V.C.6. GUIDE TO MAJOR JOURNALS IN ANTHROPOLOGY

There are many specialized fields and journals in anthropology to be found in physical anthropology, ethnology, archeology, and linguistics. The three journals of most general interest to social scientists generally are probably the following:

American Anthropologist, American Anthropological Association, 1530 P Street, N.W., Washington, D.C. 20005.

Founded 1899. Circulation 6,000.

Current Anthropology, University of Chicago Press, 5750 Ellis Ave., Chicago, Ill. 60637.

Founded 1953. Circulation 8,000.

Human Organization, Society for Applied Anthropology, Lafferty Hall, University of Kentucky, Lexington, Ky. 40506.
Founded 1941. Circulation 3,000.

V.C.7. ANNUAL MEETINGS HELD BY VARIOUS SOCIOLOGICAL AND KINDRED SOCIETIES WITH COMMON SECTION TOPICS IN SOCIOLOGY, PSYCHOLOGY, AND ANTHROPOLOGY

For information about annual meetings of the American Sociological Association and the other sociological societies write:

The American Sociological Association
1001 Connecticut Avenue, N.W.
Washington, D.C. 20036

Meetings of the American Sociological Association:
1970, August 31-September 3, Sheraton Park Hotel, Washington, D.C.
1971, August 30-September 2, Denver Hilton Hotel, Denver, Colo.
1972, August 28-31, Marriott Hotel, New Orleans, La.
1973, August 27-30, New York Hilton Hotel, New York, N.Y.
1974, August 26-29, Queen Elizabeth Hotel, Montreal, Quebec, Canada.
1975, August 25-28, San Francisco Hilton Hotel, San Francisco, Calif.

American Catholic Sociological Society
District of Columbia Sociological Society
Eastern Sociological Society
International Sociological Association
Midwest Sociological Society
Ohio Valley Sociological Society
Pacific Sociological Association
Rural Sociological Society
Society for the Study of Social Problems
Southern Sociological Society
Southwestern Sociological Association

Annual Meetings Held by Kindred Social Science and Allied Societies:
American Anthropological Association, Executive Offices, American Anthropological Association, 3700 Massachusetts Avenue, N.W., Washington, D.C.
American Association for the Advancement of Science, American Association for the Advancement of Science, 1515 Massachusetts Avenue, N.W., Washington, D.C. 20005.

American Political Science Association, American Political Science Association, 1527 New Hampshire Avenue, N.W., Washington, D.C.

American Psychological Association, American Psychological Association, 1200 17th Street, N.W., Washington, D.C. 20036.

American Public Health Association, American Public Health Association, Inc., 1740 Broadway, New York, N.Y. 10019.

American Statistical Association, Executive Director, American Statistical Association, 810 18th Street, N.W., Washington, D.C. 20036.

Canadian Sociology and Anthropology Association, Canadian Sociology and Anthropology Association, Postal Box 878, Montreal, P.Q. Canada.

International Congress of Sociometry, J. L. Moreno, Moreno Academy, Beacon, N.Y. 12508.

Population Association of America, Population Association of America, P.O. Box 14182, Benjamin Franklin Station, Washington, D.C. 20044.

Annual sociological meetings are commonly organized in sections around the following topics:

METHODOLOGY AND RESEARCH TECHNOLOGY
  Methodology (Social Science and Behavioral)
  Research Technology
  Statistical Methods
SOCIOLOGY: HISTORY AND THEORY
  Of Professional Interest
  History and Present State of Sociology
  Theories, Ideas and Systems
SOCIAL PSYCHOLOGY
  Personality and Culture
  Interaction Within (Small) Groups
  Leadership
GROUP INTERACTIONS
  Interaction Between (Large) Groups (Race Relations, Group Relations, etc.)
CULTURE AND SOCIAL STRUCTURE
  Social Organization
  Culture (Evolution)
  Social Anthropology (and Ethnology)
COMPLEX ORGANIZATIONS (MANAGEMENT)
  Industrial Sociology (Labor)
  Military Sociology
  Bureaucratic Structures

SOCIAL CHANGE AND ECONOMIC DEVELOPMENT
  Social Change and Economic Development
  Market Structures and Consumer Behavior
MASS PHENOMENA
  Social Movements
  Public Opinion
  Communication
  Collective Behavior
  Sociology of Leisure
  Mass Culture
POLITICAL INTERACTIONS
  Interactions Between Societies, Nations and States
  Political Sociology
SOCIAL DIFFERENTIATION
  Social Stratification
  Sociology of Occupations and Professions
RURAL SOCIOLOGY AND AGRICULTURAL ECONOMICS
  Rural Sociology (Village, Agriculture)
URBAN STRUCTURES AND ECOLOGY
  Urban Sociology and Ecology
SOCIOLOGY OF THE ARTS
  Sociology of Language and Literature
  Sociology of Art (Creative and Performing)

SOCIOLOGY OF EDUCATION
  Sociology of Education
SOCIOLOGY OF RELIGION
  Sociology of Religion
SOCIAL CONTROL
  Sociology of Law
  Penology and Correctional Problems
SOCIOLOGY OF SCIENCE
  Sociology of Science and Technology
DEMOGRAPHY AND HUMAN
BIOLOGY
  Demography (Population Study)
  Human Biology
THE FAMILY AND
SOCIALIZATION
  Sociology of the Child and
    Socialization
  Adolescence and Youth
  Sociology of Sexual Behavior
  Sociology of the Family

SOCIOLOGY OF HEALTH AND
MEDICINE
  Sociology of Medicine (Public Health)
  Social Psychiatry (Mental Health)
SOCIAL PROBLEMS AND
SOCIAL WELFARE
  Social Gerontology
  Social Disorganization (Crime)
  Applied Sociology (Social Work)
  Delinquency
SOCIOLOGY OF KNOWLEDGE
  Sociology of Knowledge
  History of Ideas
COMMUNITY DEVELOPMENT
  Sociology of Communities and
    Regions
PLANNING, FORECASTING,
AND SPECULATION
  Planning, Forecasting, and Speculation

COMMON SECTION TOPICS FOR PSYCHOLOGY AND ANTHROPOLOGY AT ANNUAL MEETINGS *

PSYCHOLOGY
Clinical Psychology
  Behavior problems
  Community mental health
  Crime and delinquency
  Experimental psychopathology
  Group therapy
  Individual diagnosis
  Mental deficiency
  Objective tests
  Projective techniques
  Psychotherapy
  Speech pathology
Counseling and Guidance
  Educational counseling
  Nondirective therapy
  Personal adjustment
  Rehabilitation
  Vocational counseling
Developmental Psychology
  Childhood and adolescence
  Infancy
  Maturity and old age
  Nursery and pre-school

Educational Psychology
  Educational measurement
  Programmed learning
  School adjustment
  School learning
  Special education
  Student personnel
  Teacher personnel
Engineering Psychology
General Psychology
  History and biography
  Theory and systems
Industrial and Personnel Psychology
  Employee and executive training and
    development
  Employee morale and attitudes
  Job analysis and position classification
  Labor-management relations
  Market research, advertising
  Organizational behavior
  Performance evaluation, criterion
    development
  Recruiting, selection, placement
  Safety research and training
  Salary and pay plans

* The classification shown is used by the National Science Foundation in its Register of Social Scientists.

Personality
  Development
  Measurement
  Personality and body
  Personality and learning
  Personality and perception
  Personality theory
  Structure and dynamics
School Psychology

ANTHROPOLOGY
Major Divisions
  Archeology
  Ethnology

History of anthropology
Methodology
Anthropological linguistics
Physical anthropology
Social/Cultural anthropology
Specialties
  Anthropological folklore
  Cultural ecology
  Economic anthropology
  Ethnomusicology
  Human paleontology
  Museology
  Primatology
  Psychological anthropology

V.C.8.   SELECT BIBLIOGRAPHY FOR FELLOWSHIPS AND GRANTS

1. *AIDS TO INDIVIDUAL SCHOL-ARS.* American Council of Learned Societies, 345 East 46th St., New York, N.Y. 10017.
2. *ANNOUNCEMENT OF SPECIAL AWARDS FOR LATIN AMERICA AND THE CARIBBEAN FOR THE ACADEMIC YEAR 1969-70.* Foreign Area Fellowship Program, 444 Madison Ave., New York, N.Y. 10022
3. *FELLOWSHIPS, UNITED STATES OF AMERICA AND CANADA.* John Simon Guggenheim Memorial Foundation, 90 Park Ave., New York, N.Y. 10016
4. *THE FOUNDATION DIRECTORY.* Russell Sage Foundation, 230 Park Ave., New York, N.Y. 10017
5. *THIS IS IIE.* Institute of International Education, 809 United Nations Plaza, New York, N.Y. 10017
6. *A SELECTED LIST OF MAJOR FELLOWSHIP OPPORTUNITIES AND AIDS TO ADVANCED EDUCATION FOR UNITED STATES CITIZENS.* National Academy of Sciences, National Research Council, 2101 Constitution Ave., N.W., Wash., D.C. 20418
7. *FELLOWSHIPS AND LOANS FOR STUDY ABROAD OF THE ORGANIZATION OF AMERICAN STATES.* Pan American Union, Wash., D.C. 20006

8. *FELLOWSHIPS AND GRANTS TO BE OFFERED IN 1969-70.* Social Science Research Council, 230 Park Avenue, New York, N.Y 10017
9. *FOUNDATION CENTER.* Foundation Library Center, 1001 Conn. Ave., N.W., Wash., D.C. 20036
10. U.S. Department of Health, Education, and Welfare, Office of Education, Wash., D.C. 20202
    –AIDS TO STUDENTS IN VOCATIONAL COLLEGE, ANL GRADUATE PROGRAMS.
    –LANGUAGE AND AREA CENTERS PROGRAMS.
    –OVERSEAS FOREIGN LANGUAGE AND AREA STUDIES
    –NATIONAL DEFENSE GRADUATE FELLOWSHIPS, GRAD UATE PROGRAMS.
11. National Science Foundation, Division of Social Sciences, Washington, D.C. 20550
12. For special programs refer to V.A.1 *Major Financing Agencies of Social Science Research.* Ask for Annual Report of current year. For special list of 300 opportunities for graduate students in the United States (fellowship grants, scholarships study opportunities), write Mr Martin Knudson, Indiana University, 703 E. 7th Street, Bloomington Ind. 47401.

Index